STUDIES IN CHRISTIAN HISTORY AND THOUGHT

Missionary Imperialists?

Missionaries, Government and the Growth of the British Empire in the Tropics, 1860-1885

STUDIES IN CHRISTIAN HISTORY AND THOUGHT

Missionary Imperialists?

Missionaries, Government and the growth of the British Empire in the Tropics, 1860-1885

John H. Darch

Foreword by Timothy Yates

WIPF & STOCK · Eugene, Oregon

Wipf and Stock Publishers
199 W 8th Ave, Suite 3
Eugene, OR 97401

Missionary Imperialists?
Missionaries, Government and the Growth of the British Empire in the Tropics, 1860-1885
By Darch, John H.
Copyright©2009 Paternoster
ISBN 13: 978-1-60608-596-7
Publication date 4/12/2009
Previously published by Paternoster, 2009

"This Edition Published by Wipf and Stock Publishers by arrangement with Paternoster"

STUDIES IN CHRISTIAN HISTORY AND THOUGHT

Series Preface

This series complements the specialist series of *Studies in Evangelical History and Thought* and *Studies in Baptist History and Thought* for which Paternoster is becoming increasingly well known by offering works that cover the wider field of Christian history and thought. It encompasses accounts of Christian witness at various periods, studies of individual Christians and movements, and works which concern the relations of church and society through history, and the history of Christian thought.

The series includes monographs, revised dissertations and theses, and collections of papers by individuals and groups. As well as 'free standing' volumes, works on particular running themes are being commissioned; authors will be engaged for these from around the world and from a variety of Christian traditions.

A high academic standard combined with lively writing will commend the volumes in this series both to scholars and to a wider readership.

Contents

Foreword by Timothy Yates	xiii
Acknowledgements	xv
Abbreviations	xvii
Introduction	xix

Chapter 1
Missions and Missionaries in the Mid-Victorian Era	**1**
The Foundation and Development of the 'Classical' Missionary Societies	1
London Missionary Society	4
Church Missionary Society	6
Wesleyan Methodist Missionary Society	10
New Hebrides Mission	12
Melanesian Mission	14
Universities' Mission to Central Africa	18
Missionary Motivation and Personnel	19
International and Ecumenical Relations	25
Prevalent Attitudes in the Missionary Community	29
Missionary Life in the Tropics	35

Chapter 2
Missionaries as Humanitarians? Opposition to the Recruitment of Indentured Labour for Queensland	**47**
European Exploitation of Pacific Islanders	49
Opposition from the Presbyterian Missionaries	53
The Role of Bishop Patteson	60
The Role of the Royal Navy	64
The Labour Traders' Perspective	66
Humanitarian Pressure Groups	68
The Decline and End of the Trade	73

Chapter 3
Missionary Involvement in the Annexation of Fiji	**78**
The Establishment of the Wesleyan Methodist Mission in Fiji	79
Missionary Involvement in Fijian Politics	83
Influx of Europeans	89
The Debate on Fiji's Future	91
Pressure in Parliament: The Role of William M'Arthur	95

The British Annexation of Fiji	99
Fiji under British Rule	107

Chapter 4
The Role of Missionaries in the Events Leading to the Establishment of a British Protectorate in Papua New Guinea — 112

British Government Awareness of New Guinea	117
Development of the LMS Mission	122
Britain's Interest Develops	126
Australian Intervention	129
Missionary Reaction to the Queensland 'Annexation'	133
Britain Proclaims a Protectorate	136
Missionary Reaction to the British Protectorate	138
Analysis	140

Chapter 5
The Proposed Cession of The Gambia to France — 144

The Start of Missionary Activity	145
The Development of French Interest in The Gambia	147
British Reconsideration of The Gambia's Value	149
Missionary Response	153
Opposition from the Business Community	155
The Exchange Proposals Renewed	159
Renewed Opposition	162
Assessment	168

Chapter 6
Missions and the Growth of British Power in Lagos and Yorubaland — 172

CMS, the Yoruba Mission and Henry Venn	174
Official British Involvement	176
The Yoruba Mission Expands	179
Governor Freeman and Missionary Opposition	184
Glover and the Egba	189
Glover, the Missionaries and the *Ifole*	193
The Governorship of John Pope Hennessy	196
Political Decision Making	199
Lagos and Yorubaland from 1874	202
Assessment	206

Chapter 7
The Aftermath of Slavery in East and Central Africa — 209

The Pioneer Missionaries in East Africa	209
Confronting the East African Slave Trade	211
David Livingstone	217
Livingstone and the UMCA	220

The LMS Central African Mission	222
The Troubles at Frere Town	223
The Nyanza Mission, Buganda and Bishop Hannington	228
Imperialism in East Africa	234

Conclusion:
Incidental Imperialists – Missionary Influence on the Growth of Empire   **237**

Bibliography   **247**

Index   **270**

Foreword

J.K. Fairbank, the Harvard-based historian, once called the missionary 'the invisible man of American history'. Until comparatively recently, with certain major exceptions like David Livingstone, this could have been written of British counterparts in the writings of professional historians of empire. A study like Professor Roland Oliver's *The Missionary Factor in East Africa* of 1952 stood out as exceptional in this respect. Recently, however, there has been a welcome change of stance. The work of Professor Andrew Porter, notably (but not only) his *Religion versus Empire?* of 2004; the stimulus to missionary research supplied by the generous patronage of the Pew Trust, which has issued in a series of studies edited by Dr Brian Stanley and Professor Robert Frykenburg; not to mention the continued stimulus provided by the writings of Professor Andrew Walls has meant that British colonial and imperial studies have considerably sharpened the profile both of the missions and of the missionaries. The new *Oxford History of the British Empire* has a welcome additional volume edited by Professor Norman Etherington on *Missions and Empire* (2005).

With invisibility for much of the last century went misinterpretation. It was not only the Chinese, before and after the Communist expulsion of missionaries in 1949, who referred to them as 'running dogs of the imperialists'. Dr John Darch, in this absorbing and thorough series of case studies has added the weight of his research to the widening exposure of historical caricatures which have often been treated as satisfactory accounts of the 'missionary factor'. The originals with which I am most familiar would confirm, from a part of the world not featured in these case studies, Dr Darch's profile of missionaries as 'incidental imperialists'. In New Zealand a case could be made for both the Methodist missionary John Hobbs and the Anglican CMS missionary Henry Williams exercising considerable influence towards the signing of the Treaty of Waitangi in 1840, whereby a not insubstantial piece of territory was added to the British crown. Their influence on Maori chiefs like Waka Nene, who argued in favour of the treaty, was real enough and Williams was an indisputable link between Hobson, the future governor and Maori participants in the negotiations. Nevertheless, as the original documents show conclusively, the missionaries' motives were not imperialist as such so much as willing the rule of law to be established over lawless European communities and waves of land-hungry immigrants. At most, Anglican and Methodist missionaries, if not French Roman Catholic Marists, preferred British to French authorities, once convinced that their Maori charges would be subject to some form of colonial incursion. It is a strength of Dr Darch's work that he reveals the interaction between government agencies and missionary societies for what it was and what it was not.

There is no doubt that missions were important catalysts of change and that during the nineteenth century they took with them the fruits and solvents of western technological development to societies which, often sophisticated and developed in their own terms, were still emerging into the modern age. To understand the transformation of these societies, whether in Queensland, Fiji, New Guinea or tropical Africa the impact of the missionary and the Christian message that was propagated is of historical significance and sociological importance. We can be grateful to Dr Darch for this scholarly and admirably written contribution to a growing literature of re-assessment of the missionary contribution, which is serving to correct a warped twentieth century account by means of a well-researched and more nuanced version of the missionary factor in colonial and imperial history. I hope that this fine text will be widely studied by historians of empire and missiologists alike towards a proper 'visibility' and a sounder interpretation.

Timothy Yates
Bakewell
February 2008

Acknowledgements

At the outset I am happy to record my gratitude to those who, over a number of years, have aided me in this research that has finally culminated in this book. First and foremost I should like to thank Professor Colin Eldridge of the University of Wales, Lampeter, who so ably and willingly supervised my doctoral research on which this book is based. It was a delight to work with him again some twenty years after first becoming interested in imperial and missionary history as a result of his undergraduate teaching. I well recall, as a Lampeter undergraduate in the 1970s opting for his Special Subject because it seemed the least dull of the three on offer that year! What began for the wrong motives became, through his knowledge of, and enthusiasm for, the subject, an interest that has lasted and developed over the years. He has continued to provide encouragement, academic support and critical scrutiny for my work long after his role as a supervisor was completed.

I also place on record my gratitude to other scholars in the field of mission history – especially Dr Brian Stanley and Dr Timothy Yates – who, over a number of years have willingly given me advice and encouragement and have helpfully commented on my work.

I would like to record my gratitude to the staff of a number of Libraries and Archives who have provided both primary and secondary source material for this study. Particular thanks are due to Kathy Miles of the University of Wales Library at Lampeter, and Christine Ainsley and Evelyn Pawley of St John's College Library in Nottingham. I am also grateful to the staffs of The National Archives of the UK, Birmingham University Library, the School of Oriental and African Studies Library in London, the John Rylands University Library in Manchester, the Partnership House Mission Studies Library in London, the London Library and St Deiniol's Library at Hawarden.

I would like to thank Jeremy Mudditt and Robin Parry at Paternoster Press for their readiness to accept my research for publication and Anthony R. Cross for sharing his expertise on the finer points of formatting the text.

I am grateful to those present day mission agencies – the successors of those Victorian societies who feature in this book – who have kindly given me permission to quote from their copyright archives including the Church Mission Society and the Melanesian Mission. The quotations from London Missionary Society / Council for World Mission Archives are reproduced by permission and the quotations from the Wesleyan Methodist Missionary Society archives are copyright © Trustees for Methodist Church Purposes, and used by permission of Methodist Publishing House.

This research has been conducted on a part-time basis over a number of years without major grant funding. Nevertheless small grants which have been extremely helpful have been gratefully received from the Diocese of Chester (Continuing Ministerial Education), the Trustees of St Aidan's College Charity and the London Library Trust. Two periods of study leave during the long course of this research have enabled me to concentrate on writing and for these I am grateful to the Diocese of Chester and St John's College Nottingham.

For seven years, while on the teaching faculty of St John's I contributed to the teaching of a module on the Theology and History of Mission. Over those years I greatly valued the insights of my students, who by oral questions and written reflection have helped me to explore the subject from a number of fresh angles. In this respect I am particularly grateful to Mkunga Mtingele, Nick Allen, Leigh Machell, Anne Noble and Karen Rooms. I also record my thanks to Oak Hill Theological College who made research visits to London much more tolerable by kindly providing car parking facilities.

Finally, I should like to thank my family for the help and encouragement they have given me over years it has taken for this project to come to fruition. My greatest thanks are due to my wife, Madge, for her continued love and support and, not least, for the innumerable packed lunches she made for me as I set off at unsocially early hours to distant libraries. It is with my love and gratitude that I dedicate this book to her.

Mellor Brook
Pentecost 2008

Abbreviations

BMS	Baptist Missionary Society
CHBE	*Cambridge History of the British Empire*
CMS	Church Missionary Society
CUP	Cambridge University Press
CWM	Council for World Mission
CO	Colonial Office
FO	Foreign Office
HSANZ	*Historical Studies (Australia and New Zealand)*
IBMR	*International Bulletin of Missionary Research*
JAH	*Journal of African History*
JEH	*Journal of Ecclesiastical History*
JICH	*Journal of Imperial and Commonwealth History*
JPH	*Journal of Pacific History*
JRGS	*Journal of the Royal Geographical Society*
JRH	*Journal of Religious History*
LMS	London Missionary Society
NAMP	North Atlantic Missiology Project
NZJH	*New Zealand Journal of History*
OHBE	*Oxford History of the British Empire*
OUP	Oxford University Press
PP	*Parliamentary Papers*

PRCI	*Proceedings of the Royal Colonial Institute*
PRO	Public Record Office
SPCK	Society for the Promotion of Christian Knowledge
SPG	Society for the Propagation of the Gospel
TNA	The National Archives of the UK
TRHS	*Transactions of the Royal Historical Society*
UMCA	Universities' Mission to Central Africa
WMMS	Wesleyan Methodist Missionary Society
WO	War Office

Introduction

Were missionaries, 'the earliest footsoldiers of British colonialism' or 'outriders of empire'?[1] Is it true that '"the Bible and the flag" went hand in hand in the history of Western imperial expansion'?[2] Is it correct to speak of an 'entanglement of British missions with Britain's empire'?[3] Though these might seem emotive or 'loaded' questions there is little doubt that they reflect popular conceptions and understandings of the age of imperialism, particularly in the formerly imperialized nations and among more radical thinkers in the formerly imperialist nations.

Somewhat less emotively, Professor Andrew Porter in his 1991 inaugural lecture posed the question, 'does Britain's long nineteenth century experience reveal systematic connections between religion and empire?'[4] More recently he has written an impressively detailed and thorough investigation into the relationship between religion and empire over an even longer period, from 1700 to 1914.

This study narrows down Porter's field of enquiry both chronologically, and geographically. Chronologically it is confined to the mid-Victorian years, *circa* 1860 to *circa* 1885 though, of necessity, the terminal dates are viewed with the utmost flexibility. Geographically, it is focused on tropical Africa and the South-west Pacific. It should be noted, however, that this is not an arbitrary choice: it was in these parts of the world, which W. David McIntyre has called 'the imperial frontier in the tropics', that missionaries were most closely involved in imperial expansion. We shall endeavour to examine just how closely involved they really were and the outcome of that involvement.

The case studies seek to be representative, not exhaustive, and of course there are others which would equally repay study. But lest the question be asked why, for example Bechuanaland, a very obvious example of missionary imperialism in the 1880s, is not included it should be noted that the Crown Colony of British Bechuanaland (incorporated into Cape Colony in 1895), whose annexation was largely due to the efforts of LMS missionary John Mackenzie, falls completely outside the tropics. Uganda, on the other hand, lies firmly within the tropics and the early days of the Nyanza mission are considered in Chapter 7. But the annexation of Uganda, though missionary

---

1 Jean Comaroff and John L. Comaroff, *Of Revelation and Revolution*, 2 vols (Chicago: Chicago University Press, 1991, 1997), I, xi; II, 6.
2 Brian Stanley, *The Bible and the Flag* (Leicester: Apollos, 1990), p.12.
3 Andrew N. Porter, *Religion versus Empire?: British Protestant Missionaries and Overseas Expansion, 1700- 1914* (Manchester: Manchester University Press, 2004), p.1.
4 Andrew N. Porter, 'Religion and Empire: British Expansion in the Long Nineteenth Century, 1780-1914', *JICH*, 20:3 (1992), 386.

influence was of particular importance, falls well outside even the most generous interpretation of our time frame.

The missionary factor in British imperial policy has been most extensively studied in the late Victorian years, the period of the scramble for Africa and the so-called *Pax Britannica*. Indeed Roland Oliver has dubbed the period 1884-1914 'the zenith of the missions'[5] and Richard Gray cites the traditionally accepted view that 'Christianity ... made rapid advances precisely because its emissaries, the missionaries, were so closely linked with the whole apparatus of colonial rule'.[6] But was this alleged marriage of convenience between missionary church and imperialistic state actually the case in the preceding twenty-five years, 1860-1885, on which comparatively little work has been done? If, as Max Warren observed in the 1960s, 'the nationalism of Africa is the deposit left by the receding tide of western imperialism', how important was the missionary factor in the rising tide in the mid-Victorian period?[7] To Roland Oliver, this was the 'pioneer period' of missions, a term indicating that, at least in his view, missionaries were actively involved at the leading edge of British expansion in a period of formative change.[8]

It was also in this period that missions 'came of age' and increasingly claimed the attention of the British Christian public. The death of Bishop Patteson in the south Pacific, Stanley's search for Livingstone in central Africa and the great missionary explorer's death and subsequent burial in Westminster Abbey were indications of this interest. The establishment of the first Day of Intercession for Foreign Missions on 20 December 1872 was another indication of the interest that existed within the Christian community.[9] Livingstone's books sold in vast numbers but the biographies and exploits of lesser-known missionaries were also best-sellers. A sure confidence in the inevitable triumph of Christian civilisation was as much a part of the national mood as was that of imperial expansion, for it seemed clear that the two were entwined. This complacency about the inevitability of imperial and religious progress over vast areas of the globe had a number of years to run before it was brutally pounded by Boer guns at Spion Kop and eventually ground to a halt in the mud of Flanders.

---

5 Roland Oliver, *The Missionary Factor in East Africa* (London: Longmans, Green, 1952), p.v.

6 Richard Gray, *Black Christians and White Missionaries* (New Haven & London: Yale University Press, 1990), p.79.

7 Max Warren, *The Missionary Movement from Britain in Modern History* (London, SCM Press, 1965), p.166.

8 Gallagher and Robinson concluded that, 'far from being an era of "indifference", the mid-Victorian years were the decisive stage in the history of British expansion overseas ...'. J. Gallagher and R.E. Robinson, 'The Imperialism of Free Trade', *Economic History Review*, VI (1953), 11.

9 This was inspired by the death of Bishop Patteson. The practice of prayer for missions continues to this day though the date has since been amended to coincide with St Andrew's day on 30 November.

Introduction

This book makes no claim to be comprehensive. Indeed, such an approach would be impossible. As W.P. Morrell has rightly stated, even 'the printed missionary material is a formidable mass of first-hand evidence.... To go behind it and master the vast manuscript collections of the missionary societies would take a lifetime'.[10] H.E. Maude concurs, referring to 'the prolix pens of missionaries'.[11] The sheer volume of missionary archives was caused by both the large number of missionaries in the field and also by their prolific literary outpourings. For some, the letter was a means of contact with civilization, used to powerful effect by Livingstone, for example, in bringing the needs of Africa to the British national consciousness. For others, communication, whether strictly accurate or embroidered with wishful thinking, increased chances of funding for what were, after all, entirely voluntary agencies. And for some, the letter was simply a lifeline to a home left far way and long ago and to which the writer might never return. Though a letter might take months to reach London and months more for a reply to return, the mails were a vital psychological link with the mother country, a reminder that missionaries had not been forgotten, far out of sight but not yet out of mind.[12] Of necessity, therefore, a selective approach has been adopted, with case studies taken from tropical areas of Africa and the south-west Pacific to illustrate missionary involvement with the development of the empire.

Using primary source material from the archives of several of the principal missionary societies, files from the Colonial and Foreign Offices and additional documentary evidence, especially the published accounts left by missionaries and other contemporary figures, this book will examine the missionaries of mid-Victorian England, their attitudes and methods and the influence and impact they had on those in authority. Six case studies taken from frontier areas will be examined. J.S. Galbraith has referred to the 'turbulent frontier' as both a factor in British expansion and a place where this expansion took place.[13] It was in just such frontier areas that missions were to be found, preceding the formal establishment of British political control, often the first British influence in such an area, and often a vital factor in the eventual establishment of formal political control.

---

10 W.P. Morrell, *Britain in the Pacific Islands* (Oxford: Clarendon Press, 1960), p.v. In view of the vast amounts of primary source material available it is ironical, as T. O. Beidelman observed, that 'missionary studies are among the most neglected of a wide area of potential colonial research'. T. O. Beidelman, 'Social Theory and the Study of Christian Missions', *Africa*, 44 (1974), 248.

11 Foreword to A.J. Schütz (ed.), *The Diaries and Correspondence of David Cargill, 1832-1843* (Canberra: Australian National University Press, 1977).

12 By contrast, today, two friends active on overseas mission in different parts of south and central Asia are able to make contact with individuals virtually anywhere in the world more or less instantaneously by means of e-mail.

13 J.S. Galbraith, 'The "turbulent frontier" as a factor in British expansion', *Comparative Studies in Society and History*, II (1960), 150-168.

Three areas, often overlapping, will form a particular feature of this study. First is the role of missionary supporters in Britain. It will be argued here that, because of their immediacy, the initiative of individual missionaries often had a much greater influence than the attitudes and beliefs of the home-based society in general. But the other side of the coin to immediacy was distance, isolation and difficulty of communication – all factors that militated against missionaries in the field being able to exert as much influence as they might wish on government policy and practice in Britain. How this was overcome by use of both intermediaries and influential and committed supporters will be an important theme in this book. It was largely in those cases where there were contacts between missionaries in the field and motivated supporters in positions of influence in the UK, that the missionaries were able to affect the policy and practice of the British government in general and the Colonial Office in particular.

A second feature of importance is the networking between missionaries, their supporters, other humanitarian groups and *ad hoc* pressure groups that were formed with a particular purpose in mind. Missionaries were not alone in their concerns and aims; they were happy to make common cause with others who shared similar views. Indeed some of their supporters were also simultaneously supporters of humanitarian and pressure groups.

A third feature, vitally important but often overlooked in studies of missions and imperialism, is the ongoing interaction between the missionaries and their supporters and those in official positions of authority in government, especially in the Colonial Office. The way in which the missionary lobby tackled government and sought to influence it will be one of the major strands in this book. Equally we shall be examining the reaction of both politicians and civil servants to the lobbying pressure that was exerted upon them and the processes by which policy was formulated in response to that pressure.

Finally, a word of explanation about the dates of this study is necessary. It does *not* seek to be an exhaustive study of all relevant events between the terminal dates. In any case, they are very much *circa* 1860 to *circa* 1885, but in no two case studies are those dates rigidly adhered to since each was an unplanned and uncoordinated development. Imperial expansion was, by its very nature, a piecemeal process, normally resisted by the Colonial Office in London, until pressure for annexation became intolerable or until an incident occurred which demanded British intervention. What unites apparently disparate case studies is that each found itself under discussion in the Colonial or Foreign Office during this period. In some cases it has been necessary to go back before 1860 to examine the roots of the events that took place in this period. As regards to the *terminus ad quem*, in some cases (like Papua New Guinea) it has been necessary to go slightly beyond it, but in others (Fiji and the Gambia) interest has ended before the date has been reached. In short, the case studies involve areas of expanding British influence which were live issues both for the missionary movement and for the British authorities (though not all simultaneously) during the mid-Victorian period.

CHAPTER 1

Missions and Missionaries in the Mid-Victorian Era

This book will argue that there were many approaches to imperialism – from enthusiastic endorsement of the imperial role through ignorance and indifference to outright hostility – exhibited by individual British Protestant missionaries and the societies which supported them in the mid-Victorian era. But it will also argue that, whatever their theoretical views and however hard they may have tried to avoid it, it was virtually impossible for missions to avoid being practically involved in promoting European values and influence whether actively or passively. But what of the origins of the missionary societies who were at the cutting edge of overseas mission in 1860-85?

The Foundation and Development of the 'Classical' Missionary Societies

It was a commonplace in missionary history that the foundation and growth of the 'classical' missions from the 1790s was a direct consequence of the evangelical revival earlier that the century. Recently, however, there has been a reaction against this supposed cause and effect with a theory of greater continuity being proposed in which the new, voluntary missionary societies are viewed in a wider context of both European Protestant mission and the existing statutory mission societies (SPCK and SPG) in Britain.[1] Indeed, Andrew Porter goes so far as to question the traditional understanding of a clear association of the Eighteenth-century revival and the foundation of missionary societies, suggesting that the two are 'by no means necessarily connected'.[2] And Andrew

---

1 See, for example, Walls pp.30-31 and Carson pp.47-48, both in Brian Stanley (ed.), *Christian Missions and the Enlightenment*, (Grand Rapids and Richmond: Eerdmans and Curzon Press, 2001); Andrew Porter, *Religion versus Empire?*, pp.16-28. Strictly speaking only the SPG possessed a royal charter; the SPCK was a voluntary society 'on which the bishops smiled' (Carson, p.47). Nevertheless it will be convenient to use the term 'statutory' to contrast these two societies with the 'classical' voluntary mission agencies that developed from the 1790s onwards.
2 Porter, *Religion versus Empire?*, p 28.

Walls stresses the continuity of the new impetus to mission with European precedents: 'the Protestant missionary wakening did not begin in 1792 ... what happened ... was British entry into a well-established continental tradition'.[3]

The two statutory societies, the Society for Promoting Christian Knowledge (SPCK) founded in 1698 and the Society for the Propagation of the Gospel (SPG) founded in 1701 were independent of the European tradition, though they occasionally worked in co-operation with European missions. Essentially they were foundations of their time, integrated into the first British empire, and often appearing to be imbued with a kind of spiritual mercantilism in which the religious traditions and interests of the mother country were upheld in a colonial setting, outside of which they did not normally venture.[4]

But whatever the connection between them may, or may not, have been, it is undeniable that the foundation of a new wave of missionary societies in the late eighteenth century was preceded by a sea change in religious attitudes in Britain.[5] Its heady brew of new spiritual wine first brought revival to the old wineskins of the Church of England and then burst them, spilling out to spawn new church structures such as a number of independent and Methodist sects. And just as the spiritual life of the Established Church was renewed by John Wesley and his contemporaries including his brother Charles, George Whitefield, Henry Venn Snr, and William Grimshaw, so too new life was breathed into the older dissenting congregations.[6] The Protestant missionary movement, which had begun on the continent with the Moravians, developed also in Britain in the last years of the Eighteenth century as a natural adjunct of the evangelical revival.[7] It was perhaps inevitable that out of this spiritual

---

3 Walls in Stanley (ed.), *Christian Missions and the Enlightenment*, p.34.
4 See Daniel O'Connor, et al., *Three Centuries of Mission: the USPG, 1701-2000* (London: Continuum, 2000). According to its Royal Charter the SPG sought to protect 'our loving subjects' in foreign parts who, were in danger of falling into 'atheism, infidelity, popish superstition and idolatry'. Quoted in Richard Gray, p.85. At that time their missionaries were, in effect, often little more than colonial chaplains.
5 For a most useful analysis of the beginnings of the evangelical revival see D.W. Bebbington, *Evangelicalism in Modern Britain* (London: Unwin Hyman, 1989), Chapter 2, pp.20-74. Bebbington, argues strongly that the Evangelical revival was in continuity with the Enlightenment not, as is often assumed, a 'fundamentalist' reaction against it. See also David J. Bosch, *Transforming Mission: Paradigm Shifts in the Theology of Mission* (Maryknoll, N.Y.: Orbis, 1991), pp.274-283, 344 and Stanley (ed.), *Christian Missions and the Enlightenment*, pp.1-8. John Kent seems to be alone in regarding the Eighteenth Century revival as no more than a 'persistent myth'. See John Kent, *Wesley and the Wesleyans* (Cambridge: CUP, 2002), p.1.
6 For a concise account of the revival see G.M. Ditchfield, *The Evangelical Revival* (London: UCL Press, 1998) or Mark A. Noll, *The Rise of Evangelicalism* (Leicester: Apollos, 2004).
7 Andrew Walls picturesquely describes the missionary movement as 'an autumnal child of the Evangelical Revival'. A.F. Walls, 'The Evangelical Revival, the Missionary

ferment of the eighteenth century, the desire to convert fellow countrymen to a living faith in Christ should be followed by a desire to bring the gospel to the 'heathen' overseas. But the rapidly growing churches of the dissenting tradition had nothing in common with the Anglican statutory societies and for evangelical Anglicans the SPCK and SPG were perceived as exclusive, elitist and untouched by the revival.

But it is perhaps best to regard the classical missionary societies of the 1790s as having three antecedents: the existing statutory societies, the European context and the evangelical revival. Together – and there will be continuing debate concerning their relative influence and importance – these three factors jointly formed the backcloth to the new wave of missions.

It is paradoxical, in view of the inward-looking nature of late eighteenth-century nonconformity, that modern English missions should have originated in this part of the church, and a clear indication that the revival, which had begun in the Established Church and moved outwards with Methodism, had now also taken root in older Dissent.

The Baptist Missionary Society ('the Particular-Baptist Society for propagating the Gospel among the heathen') which was formed in Kettering on 2 October 1792 was the first of the 'modern' British Protestant missionary societies.[8] The former shoe-maker, William Carey, was the moving force behind this, both by argument and persuasion within his denomination and by the publication of his small but highly influential work, *An Enquiry into the Obligations of Christians to use Means for the Conversion of the Heathens*.[9] Having established the society, Carey himself became its first missionary in the field when he travelled to India the following year. The BMS, however, did not long enjoy a monopoly in evangelical missionary work – less than three years elapsed before the formation of other societies began.

Richard Gray has noted three distinctive features common to the new missionary societies which emerged between the 1790s and the 1850s.[10] First was their financial independence of the state. Unlike the Danish Lutheran mission to Tranquebar in India (1705),[11] and unlike the English SPG and SPCK, the new missions were financially independent, being funded by local churches and individuals. Second, this financial independence gave a real

---

Movement, and Africa', in Noll, Bebbington and Rawlyk (eds), *Evangelicalism* (Oxford and New York: OUP, 1994).
8 For full details of the founding of the BMS and Carey's part in it see Brian Stanley, *The History of the Baptist Missionary Society 1792-1992* (Edinburgh: T&T Clark, 1992), pp.1-15.
9 New edn, ed. E.A. Payne, (London: Carey Kingsgate Press, 1961).
10 Richard Gray, p.88.
11 W.N. Gunson, 'Missionary Interest in British Expansion in the South Pacific in the Nineteenth Century', *JRH*, III (1965), 310n.; Bebbington, p.39. Interestingly, from 1710 they were partly funded by the English SPCK. See Carson in Stanley (ed.), *Christian Missions and the Enlightenment*, pp.47-48.

autonomy to the society. Though part of a denominational church, the missionary society was outside the official control of that church's hierarchy and there was a good deal of lay involvement in its policy making and administration. This factor was particularly apparent in the case of the CMS. Their leading members were often men of substance and considerable political influence, a fact which later proved invaluable when trying to exert pressure on government departments. Third, the missionary societies enjoyed wide-based support through countless local churches and individuals. A look at the very extensive published donation lists, usually set out regionally, in the annual reports of many of the societies, perfectly illustrates this wide support. It might be said that if the statutory societies represented the 'public sector' of missions, the new voluntary model, initiated by Carey, indicated clear shift to the 'private sector' as a more efficient basis for a society (in effect a company) for the delivery of overseas mission.[12]

It will now be appropriate to examine a number of the missionary societies which had direct involvement in the development of the empire in the mid-Victorian era. These will be first the Established Church's 'evangelical' missionary society. Then two Free Church societies, one interdenominational, one belonging solely to the Wesleyan Methodists. Then a society from Scotland and the Scottish expatriate communities. Finally, two newer Anglican societies reflecting not the tradition of the evangelical revival but the older high church tradition and the nineteenth-century Oxford movement as their inspiration.

London Missionary Society

The London Missionary Society, founded in 1795,[13] and throughout the nineteenth century the largest non-Anglican society, was interdenominational both in its foundation and its constitution, pledged to propagate, 'not Presbyterianism, Independency, Episcopacy, or any other form of Church Order and Government (about which there be many differences of opinion amongst serious persons) but the Glorious Gospel of the blessed God.'[14] But the LMS failed to encompass many missionary-minded Christians who preferred to work within their own denominations and mainly drew its support from the Congregational churches. Initially simply named 'The Missionary Society', it changed to the title by which it is better known in 1818. The LMS was administered from premises at 14 Blomfield Street in the City of London. It was governed by a large Board of Directors appointed by constituent churches and responsible to (in best Congregational tradition) an annual general meeting of

---

12 See Porter, *Religion versus Empire?*, p.45.
13 See Richard Lovett, *The History of the London Missionary Society 1795-1895*, 2 vols, (London: Henry Frowde, 1899), I, pp.3-42. For an 'official' historian Lovett is comparatively objective and, at times, even critical of the LMS Directors.
14 Quoted in Lovett, *History of LMS*, I, p.49-50.

members. From 1831 to 1891 this annual meeting was held at that mecca of Victorian evangelicalism, Exeter Hall in the Strand.

The two leading officials of the Society were the somewhat grandly-titled Home Secretary and Foreign Secretary, the former being concerned with administration and finance, the latter being the person responsible for the missionaries in the field and the person with whom they normally corresponded. Those holding the latter post in this period were Arthur Tidman (1839-68), Joseph Mullens (1868-79) and Ralph Wardlaw Thompson (1881-1914). Far from being desk-bound administrators they took the pastoral welfare of their charges very seriously. Thompson, for example, had to use all his authority and diplomacy to persuade the reluctant James Chalmers to return to Britain for a long-overdue furlough. Mullens had served on the mission field in India for twenty-one years before being recalled to assist, and eventually to succeed, Dr Tidman. His exercise of pastoral care took him first to Madagascar and later to central Africa, where he perished in 1879 on a journey to assist the ill-fated mission to Lake Tanganyika.[15]

The LMS did not limit its activities to any particular part of the globe, having missions in all continents, though those in Europe (Malta and the Greek Islands) and South America were unsuccessful, being abandoned early in the nineteenth century.

In its early days, the LMS had its own training college, first at Gosport, then at Hoxton. The Glasgow Theological Academy, founded in 1811 also trained LMS missionaries. But from the early 1830s there was a change of training policy by the Directors, who henceforth made use of existing institutions to train their candidates. In 1868, for example, the Society's twenty-eight candidates in training were farmed out to no fewer than ten different institutions.

The Congregational churches, which were the natural constituency of the LMS, tended to draw most of their support from lower-middle class and artisan sections of the community. This sociological factor meant that the LMS had fewer wealthy and influential supporters than, say, the Anglican missions. Though it certainly *had* such support (for example, the Hon. Arthur Kinnaird, who spoke for the LMS in the House of Commons and acted as the Society's Treasurer from 1864 until 1875,[16] and who was also a leading figure in the CMS) it was proportionately less. In this mid-Victorian period, before popular imperialism had taken hold of British culture, the LMS had already developed a reputation as one of the least imperialistic of missionary societies and one which worked hard to protect vulnerable indigenous peoples from the depredations of

---

15 See Mullens to Hutchinson, 7 April 1879. CMS Nyanza Mission Papers, CA6/04. *CMS Archives*, University of Birmingham Library.
16 See correspondence of March and April 1875 between Kinnaird and the LMS in LMS Home Office Papers,12/12/A. *Council for World Mission Archives*, School of Oriental and African Studies, London University.

excessive exposure to western commerce and culture.[17] The Revd J. Freeman remarked to the LMS foreign secretary in 1849 that in southern Africa, 'the missionaries are protectors of the Natives and the latter cannot be so easily outraged and driven out (by the Boers) under the direct observation and remonstrances of the missionary'.[18]

Church Missionary Society

Evangelical Anglicans found themselves in sympathy with the aims of the LMS but were unwilling to forsake the Established Church for an interdenominational body. So, right from the start, a denominational attitude intruded into British missionary enterprise, a considerable handicap which was to lead to much wasteful rivalry and duplication of effort in the years to come.[19] Yet Evangelical Anglicans were unhappy with the existing statutory Anglican missionary bodies, the SPG and the SPCK, both somewhat exclusive, both largely untouched by the evangelical revival and neither accountable to their membership. The evangelicals resolved their difficulty by founding their own 'Church Missionary Society'[20] in 1799.[21]

The Church Missionary Society was very much the product of late eighteenth-century Anglican evangelicalism and, in particular, the spirituality and practical organisational skills of the Clapham Sect. But the CMS was slow to build up momentum within the Church of England. It received no overt episcopal support until 1814 and for decades remained reliant on German and

---

17 The 'anti-imperialism' of the LMS was not, however, universal. John Mackenzie (Bechuanaland 1858-82) was the classic exception. See Anthony Sillery, *John Mackenzie of Bechuanaland,1835-1899: a study in humanitarian imperialism* (Cape Town: A.A.Balkema, 1971); Anthony J. Dachs, 'Missionary imperialism - the case of Bechuanaland', *Journal of African History*, 13 (1972) 647-658.

18 Freeman to LMS, 25 Dec 1849, LMS Home Odds, 2/4/D, quoted in Comaroff and Comaroff, I, 274.

19 Two examples will perhaps suffice. Bishop Stephen Neill told with some relish the (probably apocryphal) story of a leading Indian clergyman visiting mid-Victorian London who, on seeing St Paul's Cathedral, enquired if it was a CMS church or an SPG church. Stephen Neill, *A History of Christian Missions* (Harmondsworth: Penguin, 1964), pp. 513-514. In the flurry of missionary activity that followed the death of David Livingstone in 1873 both the main Scottish denominations set up separate missions in what was later to become Nyasaland/Malawi.

20 Originally named the 'Society for Missions to Africa and the East'.

21 Charles Simeon, the highly influential vicar of Holy Trinity Cambridge, and one of the founders of the CMS had previously sent out five Cambridge graduates to India as chaplains to the East India Company. Michael Hennell, *Sons of the Prophets* (London. SPCK, 1979), p.3.

Swiss missionaries from seminaries in Berlin and later from Basle.[22] Up to 120 subsequently attended the missionary college founded by the CMS in Islington in 1826 and were ordained into the Anglican ministry.[23]

Several Germans are involved in the case studies which follow, including Ludwig Krapf and Johannes Rebmann in East Africa and Charles Gollmer, Adolphus Mann and David Hinderer in Yorubaland.[24] W.O. Ajayi referred approvingly to this arrangement as an 'adventure of partnership in missionary manpower'.[25] David Livingstone, never one to hide his feelings, disapproved, but was more contemptuous of the lack of British men willing to serve than of the CMS for being put in the position of needing to recruit from overseas. In his Senate House speech at Cambridge in December 1857 Livingstone said that in his view it was 'deplorable to think that one of the noblest of our missionary societies, the Church Missionary Society, is compelled to send to Germany for missionaries…'.[26] Whatever the rights or wrongs of this arrangement, the German missionaries were universally loyal to the Society and, unlike some of their English colleagues, rarely complained or intrigued. Indeed, Ludwig Krapf, the pioneering missionary in East Africa, took such an interest in the work that he continued to write regular and well-informed letters to Salisbury Square from his home in Germany for twenty-four years after his retirement from the mission field in 1856.[27]

By the period of this study two vitally important factors made the CMS stand out from all other missions. First, it was the largest missionary society of the Established Church. Though other Anglican missionary societies were formed in the nineteenth century – the Melanesian Mission, the South American Missionary Society, the Universities' Mission to Central Africa – and though the SPG enjoyed something of a revival in the nineteenth century, none had the same global coverage or the kudos of being the largest mission of the largest church in Britain. Further, the CMS also benefited from the Church of England

---

22 In the period 1799-1850 more than one in five CMS missionaries came from continental Europe. Walls in Stanley (ed.), *Christian Missions and the Enlightenment*, p.35

23 See John Pinnington, 'Church Principles in the early years of the Church Missionary Society: the problem of the "German" missionaries,' *Journal of Theological Studies,* NS 20 (2) (1969), 523-532.

24 Ludwig Krapf, the pioneering missionary in East Africa was unusual in that he proceeded directly from Basle to Egypt, then Abyssinia, then Mombasa without ever passing through the missionary college at Islington or receiving Anglican ordination. Eugene Stock, *A History of the Church Missionary Society,* 4 vols (London: CMS, 1899-1916), II, 129.

25 W.O. Ajayi , 'A History of the Yoruba Mission, 1843-1880', unpublished MA thesis (Bristol, 1959), p.40.

26 Quoted in Philip Elston, 'Livingstone and the Anglican Church', in B. Pachai (ed.), *Livingstone: Man of Africa* (London: Longman, 1973), p.66.

27 Krapf's letters can be found in the CMS East African Mission papers, CA5/ O16.

being the Established Church in the sense of being the church of the establishment. This not only gave it greater clout with colonial military and naval authorities but also, vitally, in Parliament and Whitehall. The Society was always willing to exploit its social advantages.

But perhaps the greatest advantage the CMS enjoyed was not its social position but its management. For in the chair of the 'honorary clerical secretary' in its Salisbury Square headquarters, for the formative period of 1841 to 1872, sat the commanding figure of the Revd Henry Venn.[28]

Venn, born in 1796, was three years old when his father, the Revd John Venn, Rector of Clapham, friend of Wilberforce and 'chaplain' to the Clapham sect, presided at the founding meeting of the CMS. But his evangelical pedigree went back further, for his grandfather and namesake the Revd Henry Venn, was one of the leaders of the eighteenth- century evangelical revival. Curate of Clapham, Vicar of Huddersfield and lastly Rector of Yelling in Huntingdonshire, he was an associate of Wesley, Whitefield and the other eighteenth-century evangelical divines. In 1837 the younger Henry Venn declined an offer of the See of Madras, preferring the less exalted but far more influential role of directing the intercontinental work of the CMS from his desk in London.[29] Under Venn, the office routine of Salisbury Square became almost a missionary parody of the Colonial Office, with incoming letters being circulated like official despatches for minuting. All received his close attention and were initialled 'H.V.' when read.

Venn was very much a missionary theorist as well as a practical administrator. Indeed he was probably the greatest missionary strategist of the nineteenth century and his ideas were undoubtedly ahead of their time.[30] No other missionary society in this period had such a commanding figure in a position of authority.

In a new departure in missionary thinking, Venn drew clear distinctions between 'mission' and 'church', and between the role of missionary and pastor.

---

28 On Venn, see W. Knight, *Memoirs of Henry Venn / The Missionary Secretariat of Henry Venn* (London: Longmans Green & Co., 1882) and an informative brief biography in Hennell, pp.68-90. Also helpful is T.E. Yates, *Henry Venn and Victorian Bishops Abroad* (Uppsala and London: SPCK, 1978). The most detailed recent work is Wilbert R. Shenk, *Henry Venn, Missionary Statesman* (Maryknoll, N.Y.: Orbis, 1983).

29 Venn was brother-in-law of James Stephen, Permanent Under-Secretary at the Colonial Office, 1836-47. S.R. Stembridge comments on Stephen: 'His evangelical background and profound religious feeling led him to look on empire as a field for missionary work and the uplifting of backward peoples'. Stembridge, *Parliament, the Press, and the Colonies*, 1846-1880 (New York: Garland, 1982), p.40. The same words could equally have been applied to Venn.

30 See Shenk, Missionary Statesman, above, and C.P. Williams, *The Idea of the Self-Governing Church* (Leiden: E.J.Brill, 1990), pp. 1-51. For a thorough account and analysis of Venn's views in a short compass, see Shenk, 'The Contribution of Henry Venn to Missionary Thought', *Anvil*, 2 (1985), 25-42.

In his view the mission was not itself the church but was there to create an indigenous church and should, at the right time, withdraw in order to ensure that that church would be truly indigenous and not an alien institution. To Venn the great object of a mission was:

> the raising up of a Native Church – self-supporting, self-governing, self-extending. The Mission is the scaffolding; the Native Church is the edifice. The removal of the scaffolding is the proof that the building is completed.[31]

Once established, these new churches should not be dependent on missionaries from Europe. His Minutes of 1851, 1861 and 1866 spelled out his views in detail.[32] A fundamental step towards this withdrawal would be the creation of a 'native pastorate' funded by the local church rather than the European mission. Venn's vision was not always shared by white European missionaries who were liable to feel vulnerable and undervalued at being replaced by native pastors.[33] In Sierra Leone and Yorubaland in West Africa and in Tinnevelly in India, three places where the native pastorate scheme was tried, all did not run smoothly or according either to plan or timetable. Nevertheless, 'so powerful was the "Venn" orthodoxy that it was reasserted by an influential CMS committee [in the 1890s]. Only in the opening years of the twentieth century were the principles he stood for ... discarded'.[34] In the long-term, of course, Venn's views were vindicated and, since the era of decolonisation, third world churches have had indigenous leaderships. Today European missionaries, or 'mission partners' to use the current jargon, work under the authority of local leadership.[35]

In 1872 Venn's long tenure of office came to an end and he died the following year. He was succeeded by the Revd Henry Wright but no-one in the CMS had Venn's sole influence as Wright had to work in tandem with a Lay Secretary with whom he failed to develop a good working relationship. Venn had introduced this arrangement in 1867 to help share his workload without

---

31 Quoted in Shenk, *Missionary Statesman*, p. 46.
32 Venn's Minutes are printed as Appendix I of Shenk, *Missionary Statesman*, pp.118-129.
33 The fact that Venn used the phrase 'euthanasia of a mission' clearly set the alarm bells ringing among some missionaries in the field. Henry Townsend's dogged rearguard action against Venn's plans in Yorubaland can be seen in Chapter 6, below.
34 Williams, *Self-Governing Church*, p.xiv. See also Williams' 'The Church Missionary Society and the Indigenous Church in the Second Half of the Nineteenth Century: The Defense and Destruction of the Venn Ideals', in Dana L. Roberts (Ed.) *Converting Colonialism* (Grand Rapids and Cambridge: Eerdmans, 2008), pp.86-111.
35 Perhaps the sternest critic of Venn was Stephen Neill, himself a former CMS missionary and bishop, who complained that a 'sharp separation between Church and mission as implied in Venn's solution seems to lack serious theological foundation in the New Testament'. Neill, *History of Christian Missions*, pp.259-260

diminishing his authority. But with Venn's powers declining the Lay Secretary, Edward Hutchinson, had become particularly influential in Venn's last years. It was he, for example, who led the Society's campaign against the Arab slave trade in East Africa.[36] Hutchinson was regarded as the financial expert in the secretariat, which proved to be unfortunate since he was clearly allowed sufficient freedom from supervision to become involved in serious financial irregularities and, after hurriedly resigning his position in May 1881, he fled to Paris to escape possible criminal proceedings.[37]

When Roland Oliver analysed the donations list of the CMS for the year 1882 he discovered that in a church which by that date had a number of different missionary societies, the CMS was supported by about one third of the country's 15,700 parishes.[38] It would be incorrect to deduce from this that two thirds of the parishes supported other missions since the CMS was by far the largest Anglican society. What is clear is that only a few short years before the 'new imperialism' became popular in Britain the majority of English and Welsh Anglican parishes still had no interest in overseas missions.

Wesleyan Methodist Missionary Society

During his lifetime John Wesley, possibly influenced by memories of his own fruitless time in Georgia, was said to have discouraged overseas missions on the grounds that there were more immediate prospects of success at home, though he had sent Francis Asbury and Thomas Coke to North America.[39] But as far back as 1778 the Methodist Conference first debated the possibility of sending a mission to Africa,[40] and in 1783 Thomas Coke published his *Plan of the Society for the Establishment of Missions among the Heathens*, eight years before the publication of William Carey's *Enquiry*. By 1813, twenty years after Wesley's death, the interest in foreign missions had led to various Methodist Districts forming their own local missionary societies. The Methodist Conference eventually harnessed this enthusiasm and the Wesleyan Methodist Missionary Society was officially founded in 1818.[41] But, as the Society's official

---

36 As well as much parliamentary lobbying Hutchinson published *The Slave Trade of East Africa* (London: Sampson Low, 1874).
37 For details of the 'range of ... doubtful actions' pursued by Hutchinson, see Williams, *Self-Governing Church*, pp.96-97. Eugene Stock, the Society's official historian, is much more circumspect about the affair referring only to 'circumstances ... which led to his retirement'. Stock, III, p.261.
38 Oliver, p.5n.
39 See Bebbington, *Evangelicalism*, p.42.
40 Henry Rack, *Reasonable Enthusiast: John Wesley and the Rise of Methodism*, 3rd edn (London: Epworth, 2002) p.478.
41 The Wesleyan Missionary Society (WMS) became, on Methodist reunion in 1933, the Methodist Missionary Society (MMS) and, by the 1970s, the 'Overseas Division' of

historians note, the foundation of the WMMS in 1818 merely made official what had been happening spontaneously and 'gave formal signature and incorporation to the missionary work which Methodists of their own accord had already carried forward successfully for fifty years'.[42] David Hempton has recently emphasised this 'bottom-up' development:

> Methodism had a mobile laity before it had missionaries, it had missionaries before it had a missionary society, and it had locally based missionary societies before it had a national missionary society.[43]

Interestingly, when the official foundation of the WMMS took place, it was not a voluntary body of subscribing members but 'none other than the Methodist Church itself organised for overseas missions ... and every member of the Methodist Church as such is a member of the Methodist Missionary Society'.[44] The Wesleyan Methodist Conference concerned to safeguard centralised control of the society and its constitution ensured that the WMMS and its missionary activity came explicitly under the control of the Methodist Conference.[45] This was a unique arrangement among the British missionary societies.

It should be noted, however, that Bernard Semmel has postulated an ulterior motive for the foundation of the WMMS.[46] In his view, foreign missions were actively promoted by the Methodist leadership, especially Jabez Bunting, in order to siphon off excess evangelising energy at home. The alleged reason for this was to reassure Lord Sidmouth's Home Office that Methodist activity was not part of a wider pattern of civil unrest. This thesis was subsequently challenged by Stuart Piggin who went on to suggest that the development of missionary activity actually revitalised the British Methodism.[47]

The WMMS was governed by a Missionary Committee consisting of the President and Secretary of Conference together with forty-eight other members. No fewer than three General Secretaries were to be in office at any one time

---

the Methodist Church. Here, the convention adopted by most modern historians in the field, of referring to the society as the 'Wesleyan Methodist Missionary Society' (WMMS), will be followed.

42 G.G. Findlay and W.W. Holdsworth, *The History of the Wesleyan Methodist Missionary Society*, 5 vols, (London: Epworth, 1921-4), I, 35. Though the most detailed book on the WMMS, Findlay and Holdsworth are sometimes rather vague about dates and far from impartial when analyzing contentious issues.

43 David Hempton, *Methodism: Empire of the Spirit* (New Haven and London: Yale University Press, 2005), p.30.

44 Minutes of the Methodist Conference, 1943, Appendix III, quoted in John Vickers, *The Genesis of Methodist Missions*, (Cambridge: NAMP, 1996), p.1.

45 This proved remarkably durable and was not revised until 1884.

46 Bernard Semmel, *The Methodist Revolution* (London: Heinemann, 1974).

47 Stuart Piggin, 'Halévy Revisited: The Origins of the Wesleyan Methodist Missionary Society: An Examination of Semmel's Thesis', *JICH*, 9 (1980), 17-37.

with one always, like canons in an Anglican cathedral, 'in residence' at mission headquarters. This was 17 Bishopsgate Street in the City of London, acquired in 1841 with a newly-built centenary hall attached as a centre for WMMS missionaries on furlough in London. From 1855 the Pacific work of the WMMS was devolved, for convenience,[48] to the Australian Wesleyan Missionary Conference. This was a propitious move, given the considerable Methodist influence in the New South Wales Assembly.[49] Links between British and Australian Methodists were strengthened and W.B. Boyce, General Secretary from 1861 to 1876, was a past president of the Australian Methodist Conference. When Shirley Baker, a Methodist missionary turned politician, began from 1869 to build up what eventually became a personal dictatorship in Tonga, it was the Australian WMMS that had to deal with the situation and any odium was incurred by them and not the parent society.[50]

The Society had its well-placed supporters in the House of Commons, Admiral J.E. Erskine, and the M'Arthur brothers, Alexander and William, the former having first served in the New South Wales Assembly and the latter, serving as WMMS Lay Treasurer from 1883, proved highly influential in bringing missionary concerns before Parliament.

New Hebrides Mission

The Presbyterian mission to the New Hebrides (modern Vanuatu) was quite unlike any of the other missionary societies in this study in that it was never 'founded' in a formal sense but grew piecemeal from the work of one man, the Revd John Geddie, sent to the mission field by a group of local churches in Nova Scotia in 1847.[51] It was, as Geddie's admiring neighbour, Bishop Selwyn

---

48 John Garrett contends the motive was primarily financial. Garrett, *To Live Among the Stars: Christian Origins in Oceania* (Geneva and Suva: World Council of Churches, 1982), p.128.
49 See W.D. McIntyre, *The Imperial Frontier in the Tropics 1865-75* (London: Macmillan, 1967), pp.215-216.
50 See Morrell, *Pacific Islands*, pp.317-329.
51 Like William Carey before him, Geddie had urged the local presbytery to take their responsibility for world mission seriously and, having achieved that, he became their first missionary. The New Hebrides Mission is also unique in neither having had its history written nor even possessing an archive, factors probably accounted for by its disparate nature and the convoluted history of its Scottish branch, the Reformed Presbyterian Church of Scotland. This body united with the Free Church of Scotland in 1876, which in turn united with the United Presbyterian Church in 1900, which in turn joined the Church of Scotland in 1929. No official records of this diversely-parented mission have survived. Yet, as O.W. Parnaby points out [*Britain and the Labor Trade in the Southwest Pacific* (Durham, N.C.: York University Press, 1964), p.212] much of their correspondence is extant in Colonial Office files and Parliamentary Papers. The best, though incomplete, accounts of the mission in this period are an appendix in

of New Zealand, correctly noted, 'the first instance of any Colonial body sending out its own mission to the heathen without any assistance from the mother country'.[52]

In time the news of Geddie's achievements spread and he was joined in the New Hebrides by others inspired by his remarkable work and eager to participate in it. This mission was an amalgam of missionaries from several Presbyterian churches, in Scotland, Nova Scotia and Australia. Very much a Scottish mission (both of native Scots and expatriates from the colonies of the first British empire), its supervisory body in Britain was the Foreign Missions Committee of the Reformed Presbyterian Church of Scotland, whose secretary, John Kay, both publicised the work of the mission and made representations to Parliament and the press in order to support the mission's robust campaign against the Pacific labour trade. In fact, the individual missionaries were virtually independent on their respective islands and the mission ran itself by means of an annual synod of the missionaries in the field, held in rotation at the various mission stations in the New Hebrides. By 1879 there were eleven missionaries on the active staff. John Geddie took the chair and John Inglis acted as vice-chairman, but the missionaries had a good deal of autonomy and frequently acted individually in their campaigns against the labour trade. Because of aggressive campaigning and his flair for publicity John Paton became well-known in Britain and Australia. Dr Robert Steel in Sydney acted as the Mission's agent in Australia and link with Europe.

It is interesting to note that, though comprising men of a fairly rigid Presbyterian background, and though highly confrontational to the labour traders of the south-west Pacific, the New Hebrides missionaries maintained good relations with other missionary societies operating in the area. Good relations with the largely Congregational LMS were, no doubt, *de rigueur* since Geddie had actually taken over the mission from the LMS who had had very little success since establishing it in 1840.[53] Subsequently the LMS aided Geddie, initially working entirely alone, in establishing himself on Aneiteum and in sending Thomas Powell from Samoa to assist him in the early days. It also seems that, for a number of years subsequently, Geddie used the larger mission's supply network in order to obtain supplies.[54] Rather more surprising

---

Commander Albert Markham, The *Cruise of the 'Rosario' amongst the New Hebrides and Santa Cruz Islands* (London: S. Low, Marston, Low and Searle, 1873), and Robert Steel, *The New Hebrides and Christian Missions* (London: J. Nisbet, 1880). See also the missionaries' own survey: John Kay, (ed.), The *Slave Trade in the New Hebrides* (Edinburgh: Edmonston and Douglas, 1872).

52 G.A. Selwyn, 'Letters on the Melanesian Mission in 1853', p.33, quoted in David Hilliard, *God's Gentlemen* (St Lucia, Queensland: Queensland University Press, 1978), p.4.

53 Garrett, *Stars,* pp.167-168.

54 See Geddie to Tidman, 12 December 1859. LMS South Seas Correspondence, 23/5/E.

were the good relations the Presbyterians enjoyed with the High Anglican Melanesian Mission, involved in the Banks and Santa Cruz groups in the northern New Hebrides. This friendly relationship would seem to date from Bishop Selwyn's comments in November 1850 when he held up Geddie's work as an example to the Australian churches.[55] Selwyn found relations with the WMMS more difficult, however, branding them 'schismatics' and complaining of 'the popery of their system, in spreading the name of Wesley, and the authority of their conference over the whole mission field'.[56] But Selwyn sought unity rather than competition in mission work, even when other missions were not entirely to his theological taste. Thus he made informal comity agreements leaving the Loyalty Islands to the LMS and the southern New Hebrides to Geddie's Presbyterians.[57]

Stephen Maughan has asserted that 'the core ideologies of the Victorian Anglican missionary movement [were] rooted heavily in an evangelical impulse and a parallel High Church reaction'.[58] We now turn to that High Church 'reaction'.

Melanesian Mission

Though the 1850s, 60s and even 70s were largely years of stagnation for the classical evangelical missionary societies – what Porter calls a 'mid-century waning of missionary enthusiasm'[59] – and the concept of 'faith' missions propagated by Hudson Taylor and others began to develop a momentum, this period nevertheless saw the foundation of two new classical societies, both with a more High Church ethos. The origins of the Melanesian Mission may be traced back to the consecration of George Augustus Selwyn as the first Anglican Bishop of New Zealand in 1841. Whether or not the Letters Patent delineating his new diocese contained a glaring error has been much discussed.[60] Nevertheless, whether by mistake or intention, the New Zealand

---

55 See George Patterson, *Missionary Life among the Cannibals, being the Life of John Geddie, DD, First Missionary to the New Hebrides* (Toronto: J. Campbell, J. Bain and Hart, 1882), p.256.
56 See Allan K. Davidson in Kevin Ward and Brian Stanley (eds), *The Church Mission Society and World Christianity 1799-1999* (Grand Rapids and Richmond: Eerdmans and Curzon Press, 1999), p.212. and Geoffrey Rowell, *The Vision Glorious: themes and personalities of the Catholic revival in Anglicanism* (Oxford: OUP, 1983), p.173.
57 Ian Breward, *A History of the Churches in Australasia* (Oxford: OUP, 2001), p.89.
58 Stephen Maughan, 'Imperial Christianity? Bishop Montgomery and the Foreign Missions of the Church of England, 1895-1915', in Andrew Porter (ed.), *The Imperial Horizons of British Protestant Missions, 1880-1914* (Grand Rapids and Cambridge: Eerdmans, 2003) 32-57.
59 Porter, *Religion versus Empire?*, p.224.
60 See, for example, C.E. Fox, *Lord of the Southern Isles* (London: Mowbray, 1958), pp.2-3 and Hilliard, *God's Gentlemen*, p.1. The latter is an extremely useful study, one

diocese extended from latitude 47 degrees South to latitude 36 degrees *North* (the supposed mistake) so placing under his episcopal care a wedge of the globe extending nearly from Antarctica up into the northern Pacific. Thus John Coleridge Patteson, Selwyn's prize recruit, joined him in New Zealand in 1854 with the specific brief of relieving him of the responsibility for the Melanesian part of his enormous diocese so that Selwyn could concentrate on New Zealand.[61]

On a visit to the Solomon Islands in 1852 Selwyn had noted in his diary that 'the careful superintendence of this multitude of islands will require the services of a missionary bishop, able and willing to devote himself to this work.'[62] In due course the diocese was legally divided and Patteson was consecrated first Bishop of Melanesia in 1861.[63] Under Patteson the mission moved closer to the people it served. Its initial headquarters had been Auckland – the nearest part of New Zealand to Melanesia – to which hand-picked Melanesian boys were taken for part of the year to be educated in a Christian community. In 1867 Patteson moved the school community to Norfolk Island, 600 miles closer to the boys' homes. Eventually Patteson himself moved to the island of Mota in the Banks Group of the northern New Hebrides, which he considered to be the most central part of his diocese. He also began to use the Mota language as the mission's *lingua franca*. Like Venn, Selwyn, Chalmers and Livingstone, Patteson was an innovator in missionary work. Two areas in particular are worthy of note. Firstly, he began to examine the traditional Victorian connection between Christianity and literacy, by the end of his life questioning whether or not it was an unnecessary burden for adults in a non-literate society.[64] Secondly, like Bishop Selwyn before him, he affirmed the value of native cultures:

---

of the two best currently available on the Melanesian Mission. The other is Darrell Whiteman, *Melanesians and Missionaries* (Pasadena: William Carey Library, 1983).

61 Patteson's remarkable facility for linguistics was shown on the outward journey, during which he learned Maori so as to be able to converse freely with the natives he met upon landing. E.S. Armstrong, *The History of the Melanesian Mission* (London: Isbister, 1900), p.24. In due course he mastered twenty-four languages and reduced many of them to writing. Whiteman, p.119. However, a total of ninety-six different languages were spoken in the Solomon Islands and the New Hebrides.

62 Quoted in Rowell, p.175.

63 Not *second* bishop as Parnaby suggests. See O. W. Parnaby, 'Aspects of British Policy in the Pacific: the 1872 Pacific Islanders Protection Act', *HSANZ*, VIII (1957), 64.

64 Hilliard, 'John Coleridge Patteson, Missionary Bishop of Melanesia', in J.W. Davidson and Deryck Scarr (eds), *Pacific Island Portraits* (Canberra: Australian National University Press, 1970), p.195. This was radical thinking since the connection between the two was taken as read by all missions including the Melanesian. Indeed Henry Venn had previously taken Bishop Selwyn to task for insisting that Maoris should

> I have for years thought that we seek in our missions a great deal too much to make English Christians of our converts. We consciously and unanimously assume English Christianity to be necessary. One mistake of this kind was to suppose clothing essential. Aesthetically, clothes are no improvement; there is almost always a stiff, shabby-genteel look.[65]

Two years before his death he returned to this theme:

> It is easy for us now to say that some of the early English Missions, without thinking at all about it, in all probability, sought to impose an English line of thought and religion on Indians and Africans. Even English dress was thought to be almost essential, and English habits &c., were regarded as part of the education of persons converted through the agency of English Missions. All this seems to be burdening the message of the Gospel with unnecessary difficulties.... If we treat them as inferiors they will always remain in that position of inferiority.[66]

Consequently he aimed to disturb as little as possible the manners and customs of the people among whom he worked.

Patteson's refined manners and privileged upbringing made him regard as distasteful the very idea of publicising the mission in the way other missionary societies did, since he felt it would cheapen both his own activities and the spiritual experiences of his converts. But his cousin, the writer Charlotte M. Yonge, ensured that Melanesia – and Patteson – were not unknown in Britain. Her efforts were not wasted and the fact that Patteson was very much one of their own at last made missions respectable in polite society in Britain.

His tragic death – discussed in Chapter 2 – did even more to raise the profile of missionary work and the dangers with which it had to contend. Indeed, its recruits in Patteson's time were very much drawn from the upper strata of society and most were the products of a public school and Oxbridge education. It is easy to smile – or even cringe – at Patteson's plaintive cry, 'Oh! for good Eton fellows to pull together with me on the Pacific, as on the Thames'.[67] But aside from overtones of snobbery or class consciousness there was the real pain of a highly cultured and educated individual who had given his life to missionary work in an obscure and dangerous corner of the globe, who longed for others of the same social standing and educational background to work with him in order to provide both companionship and mental stimulus.

---

know both English and Greek before being eligible for ordination. Venn to Selwyn, 12 July, 1851, quoted in Williams, *Self Governing Church*, p.7.
65 Quoted in Fox, pp.18-19.
66 Patteson to Miss Mackenzie, 26 February 1869, quoted in Charlotte M. Yonge, *Life of John Coleridge Patteson, Missionary Bishop of the Melanesian Islands*, 2 vols (London: Macmillan, 1874), II, pp.358-360.
67 Patteson to his father, 4 June 1861, quoted in Hilliard, 'John Coleridge Patteson', p.195.

The posthumous tribute paid to Patteson by the Presbyterian New Hebrides missionaries, men of very different theological and social antecedents, though smacking somewhat of the kind of stylised tribute that Victorian working men paid to their social superiors, was nevertheless genuine and an indication of the central place he had acquired in all missionary activity in the Pacific:

> Bishop Patteson's talents, acquirements, social position, and earnest piety, with his abundant and wisely-directed labours have greatly elevated the character of missions in the estimation of all classes, both in the colonies and throughout the British Empire, and have conveyed unspeakable benefits to the degraded natives in Western Polynesia.[68]

Their tribute was particularly apt since it was because of the Pacific labour trade against which both Patteson and the New Hebrides missionaries waged a fervent campaign – though in very different styles – that Patteson lost his life, clubbed to death by the very people he had come to help, whose hostility had been aroused by their treatment at the hands of the white labour traders.

Unlike virtually all the other missions founded in the late eighteenth and early nineteenth centuries, the Melanesian Mission did not owe its roots to the evangelical movement, but to a pre-Tractarian form of High Church Anglicanism in the tradition of Andrewes, Laud, Cosin and Sancroft. Patteson was wary of the Oxford Movement and the introduction of both theology and ritual from Roman Catholicism that was becoming increasingly fashionable in those Tractarian circles as the nineteenth century progressed. Though he is known to have corresponded with John Keble, he was neither a close friend nor a disciple.[69] It was not until the early twentieth century, long after Patteson's death, that the Melanesian Mission began to acquire the trappings of contemporary Anglo-Catholicism.[70] The Mission *per se* was finally wound up in 1975 when it became the autonomous Province of Melanesia within the Anglican Communion.

---

68 Quoted in Steel, p.424.
69 At least one letter from Keble survives in the mission archives. Keble to Patteson, 15 July 1862. *Melanesian Mission Archives*. Bishop Patteson Papers. Mel/M 2/8. Perhaps the link was through Charlotte Yonge, Patteson's cousin and a staunch supporter of the mission who was prepared for confirmation by Keble. Rowell, p.33.
70 For this change in the mission's churchmanship see Whiteman p.333; Hilliard, pp.232-234.

Universities' Mission to Central Africa

The Universities' Mission to Central Africa was the last of the major classical missionary societies to be founded.[71] Its inspiration, ironically, since the UMCA was the most high-church of all the Anglican missionary societies in the nineteenth century, was the Scots Presbyterian, David Livingstone. The challenge by this near-legendary Christian explorer, who had only recently left the employ of the LMS, was made in the Senate House at Cambridge on 4 December 1857.[72] After painting a stark picture of the effect the slave trade was having on East and Central Africa, he challenged the two ancient universities to send their finest and best to provide missionaries for Africa. Within three years the mission had been formed;[73] the Revd Charles F. Mackenzie had been chosen to lead the mission; and, in startling contrast to the somewhat lower-key starts experienced by the other missions, the mission party was sent out in October 1860 via a valedictory service in no lesser setting than Canterbury Cathedral.

The UMCA was also the first mission to be influenced from its foundation by the Oxford Movement, clear evidence of the rapid growth of Tractarianism in the ancient universities. At this period, any new departure in the Anglican church inevitably exhibited Tractarian influence and consequently a bishop at the head of the new mission was considered to be *de rigueur*. Therefore on New Year's Day 1861, seven weeks *before* J.C. Patteson's consecration as missionary bishop of Melanesia, Mackenzie was consecrated in St George's Cathedral, Cape Town, the first missionary bishop of the Anglican church.[74] However, the UMCA differed from the two other Anglican societies already discussed. After all, the traditional high church Melanesian Mission as the

---

71 The UMCA has published two official histories of this period, G.H. Wilson, *The History of the Universities' Mission to Central Africa* (London: UMCA, 1936) and A.E.M. Anderson-Morshead, *The History of the Universities' Mission to Central Africa*, Vol. 1, 1859-1909 (London: UMCA, 1955). The former is to be preferred. For a very useful brief critical overview of the UMCA see Andrew Porter, 'The Universities' Mission to Central Africa: Anglo-Catholicism and the Twentieth-Century Colonial Encounter', in Brian Stanley, (ed.), *Missions, Nationalism and the End of Empire* (Grand Rapids and Cambridge: Eerdmans, 2003), pp.79-107.
72 Livingstone's speech is printed in several places. See, for example, George Seaver, *David Livingstone: his Life and Letters* (London: Lutterworth, 1957), pp.292ff.
73 The mission's name was initially in a state of flux. After Livingstone's speech had had a wider than expected impact, other universities also took up the challenge and the 'Oxford, Cambridge, Durham and Dublin Mission to Central Africa' was formed in 1860. But the two newer universities soon dropped out leaving the 'Oxford and Cambridge Mission to Central Africa'. By 1865 this had been shortened to the 'Universities' Mission to Central Africa' This title remained for precisely a century until the UMCA merged with the SPG in 1965 to form the USPG.
74 This was the very opposite of Henry Venn's policy of building a mission from the bottom up.

offshoot of the diocese of New Zealand represented the main stream of Anglicanism; the CMS had consciously been founded on what John Venn called the 'church principle', in other words as a missionary society for the whole Church of England.[75] In contrast, the UMCA represented a tradition within the Church of England rather than that church as a whole.

The early years of the mission were particularly traumatic ones. The unnecessary death of Mackenzie was no martyrdom, but tragic nevertheless, and the drastic but necessary changes to the mission made by his successor, Bishop Tozer, were all the more difficult to accept because they contained the implication that Mackenzie had been wrong from the start to follow Livingstone's suggestion and establish the mission in the Shiré highlands. However, though not universally recognised or appreciated at the time, Tozer, in abandoning the Shiré highlands and moving its headquarters to Zanzibar, gave the mission a new lease of life and, with a secure base, allowed expansion under his successor, Bishop Steere. The UMCA was now firmly established though, much to his chagrin, not in the location originally envisaged by Livingstone.

Missionary Motivation and Personnel

Having briefly surveyed the relevant missionary societies it is now appropriate to examine in some detail the factors common to the different societies and, in particular, to their missionaries in the field. Were they all of one mind or did their approach to missionary work differ, and if so were these differences substantial or merely cosmetic? Were there any differences in personnel and organisation, and in their attitudes to indigenous peoples and their culture? What hardships and dangers did missionaries face? After all, the nineteenth century saw the beginnings of mission work on a large scale. For the first time a significant number of people from the western world became active in underdeveloped parts of the globe as messengers of the Christian gospel and its associated values of an educated mind and a healthy body. What motivated this vast army of missionaries and from what part of British society did they come?

In an introduction to 2,000 years of Christian mission, David Bosch produces two lists of missionary motives (the first he refers to as 'impure' motives) culled from the writings of a number of missiologists. There are an imperialist motive, a cultural motive, a romantic motive and the motive of ecclesiastical colonialism. His second list (of presumably less impure motives) comprises a motive of conversion, an eschatological motive, a church planting motive and a philanthropic motive. All these, he suggests, have played some

---

75 It was because of this inclusiveness that the CMS suffered its only major schism – the departure of a substantial number of conservative evangelicals to form the Bible Churchmen's Missionary Society (BCMS) in 1922.

part in Christian missions, despite a degree of ambiguity in the motives he has identified.[76]

A seminal study of missionary vocation is that by Ruth Rouse, published as far back as 1917.[77] Rouse examined the circumstances of over 300 men who were called to the mission field in the nineteenth century and had left written accounts of their calling. From this research she concluded that though her subjects came from a wide spread of missionary societies and several nations the central motive was constant. Discounting possible subsidiary motives of status, family circumstances or emotional pressure, she identified the basic underlying motive for missionary service quite simply as a 'loyalty to Jesus Christ'. However, other than the presence of a specific 'call' to missionary work, Rouse failed to explain the motivation of those who went overseas over and against those (the vast majority) with a similar loyalty who remained at home. Also, by suggesting that 'the heathen are no longer thought by missionaries of as "perishing" but as "suffering" and "neglected"', Rouse greatly generalised the development of missionary thought. It would not, for example, apply to the Presbyterian New Hebrides missionaries. J.W. Burton, who by the 1930s was the general secretary of Australian Methodist Overseas Missions recorded an event in 1901 when he, as a young missionary, was denounced by the venerable John Paton for having the temerity to suggest that the heathen were not actually 'perishing' without the light of the gospel.[78]

In an independent piece of research published in 1974 concerning the motivation of LMS missionaries in India in the second half of the nineteenth century G.A. Oddie has in many ways confirmed Rouse's research, though suggesting that a complex of motives was more likely than a single one.[79]

More recently Peter Williams has gone some of the way to filling in the gaps left by Rouse in her study of missionary vocation, but unlike Rouse he does not discount the importance of status. While at no point denying the presence or the validity of specific calls to the mission field, he looks at some of the social attitudes and assumptions that might have influenced the Christians in relation to missionary work. In particular Williams has drawn attention to the social origins and expectations of nineteenth-century missionaries, observing from a study of four of the major societies that even in the second half of the century 'they were still most frequently drawn from the ranks of the artisans, the *petit bourgeoisie* and the newly professionally conscious'.[80] This group he

---

76 Bosch, *Transforming Mission*, p.5.
77 Ruth Rouse, 'Missionary Vocation', *International Review of Missions* (April 1917), 244-257.
78 J.W. Burton, *Modern Missions in the South Pacific* (London: Livingstone Press, 1949), pp.11-12.
79 G.A. Oddie, 'India and Missionary Motives c.1850-1900', *JEH*, 25 (1974), 61-74.
80 C.P. Williams, '"Not Quite Gentlemen": An Examination of "Middling Class" Protestant Missionaries from Britain c.1850-1900', *JEH*, 31 (1980), 301-315. Max

identifies as corresponding with the 'middling class' category of R.S. Neale.[81] Aspiring social climbers could often find on the mission field a status which was denied to them at home. But if most missionaries were 'not quite gentlemen', the two newer Anglican missions, the Melanesian and the UMCA, undoubtedly raised the average social class of missionaries. Bishop Patteson, for example, educated at Eton and Balliol, and cousin of the Attorney General at the time of his death, showed that mission personnel were not always lower middle class or artisan and made missions socially respectable. And the UMCA was specifically drawn from the socially elitist ranks of Oxford and Cambridge graduates.[82]

To supplement missionaries from Britain, virtually all missions made use of aboriginal people whom they had trained in order to further the teaching work of the mission. The first bringers of the Christian gospel to Fiji were not the Methodists from Britain in 1835 but Hanea and Atai, two native teachers from Samoa, sent by the LMS in 1830. LMS pioneer John Williams had quickly grasped the importance of using indigenous teachers wherever possible: 'So great are the advantages on the side of a native teacher at the commencement of a Mission over a European; one colour. Almost one language, and a oneness of habit gives them these superior advantages.'[83]

In fact, the Wesleyan mission in Tonga had also made use of native teachers and the WMMS Annual Report for 1834 referred approvingly to 'a noble host of native helpers, whom God has raised up and qualified to spread the knowledge of the truth among their fellow countrymen.'[84] More than a hundred were employed in that category in Tonga in the 1830s and the practice was continued when the mission was established in Fiji. In due course, the most outstanding of the Tongans in Fiji, Joel Bulu, was ordained, and even published an autobiography.[85] In order to increase the supply of native teachers a number

---

Warren used the phrase 'aristocracy of labour' to describe missionaries' social origins and claimed that the missionary movement was responsible for 'the social emancipation of the underprivileged classes'. Max Warren, *Social History and Christian Mission* (London: SCM Press, 1967), pp.37-55.

81 R.S. Neale, *Class and Ideology in the Nineteenth Century* (London, 1972), pp.26-27 and 30, quoted in Williams, 'Gentlemen', *passim*.

82 Robert Strayer has suggested, based on his study of East Africa, that the mission field provided a 'back-door' to ordination as colonial bishops were not so thorough in their examination procedures as were those in Britain. By ordination, lay missionaries could enhance their social status. *The Making of Mission Communities in East Africa* (London: Heinemann, 1978), p.5.

83 Quoted in Garrett, *A Way in the Sea: aspects of Pacific Christian history with reference to Australia* (Melbourne: Spectrum Publications, 1982), p.55.

84 WMMS *Annual Report* 1834, p.35.

85 S.G. Rowe (ed.), *Joel Bulu: the Autobiography of a Native Minister in the South Seas* (London: T. Woolmer, 1871).

of training institutions grew up in the Pacific: Tonga and Fiji (WMMS), Lifu, Rarotonga and Port Moresby (LMS) and Norfolk Island (Melanesian Mission).

The Church of England was quite happy to ordain non-Europeans, provided they were suitably qualified. After all, Samuel Crowther was ordained in 1843 by the Bishop of London.[86] But the crunch came, for the white missionaries, when it was proposed handing over missionary power to non-Europeans. In Yorubaland, Henry Townsend conducted a long rearguard action to prevent Samuel Crowther being consecrated Bishop of the Niger and though this failed, Townsend's efforts made such an impression on the CMS committee that Crowther's jurisdiction was considerably curtailed. Similarly, Henry Venn's proposals to establish 'native pastorates' in Sierra Leone and Lagos did not meet with ecstatic approval by all white missionaries, who saw such appointments as a threat to their status and security of employment. Though Venn's ideas were vindicated by the end of the twentieth century, they were well ahead of their time, and Stephen Neill was highly critical, asserting that 'enthusiasm is no substitute for common sense; and once again the doctrinaire principles of Henry Venn proved themselves disastrous when applied to recalcitrant reality'.[87] Certainly the Sierra Leone experiment was a slow one, taking from 1860 to 1877 for all churches to be part of the pastorate, but it was never fully independent in the nineteenth century, still having a European bishop in 1899.[88]

In New Guinea Captain Moresby was critical of the LMS for leaving Polynesian teachers virtually unsupported in highly dangerous pioneering situations, asserting that 'zeal overruns prudence, and new stations are occupied before a proper staff has been organised or means of support ensured'.[89] Consul Layard was concerned in 1875 that young Fijians were being trained by the Australian WMMS to be sent as pioneers to New Britain, 'where cannibalism prevailed, where fever and ague were rife and where they would be subject to privation and hardships'. He concluded, with bitter irony, 'if they succeed in establishing themselves in the islands, I hear it is the intention of white missionaries to follow. If they are clubbed and eaten I presume the white missionary will not deem the time come for him to venture'.[90]

James Chalmers recognised the debt owed to the Polynesian teachers and the disproportionate risks they faced: 'They have to bear the brunt of the fight,

---

86 But Crowther was certainly not the first. An African, Philip Quaque had been ordained in England in the eighteenth century and sent by the SPG to serve as chaplain at Cape Coast Castle. Jesse Page, *The Black Bishop: Samuel Adjai Crowther* (London: S.W. Partridge, 1908), p.53.
87 Neill, *History of Christian Missions*, p.377.
88 Stock, II, pp. 445-446.
89 John Moresby, *Discoveries and Surveys in New Guinea* (London: J. Murray, 1876), p.34.
90 Layard to Carnarvon, 15 June 1875. C.O. 881/4, Confidential Print Australian No.49A.

and we, the white missionaries, follow in and get the bulk of the credit'.[91] But the freelance explorer and trader, Wilfred Powell, questioned the missionaries' wisdom in using native teachers at all:

> I think that many of the troubles that missionaries have to contend with arise from having native teachers. They are but lately reclaimed from savage life themselves ... their colour is against them; their habits are too much like those they come to live amongst to raise them to that height of superiority that is necessary.... Do not think for one moment that I do not give all credit due to those noble fellows, who try to do their duty as far as their light goes, but what I contend is, that their light is not *sufficient*. White men are undoubtedly the men to send as missionaries.[92]

The two High Church missions were in fact the most progressive as far as ordaining indigenous peoples to the ministry was concerned. The UMCA, for example, ordained its first African deacon in 1879, though the person concerned, John Swedi, had served a long apprenticeship as sub-deacon before the step was taken.

Most Victorian missionaries lived and died in obscurity. Nevertheless, to the Victorians the missionary was often a heroic figure, and a few particular missionaries achieved a reputation approaching cult status. Those who returned to Britain were often instant public celebrities and were in much demand as deputation speakers and those with a 'name' would be persuaded to venture into print (or allow someone else to do the writing for them).[93] John Paton's frequent letters to the British and Australian press denouncing the Pacific labour trade made him something of a celebrity, much in demand for deputation preaching. A.A. Koskinen described him as 'a militant journalist for Jesus'.[94]

David Livingstone was commonly regarded as the Victorian missionary *par excellence*. Certainly the combination of explorer and medical missionary caught the contemporary public imagination and was fed, first by his own writings, then by those of others. In his few visits home he was lauded as something of a national hero.[95] But in his revisionist biography, Tim Jeal pricked the bubble of the Livingstone myth, showing the great man to have feet of clay.[96] Jeal portrays him as ambitious, overbearing, and prone to look for scapegoats when disasters of his own making loomed. With one eye always

---

91 Richard Lovett, *James Chalmers: His Autobiography and Letters* (London: Religious Tract Society, 1902), p.167.
92 Wilfred Powell, *Wanderings in a Wild Country* (London: Sampson Low, Marston, Searle and Rivington, 1883), pp.145-146.
93 See Chalmers to the Revd Gilbert Meickle, n.d., quoted in Lovett, *Chalmers*, p.231.
94 Aarne A. Koskinen, *Missionary Influence as a Political Factor in the Pacific Islands* (Helsinki: Academia Scientiarum Fennica, 1953), pp.206-207.
95 It would be more correct to say *inter*national, since Stanley's expedition to find Livingstone was funded by the *New York Herald*.
96 Tim Jeal, *Livingstone* (London: Heinemann, 1973).

focused on posterity Livingstone, says Jeal, was highly selective in what he committed to paper, routinely accentuating the positive and soft-pedalling the unpleasant.

Livingstone was, of course, a medical doctor, with a degree from Glasgow University. But as the century progressed and missionaries came to have a public profile, the tendency increased for honorary doctorates to be awarded to men who were not even graduates. John Geddie of the New Hebrides, Samuel McFarlane of the Loyalty Islands and W.G. Lawes of Papua New Guinea were among those so honoured.

The vulnerability of missions, particularly high-profile ones, is shown by the public reaction to the UMCA. Sent out with a bishop at their head in 1861, with high hopes and amidst much publicity, fickle public opinion turned against them and voluntary contributions dropped alarmingly when news leaked out that the supposedly saintly Bishop Mackenzie had led the missionaries into battle having taken sides in a tribal war.[97] And when, three years later, withdrawal from the initial mission site in the Shiré highlands was deemed necessary, Tozer, the second bishop, was vilified by many including David Livingstone. Although Tozer's strategic withdrawal undoubtedly contributed to the immediate survival and long-term growth of the mission, it was at the expense of his own health. A nervous breakdown from which he never recovered caused his premature retirement. The Victorian public demanded success in missionary activity. This had been perfectly illustrated years before at the CMS Anniversary Meeting in 1820. When a returning missionary advised the audience not to expect too much from missionary endeavours in India, William Wilberforce immediately rose to protest. Like Captain Mainwaring, of the British television comedy series *Dad's Army*, scorning any hint of defeatism in the dark days of 1940, Wilberforce stated: 'We know nothing of despondency here. We proceed as the word of God directs us; we must, we can, we will, we ought, we shall prosper.'[98] This predisposition to deny unpalatable facts no doubt explains the refusal of the Directors of the LMS to admit a mission failure in Central Africa in the late 1870s.[99]

Dr R.N. Cust was a leading lay member of the CMS who found himself out of step with prevailing mission publicity practice. He complained that many missionary publications were 'so full of worship of their particular missionary-hero, they are ... unwilling, or fearful, to state the failure, the difficulties, the gross errors...'. In a surprisingly modern sounding critique, he attacked deputation speakers, 'such as abuse the poor Heathen races, their religious

---

97 Owen Chadwick, *Mackenzie's Grave* (London: Hodder and Stoughton, 1959), p.192.
98 Quoted in Ian Bradley, *The Call to Seriousness* (London: Jonathan Cape, 1976), p.143.
99 Lovett, History of the LMS, I, Ch. XXVII. See also Doug Stuart, *The Making of a Missionary Disaster, the London Missionary Society and the Makololo*, (Cambridge: NAMP, 1997).

beliefs spoken of in terms of derision, and perhaps their objects of worship exposed to be laughed at'. He also pointed out that only those who were 'ignorant of the sins of Christian Europe' could portray 'the non-Christian world [as] living in the practice of shameless and abominable sins'.[100] This was a valid, but for its time, quite radical, observation since it was a common practice for mission publicity to play up the depravity of 'backward' races. A sensationalist tone was clearly designed to arouse interest in missions, to make them seem exciting, and the more depraved the native peoples were made to appear, the more missionary supporters would be inclined to contribute to mission funds in order to bring the light of the gospel to such places of darkness.[101]

International and Ecumenical Relations

The nineteenth century was still an age of mutual suspicion and intolerance between Christian denominations. As an example of this pre-ecumenical spirit Adrian Hastings cites an occasion in 1899 when Bishop Talbot of Rochester refused an invitation to the centenary celebrations of a Baptist Sunday School in his diocese, since to give any recognition to the Baptists would be to countenance 'the breach of unity which is so colossal an evil'. In other words, to him, the Baptists had no right to a separate existence outside the Established Church.[102]

That such prejudiced attitudes should be carried overseas by missionaries was hardly surprising and most obvious was the unseemly competition between Protestants and Roman Catholics. The arrival of the White Fathers in Buganda, for example, before the CMS Nyanza Mission was properly established was a source of much frustration for the missionaries and confusion for the Baganda.[103] The same hostility was apparent in Fiji where a Catholic mission sought to convert people from the errors of Methodism as much as from

---

100 R.N. Cust, *Essay on the Prevailing Methods of the Evangelization of the non-Christian World* (London: Luzac & Co., 1894), pp.7 and 146. Stock describes Cust as 'an independent and a fearless critic'. Stock, III, p.668.

101 One example may suffice, from the Wesleyan *Missionary Notices* of October 1839, p.152: 'Let your ears be pierced with the dying groans of strangled widows, and the wild shrieks of the victims of a horrid superstition, who are either roasted alive, or otherwise cruelly murdered. Paint to your imaginations the awfully horrifying spectacle of multitudes of human beings fattened and slaughtered to be roasted and eaten! Look at enraged warriors cutting out the tongues of their fallen enemies and eating them raw. See some of them quaffing the still reeking blood, and proudly retaining the skull of their vanquished foe as a drinking vessel.'

102 Adrian Hastings, *A History of English Christianity*, 1920-1985 (London: Collins, 1986), p.86.

103 See John V. Taylor, *The Growth of the Church in Buganda* (London: SCM, 1958), pp.39-40.

paganism.[104] But the Methodists responded in kind and noted with some satisfaction that in 1873 'in one circuit 214 have come over to us from the ranks of Popery'.[105] The LMS missionaries on the Loyalty Islands found themselves opposed by a combination of Roman Catholic priests and official harassment by the French colonial authorities after the annexation of the islands by French troops in 1864. Representations by the Directors of the LMS to Emperor Napoleon III produced a sympathetic reply but made no difference to the way the missionaries were restricted and as a result the mission on the Loyalties was wound down.[106]

Relations between the British Protestant missions, however, seem to have been much more cordial. There were, of course, occasional problems. A minor disagreement arose over the best course of action against the labour traders, when the New Hebrides missionaries' refusal to divulge information to their Wesleyan counterparts in Fiji, caused the exasperated Consul Thurston to comment: 'I regret to learn the Mission in the New Hebrides cannot co-operate with the Mission on Fiji'.[107] It must be remembered that there was no ecumenical movement in the mid-nineteenth century and Christians were not noted for their generosity of spirit to those of differing denominations. So it is noteworthy that the hardships and privations of missionary life often led to a sympathy and co-operation that may not have been forthcoming in Britain. In some cases this could be no more than the natural inclination of British people abroad to offer support to one another, but in other cases there was genuine sympathy and mutual admiration.

In a remarkably advanced attitude of ecumenism, Rule XX of the CMS at its foundation in 1799 required that 'a friendly intercourse shall be maintained with other Protestant Societies engaged in the same benevolent design of propagating the Gospel of Jesus Christ'.[108] Also from the Anglican stable, the Melanesian Mission showed considerable openness to other denominational missions. Their founder, Bishop Selwyn, had laid down the principle that he would 'never interfere with any Christianization already undertaken by any religious body or sect whatever' because he 'wanted to avoid the scramble for souls and divided Christianity which he felt characterised much of the missionary work elsewhere in the Pacific'.[109] Bishop Patteson continued this principle and the Melanesian Mission appears as the most irenic of the

---

104 See A.W. Thornley, '"Heretics and Papists": Wesleyan-Roman Catholic Rivalry in Fiji, 1844-1903', *JRH*, 10 (1979), 294-312.
105 WMMS *Annual Report* 1873, p.131.
106 See Samuel McFarlane, *The Story of the Lifu Mission* (London: J. Nisbet, 1873), and Lovett, *History of the LMS*, I, pp.410-417.
107 Report on the introduction of labourers ... into Fiji, enc. in Thurston to Commodore Lambert, 4 September 1868. CO 234/21.
108 Quoted in Stock, I, p .71.
109 Whiteman, p.101.

missionary societies, especially significant in view of the mission's High Church and establishment origins. Bishop Selwyn's approving comments on John Geddie have already been noted and in 1852 he gave the Presbyterians practical help by providing a free passage from Auckland for Geddie's first colleague, John Inglis, in the mission vessel, *Border Maid*.[110] Despite their theological polarities both missions had a warm regard for each other.

Practical co-operation was in evidence elsewhere in the Pacific. When the LMS moved towards Samoa and Fiji from their base in Tahiti at the same time as the WMMS did the same from their base in Tonga, to avoid wasteful duplication of effort and possible rivalry, a deal was struck in 1836 which resulted in the withdrawal of the LMS from Fiji, leaving the field open to the Methodists. The WMMS simultaneously withdrew from Samoa, leaving it to the LMS. This was, in the words of the Wesleyan *Missionary Notices,* 'a friendly arrangement with the Directors of the London Missionary Society, dictated on both sides by principles of Christian prudence and catholic generosity'.[111] Arrangements of this kind became know as 'comity agreements'. And it was not just on the mission field that friendly contacts were maintained: the archives of the various missionary societies contain many examples of correspondence between the leaders and headquarters staff of a number of the missions.[112]

It was perhaps only natural that missionaries, often isolated and inevitably far from home, proudly retained their national characteristics in an alien environment. Alan Cairns has detected 'a natural predisposition for British missionaries to favour the assumption of imperial control by their own government rather than by some other European nation'.[113] In different mission stations this took different forms. James Chalmers, concerned at possible German interest in New Guinea, was open about his views, which were certainly not those of the LMS: 'As Britons, we may be pardoned for wishing to see the influence of Britain supreme rather than that of any other Power'.[114]

---

110 Patterson, pp.333-334.
111 *Missionary Notices*, March 1838. The 'amicable' exchange was marred by the feeling of betrayal of the substantial Methodist community in Samoa who refused to join the LMS and kept their own tradition alive until the Australian WMMS took pity on them, reneged on the 1836 agreement made in London and sent the Revd Martin Dyson to Samoa to minister to the Methodist rump. See Martin Dyson, *My Story of Samoan Methodism* (Melbourne: Fergusson & Moore, 1875); Findlay and Holdsworth, III, pp.341-362.
112 See, for example, Mullens to Hutchinson, 7 April 1879. CMS Nyanza Mission papers, CA6/04. The LMS Foreign Secretary informed his opposite number at the CMS that he would shortly be returning to the mission field on a relief expedition to assist Central African Mission. In fact, Mullens never returned.
113 H.A.C. Cairns, *Prelude to Imperialism* (London: Routledge & Kegan Paul, 1965), p.244.
114 Chalmers, 'New Guinea – Past, Present and Future', *PRCI*, XVIII (1886-7), 102.

As Bismarck's first bid for colonies began to build up a head of steam in the mid 1880s, concern was also expressed in East Africa, more at the behaviour of individual Germans and the possible adverse effect on mission work rather than any fear that Germany might establish a colonial government. At the end of 1885 one CMS missionary with an indecipherable signature wrote to London that 'the Germans are causing trouble in this part already'. Describing an atrocity on two native porters which backfired on two Germans, leaving one of them dead, he reflected, 'I can't say what effect this will have on our own work. Most of the natives here know these men belong to a different nation to us and this will I hope spread'.[115]

But missionaries did not always adopt a nationalistic stance. A different reaction to German imperialism came from the Australian Methodists in New Britain, which was annexed by Germany in December 1884. Benjamin Danks was positive about the new colonial power which left the mission alone and allowed it to continue its work without interference or restriction.[116] In Yorubaland in 1885, Charles Phillips, trapped at Ode Ondo both by the Yoruba wars and the inability of the Lagos government to interfere positively to relieve his plight, also supported the cession of the whole of the Mahin beach and the country inland to the Germans as a fitting opportunity to enhance the work of the CMS in those parts.[117]

In addition, Eugene Stock in the fourth and final volume of his history of the CMS, written in 1916 after events had been overtaken by war *against* Germany, commented on 'the utmost friendliness between the missionaries and the German authorities' in Tanganyika – a clear indication that, even at a time of rabid anti-German feeling in Britain, the CMS headquarters would have no part in unthinking nationalism.[118]

Nevertheless, from time to time missionary societies and individual missionaries found it necessary to lobby British officialdom in aid of a particular cause. To individual missionaries, isolated often thousands of miles from Britain, the letter (whether to a government department, an individual minister, an MP, or the press) was the only means of immediate influence, despite a frequent time-lag of several weeks or months.[119] The use of an

---

115 ? to Lang, 11 November 1885. CMS Nyanza Mission papers, G3/A6/ 0.
116 Wallace Deane (ed.), *In Wild New Britain: the Story of Benjamin Danks, Pioneer Missionary* (Sydney: Angus and Robertson, 1933), Chap XIV.
117 A.A.B. Aderibigbe, 'Expansion of the Lagos Protectorate, 1863-1900', unpublished PhD thesis (London, 1959), p.85.
118 Stock, IV, pp.579-580. It is significant that in the same section Stock wrote of the hostility of the French authorities in Madagascar to the CMS mission.
119 W.G. Lawes wrote from New Guinea on 15 September 1884 to the editor of *The Times* to complain about kidnapping in eastern Papua. The letter was eventually published on 5 December 1884. Similarly, H.M. Stanley's letter to the *Daily Telegraph* requesting missionaries for Buganda was published on 15 November 1875. It was dated 14 April.

intermediary often speeded up the process; for example Dr Robert Steel and J.P. Sunderland, both resident in Sydney, acted as agents for the New Hebrides missionaries and the LMS New Guinea missionaries respectively.

The use of influential supporters at home, often MPs, has already been mentioned, and questions asked or motions moved in the House of Commons could have considerable effect on opinion.[120] Headquarters staff could make their influence felt. Dr Mullens of the LMS and John Kay of the board of missions of the Reformed Presbyterian Church of Scotland, sponsors of the New Hebrides Mission, were frequent correspondents of the Colonial Office. Henry Venn was on social terms with Colonial Office staff and did not hesitate to use this informal influence when necessary.[121] He was known to drop in at the Colonial Office to deliver mail by hand as a pretext to be able to talk with officials. Venn attended four sittings of the 1865 Select Committee on the West African Settlements and corresponded with Sir Harry Ord, the special commissioner to West Africa. His colleague, Edward Hutchinson, was a major influence in pressing for the establishment of the 1871 Select Committee on the East African slave trade.

The missionary societies were happy to make common cause with other interested pressure groups. The Anti-Slavery Society and the New Hebrides missionaries co-operated over the Pacific labour trade and the WMMS worked with the Aborigines Protection Society and others in the Gambia and Fiji Committees. The fact that William M'Arthur was on the committees of both societies made him a natural link between the two. This link with the humanitarians, however, did not mean that missionaries were necessarily free from the prejudices of their day.

Prevalent Attitudes in the Missionary Community

Towards the end of his life, Bishop Samuel Crowther wrote, 'I know my place as a Negro, but I have ever paid my respects to Europeans, whether old or young, missionaries or those in secular occupations, as the race of our benefactors'.[122] That such a distinguished bishop of the church should feel it necessary to speak freely in such terms is an indication of the racism that, to a greater or lesser extent, was a natural part of missionary culture in the nineteenth century. This was not, of course, because missionaries were racists *per se,* or more racist than the rest of contemporary society, merely that the

---

120 See, for example, the Fiji debate of 25 June 1872, proposed by William M'Arthur and seconded by Admiral Erskine, both supporters of the WMMS. *Hansard*, Third Series, CCXXII, cols 192-219.

121 He also had the ear of the leaders of the Anglican church: 'Venn always knew he had an entrée to Lambeth palace, and also to Fulham palace'. [the residence of the Bishop of London] Hennell, p.89.

122 Crowther to CMS Secretary, 30 January 1884, quoted in Page, p.369.

whole relationship between European and Pacific islander or African was viewed, by both sides, as a relationship between superior and inferior. Writing of a common attitude shared by missionary societies and government officials, J.S. Galbraith states that 'their concern was not with understanding African societies but with the relationship of these societies to British interests (slave trade and commerce)'.[123] The missions varied in their racist attitudes with the Wesleyans in Fiji being among the least enlightened. By 1871 they had allowed a kind of spiritual apartheid, providing separate worship facilities in Levuka for natives and Europeans, the latter being able to obtain the exclusive services of the missionaries whenever they were present in sufficient numbers.[124] Among the most enlightened were the Anglican High Church missions in Melanesia and Central Africa. Because their missionaries were celibate, there was no mission compound kept at a distance from the local people, no wives or families to protect from real or imagined violence or moral pollution. Their missionaries, therefore, had much closer contact with the native helpers, often living and working in a multi-racial community and this clearly helped to break down any latent racist tendencies.

Attitudes to indigenous culture were often a practical measure of missionary racism. Writing in a 1983 Church of England report, John Tiller commented:

> The history of Christian mission, though littered with awful mistakes, nevertheless proves that the minister of the Gospel is called to cross cultural boundaries. To do so effectively he or she must (i) respect the culture which already exists; (ii) distinguish between the Gospel and cultural expressions of it; (iii) be committed to long-term and practical involvement in a particular culture.[125]

The story of missions in this period indicates clear divisions between those who worked according to the enlightened principles outlined by Tiller and those who saw Christianity as inextricably bound up with western cultural norms and missionary work as an opportunity to impose those norms on 'backward' races.

Henry Venn saw the object of missions as the creation of truly national churches, and missionaries as a temporary means to that end. He therefore counselled his missionaries to avoid any form of cultural imperialism. Writing to J.C. Taylor, he advised 'let all European habits, European tastes, European ideas, be left behind you. Let no other change be visible in your tone of mind or

---

123 J.S. Galbraith, *Mackinnon and East Africa, 1878-1895* (Cambridge: CUP, 1972), p.16.

124 John Young, 'Evanescent Ascendancy: the planter community in Fiji', in Davidson and Scarr, p.160. *The Fiji Times* (3 December 1870) gave a flavour of the arrangements: 'In the forenoon Mr Brooks harangued about five hundred of the "devils", and made an evident impression. During the afternoon he preached to the whites.'

125 John Tiller, *A Strategy for the Church's Ministry* (London: CIO Publishing, 1983), p.41.

behaviour than that of a growth in grace and in the knowledge and love of God'.[126] This was particularly significant since Taylor was an ordained African in the Niger Delta who might have been expected to emulate European ideas and distance himself from African culture, the very thing that Venn wanted to avoid. Similarly, the Melanesian Mission and the UMCA also sought to disturb as little as possible the manners and customs of the people among whom they worked, regarding Christianity not as an adjunct of western civilization but as a supra-national faith that came both to enhance and reform a culture rather than to destroy it.

It was suggested by J.D. Legge that missionary attitudes to tribal society and indigenous cultures depended on their concept of the church. In his view, because Anglicans saw the church as inclusive, able to encompass all people, this made them more tolerant of tribal cultures; nonconformist concepts of individual salvation and a gathered church, on the other hand, led to a greater emphasis on moral and ethical standards and a consequent hostility to tribal cultures.[127] Because Legge's researches were in the Pacific arena, he naturally compared the attitude of the Anglican Melanesian Mission with that of the nonconformist WMMS and LMS.[128] And here lies the reason for his conclusion being somewhat off target. The difference, which he rightly detected, was not between Anglican and nonconformist, church and chapel, but between the evangelical and catholic strands which, particularly in the case of the Anglican church, ran through churches rather than coincided with their boundaries. The Melanesian Mission in the south-west Pacific was from the high church tradition and therefore had a more catholic view of the church. Had Legge examined the CMS, also Anglican but of an evangelical tradition, he would have found that, whatever Henry Venn might have wished far away in London, attitudes to native culture approximated more to those of fellow evangelicals in, say, the WMMS or LMS, than those of fellow Anglicans in the high church missions, the Melanesian Mission or the UMCA.

From his studies of Central Africa, Alan Cairns adds another factor. He notes that 'the UMCA missionaries were drawn from the upper and upper middle classes of British society, and they tended to be well educated, frequently at the better public school, followed by Oxford and Cambridge'. He therefore concludes 'their educational and class background probably helped to induce a certain appreciation of diversity with an accompanying tolerance and comparative respect for other cultures'.[129] This factor could also have been

---

126 Quoted in Shenk, *Missionary Statesman*, p.33.
127 J.D. Legge, *Britain in Fiji 1858-1880*, (London: Macmillan, 1958), pp.147-148.
128 The LMS also had its progressives and James Chalmers was very much ahead of his time in preferring loin cloths or even nudity to western clothing for the inhabitants of New Guinea. 'My experience,' said Chalmers 'is that clothing natives is nearly as bad as introducing spirits among them'. Cuthbert Lennox, *James Chalmers of New Guinea* (London: Melrose, 1902), p.142.
129 Cairns, p.221.

cited by Legge and would have supported his contention, since the Melanesian Mission drew its personnel from the same social class as the UMCA, whereas no Pacific missionaries from LMS or WMMS were from a high social stratum, nor were many highly educated.[130]

Missionaries were essentially men of peace. Occasionally, however, they became involved in acts of violence, either at the receiving end, or carried out on their behalf (but usually against their will) by the Royal Navy for punitive purposes. For example, following the murder of Bishop Patteson, his former chief, Bishop Selwyn, speaking in the House of Lords on 3 May 1872, urged that there should be no official retribution on the islanders of Nukapu.[131] When this advice was ignored and HMS *Rosario* was dispatched to the island, Commander Markham received a written protest from the Melanesian missionaries 'protesting against the use of force under my command, for the purpose of chastising the natives of Nukapu, in retaliation for the murder of Bishop Patteson'.[132]

Missionaries knew the risks they were taking and by and large did not feel that armed force would help them in the long term. Yet there are too many examples to be ignored of missionaries refusing to turn the other cheek and approving the use of punitive force against recalcitrant native peoples. Sometimes they, or their mission staff even used it themselves to maintain order and discipline in the mission community. It was clearly an area where there was some division of opinion in missionary ranks.

In Yorubaland, the CMS missionary Charles Gollmer saw the bombardment of Lagos as 'God's interposition for the good of Africa' and later asked for military intervention against the Ijebu.[133] George Brown, head of the WMMS mission in New Britain, went a step further and in 1878 personally led a punitive expedition against a tribe that had killed and eaten three of his native teachers. Brown's expedition of some sixty armed men burned three towns and fought two brief battles. Chief Justice Gorrie of the Western Pacific High Commission began proceedings against Brown, but the High Commissioner Sir Arthur Gordon overruled him.[134]

---

130 David Cargill, WMMS missionary in Tonga and Fiji earlier in the century was highly unusual in having an MA from Aberdeen University. See John H. Darch, 'William Cross, David Cargill and the Establishment of the Wesleyan Methodist Mission in Fiji, 1835-1843', unpublished MA dissertation (Birkbeck College, London, 1977).
131 *Hansard*, Third Series, CCXI, cols 184-189.
132 Markham, p.68.
133 Gollmer to Venn, 7 January 1852. CMS Yoruba Mission papers. CA2/043(a). F.A. Ayandele, *The Missionary Impact on Modern Nigeria, 1842-1914* (London: Longmans, 1966), p.8.
134 Morrell, Pacific Islands, pp.246-247; Gorrie to Hicks Beach, 11 November 1878. CO 225/1. The labour trader William Wawn, commented, 'if such reprisals had been undertaken by a layman, a howl of indignation would have arisen from Exeter Hall.

Another interesting incident occurred in the New Hebrides in 1865 when Commodore Wiseman used the guns of HMS *Curaçoa* to bombard Port Resolution on the island of Tanna for a two-hour period. It was the missionaries who had originally asked for the naval intervention which got out of hand and resulted in the bombardment.[135] There was a clear division of opinion among the New Hebrides missionaries on the rightness of this action. On his return to the islands (the other missionaries had sanctioned the use of force in his absence), John Geddie condemned the action without condemning his brother missionaries:

> I believe the punishment of the Tannese was a great but unintentional mistake. The weapons of our warfare ... must be spiritual, and not carnal. We shall do far more to subdue, humanize and elevate these natives with Bibles in our hands than with the whole British navy at our backs. Natives walk by sight rather than by faith, and understand actions better than words. We may now tell these islanders that we come to them with a message of love, but the case of Tanna will raise doubts in their minds. The mission on these islands has now a character to redeem as well as a character to maintain.[136]

But Geddie was in the minority and the Foreign Missions Committee of the Reformed Presbyterian Church in Scotland officially endorsed the action as being 'of considerable advantage to the New Hebrides Mission'.[137]

After north-east New Guinea and New Britain had come under German authority, the Methodist Benjamin Danks was equally emphatic in his support of a German punitive expedition:

> On 15 June 1884 a German squadron arrived .... The governor of the colony kindly sent us word ... so that if we thought it desirable Mrs Danks could leave immediately the fleet arrived .... Only houses were burnt and some plantations destroyed ... they were anxious to avoid bloodshed ... and took every precaution to save the people from the consequences of their own savage folly. In this we, as

---

Likely enough, too, the leader of the expedition would have been hanged when he got home'. William T. Wawn, *The South Sea Islanders and the Queensland Labour Trade* (London: Swan Sonnenschein, 1893), pp.169-170. For Brown see also Garrett, *Stars,* pp.220-232.

135 Accounts of the bombardment reached the British press via the pen of Julius Brenchley, the botanist on board the *Curaçoa,* Julius L. Brenchley, *Jottings during the Cruise of HMS Curaçoa* (London: Longmans, Green & Co., 1873), p.204.

136 Quoted in James W. Falconer, *John Geddie* (Toronto: Board of Foreign Missions, Presbyterian Church in Canada, 1915), pp.98-99.

137 Paper issued by the Foreign Missions Committee , 25 June 1872, printed as an appendix in Markham, pp. 268-272. For an impartial account of the events see Morrell, *Pacific Islands,* pp.99-100.

interpreters, seconded their efforts. And our efforts were very warmly appreciated.[138]

Appreciated by the Germans, presumably. Danks did not seem concerned that such an action would be in any way detrimental to the work of the Wesleyan mission.

In the south of the island, however, the LMS missionaries opposed punitive force and when, in March 1881, four Polynesian teachers and their families were murdered at Kalo, the missionaries did not report the incident to the authorities in order to prevent further violence and bloodshed. But the secrecy was not maintained and, some months later, HMS *Wolverine* arrived to punish the village responsible. James Chalmers complained:

> indiscriminate shooting down of innocent natives, burning villages and cutting down cocoa-nut trees, I think [is] mere barbarism. It ought not to be done by our navy ... is it right that a great nation should do such things to savages? Better far that we should suffer than that we should do wrong.[139]

The CMS Nyanza mission also opposed retaliation. Indeed, six months after the murders of O'Neill and Shergold Smith in 1877, Alexander Mackay assured their murderer, Chief Lukongeh, that 'the followers of Jesus did not avenge wrongs, but forgave them'.[140]

Just as there was a difference of opinion in the missionary community over the use of punitive force, the same spread of opinion applied to physical punishment, though in this case only a minority supported and administered it. The actions of James Streeter, Lay Superintendent of the CMS settlement for freed slaves at Frere Town near Mombasa, are fully discussed in chapter seven. Streeter's use of particularly brutal punishments on those in his care led to the Vice-Consul being called in to report, since the incidents were affecting relations with the Sultan of Zanzibar. Streeter's actions were then disowned by the CMS and he was recalled.

Another *cause célèbre* of missionary cruelty was that of the Church of Scotland missionaries at their Blantyre settlement in Nyasaland. The mission, overwhelmed by runaway slaves who had been allowed to take sanctuary there, took civil authority upon itself and in response to crime treated wrongdoers to severe floggings and even administered the death penalty. A visitor to Blantyre, Andrew Chirnside, observed the punishments being meted out and, on his return to Britain, published the story.[141] The Church of Scotland's Foreign Missions Committee ordered an immediate enquiry by one Dr Rankin. The outcome was

---

138 Deane, pp.270-271.
139 Quoted in Lennox, p. 97.
140 Quoted in Stock, III, p.104.
141 Andrew Chirnside, *The Blantyre Missionaries: Discreditable Disclosures* (London: William Ridgway, 1880).

that Duff Macdonald, the mission leader, was replaced. The committee commented: 'Government is indispensable; evildoers must be restrained and punished, but the power should not be in the hands of those who have gone forth as the Ambassadors of Christ's Gospel'.[142]

R.N. Cust went even further. In a book published in 1889 he complained about savage beatings administered by one missionary in East Africa and concluded:

> if it is agreed that an expedition cannot be carried on, unless the leader of it commits day by day acts of brute violence, the reply is, that *missionary expeditions had better not be undertaken.* If missions can only be worked by methods which no supporter of the mission would dare to state in detail on a mission-platform, then missions had better not be undertaken.[143]

Cairns notes that the missionary so criticised, though not named, is clearly identifiable as Bishop James Hannington. If correct, this information goes some way to tarnish the saintly aura that surrounded Hannington's reputation following his martyrdom in October 1886.[144]

Missionary Life in the Tropics

The dangers, isolation and deprivations of life on distant mission stations[145] have sometimes been held to account for the occasional acts of barbarity carried out by missionaries. The impact of such conditions should not be ignored.[146] For example, John Geddie, pioneer missionary in the New Hebrides, commented on one of his junior colleagues, James McNair: 'he is a very excellent man, but he is unfit for the hardships of missionary life'.[147] By

---

142 Minute of Foreign Missions Committee, 1 June 1860, quoted in A.J. Hanna, *The Beginnings of Nyasaland and North Eastern Rhodesia, 1859-1895* (Oxford: Clarendon Press, 1956), p.32. See Hanna, pp.28-34 for a full account of the Blantyre atrocities, and A.J. Temu, *British Protestant Missions* (London: Longman, 1972), pp. 16-17, for a discussion of missionary brutality in East Africa.
143 R.N. Cust, *Notes on Missionary Subjects* (London, 1889), pp.29-30, quoted in Cairns p.40.
144 Unlike Rome, the Church of England has no machinery for canonization. Nevertheless Hannington has been honoured as far as is possible, since the date of his death, 29 October, is listed on the church's calendar of 'Lesser Festivals'. *Common Worship* (London: Church House Publishing, 2000), p.14.
145 See, for example, Hannington to Lang, 9 February 1885. CMS. G3/A5/?L1 1885/25, quoted in Strayer, p.15.
146 This section closely follows John H. Darch, 'Love and Death In the Mission Compound: the hardships of life in the Tropics for Victorian missionaries and their families.' *Anvil*, 17 (2000), 22-39.
147 Quoted in Patterson, p.483, see also p.484.

contrast Bishop James Hannington remarked, with some disapproving surprise, on the 'palatial residences' he observed at Frere Town and the fact that the missionaries lived 'in every comfort'.[148] Such an observation was, however, very much the exception rather than the rule. Henry Venn had recorded in 1867: 'I often plead before the throne of grace that those who have sacrificed home comforts for the Lord's sake may experience such *comforts* abroad as may be consistent with the brightening of their final crown of glory. But *there* our hopes must be fixed – all short of final glory is such a poor thing'.[149]

However, two points need to be borne in mind as the hardships of missionary life are examined. First, the danger (which, of course, applies to all periods of history) of viewing the past through contemporary experience and assumptions. Many industrial workers and farm labourers in Britain endured living conditions and faced hardships (though not, of course, the same isolation and loneliness) akin to those on the mission field. Second, the faith and vision of the missionaries must not be underestimated. Though ordinary men with the inevitable frailties of human nature, a sense of divine calling permeated their job description and organisational structure, if not their personal experience.[150] As J.F.A. Ajayi has observed, 'by definition, missionaries were incurable optimists with severely limited funds and resources but unlimited hopes and aspirations'.[151]

Isolation and loneliness should be seen as key determining factors, underpinning and to a large extent exacerbating, all the other hardships of missionary life. Livingstone's relationship with Stanley can only really be fully understood when it is realised that Stanley was the *only* white man he saw in the last five or six years of his life. Even when working with others, missionaries were often isolated as the only white person (or family) on a particular island or in a particular mission station.[152] W.G. Lawes wrote to the LMS Directors from Niue in 1867 asking for leave to come home after nine years as the only missionary family on the island. He noted that 'we have never had an

---

148 Hannington to Lang, 9 February 1885. CMS. G3/A5/?L1 1885/25, quoted in Strayer, p.15.
149 Venn to Lamb, 23 September 1867. CMS Yoruba Mission Papers, CA2/L4
150 For a useful survey of missionary service motivation see Rouse, 244-257.
151 J.F.A. Ajayi, *Christian Missions in Nigeria, 1841-1891: the Making of a New Elite* (London: Longmans, 1965), p.57.
152 The CMS Yoruba Mission papers, for example, are full of 'resolutions passed by correspondence'. This device, which meant that business could be transacted, albeit slowly, was also an indication of the isolation of individuals. Unrest and warfare among the native population could exacerbate this isolation and David and Anna Hinderer trapped in Ibadan for five years during the Yoruba wars were so short of food they were obliged to sell their possessions in order to survive. Anna Hinderer, *Seventeen Years in the Yoruba Country*, (London: Religious Tract Society, 1873), Ch. 6.

opportunity of visiting our brethren on other islands, not even those in Samoa. Our life here has been one of more than ordinary isolation'.[153]

In 1871, Commander George Palmer, who had had close dealings with the New Hebrides missionaries during his tour of duty on HMS *Rosario*, commented:

> Doubtless the sketches of the missionary settlement look very pretty on paper, but unfortunately there are some things you cannot portray, such as insufficient food, brackish water, together with swarms of mosquitoes and other insects, and often, as at Dillon's Bay, a sweltering poisonous atmosphere, accompanied by fever and ague. The missionary schooner is often delayed on her annual trip; and then the stores of flour, etc., are at a low ebb, and frequently injured by the damp, and the sugar swarming with ants. An English labourer would often turn up his nose at their daily fare.[154]

One of the greatest trials, for those missions without a resident doctor, was the distance from qualified medical attention when a family member was sick. Would John Paton, for example, have lost his first wife and baby son if there had been a doctor on Tanna in February 1859?[155]

One therapy for isolation was the writing of letters. This was not only the missionaries' sole method of communication but also a means of influencing events and (not to be underestimated) a means of inducing letters in reply to alleviate loneliness. Small wonder that missionary archives are so voluminous.

Furthermore, missionaries were no different from any other vocation, profession or trade in that disagreements broke out between them from time to time. There is little doubt that the isolation and loneliness they endured, combined with the often close living arrangements with other individuals from whom they could not easily escape, resulted in occasional outbreaks of hostility. Indeed, it should be remembered that few missionaries were as irritable and contentious as David Livingstone. Another obvious example is when, despite being chided by Ralph Wardlaw Thompson, the LMS Foreign Secretary, the New Guinea missionaries gave up convening a mission meeting, largely because Samuel McFarlane always disagreed with W.G. Lawes and James Chalmers. McFarlane used his more frequent visits to London to influence the Directors in his favour. In effect the mission split into an eastern and western

---

153 Lawes to Mullens, 6 July 1869. LMS South Seas Letters, Box 32.
154 George Palmer, *Kidnapping in the South Seas* (Edinburgh: Edmonston and Douglas, 1871), p.56.
155 John G. Paton, *Missionary to the New Hebrides. An Autobiography,* 2 vols., (London: Hodder & Stoughton, 1889), pp 129-137.

section pursuing sometimes wildly different objectives. Only after McFarlane's retirement was the situation normalised.[156]

Frequently disputes were referred to missionary headquarters for arbitration and missionary society secretaries in London were obliged to exercise the wisdom of Solomon, in the near impossible task of settling, by post, petty disputes that had begun months ago and thousands of miles away. Henry Venn, for example, had to deal with unrest in the Yoruba mission when Henry Townsend complained about Samuel Crowther ('improper conversation with a young female') and Charles Gollmer complained about James White ('oppressive conduct towards certain natives and writing improper letters'). Venn dismissed the charges on the grounds of unsatisfactory evidence.[157]

There was also an unpleasant tendency for missionaries, like schoolboys 'sneaking' to a master, to report fellow missionaries to headquarters behind their backs. James Calvert wrote from Fiji to the WMMS General Secretaries concerning a fellow missionary, John F. Horsley. Though the nature of the revelation remains obscure, Calvert had no hesitation in proclaiming, 'I fully believe that he is a doomed man as regards the ministry'.[158] Similarly Charles Barff of the LMS in Tahiti, wrote to Dr Tidman reporting his fellow missionary, Alexander Simpson, Principal of the South Sea Academy on Tahiti, as a notorious drunkard.[159] Barff's letter was to no avail, however, since the LMS Directors were clearly already aware of Simpson's failings and dismissed him on 9 December 1850, *before* Barff's letter could have arrived in London.[160]

Whilst references to alcohol as 'an obstacle to missionary progress' and 'a traitor which will do its best to blot out every blessing Christianity may bring',

---

156 See LMS Papua Correspondence, boxes 2 and 3; Diane Langmore, *Tamate– a King. James Chalmers in New Guinea 1877-1901* (Melbourne: Melbourne University Press, 1974), pp.29-34.
157 Venn's circular letter to Yoruba conference, 19 April 1861. CMS Yoruba Mission papers, CA2/L3.
158 Calvert to Gen. Secs., (Private), 1 October 1864. WMMS Australian Correspondence, Box 532. *WMMS Archives*, School of Oriental and African Studies, London University. Calvert also wrote letters in order to try to engineer the dismissal of the British Consul in Fiji. *Ibid*. Calvert to Boyce, 4 March 1869 and encs.
159 Barff to Tidman, 26 November 1850. LMS South Seas Correspondence, 23/3/B.
160 Entry for Alexander Simpson in the Register of LMS Missionaries held at the School of Oriental and African Studies in London. It is interesting to note that apart from a single gentlemanly disagreement over the use of punitive naval force against the island of Tanna in 1865 there is no evidence that any of the Presbyterian missionaries in the New Hebrides ever fell out with one another in such high-profile ways as frequently happened elsewhere on the mission field. Could it be that their common hostility to the labour trade absorbed all their aggressive tendencies, which might otherwise been turned inwards towards one another?

normally concern its adverse effect on indigenous peoples,[161] Niel Gunson has noted the unfortunate effects of alcohol on the missionaries themselves:

> it was under frontier conditions that alcoholism made its greatest ravages, ministers of religion no more excepted than other groups. Removal from a familiar environment, the absence of familiar family patterns, and the sheer experience of vastness and strangeness, were but some of the conditioning factors.[162]

The death of David Cargill on Tonga in 1843 was *assumed* by the WMMS to be suicide occasioned by alcoholism and the Society duly covered up the circumstances so as not to scandalise their supporters. G.C. Henderson, Niel Gunson and the present author have all independently accepted this version of events.[163] But another interpretation has been put forward by Albert J. Schütz suggesting that Cargill's illness was dengue fever, a tropical disease with depressive side-effects.[164] Whatever his cause of death, there was no doubting that Cargill's spirit-drinking habits were a source of discomfort to his fellow missionaries. James Chalmers in New Guinea was fortunate in being able to enjoy whisky in moderation.

The fact that most Protestant missionaries were married meant that problems occasioned by sexual deprivation were not as great as they might have been, and cases of adultery with other missionaries' wives are rare. One unusual case was that of a Methodist native minister in the Gambia, Yorke Clement. He admitted adultery in 1874 and resigned from his post on McCarthy's Island, though this was never spelt out for missionary supporters at home, who were merely told about 'painful circumstances' occasioning his departure from office.[165]

In the New Hebrides, John Geddie's lay catechist, a married missionary named Isaac Archibald, misbehaved himself with a local girl and left the mission, joining the nearby sandalwood station. Geddie refused to baptise his child and it was left to Bishop Selwyn to administer baptism.[166] In Fiji Thomas Jaggar, who was Superintendent of the Rewa circuit, had an affair with a part-Fijian woman and was dismissed from his post in 1848. Eighty years later the

---

161 Page, p.274.
162 W.N. Gunson, 'On the incidence of alcohol and intemperance in early Pacific missions', *JPH*, I (1966), p.45.
163 See G.C. Henderson, *The Journal of Thomas Williams, Missionary in Fiji, 1840-53* (Sydney: Angus & Robertson, 1931), pp.195-196; Gunson, 60; John H.Darch, 'Missionaries to the Cannibals,' *Trivium* 17 (1982), 103-117.
164 Schütz, (ed.), pp.244-246.
165 See correspondence in WMMS West Africa - Gambia Correspondence Box 295 and WMMS Annual Reports, 1875 p.123 and 1876 p.113. Recent research by Martha T. Frederiks points to a possible brain tumour being the reason for Clement's uncharacteristic behaviour. *We have Toiled all Night: Christianity in the Gambia, 1456-2000* (Zoetermeer: Uitgeverij Boekencentrum, 2003), p.257.
166 Garrett, *Stars*, pp.69-70.

official history of the WMMS still clothed that matter with discretion, merely informing its readers that Jaggar 'through temptation ... fell out of the ranks' and 'returned from the field under discipline'.[167] But at least one such case had a happy ending. This concerned George Grenfell, a bachelor serving with the Baptist Missionary Society in the Cameroons. He resigned from the BMS because Rose Edgerley, his young Jamaican housekeeper was found to be pregnant with his child. Grenfell kept his promise to marry Rose and, after two years of secular employment, he was reinstated by the mission, which he served with distinction until his death in 1906.[168] But the fact that those missionary wives who survived the ravages of life in tropical climes were often in poor health and may well have wished to avoid frequent childbirth in primitive conditions, may have imposed strains that were not always apparent in the domesticity of the missionary compound.[169]

For the High Church missions, the Melanesian and the UMCA, the celibacy of the missionaries no doubt brought its own strains. One recorded incident was on the island of Nggela in the Solomons. Charles H. Brooke of the Melanesian Mission found solace for his loneliness in forming emotional attachments with his male pupils. When his overt homosexuality was discovered by the mission authorities in 1874 he was promptly dismissed.[170]

In general, for the Victorian missionary, family life was, of necessity, subordinated to the needs of the mission. One of the greatest Victorian missionaries was also one of the most notorious examples. David Livingstone's prolonged absences from home played havoc with his family's life. His wife Mary suffered financially and mentally, becoming moody and resentful. She took to drink and died on a rare visit to see her husband in 1862.[171] His eldest son, Robert, clearly suffered from being neglected by his father. He became quite uncontrollable and, as soon as he could, left Scotland to enlist in the Union forces in the American Civil War, where he died from his wounds, aged eighteen.[172]

From the New Hebrides, John Geddie bewailed 'the most painful sacrifice which missionaries are called on to suffer in these islands is separation from their children, whose interest and welfare demand their removal to a less polluted moral atmosphere'.[173] When Geddie next saw his daughter eight years had elapsed, she had grown up and there was no mutual recognition.[174] But at

---

167 Findlay and Holdsworth, III, pp.386, 432
168 Brian Stanley, *History of the BMS*, pp. 119-121.
169 See Sir Harry Johnston's caricature of life in a mission settlement, which is surprisingly accurate. *The Nineteenth Century*, XXII (1887), 708-724.
170 Hilliard, *God's Gentlemen*, p.90.
171 See Chadwick, *Mackenzie's Grave*, pp.110-111.
172 See Jeal, pp. 279-280.
173 Quoted in Falconer, p.40
174 George Patterson, p.416.

least she was alive, the mortality rate in missionary children in the tropics being high, though it needs to be viewed against the background of a not insignificant infant mortality rate in England at this time. Nevertheless, missionary correspondence is laden with accounts of the deaths of children.

James Calvert sent his eldest child, Mary, back home from Fiji, only to hear of her death soon after reaching England.[175] Samuel McFarlane's daughter, Maggie, died and was buried at sea on the way to New Guinea.[176] On 25 August 1876, W.G. Lawes plaintively recorded in his diary the death of his young son from malarial fever:

> Our dear little Percy left us this afternoon. His little life has been full of suffering, and we cannot be sorry that it is exchanged for peace. How desolate our home will be now. He has been so much with us day and night and the house is so full of his mementoes.[177]

In a smallpox outbreak in Yorubaland at the beginning of 1880, CMS native pastor (and later bishop) Charles Phillips lost three of his four children.[178] In Mombasa, William Chancellor found solace for the death of his baby daughter by writing to CMS headquarters:

> The Lord has laid his heavy hand upon us. On the 24th of May my dear wife gave birth to a strong healthy daughter, but on May 30th our little treasure went home to Jesus. Our windows having been so badly constructed, admit a great draught which struck our little darling.... We felt very much the want of medical aid, but that was impossible; the nearest medical man being ten days journey away. It was the Lord's will that our sweet bud should be culled and now it blooms in the fields of light above.[179]

Little wonder that the CMS missionary, James Lamb, writing from Frere Town in 1876 advised against a new mission teacher bringing his children with him: 'On the whole I think it would be the wisest plan to leave their children at home. There must be considerable risk in bringing them to the tropics'.[180] James Hannington left his family at home in Sussex, but he had only 'signed on' for a period of three to five years on his first tour of duty in East Africa.[181]

---

175 Findlay and Holdsworth, III, p.451
176 McFarlane to Whitehouse 13 Nov 1874. LMS Papua Correspondence 1/2/B.
177 Quoted in Joseph King, *William George Lawes of Savage Island and New Guinea* (London: Religious Tract Society, 1909), p.92.
178 W.O. Ajayi, p.242.
179 Chancellor to Henry Wright, 12 June 1874. CMS East African Mission papers, CA5/05.
180 Lamb to Wright, 4 Nov 1876. CMS East African Mission papers, CA5/017.
181 E.C. Dawson, *James Hannington, a History of His Life and Work* (London: Seeley & Co., 1887), p.199; Hannington to CMS Committee, 23 February 1882, quoted in Dawson, pp.191-192.

Missionary parents had the unenviable choice of splitting their families or risking the lives of their children. This was not, however, a problem exclusive to missionaries, but to all who worked in the tropics. Despite advice to the contrary John Pope-Hennessy could not bear to be parted from his infant son during his short tour of duty as Governor-in-Chief of the West African Settlements. The child soon died. [182]

But if children presented a problem on the mission field, wives were essential for Protestant missionaries of a non-celibate tradition and there were two particularly noticeable trends. First, for missionaries to marry in the brief period between receiving their posting and actually leaving Britain; second, for those who had been widowed on the mission field to acquire another wife, at the first possible opportunity, on their next furlough home.

The official history of the WMMS reveals that James Calvert got married in 1838 only because missionaries to Fiji were expected to be married.[183] One of James Chalmers' biographers was equally frank: 'At last the ship was ready, and the young missionaries were told to prepare for ordination, which was also to be followed by their marriage, and a speedy departure'.[184] The experience of the Presbyterian, Peter Milne, may have been extreme, but is a stark indication of the way in which the severely practical Protestant missionary mind worked with regard to matrimony. Having been 'ordained to the work of the ministry and as a missionary to the New Hebrides on 26 November 1868', he recorded: 'One important question still remained to be answered – viz.: how was I to get married? For it was not considered expedient for me to go alone'. Milne was clearly a man of action and after two unsuccessful attempts he married Miss Mary Jane Vietch three weeks later on 18 December 1868. The couple left London docks on 29 December.[185] John Paton returned to Scotland in 1864, his first furlough after his wife's death, and did not leave without acquiring a second wife.[186]

Things were much the same for missionaries in Africa. Having done one tour of duty in Yorubaland as a bachelor, David Hinderer married Anna Martin while on furlough in October 1852.[187] David Livingstone had no romantic illusions and seemed to regard a wife as a necessary part of a missionary's equipment. He drily informed the Directors of the LMS that,

---

182 James Pope Hennessy, *Verandah: some episodes in the Crown Colonies 1867-1889*, (London: George Allen and Unwin, 1964), p.116.
183 Findlay and Holdsworth, III, p.391.
184 William Robson, *James Chalmers* (London: Pickering & Inglis, n.d.), p.20.
185 Alexander Don, *Peter Milne of Nguna* (Dunedin: Foreign Missions Committee of the Presbyterian Church of New Zealand, 1927), pp.65-66.
186 J.G. Paton, I, p.86. The two pioneer missionaries on Fiji, William Cross and David Cargill were both widowed and both subsequently remarried.
187 W.O. Ajayi, p.87.

various considerations connected with this new sphere of labour ... having led me to the conclusion that it was my duty to enter into the marriage relation, I have made the necessary arrangements for union with Mary, eldest daughter of Mr Moffat ....[188]

John Bowen, whose early death on the mission field is referred to later in this chapter, was consecrated Bishop of Sierra Leone on 21 September 1857, married Catherine Butler on 24 November and almost immediately embarked for Freetown, arriving on 13 December.[189] A rare case of a missionary marrying a native woman was that of Charles Stokes of the Nyanza mission. This happened after the death of Stokes' first wife and was so unusual a step and so completely unacceptable to his colleagues that it brought to an abrupt end Stokes' association with the CMS.[190]

James Chalmers married his first wife, Jane Hercus, two days after his ordination in 1865.[191] After her death, in 1879, Chalmers remained single for eight years until his second marriage to Lizzie Harrison. However, it is probable that this gap indicates not so much his reluctance to remarry, as a lack of opportunity, since he failed to take a furlough until ordered to do so by his superiors. Thomas Beswick resigned from the New Guinea mission after two years' service in 1881 when the LMS Directors refused to sanction his marriage to Clara Coombes on the grounds of her ill-health. After he had married Clara, Beswick was reappointed to the mission but died at Townsville, Queensland in August 1883 whilst returning to New Guinea.[192]

The very first despatch from Ludwig Krapf, the pioneer CMS missionary in East Africa, contained news of the death of his wife before they had even arrived in Mombasa: 'the mysterious but ever sweet hand of our Heavenly Father thought good to make me mourn for my beloved wife whom he has removed by death to the blessed abode of his immovable kingdom'.[193] David Livingstone's brother-in-law, J.S. Moffat, expressed his views about missionary wives to LMS headquarters in 1876:

> My convictions have grown deeper for years that our pioneering work ought to be done by men alone. It is useless cruelty to take a lady into an undertaking where she

---

188 Livingstone to LMS Directors, 2 December 1844, quoted in Jeal, p.60.
189 W.O. Ajayi, p.147.
190 Whether he resigned (Stock, III, p.403n) or was expelled (T.O. Beidelmann, *Colonial Evangelism*, p.56, quoted in Elizabeth Isichei, *A History of Christianity in Africa* (London: SPCK, 1995), p.82), is almost beside the point.
191 Lovett, Chalmers, pp. 57-58.
192 Diane Langmore, *Missionary Lives: Papua 1874-1914* (Honolulu: University of Hawaii Press, 1989), Appendix 3, p.284.
193 Krapf to Dandeson Coates, 13 August 1844. CMS East African Mission papers, CA5/016.

does no good beyond affording a spectacle of resigned and devoted suffering: and possibly a hindrance rather than a help to the cause she would die to promote.[194]

Life was undoubtedly hard and death was a common feature of missionary existence. Some missionaries would, no doubt, have agreed with Tertullian that 'the blood of the martyrs is the seed of the church'. But there were very few European missionary martyrs *per se* in the south-west Pacific and even fewer in tropical Africa. Considering the opposition, threats and intimidation that they had to endure, remarkably few missionaries suffered violent deaths at the hands of indigenous peoples. Fiji was notorious as the 'cannibal islands' yet only one missionary was ever murdered by cannibals: Thomas Baker was killed and eaten by a mountain tribe in central Viti Levu in 1867. The cannibal tribes of New Guinea also had a bad reputation, but the mission there had to wait until the dawn of the twentieth century for their first martyrs, the veteran James Chalmers and his young colleague, Oliver Tomkins, in 1901. The 'martyrs' isle' of Erromanga in the New Hebrides saw the death of LMS pioneer John Williams in 1839. Later the Gordon brothers, both in the service of the New Hebrides mission, were also murdered by the islanders, George in 1861 and James in 1872. The death of Bishop J.C. Patteson on the island of Nukapu in September 1871 was the most publicised, and brought the south Pacific and its problems before the British Parliament and public.

In those parts of Africa that will be examined, actual martyrdoms of European missionaries are even fewer and all were in Buganda. Though it was eventually to become one of the greatest missionary success stories of the late nineteenth century, the initial attempt to establish the Nyanza mission was a painful and bloody process. The first to suffer death were Lieutenant George Shergold Smith and Thomas O'Neill. Having been invited to enter Buganda by Kabaka Mutesa, they perished when their camp on the island of Ukerewé on Lake Victoria was attacked by the local chief in December 1877.[195] Bishop James Hannington of the CMS, the first bishop of East Equatorial Africa, was captured on arrival in Busoga by a local chief and imprisoned for eight days. He was murdered in October 1885 on the orders of Kabaka Mwanga, thus becoming the best known of the victims of the persecution of Christians at the beginning of Mwanga's reign.[196]

To speak exclusively of British martyrs, however, is to ignore the great number of indigenous Christians who suffered martyrdom for their faith, for whereas those who opposed the introduction of Christianity might think twice about taking the life of a white man, thus risking retribution from the British armed forces, there was no such risk in putting to death their own people who had forsaken tribal religion for the white man's creed. The massacres of

---

194 Moffat to Mullens, 6 July 1876, quoted in Cairns, p.58.
195 Stock, II, p.104.
196 See J.V. Taylor, pp.56-57.

Christian converts in Buganda at the beginning of Mwanga's reign in 1885-86, and the deaths of probably several hundred of the Polynesian teachers in New Guinea and the Pacific islands, are an indication that the real martyrs of this period (in terms of sheer numbers) were local converts rather than European missionaries.

As far as the European missionaries were concerned, their lives were infinitely more at risk from disease than from physical attack. The Gambia, for example, which was a highly unpopular posting for British officials because of its unhealthy conditions, also took its toll of missionaries. The Revd J.W. Bell lasted but three weeks in the Gambia in 1874. An unnamed colonial chaplain survived for only a month in 1869.[197] Along the coast in Lagos, conditions were also very unhealthy: Joseph Rogers, Chairman of Lagos Methodist District died of fever in 1882 after only one year in office;[198] Richard Paley, a young Cambridge graduate who travelled to Africa with the Hinderers to serve with the CMS at Abeokuta, died of fever shortly after arrival at Lagos; his wife died before reaching Sierra Leone on the return journey.[199]

The tropical climate was no respecter of persons and bishops were no more immune than any other missionaries to the rigours of the climate and the diseases it harboured. Bishop Mackenzie of the UMCA died at the mouth of the Zambesi in 1862, less than a year after his arrival in Africa.[200] The first Bishop of Sierra Leone, Owen Emeric Vidal, left England in December 1852 and died exactly two years later.[201] His successor, Bishop John Bowen, died of fever at the age of forty-four in May 1859 after only eighteen months in post. Henry Townsend reported to CMS headquarters, 'it is not unusual for us to see our friends die around us'.[202] Bishop Henry Parker, who replaced the murdered James Hannington in East Africa in 1886, lasted less than eighteen months.[203] Dr Joseph Hill, Samuel Crowther's successor as Bishop of Western Equatorial Africa, survived less than one month, both he and Mrs Hill dying within a few hours of each other in January 1894, a month in which seven European missionaries in his diocese died of malaria or dysentery.[204]

The focus of this study now turns from the preceding general observations concerning missionary societies and missionary life, to a series of six specific case studies of missionaries on the frontiers of empire in the tropics, three from

---

197 Administrator Patey's report of 4 August 1869, enc. in Kennedy to Granville, 9 August 1869. *PP* 1870, XLIX [C.149].
198 Findlay and Holdsworth, IV, p.207.
199 Hinderer, pp. 45-47; Stock, II, pp. 63-65.
200 Jeal, pp.247-248; Wilson, p. vii.
201 W.O. Ajayi, p.104
202 Townsend to Col. Dawes, 30 September 1859. CMS Yoruba Mission papers, CA2/085 (a).
203 Stock, III, pp.418-420.
204 W.O. Ajayi, p.253

the south-west Pacific and three from Africa. They will show in detail missionaries from a number of societies working in different areas of the imperial frontier and, since no two situations were alike, mission personnel will be seen to respond in varying ways to the different circumstances which they faced. These case studies will enable the effect of missionaries on imperial development to be accurately assessed.

CHAPTER 2

Missionaries as Humanitarians? Opposition to the Recruitment of Indentured Labour for Queensland[1]

Opposition to slavery was buried deep in the Victorian psyche. The long battle of Wilberforce and the Clapham Sect, culminating in the abolition of the slave trade in 1807 and of slavery in the British Empire in 1833, was a source of great pride to the Victorians. Slavery was an unmixed evil, which might be tolerated or even practised by lesser races, but to the British it was to be suppressed whenever it was encountered and replaced with 'legitimate' trade. Tsar Alexander II's abolition of serfdom in Russia in 1861 and Lincoln's Emancipation Proclamation of 1862 were, to the Victorian mind, two indications that the argument against slavery had been won world-wide and that it was only a matter of time before it was everywhere abolished. To many in Britain, the extension of her empire was a God-given opportunity to deal a mortal blow to slavery and this was a major factor in British involvement in both west and east Africa. But here there was a problem, for to define 'slavery' accurately was far from straightforward. This was particularly the case in the grey area that was indentured labour, which could be recruited entirely legitimately or could be little better than the slave trade.

The Australian journal, *The Mudgee Liberal*, had no doubts:

> That noble, generous England should pay twenty millions to emancipate the West Indian slaves; that she should keep a squadron on the West coast of Africa, at an enormous amount in men and money; that gallant officers and noble-minded men should, in defiance of one of the worst climates on the earth, unite all their energy and zeal for the suppression of the infamous slave trade, and yet find it being resuscitated in a British colony, and carried out in British owned and registered vessels, is enough to make the blood boil with indignation. When the American civil war gave the death-blow to slavery in the southern States of America we

---

1 This chapter is an expanded version of a paper of the same name given at the Henry Martyn Centre, Westminster College, Cambridge on 2 March 2006, <http://www.martynmission.cam.ac.uk/ CJDarch.html>

imagined the word *slave* was a word only to be used in connexion with the past, little dreaming that Australia was to be disgraced by such a traffic.[2]

This paradox was not unnoticed in Whitehall. Robert Herbert, Permanent Under-Secretary at the Colonial Office from 1871, observed that 'it seems strange that we should go to trouble and expense in Africa and consider ourselves under no similar obligation in other seas in which Her Majesty's ships are stationed'.[3]

The abolition of slavery throughout the British Empire in 1833 had, however, left certain fundamental questions unanswered.[4] Slavery had, after all, only grown up because of the need for labour in tropical climates where Europeans were unwilling to labour physically for any length of time in the adverse climatic conditions. How were plantations growing crops like cotton and sugar, both requiring hot temperatures and intensive cultivation, to be economically staffed? As it became clear that freed slaves were quite as likely to exercise their freedom by choosing not to work for their former masters as employees, a system of indentured labour from India began to develop to relieve shortages.[5] But this was clearly open to abuse as two Royal Commissions on the operation of indenture in British Guiana and Mauritius pointed out.[6] Nevertheless, it came to be regarded as an acceptable means of recruiting labour since the migrants' journey was under the supervision of British officials at both ends.[7] An *ad hoc* system of transferring labour between the Pacific islands was certainly happening in the 1850s but the *Two Brothers* incident, when colonial courts were found to be powerless, prompted the Colonial Office in London to consider imperial legislation to bring kidnappers to justice.[8]

The start of an organised Pacific labour trade seems to have begun following the abolition of slavery in Peru in 1855. At first, Chinese coolies were used to fill the gap in the labour market, but before very long a cheaper and easier alternative came into play, namely the importation of islanders from the New Hebrides (modern Vanuatu). J.C. Byrne, an Irish-born French citizen, who had already been responsible for transporting over 3,000 New Hebrideans into

---

2 *The Mudgee Liberal*, May 1869, quoted in Palmer, p.169.
3 Min., 20 October 1871, on Belmore to Kimberley, 9 August 1871. CO 201/564.
4 For the continuing opposition to slavery in the years following emancipation see H. Temperley, *British Antislavery 1833-1870* (London: Longman, 1972).
5 For the use of indentured Indian labour overseas, see H. Tinker, *A New System of Slavery* (London: OUP for The Institute of Race Relations, 1974).
6 See Report of Commission appointed to enquire into treatment of immigrants into British Guiana. *PP* 1871, XX, [C.393] and Correspondence respecting Royal Commission to enquire into the treatment of immigrants into Mauritius. *PP* 1875, LII, [C.1118].
7 F.W. Chesson, 'The Polynesian Labour Question', *PRCI*, III (1871-2), 36.
8 FO to CO, 24 August 1860, CO201/514. Also see O.W. Parnaby, 'Aspects of British Policy in the Pacific', *HSANZ*, VIII (1957), 55-57.

the French occupied island of New Caledonia, was licensed by the Peruvian government to import labourers for a period of five years.

The warning that this dubious trade had begun came to London from the British representative in Lima in May 1862.[9] His superior, W.S. Jerningham, on leave in London at the time, returned to Lima with instructions from the Foreign Secretary, Earl Russell, to keep a close eye on developments. Russell's comment that 'the system to which I have now called your attention may well degenerate into the slave trade in disguise'[10] had a prophetic ring about it and exactly sums up the fears not only of the British government and its representatives, but also of the missionaries who served in the south-west Pacific and their parent societies. In view of their concerted opposition to the labour trade, it is interesting (and not a little ironical) that the first missionary to appear in the events of the labour trade was the unnamed missionary on Rakaan who, along with the local chief, prepared the contract signed by the islanders who were landed at the Peruvian port of Callao early in 1863.[11] But the arrival of recruiting vessels on the remote Polynesian island of Niue later in 1863 drew protests from the resident LMS missionary W.G. Lawes.[12]

The missionaries could claim no credit for the Peruvian government's subsequent abolition of the labour traffic in the spring of 1863: pressure from the diplomatic community would seem to have been the reason.[13] But any sense of moral victory would have been short-lived, for the labour trade merely found new outlets for its human cargoes, this time on British territory. In May 1863, Robert Towns, who had already had experience of the use of New Hebridean labour on the plantation in French New Caledonia in which he was a partner, sent the *Don Juan* to the New Hebrides to recruit for his Queensland plantation.[14] Towns was well aware that this move was likely to encounter considerable opposition from the missionary community.

European Exploitation of Pacific Islanders

The missionaries had first arrived in the south-west Pacific before the eighteenth century was over,[15] but they were not the first Europeans to come to the area. They were preceded by Spanish, Dutch and French seamen, though the nature of the island groups was imperfectly understood until James Cook made

---

9 Barton to Russell, 29 May 1862. CO201/514.
10 *Ibid*. Russell to W.S. Jerningham, 26 November 1862.
11 *Ibid*. E.W. Robertson to Jerningham, 11 January 1863.
12 Garret, *Stars,* p.137.
13 Encs. in Jerningham to Russell, 12 May 1863 and 29 May 1863. CO201/514.
14 O.W. Parnaby, *Britain and the Labor Trade,* pp.54-55. See also E.W. Docker, *The Blackbirders* (Sydney: Angus and Robertson, 1970), pp. 9-11.
15 For an overview of early missions in the area see W.N. Gunson, *Messengers of Grace* (Melbourne: OUP, 1978).

his detailed exploration of the area in the 1760s and 1770s.[16] The navigators had been followed by traders. First came whalers, who made occasional stops in order to replenish their supplies. Next came sandalwood traders, who stripped the islands of all the wood they could find between the years 1840 and 1865. Inhumanity towards the native peoples and a cavalier disregard of their rights were widespread, with unfortunate consequences for the next group of white men to arrive, the European missionaries. The legacy of the sandalwood and other traders was threefold, suggested an early twentieth-century missionary writer:[17] the introduction of disease, firearms and alcohol played havoc with the social fabric of the islands, already weak through cannibalism and inter-tribal warfare.

Despite the bad reputation of his colleagues, however, one sandalwood trader drew plaudits from both Presbyterian and Anglican missionaries. Captain James Paddon, involved in the sandalwood trade on Aneiteum, Tanna, and New Caledonia, proved a friend to both John Geddie, the pioneer Presbyterian missionary in the New Hebrides, and Bishop Selwyn. Paddon donated to Geddie the timber frame for the first chapel and school house on Aneiteum;[18] his methods of mixing people from different islands and using them away from the influence of their home environment in order to improve their work were noted by Bishop Selwyn and adopted in his missionary college for Melanesian youths, first at Auckland, then at Norfolk Island.[19]

In order to understand the initially hostile attitude of many of the island peoples to the missionaries, it has to be remembered that their only experience of white men was that of the sandalwooders and other traders whose aim was to exploit the resources of the islands and for whom the islanders were treacherous savages who would apparently attack and kill white men at random. Eighty years earlier, William Carey, the father of the British missionary movement, had posed the uncomfortable question as to whether native peoples were inherently savage or whether they were merely reacting in self-defence to their treatment at the hands of European traders: 'I greatly question whether the barbarities practiced [sic] by them, have not originated in some real or supposed affront and are therefore, more properly, acts of self-defence, than proofs of inhuman and bloodthirsty dispositions'.[20] The prime example of European missionaries being caught up in this cycle of violence, the murder of the 'Apostle of the South Seas', the LMS missionary John Williams, on Erromanga in the New Hebrides in 1839 was well known throughout Christendom and was particularly

---

16 For the early explorers see Morrell, *Pacific Islands*, pp.12-25.
17 F.H.L. Paton, *The Kingdom in the Pacific* (London: Young People's Missionary Movement, 1913), pp.31-32.
18 Patterson, p.180.
19 John Inglis, *In the New Hebrides* (London: Nelson, 1887), p.201.
20 Carey, p.64. See also p.71.

remembered by his missionary successors on the islands of the south-west Pacific.[21]

Lieutenant-Colonel W.J. Smythe, sent to Fiji in 1860-61 to report on the possibility of annexation, noted the problem of lawlessness and commented, 'the great hindrance to the progress of civilisation and Christianity among the inhabitants of the Pacific islands is the conduct of the whites residing or roving among them'.[22] As the missionaries sought to convince the islanders of their good intentions, their work was undermined by the next wave of European exploiters, the labour traders.

Robert Towns was aware of the missionaries in the New Hebrides, where his vessels principally recruited. He was also shrewd enough to realise their influence and authority over the islanders. Hence the open letter to the missionaries which he sent with his recruiters:

> as I have told your worthy brotherhood, Messrs Inglis and Geddes [sic], that I with my cotton emigration (returning every six or twelve months) will do more towards civilising the natives in one year than you can possibly in ten; they will see what civilisation is, and aim to follow it.[23]

Not unnaturally, the missionaries who received this letter failed to agree with its contents.[24] But whereas they regarded Towns as an unwelcome competitor for the attention of the islanders, Towns regarded himself (or at least tried to portray himself) as a fellow civiliser of the uncivilised, endeavouring to make this clear later in his letter when he appealed: 'if you can supply me with a native teacher or reader ... it will very much hasten the object'.[25] Not surprisingly, the missionaries were unimpressed and defended their influence over their converts with such a fierce jealousy that it led to open hostility towards the labour traders and to repeated clashes during the years in which the trade took place.

The native peoples found themselves in demand by two very different kinds of Europeans. On the one hand, there were the missionaries who sought the good of the indigenous population and showed them kindness and provided both education and medicine. On the other hand, there were the labour traders who sought to recruit, sometimes by fair means, often by foul, native men, women and boys to work in the plantations of Queensland, Fiji or New Caledonia. To make matters even more confusing for the islanders, some of the labour traders were known to pose as missionaries for the purpose of disarming

---

21 Lovett, *History of the LMS*, p.377.
22 Smythe to Newcastle, 1 May 1861. *PP* 1862, XXXVI [2995].
23 Towns, 'To any Missionary into whose hands this may come', 29 May 1863, enc. in Bowen to Newcastle, 16 September 1863. *PP* 1867-8, XLVIII [391].
24 Inglis, p.204.
25 Towns, 29 May 1863, enc. in Bowen to Newcastle, 16 September 1863. *PP* 1867-68, XLVIII [391].

and deceiving their prey,[26] and on at least two occasions missionaries became involved in punitive attacks on native villages.[27] Little wonder that the response of the islanders to white men was confused and unpredictable. Nevertheless, the islanders were often more perceptive than the missionaries realised. John Garrett notes the paradox:

> many local men went willingly. They wanted to be free to learn better English, use white men's tools, wear white men's clothes, build better boats, and improve their skills in planting. Missionaries tried to prevent them going. They did not want them to be corrupted by the white man's profanity, lechery and acquisitiveness and power....[28]

Benjamin Danks, of the Methodist mission in New Britain referred approvingly to the attitude of one of his converts to the dilemma posed by the labour trade to Christian converts – should they go with the traders or stay with the missionaries?

> They have thrown away their own country to come here to us in a country of sickness to teach us the *lotu* and it is not good that we should run away from them in these ships; for they have come here in love to us, not like the traders for coconuts, or like the ships for our work.[29]

When concern about possible abuses in the labour trade led the Queensland government, in February 1868, to legislate for its regulation, missionaries were given an unrequested and unwanted supervisory role. The Polynesian Labourers Act provided for a form to be signed by a missionary, consul or other white resident at the place of recruitment to certify that people leaving their island for Queensland had assented freely and willingly to their engagements.[30] To a man the New Hebrides missionaries refused to co-operate with the Queensland government, fearing that to do so would be to legitimise the trade and undermine their opposition to it. But the result of the boycott was that the unregulated trade flourished. Yet Lorimer Fison of the Wesleyan mission in Fiji was also unimpressed by regulation, shrewdly perceiving that 'no licence granted to any vessel by the Queensland, or any other government, can be a

---

26 *Southern Cross*, 6 Nov 1869, quoted in *PP* 1871, XLVIII [468].
27 See Commodore W.S. Wiseman to Admiralty, 16 October 1865. FO58/106 and Morrell, *Pacific Islands*, pp.246-247.
28 Garrett, *A Way in the Sea*, pp.24-25.
29 Quoted in Deane, p.245. *Lotu* was originally a Tongan word which became widely used throughout the south Pacific islands. As a noun it signifies Christianity, as a verb, conversion to Christianity.
30 'A Bill to Regulate and Control the Introduction and Treatment of Polynesian Labourers', *PP* 1867-8, XLVIII [391]. See also Murdoch to Rogers, 14 April 1869. *PP* 1868-9, XLIII [408].

guarantee against any such barbarities'.[31] Parnaby suggests that the two inherent weaknesses in the Act were, first, the assumption that islanders had a sufficient understanding to enter into a fair and legal contract and, second, the absence of any provision for effective supervision at the place of recruitment.[32]

The Colonial Office concurred with the proposed amendments to the Act, expressing its satisfaction in what was being done to prevent abuses and no doubt felt relief that the Queensland government had acted without the necessity of pressure from London.[33] But on behalf of the Presbyterian missionaries, John Inglis challenged the right of a colonial government to regulate the trade at all:

> What moral right has the government of Fiji or Queensland to license the rowdyism of their respective populations, to go down and prowl about and plunder our mission of its best natives, and carry into captivity the poor defenceless inhabitants of these islands, in order that their thews and sinews may be transmuted into colonial gold?[34]

To many of the missionaries, for whom black and white were the only necessary colours in their moral palette, the labour trade was nothing more than a new slave trade and, although the different missionary societies varied in their approach, they all opposed the way in which it was being carried on. The problem for the historian – as it was for the authorities in the 1860s and 1870s – is this: was the Pacific labour trade nothing more than slavery or was it the legitimate recruitment of labour?

In examining missionary opposition to the labour trade, it will be appropriate to consider several individual cases of missionary involvement and then, for a wider perspective, to examine the reactions of other interested parties who encountered the missionaries and observed them in their opposition to the labour trade: naval officers, humanitarians, and the only labour trader who wrote a detailed contemporary account. Interwoven with these will be the reaction of the officials in the Colonial Office to whom complaints and representations were made.

Opposition from the Presbyterian Missionaries

Three missions covered the area of the Pacific which the labour traders used as their main recruiting grounds. The London Missionary Society had been first in the field in its attempts to move from Samoa to the southern New Hebrides. But the murder of John Williams in 1839 marked the failure of this strategy. The

---

31 Lorimer Fison to William Fison (copy), 27 August 1870. CO 201/562.
32 Parnaby, *Britain and the Labor Trade*, pp.66-67. Bishop Patteson asserted that 'statements of "contracts" made with wild native men are simply false'. Patteson to Bishop of Sydney, enc. in Kinnaird to Clarendon, 27 May 1869. *PP* 1868-9 XLIII [438]
33 Earl Granville to Governor Blackall, 18 Feb 1870. *PP* 1871, XLVIII [468].
34 Inglis, p.212.

LMS managed to gain a foothold in the Loyalty Islands which, despite the French occupation of the islands in 1864, it retained tenaciously until 1884. The LMS also selflessly assisted the re-establishment of the mission on the New Hebrides in Presbyterian guise in 1848. The LMS sent Thomas Powell from Samoa to accompany John Geddie and to remain with him on Aneiteum until he was settled. After Powell's return to Samoa and the arrival of John Inglis in 1852, the New Hebrides Mission was a purely Presbyterian affair, though the missionaries who came to the islands as the mission developed were from a number of different Presbyterian churches in Scotland, New Zealand and Nova Scotia.

The Melanesian Mission was the last on the scene, developing out of the Anglican diocese of New Zealand in 1849 and becoming a separate missionary diocese in 1861. Missionary evidence of the abuses in the labour trade was vital in vast areas of the Pacific where there were no resident British consuls and where Royal Navy patrols were few and far between. Though taking different views on the principle of indentured labour, all three missions opposed the labour trade, but to different degrees and in practical terms reacted to it in different ways. From their bases in Samoa and the Loyalty Islands, the LMS encountered the trade far less than the other two societies, though it was on Samoa that the notorious recruiter 'Bully' Hayes was first arrested and then escaped from custody in 1870. The veteran missionary, Thomas Powell, commented:

> It will be a lamentable inconsistency on the parts of the British and French governments if this iniquitous traffic be allowed under their flags after their intervention, only a few years ago to put a stop to Peruvian proceedings of the same character.[35]

And he added:

> I hope the Directors of the London Missionary Society will use their influence with the responsible authorities to get this new form of slavery - or rather slavery under a new name –"*labour*" – put to an end.

Samuel McFarlane, from the Loyalty Islands and later Papua New Guinea, took a less doctrinaire view:

> I have always maintained, I said so in Brisbane as long ago as 1863, that recruiting is to the benefit of natives and planters alike ... but I should not like to see the traffic carried on as it is in the South Seas.[36]

---

35 Powell to Mullens, 20 January 1870. LMS South Seas Letters 32/5/A.
36 McFarlane to Wide Bay Farmers' and Planters' Association, 14 February 1883. Quoted in Docker, p.172. See also William T. Wawn, *The South Sea Islanders and the Queensland Labour Trade* (London: Swan Sonnenschein, 1893). p.350.

The New Hebrides Mission found itself in the thick of the arguments over the labour trade and took a robust line in opposition. They held that the trade could never be effectively regulated and that it would always hinder their work by taking native converts away from missionary influence. With dogged determination they opposed the trade root and branch and took every opportunity to denigrate it publicly.

In early October 1868,[37] a kidnapping incident involving the Queensland-licensed recruiting vessel *Lyttona* on the New Hebrides island of Erromanga resulted in a letter of complaint from the local missionary, James McNair, to the senior naval officer of the Australian Squadron.[38] McNair alleged that Captain George Smith of the *Lyttona* had been responsible for the kidnapping of nine Erromangans and that despite his efforts to rescue them by temporarily impounding the landing boat, the recruiters had, by deception, regained their vessel and put to sea without returning the islanders as promised.

The *Lyttona* case was probably no worse than many other 'blackbirding' incidents, and although human liberty was infringed, no human life was lost. But three factors make it particularly interesting for this study. Firstly, it was the earliest major case of missionary involvement in, and opposition to, the labour trade. Secondly, the stir caused in official circles by McNair's allegations of kidnapping showed just how important missionary evidence could be and how much pressure the missionaries could exert in the corridors of power by the judicious use of their influence. Thirdly, it also showed how easily the missionaries' righteous enthusiasm for the cause could result in them overplaying their hand and undermining their own credibility. Moreover, the *Lyttona* case showed the weakness of current legal sanctions. As William Dealtry observed in an oft-quoted minute in the Colonial Office files, 'I am afraid that the Colonies possess no legal power to punish those engaged in this trade for the mere act of kidnapping if unaccompanied with acts of atrocity'.[39]

Commodore Lambert, the senior naval officer on the Australasian station, had informed the Governor of Queensland of McNair's complaint,[40] and Governor Blackall, after dutifully making enquiries about the matter, reported back to the Colonial Office.[41] McNair, however, had not waited for the wheels of officialdom to grind, but neatly short-circuited the system by sending a copy of his letter (probably by way of the mission's agent in Sydney, Dr Robert Steel) to the Revd John Kay in Coatbridge, Scotland. Kay, the Secretary of the Foreign Missions Committee of the Reformed Presbyterian Church of Scotland, passed McNair's letter to the Hon. Arthur Kinnaird, Liberal Member for Perth, and a highly influential supporter of the missionary movement. Kinnaird's

---

37 Parnaby incorrectly dates the incident as July 1868. Parnaby, *Labor Trade*, p.16.
38 McNair to Lambert, 22 October 1868. CO 234/23.
39 Min., 10 June 1869, by Dealtry on FO to CO, 5 June 1869. CO 234/23.
40 Lambert to Blackall, 28 January 1869. *PP* 1868-9, XLIII [408].
41 Blackall to Granville, 16 April 1869. CO 234/22.

influence at the Foreign Office meant that he had only to present them with the information for it to be forwarded, now with all the authority of the Foreign Office, to the Colonial Office:

> I am directed by the Earl of Clarendon to transmit to you, to be laid before Earl Granville, some extracts of a letter from Mr James McNair together with other papers which have been placed in Lord Clarendon's hands by Mr Arthur Kinnaird....[42]

This arrived on Sir Frederic Rogers' desk in the Colonial Office a fortnight *before* the official despatch from the Governor of Queensland and it was the first the Colonial Office had heard of the matter.[43] Having been warned that the matter would be raised in the House of Commons, the Colonial Office gave it prompt attention.[44] The high profile given to McNair's allegations and the subsequent investigations into the *Lyttona* case in two Parliamentary Papers is perhaps indicative of the way in which the Colonial Office had been caught off guard and sought to atone for this by being conspicuously open in agreeing to the requests for the publication of the correspondence.[45] It was the Quaker P.A. Taylor, Radical Member of Parliament for Leicester, who had forewarned the Colonial Office of the question he asked in the House on 28 June 1869.[46] John Inglis was incorrect in suggesting that 'this was the first time that the labour traffic was brought under the notice of the Imperial Legislature',[47] since Taylor himself had asked two previous questions on the subject before the *Lyttona* incident.[48]

It was an important tactical *coup* for the missionary movement, though any jubilation was short-lived. For the arrival of the official despatch from the Governor of Queensland cast some doubt on the accuracy of McNair's allegations.[49] The papers were examined in London by Sir Clinton Murdoch of the Emigration Board. Murdoch summarized the case put by McNair, contrasted it with the enquiry made by the Queensland Immigration Agent, and concluded significantly: 'it is clear that either Mr McNair or the Immigration

---

42 FO to CO, 5 June 1869. CO 234/23.
43 'Mr McNair's complaint has already been received through the Foreign Office.' Min. by Dealtry, 21 June 1869, on Blackall to Granville, 16 April 1869. CO 234/22.
44 *Ibid.*, 'I understand from Mr Monsell that a question is to be asked in the House respecting these labourers on Friday next'.
45 See *PP* 1868-9, XLIII [408, 438].
46 *Hansard*, Third Series, CXCVII, cols 633-648.
47 Inglis, p.239.
48 *Hansard*, CXCL, col.1882, 13 March 1868 and CXCII, col.816, 25 May 1868. Sir John Simeon had previously asked a similar question, CXCVI, cols 574-575, 11 May 1869.
49 '...a searching enquiry throws considerable doubt on the correctness of the Rev Mr McNair's statement'. See Blackall to Granville, 16 April 1869, and encs. CO 234/22.

Agent was deceived in the matter; and the circumstances appear to make it more probable that it was Mr McNair than the Immigration Agent'.[50]

There is no evidence, indeed it is highly improbable, that McNair sought, by deceit or inaccuracy, to prod the Colonial Office into action against the labour trade. The effect, however, was the same and Owen Parnaby's comment that 'McNair's purpose in stirring the Colonial Office to action ... was accomplished before the inaccuracy of his report was known', is substantially correct.[51] It later became a common feature of attacks on reports by the New Hebrides missionaries that they appeared to be excessively credulous in believing what they were told by the islanders and in repeating these accusations as though they represented the whole truth.[52] To have been more discriminating in their use of native evidence and to have been more sparing in their accusations would have enhanced their influence.

The practical outcome of the enquiry into the *Lyttona* case was that public meetings held in Sydney and Brisbane in February and March 1869 showed considerable public disquiet with the working of the Act. At the meeting on 8 February, speakers included the LMS representative in Australia, J.P. Sunderland, and the Bishop of Sydney. In his address the latter quoted from a letter of Bishop Patteson. A letter from McNair was also read out.[53] The meetings and their attendant publicity aroused public opinion to the extent that the Queensland government accepted amendments to the Polynesian Labourers Act. A Select Committee, which reported in September 1869, made seven recommendations for better enforcement of the Act, including the appointment of Government Agents to sail on each recruiting ship and the admissibility of the unsworn evidence of native islanders in court cases.[54] This apparent tightening up of the regulations cut no ice with the New Hebrides missionaries, however. John Inglis commented that, 'it looks as if Acts were passed rather with a view to blind the public than to operate as a means of protecting the poor natives'.[55]

The moral seemed to be that what was most effective in shaping opinion and forming official action was not so much the quality of missionary evidence as the way in which that evidence was presented. This lesson was not lost on John Paton, McNair's Presbyterian colleague. As McNair faded from the limelight after the *Lyttona* case his mantle fell, even before his premature death

---

50 Murdoch to Rogers, 27 July 1869. *PP* 1868-9, XLIII [408].
51 Parnaby, 'Aspects of British Policy in the Pacific', 59 n.27.
52 See, for example, Agent General for Queensland to Kimberley, 10 May 1871: 'Mr Paton seems willing to take the bare word of any of them [i.e. islanders] as it tells on that side of the question he wishes to establish'. *PP* 1871, XLVIII [468].
53 Extract from *Sydney Morning Herald*, 9 February 1869, enc. in Belmore to Granville, 26 February 1869. *PP* 1868-9, XLIII [408].
54 Rogers to Kinnaird, 30 March 1870. *PP* 1871, XLVIII [468]. Also see F.W. Chesson, 'Polynesian Labour Question', 38-39.
55 Inglis to Steel, 15 June 1871. Printed in Kay, p.6.

in 1872, upon Paton who turned opposition against the labour trade into a cottage industry. Paton, first Presbyterian missionary on the New Hebridean island of Tanna, had been driven off that island in 1862 and had subsequently taken up residence with the less aggressive inhabitants of Aniwa, where he served for thirty years, constantly battling against the labour trade and all who supported it. A man of patriarchal appearance with his flowing beard and strident manner, Paton seemed to arouse intense feelings in those who encountered him. Anger or adulation, never indifference, seemed to be the order of the day.

Paton's notoriety began with another complaint against the *Lyttona*, published in the *Sydney Morning Herald* on 13 February 1871. In the same letter he accused the captain of the *Spunkie* of kidnapping and, for good measure, he also involved himself in controversy over another ship, the *Jason*.[56] Paton's *modus operandi* seemed to be that where a manifest injustice needed to be righted, accuracy in matters of detail was a luxury not to be indulged in. It was not so much that Paton was economical with the truth, rather that he was profligate with his accusations. As one contemporary Melbourne clergyman put it, Paton 'appears to combine enthusiasm in a good cause with a perfect genius for scandal-mongering and the imputation of bad motives'.[57] The labour trader William Wawn chronicled three separate occasions when he clashed with Paton, commenting drily about one of them:

> I suppose it was not worth his while to sift the matter properly, so long as he could get a good story to tell against a "slaver". Many of the stories told by this gentleman about "labour" vessels have just as good a foundation and no better. [58]

An able publicist, frequently using Robert Steel in Sydney as his intermediary, Paton variously used letters both to individuals and to the press (especially the sympathetic Congregationalist-owned *Sydney Morning Herald*), petitions, meetings, the lobbying of politicians, making common cause with trade unions and deputation work in Australia and Great Britain to whip up support against the labour trade. His reputation was, however, double-edged. Though he was a figure of heroic stature to his own supporters, his campaign, which continued unabated until the turn of the century, merely antagonised the authorities and failed to move them. Protesting vociferously at every possible opportunity only had the effect of making the authorities deaf to his complaints.[59] Docker refers

---

56 See Immigration Agent to Colonial Secretary of Queensland, 21 February 1871. *PP* 1871, XLVIII [468].
57 *Brisbane Courier*, n.d., quoted in Wawn, p.267.
58 *Ibid.*, p.29.
59 'I cannot help thinking that if the other statements in Mr Paton's letter are made with as little regard to the truth as this one, the Government should hesitate before giving credence to any of them.' Immigration Agent to Colonial Secretary of Queensland, 21

to Paton's 'staggering verbosity' and his 'utter disregard for fact', concluding that 'for most of the time he harmed his own cause more than those he opposed'.[60] Even an observer as objective as Niel Gunson does not hesitate to label Paton 'an agitator frequently deluded by his own propaganda'.[61] With John Paton in full flow, 'evidence' of malpractice and kidnapping by the labour traders was becoming indistinguishable from abolitionist propaganda. James McNair, in his one foray against the labour trade, had brought the matter forcefully to the attention of the Colonial Office and begun a train of events which led in time to the passing of the Pacific Islanders' Protection Act. John Paton, however, in thirty years of vociferous campaigning achieved little more than a dubious personal reputation and countless column inches in the colonial press.

Another Presbyterian missionary, Peter Milne of Nguna, found himself in the media spotlight after Captain Coath and J.C. Irving of the *Jason* turned the tables on the missionaries and lodged a complaint against Milne claiming that he had incited Nguna natives to fire on the *Jason*.[62] In the ensuing controversy the Aborigines Protection Society supported the missionaries.[63] Not surprisingly, Commander Markham of HMS *Rosario* took Milne's side[64] and, after claim and counter-claim, the Queensland government eventually accepted that the charges against Milne were worthless.[65] But it is interesting to note that Commander Markham, normally a staunch defender of the missions, assumed that the alleged attack *had* taken place but that it was a justifiable retaliation.

The *Jason* case was significant because it came after government agents had been appointed to labour recruiting vessels. Investigations showed that Captain Coath and the agent Meiklejohn had been at odds with one another throughout the voyage in question and the integrity and authority of the latter had been put in doubt. Whether or not he had, as he claimed, been locked in the hold and threatened by the captain, the agent's presence had clearly had no effect whatsoever on the recruiting practices of that particular vessel. The presence of a government agent was shown to be no guarantee of lawful recruiting. The view of William Dealtry of the Colonial Office that the

---

February 1871. *PP* 1871, XLVIII [468]. See also Min., 3 June, by Knatchbull-Hugessen on O'Connell to Kimberley, 20 March 1871. CO 234/26.
60 Docker, p.244.
61 Gunson, 'Victorian Christianity in the South Seas: a survey', *JRH*, VIII (1974), 189.
62 Statements by Master and Chief Officer of Jason enc. in Agent General for Queensland to Under- Secretary for the Colonies, 25 May 1871. *PP* 1871 XLVIII [468]. For a detailed account of the incident see Steel, pp. 243-250. For Milne's account see Don, pp.101-4.
63 Aborigines Protection Society to Kimberley, 14 August 1871. *PP* 1871 XLVIII [468].
64 Markham, pp.97-98; Markham to Commodore Stirling, 14 November 1871. *PP* 1872 XXXIX [C.542].
65 Normanby to Kimberley, 21 March 1872. CO 234/26.

appointment of government agents would check recruiting abuses appeared to be over optimistic and unduly complacent.[66]

A virtually identical incident took place on Aniwa in 1879. This time the ship's captain made a complaint against Paton. For once the latter does not appear to have made any political capital out of the affair and it came to light only through the published letters of his second wife.[67] One can only speculate as to why the habitually verbose Paton remained uncharacteristically silent on this occasion.

The Role of Bishop Patteson

Without doubt the most influential of all missionaries in the south-west Pacific in this period was John Coleridge Patteson, missionary Bishop of Melanesia from 1861 to his untimely but ultimately highly propitious death in September 1871. Patteson was held in high regard for three reasons. First, he was an Anglican and a bishop – most other missionaries in the area were neither. Secondly, whereas most missionaries in this period were from the artisan classes, Patteson's pedigree and connections were impeccable: scion of a wealthy family, educated at Eton and Oxford, he was a friend of Gladstone and other establishment figures while his cousin, Sir John Duke Coleridge, was Attorney General in Gladstone's first cabinet. Thirdly, Patteson had such a warm personality and saintly aura and exuded so little episcopal pomp that he was loved and respected even by those who would normally have little truck with Anglican bishops. John Geddie, for example, greatly respected Patteson, describing him as 'a man of the most lovely Christian character and singular devotedness'.[68] John Paton's views on Patteson are not recorded, but Patteson records his visit to the fiery Scot on Tanna shortly after the death of his first wife and child and expresses feelings of heart-felt sympathy and humility.[69]

Few missionaries were more fair-minded with regard to the labour trade than Patteson. Because of his peripatetic episcopal ministry over the countless islands of his vast diocese, he was in the position to view the labour trade in its broader context, not merely its effect on one island or group of islands. His phenomenal gift for acquiring native languages also gave him a wider perspective as to what was going on over a large area of the Solomon Islands and the New Hebrides.[70]

---

66 Min., n.d., by Dealtry on Blackall to Kimberley, 27 December 1870. CO 234/24.
67 Margaret W. Paton, *Letters and Sketches from the New Hebrides* (London: Hodder and Stoughton, 1896), pp.311-312.
68 Quoted in Patterson, p.420.
69 Patteson to Bishop of Wellington, 9 October 1859, quoted in Charlotte M. Yonge, *Life of John Coleridge Patteson, Missionary Bishop of the Melanesian Islands*, 2 vols (London: Macmillan, 1874), I, p.420.
70 'Patteson spoke twenty-four languages and reduced many of them to writing'. Whiteman, p.119.

With a greater breadth of vision and a more educated and subtle mind than many of the Pacific missionaries, Patteson was hesitant in condemning the labour trade out of hand. His cousin and biographer, Charlotte Yonge, believed he 'was not at all averse to the employment of natives, well knowing how great an agent in improvement is civilisation. But to have them carried off without understanding what they were about, and then set to hard labour, was quite a different thing'.[71] The tension Patteson felt between the possibilities for advancement offered by plantation life and the brutal realities of the labour trade is nowhere made clearer than in a letter written in 1868:

> ... I feel almost sure that there is, or will be, injuries done to the natives, who (I am sure) are taken away under false pretences. The traders don't know the Tannese language, and have no means of making the people understand any terms, and to talk of any contract is absurd. Yet, a large number of Tanna men, living on really well-conducted plantations, owned by good men, might lead to a nucleus of Christian Tannese.[72]

Patteson's dictum, 'I do not advocate the suppression but the regulation of this traffic', was well known and frequently quoted.[73]

Whereas the evidence of the Presbyterian missionaries against the labour traders usually relied on native accounts of malpractice, Patteson was more cautious and less credulous: 'it is not possible to obtain from the great majority of the islanders of the Western Pacific any trustworthy account of what may have taken place among them'. He was similarly disbelieving of the point of view put forward by the labour traders themselves.[74] As time progressed, Patteson increasingly saw for himself the effects of the labour trade in depopulating islands and leaving violence and distrust in its wake, disrupting and even destroying the everyday life of families and whole communities. His views began to harden and he became particularly angry when his name was used by the traders to entice gullible islanders on board their ships.[75]

By the year of his death his views had hardened further but still retained their characteristic moderation and balance. In a memorandum to the General Synod of the Anglican Church in New Zealand, he refused to condemn indentured labour as such but attacked the cruelties of the labour trade and the ill effect it had on the islanders of his diocese. He commended law-abiding labour ships, called for imperial legislation to regulate the trade effectively and for two Royal Navy ships to cruise in the islands and enforce the regulations. Whether unenforced or unenforceable, current regulations were 'absolutely no check whatever' on the trade. He called for no retaliation against islanders who

---

71 Yonge, II, p.438.
72 Patteson to ?, 6 May 1868. Quoted in Yonge, II, p.321.
73 Quoted, for example, in Yonge, II, p.442
74 Patteson to Bowen, 4 July 1870. *PP* 1871, XLVIII [468].
75 *Ibid.* Extract from *Southern Cross*, 6 November 1869.

attacked labour ships, 'until it is clearly shown that these acts are not done in the way of retribution for outrages first committed by white men'. He now accused many of the labour traders, 'whether they are technically or legally slavers or not', of 'acting in the spirit of slavery'.[76]

Five months later, he spoke of 'the general suspicion and distrust admitted to exist by the traders themselves' as being 'sufficient proof that there are lawless practices going on', and continued gloomily, 'it was not so a few years ago in many places where I see with my own eyes that it is now so'. But even at this late stage Patteson refused to issue a blanket condemnation. The problem was not treatment of the labourers on the plantations, nor even recruiting *per se*, but 'the mode of procuring the labourers which is practised by *some* of the traders'.[77]

Patteson knew that revenge for the activities of the labour traders might well be exacted on missionaries and his last, unfinished, letter had a prophetic, even fatalistic, ring to it:

> I am fully alive to the probability that some outrage has been committed here by one or more vessels. I am quite aware that we *may* be exposed to considerable risk on this account.... If any violence has been used, it will make it impossible for us to go thither now. It would simply be provoking retaliation.... It is *very* sad. But the Evil One is everywhere and always stirs up opposition and hindrance to every attempt to do good.[78]

The circumstances of Patteson's death – regarded by many as a martyrdom – are well known.[79] Landing on the island of Nukapu in the Santa Cruz Islands on 20 September 1871, he was clubbed to death while resting in a native hut. When the body was later recovered by his companions, it was found to bear five wounds clearly caused after death, and the hands held a palm branch with five knots. To the faithful, a comparison with the *stigmata* of Christ was irresistible; to the more practically minded, the signs that Patteson had been killed in revenge for the recent kidnapping of five natives from Nukapu were clear. Deryck Scarr's researches indicate that the *Emma Bell* was the ship responsible and that five men of rank on Nukapu had been kidnapped when they came aboard the ship as visitors.[80] David Hilliard is unhappy with what he calls the

---

76 Memorandum, 11 January 1871. *PP* 1872 XLIII [C.496].
77 Patteson to Floyd, 26 May 1871. *Melanesian Mission Archives.* School of Oriental and African Studies, London University. Bishop Patteson Letters. Mel/M 2/8.
78 Patteson, unfinished letter, 16 September 1871, quoted in Yonge, II, p.560.
79 For Patteson's death, see PP 1872 XLIII [C.496]. Docker, p.90; Yonge, II, pp.566-572; Hilliard, pp.66-71.
80 Deryck Scarr, 'Recruits and Recruiters, a Portrait of the Pacific Islands Labour Trade'', *HSANZ*, II (1967), 5-6. The Methodist missionary Lorimer Fison was of the opinion that the five knots might indicate that five days had elapsed since the kidnapping rather than that five persons had been kidnapped. Belmore to Kimberley, 22

'revenge theory', suggesting that 'it was ... born ... out of a desire to condemn the activities of labour recruiters'. He favours the idea that Patteson may have been murdered after unintentionally violating a local custom. This theory was first put forward some twenty years after the event by lay missionary A.E.C. Forrest. He opined that Patteson was actually murdered by Santa Cruz natives who felt slighted that the bishop's gift to the chief of Nukapu was greater than that to their chief, who considered himself a more important personage. This however fails to explain adequately either the presence of Santa Cruz men on Nukapu, or their formulation of a murder plot when the bishop's visit was not known in advance. Neither does it explain how they gained access to such an important guest or why there was no apparent retribution against them or even their naming and shaming by the people of Nukapu by way of exonerating themselves from the deed. Perhaps Hilliard is most accurate when he admits that 'the truth is far from clear'.[81]

But perhaps no one should have been really surprised by the death of a white missionary. Patteson's peripatetic ministry among many imperfectly known islanders probably made him far more vulnerable than those who laboured continually amongst the same people. In this context it must be remembered that every year, following the strategy long established by Selwyn, Patteson himself carried off a steady number of the ablest native boys from the islands for training at the mission school on Norfolk Island. He was known to describe this work as 'recruiting' and in effect, if not always in method and certainly not in motive, it closely resembled what the labour recruiters were doing. Clearly, here was further scope for confusion about the motives of white men in the minds of the Melanesian peoples.[82]

Patteson's deputy, R.H. Codrington, was quick to apportion the blame:

> There is very little doubt that the slave trade which is desolating these islands was the cause of this attack.... Bishop Patteson was known throughout the islands as a friend, and now even he is killed to revenge the outrages of his countrymen. The guilt surely does not lie upon the savages who executed, but on the traders who provoked the deed.[83]

Commander Markham, the first naval officer on the scene, concurred.[84]

Ironically, Patteson did more in turning public opinion against the labour trade by the circumstances of his death than he, or any other missionary, had done during their lifetime. The brutal death of a revered and saintly figure

---

November 1871. *PP* 1872 XLIII [C.496]. Either way, Patteson's death was clearly bound up with abuses in the labour trade.
81 Hilliard, pp.68-69.
82 Docker, p.88.
83 R.H. Codrington. Letter in *Hobart Mercury*, 18 Nov 1871, quoted in Whiteman, p.21. See also Codrington to Belmore, 17 October 1871. *PP* 1872 XLIII [C.496].
84 See n.94, below.

caused a wave of horror in the colonies and in Britain. This resulted in a near universal desire to control a trade that was seen as the prime cause of Patteson's death.

The Role of the Royal Navy

That naval officers tended to be strong supporters of the missionaries in their robust opposition to the labour trade ought to be a commonplace. Indeed, Jane Samson has noted the strength of evangelical and humanitarian influences on naval officers of this period.[85] Having wide experience of pursuing slaving ships between Zanzibar and the east coast of Africa, naval personnel saw the labour trade in the Pacific as being nothing more and nothing less than a slave trade. Because successive governments had declined to pay for naval bases and regular patrols in the area, the navy had to be content with sending the occasional warship from Sydney. But such voyages were so infrequent that they made little impression on the abuses inherent in the labour trade. To examine the writings of those naval officers involved with the missionaries and the labour traders in this period is to observe their uncritical endorsement of the work of the missionaries and their abhorrence of the labour trade and those involved in it.

Two successive captains of the naval patrol ship, HMS *Rosario*, George Palmer and Albert Markham, both of whom rushed to publish their experiences immediately after their tour of duty was over, appear to speak with a single voice, but Markham is perhaps the more thoughtful and perceptive of the two. George Palmer's partiality was never in doubt when he spoke of the missionaries and their reaction to the labour trade in the following terms:

> these noble men and women, who have in every age gone forth from their country and friends, often bearing their lives in their hands, to do their Master's bidding, and preach the glorious gospel of Christ to the heathen.... What concerns them most is to see the little work they have been permitted to do among these savages, after weeks and months of prayer and patience dashed to the ground and indefinitely thrown back by the shameful acts of their own countrymen.[86]

Palmer suggested that without the interference of the 'slavers' the Tannese, for example, would soon come under effective missionary control,[87] a seemingly over-optimistic assessment since Paton and Mathieson had been driven off that island in 1862 *before* the labour trade became established. To Palmer, the

---

85 See Samson, *Imperial Benevolence: making British authority in the Pacific Islands* (Honolulu: University of Hawai'i Press, 1998), Ch.8, pp.130-147.
86 Palmer, p.57.
87 Palmer to Lambert, 5 April 1869. CO 234/23.

problem for the missionaries was that their converts would 'get contaminated with the mean whites of Queensland'.[88]

Palmer achieved fame by his arrest of the Queensland-licensed labour ship *Daphne* on charges of slave trading. Licensed to transport fifty New Hebridean labourers to Queensland, Palmer found it in Fiji with twice that number on board. In Sydney both the Water Police Court and the Vice-Admiralty Court threw out the charge of slave trading and awarded costs against Palmer. The failure of Palmer's prosecution of the *Daphne* was significant. It showed that the Slave Trade Acts[89] did not cover this kind of recruiting when the islanders had been lured on board by deceit and tricked into signing 'contracts'. It showed that the Queensland Act was largely ineffective (as the missionaries had claimed all along) and cast doubt on the sincerity of the Queensland authorities to make the Act work in anything more than a cosmetic sense. Further, following the *Daphne* judgment, naval officers would be reluctant to act against labour ships. The truth of Bishop Patteson's assertion that 'imperial legislation is required to put an end to this miserable state of things' was becoming increasingly clear.[90]

As far as his personal circumstances were concerned, Palmer was clearly aware how much influence the parliamentary supporters of the missionary and humanitarian societies were able to exert. He wrote for help to his brother-in-law, one Captain King. King duly wrote to Kinnaird to enlist his support. Kinnaird wrote to Granville and followed this up with a question to the First Lord of the Admiralty in the House of Commons. As a result the Admiralty reimbursed Palmer's costs of £179.5s.5d. and promoted him to captain.[91] But his campaign did not stop there. In 1871 he published his book, *Kidnapping in the South Seas*, in which he expressed sympathy and admiration for the missionaries and contempt and outrage for the labour traders and their trade. So outspoken were his statements that they occasioned a correspondence between Kimberley and the Governor of New South Wales, which was published in 1872 as a Parliamentary Paper.[92] In the interests of objectivity, however, Palmer might profitably have reflected on the Duke of Newcastle's words of advice to Colonel Smythe in 1862: 'I must caution you not to suffer your sympathy with the missionaries or your admiration of their achievements to affect your judgment...'.[93]

---

88 Palmer, p.160.
89 5 George IV c.113; 6 and 7 Victoria c.98.
90 Patteson's Memorandum to Synod of Anglican Church in New Zealand, 11 January 1871. *PP* 1872, XLIII [C.496].
91 See Palmer to King, 3 December 1869; King to Kinnaird, 12 March 1870; Kinnaird to Granville, 18 March 1870; all in *PP* 1871, XLVIII [468]. *Hansard,* CC, col.1427, 7 April 1870. Palmer, p.152.
92 *PP* 1872, XLIII [C.479].
93 Newcastle to Smythe, 23 December 1859. *PP* 1862, XXXVI [2995].

Albert Markham, who succeeded Palmer as captain of HMS *Rosario* in October 1871, less than a month after the murder of Bishop Patteson, took the same line as his predecessor in robustly supporting the missionaries against the labour traders. He spoke of 'the almost unheard-of enormities committed by those involved in the so-called "Labour trade" and its attendant organised system of kidnapping' and condemned 'the deeds perpetrated by the lawless and unscrupulous ruffians who infest these beautiful islands for the purpose of procuring natives ... [which] are unparalleled for cruelty and treachery'.[94] Markham was the first naval officer to visit the headquarters of the Melanesian Mission after Patteson's death. He both accepted and propagated Archdeacon Codrington's view that the Bishop's murder was retaliation for a kidnapping incident:

> The only reason that can be given for this treacherous and wholesale attack upon the Bishop and his party by the islanders of Nukapu – and unhappily this reason is verified by all that we hear – is that a 'labour vessel' had some short time previously visited the island for the purpose of adding to her human cargo, and that probably some outrage had been committed upon the natives, who had in consequence resolved to attack and take the lives of the first white men that happened to fall into their power.[95]

But Markham was sufficiently experienced to realise that this was not just arbitrary savagery, but a measured response strictly according to the way the islanders approached the avenging of wrongs committed against them:

> It is their law, when a man belonging to a tribe commits any offence, to punish the guilty *tribe* and not as in our law the guilty *individual* ... they look upon all white men as belonging to one tribe.[96]

The Labour Traders' Perspective

Unlike the missionaries and naval officers, who were inveterate writers and able publicists of their respective points of view, the men who were actually involved in the labour trade were, not surprisingly, virtually silent in stating their position. Coming from the least respectable sections of the Queensland merchant fleet, sailing close to the wind legally as well as nautically, they were not eager to go into print; some indeed would have been barely literate.[97] Some

---

94 Markham, p.67.
95 *Ibid.*, p. vi.
96 *Ibid.*, p.98.
97 A naval officer remarked that the masters of labour ships were mostly 'men of inferior character, generally drunkards, and not unfrequently (sic) of the worst possible moral habits'. 'Remarks on the Labour Traffic etc., by Commander W. Dyke Ackland, RN', 20 October 1884, quoted in Scarr, 'Recruits and recruiters', 10.

were forced to defend their actions in legal depositions, but only one voluntarily produced a book devoted to his role in the Queensland labour trade. For this reason William Wawn, who was involved in the labour trade from 1875 to 1891 as the master of a number of recruiting ships, must be regarded as less than typical of the labour traders. Although his seems to be the acceptable face of 'blackbirding', since he represents himself as a humane man, his account of his experiences, however sanitized (he is known to have been debarred several times by the Immigration Department for recruiting misdemeanours),[98] provides an eye-witness account from a position diametrically opposed to that of the missionaries.

Though much maligned by Paton, Wawn had cause to be grateful to at least one missionary. As master of the *Bobtail Nag* on its last voyage from Brisbane in September 1877,[99] he was shipwrecked the following January at Vila in the New Hebrides. The local missionary got his people to provide food for the crew. Wawn, in his warmest remarks about any missionary, commented, 'He was as good as his word, and better. I am glad to have it in my power to express my sense of gratitude to this good man and his "worshippers".'[100] Otherwise, his comments on missionaries tend to be negative ones, not surprisingly, since their aim was the extirpation of his livelihood. Nevertheless he commented:

> I do not wish to create the impression that I 'have a down' on missionaries. During my travels I have only become personally acquainted ... with eight. Four of these were Presbyterians, the others belonged to English church missions. The latter were, I believe, good earnest men, though not angels. They were men willing to give and take; not devoid of some weaknesses, or even faults, for which we laymen could make allowance, since they did the same for our frailties. The Presbyterian missionaries, as far as I could judge, were, with one exception, narrow-minded, bigoted and intolerant. They were men who looked only to one side of a disputed question, which was invariably that side which suited their own interests; *while to gain their own ends they would rush into exaggeration, sometimes even to the extent of downright untruth.* [my italics] [101]

Wawn argued strongly that a spell working on a plantation in Queensland actually had a beneficial effect on Polynesian labourers, leaving them stronger, fitter, less gullible and more experienced than their fellows who stayed at home. He criticised the proprietary attitude of missionaries to their converts and their dislike of returnees: 'It is this last fact which has made some missionaries so bitter against us. The raw untravelled "nig" is a very pliable article in their hands.'[102]

---

98 Scarr, 'Recruits and recruiters', 11.
99 Not 1878. Wawn, p.119 is incorrect.
100 *Ibid.*, p.145.
101 *Ibid.*, pp.271-272.
102 *Ibid.*, p.17.

To counter missionary charges of 'buying' or 'stealing' recruits from their villages, Wawn claimed a misunderstanding of native terminology.[103] The practice of giving presents to relatives of the recruits or their village elders (forbidden by the Queensland government in 1878) was but a recognition of the Melanesian custom of reciprocity.[104] 'The term "steal"', he opined, 'is frequently misunderstood. If you take away a recruit from his home without "buying" or "paying" for him ... they will say you "steal" him. This free use of the term "steal" among the islanders accounts for numbers of unfounded charges of kidnapping made against us'. However, he conceded, apparently without irony, that 'kidnapping has been occasionally perpetrated in these waters'.[105]

Wawn, then, provides valuable insights into the labour trade from a recruiter's perspective and an irreverent alternative view of the missionaries far removed from the near sycophantic line taken by the naval officers. Though he himself was clearly literate and, by his own account, humane and decent to the men he transported, he provides no account of the illegalities and cruelties practised by other recruiters, other than the occasional admission that irregularities in the trade were not unknown. Wawn claimed to have personally always acted with perfect propriety. Docker describes him as 'honest William Wawn',[106] though not without implying a certain naïveity. It should also be remembered that Bishop Patteson referred approvingly to 'some two or three vessels honourably distinguished from the rest by fair and generous treatment of the natives'.[107]

Humanitarian Pressure Groups

Supporting the missionary societies in seeking to press the government to action on the abuses in the labour trade were two pressure groups, the Anti-Slavery Society and the Aborigines Protection Society. In order to obtain information about the labour trade and its abuses both societies were obliged to rely on the missionaries who resided in the south-west Pacific and, inevitably, this resulted in the humanitarian societies often receiving evidence with an in-built missionary bias.

---

103 See, e.g., Reply of Peter Milne to Anti-Slavery Society Questionnaire. Kay, pp. 64-65.
104 Scarr, 'Recruits and recruiters', 15. Missionaries in Central Africa had similar problems with the custom of bride or dowry, known as *lobola*, the payment of cattle or services to a bride's family, which they frequently interpreted as wife purchase. See Cairns, p.177.
105 Wawn, pp.11-12.
106 Docker, p.192.
107 Memorandum to Synod of Anglican Church in New Zealand, 11 January 1871. *PP* 1872, XLIII [C.496].

Supporters in Britain of the Aborigines Protection Society and of the missionary movement were often the same people. The Anti-Slavery Society also attempted to develop closer links with the missionaries in the Pacific. In 1870, in order to get first-hand information about the abuses in the labour trade, the society sent out a questionnaire to the missionaries in the New Hebrides.[108] The Presbyterian missionaries availed themselves of this opportunity to gain publicity and wider support for their campaign against the labour trade. Their replies were instrumental in providing the humanitarians with abundant accounts of kidnapping in the islands.[109]

Even before the replies to the questionnaires were received and processed by the Anti-Slavery Society, the Aborigines Protection Society was busy using missionary evidence in its own campaign. A letter of 3 January 1871 to William Monsell, the Parliamentary Under-Secretary, made further charges against the *Lyttona* and a letter to Lord Kimberley of 14 August 1871 made accusations against the *Jason*.[110] At a meeting of the Royal Colonial Institute on 1 May 1871, F.W. Chesson, Secretary of the Aborigines Protection Society, read a paper on 'The Polynesian Labour Question in relation to the Fiji Islands and Queensland'. Several Members of Parliament attended the meeting, including Arthur Kinnaird. The council of the Royal Colonial Institute were clearly concerned about the outspoken nature of Chesson's paper, inserting a disclaimer at the foot of the first page of the printed edition.[111] The fact that both Chesson's paper and the letter to Kimberley were obviously based on evidence provided by John Geddie and John Paton is an indication that the humanitarians generally accepted missionary evidence at face value without necessarily being aware of possible prejudice. The pressure groups continued to press the Colonial Office. On 10 September 1873, long after the Pacific Islanders' Protection Act had become law, Kimberley wearily minuted, 'No one would even dream of being able to "satisfy" these gentlemen', but conceded, 'they perform a useful function as a perpetual "opposition"'.[112]

The *modus operandi* of the humanitarians was both to bombard the Colonial Office with evidence of malpractice and to use influential supporters in Parliament. There is no evidence that the former was of great avail. The only missionary who tried this method, John Paton, also had little effect, since constant repetition from the same source tended to deaden the Colonial Office's response. The latter approach, on the other hand, was much more effective, but

---

108 Printed in Kay, p.48.
109 *Ibid.*, pp.48-65; S.M.K. Willmington, 'The Activities of the Aborigines Protection Society as a pressure group on the formulation of colonial policy, 1868-1880', unpublished PhD thesis (Wales, 1973), pp.45-46.
110 Aborigines Protection Society to Monsell, 3 January 1871. *PP* 1871, XLVIII [468]. *Ibid.* Aborigines Protection Society to Kimberley, 14 August 1871.
111 Chesson, 'Polynesian Labour Question', 34-56.
112 Min., 10 September, on Anti-Slavery Society to Kimberley, 6 September 1873. CO 234/26.

it must be noted that the missionaries also used parliamentary pressure, *often by the same people*, since several MPs supported both groups.

In her unpublished thesis on the role of the Aborigines Protection Society as a pressure group, Susan Willmington contends that, irrespective of the murder of Bishop Patteson and its effect on informed opinion in Britain, 'there is more than a probability that the Aborigines Protection Society would have intervened successfully in this situation and forced the Colonial Office into legislation ...'.[113] This sweeping assertion appears to reflect an understandable vested interest in establishing the importance of that Society. Clearly, it must be questioned. It must be remembered that public opinion was shocked to an almost unprecedented degree by the bishop's death, which gave the Colonial Office new resolve and shook the opposition of the Treasury to the necessary expenditure. More to the point, what grounds are there to suggest that the Aborigines Protection Society *alone* could, or indeed did, force the Colonial Office to legislate against the labour trade? Kimberley's minute about a 'perpetual opposition' was, after all, written on a letter from the Anti-Slavery Society. It must be borne in mind that the missions were equally involved in pressing the Colonial Office and when that pressure came from the floor of the House of Commons it was impossible to tell whether some members, like Kinnaird and the M'Arthur brothers, were wearing humanitarian or missionary hats, or indeed (since a distinction between the two is more likely to occur in the mind of the historian than it was in theirs) both simultaneously. Willmington cannot therefore justifiably cite the influence of the parliamentary pressure group as a factor which helped *only* the Aborigines Protection Society in its opposition to the labour trade.[114] It must not be forgotten that but for the willing co-operation of the missionaries the humanitarians would have had precious little evidence of irregularities in the labour trade to complain about.

Indeed, it is possible to argue that the missionary movement actually had more effect on the Colonial Office than the humanitarians, since McNair's complaint about the *Lyttona* began a train of events which culminated in the tragic death of the senior British missionary in the south-west Pacific and this impelled the Colonial Office into a renewed determination to legislate, this time speedily and successfully. That point, however, will not be argued here since the evidence points not to competition but to harmonious co-operation between the missionary and humanitarian lobbies to press for legislation to end abuses in the labour trade. For the Colonial Office the problem caused by the labour trade was similar to that elsewhere in the mid-Victorian period – the problem of lawlessness on the imperial frontier, where the interaction of Europeans and indigenous peoples was unsupervised by a legal framework; where Britain had much influence, often military or naval power, but no legal authority; and where lawlessness threatened to destabilise nearby British colonies. The ultimate

---

113 Willmington, p.84.
114 Willmington, p.85.

solution to the problem was annexation, but this was generally avoided unless there was no alternative.[115] In the Pacific islands, Britain had for some years pursued a policy, dubbed 'minimum intervention' by J.M. Ward, which by the early 1870s was beginning to break down under the pressure of calls for action to prevent abuses in the labour trade and to annex or establish a protectorate over Fiji. The missionary movement and its supporters were much involved in both issues.[116]

'Minimum intervention' was well established at the Colonial Office where there was an inherent reluctance to act unless pressed to do so. For example, it was only the advance notice of Taylor's question to Monsell for 18 February 1870 that persuaded the Colonial Office to grant belated approval for the Queensland 1868 Polynesian Labourers Act, judgement on which had been suspended in June 1868.[117] There was also a somewhat complacent tendency to assume that all was well in the colonies unless a considerable weight of evidence proved otherwise.[118] Willmington detects, in the second half of 1869, 'a hardening of the attitude of the Colonial Office towards the Australian colonies who were involved in the prosecution of British offenders, and whose people were allegedly engaged in the labour traffic'.[119] However real this attitude may have been, it failed to translate into action and she goes on to accept that 'right up to the time of Patteson's death the Colonial Office displayed no urgency in its dealings with the kidnapping problem'.[120]

As Owen Parnaby has pointed out, any regulation of the labour trade by the imperial Parliament was inhibited by two factors: the advent of responsible government in the colonies – it came to Queensland in 1859, and by the long-established Whitehall practice of the Treasury holding the purse strings of expenditure by government departments.[121] That the latter was the more intractable problem is illustrated by the fact that the issue of controlling the labour trade was not being raised for the first time. In 1861, following the *Two Brothers* incident, a bill to 'facilitate the conviction of persons guilty of criminal offences in the Australian Colonies and in the Islands of the Pacific' was drafted by the Colonial Office and agreed by the Foreign Office. But the draft bill got no further than the Treasury, which refused to sanction expenditure for the transport of witnesses to Australia.[122] Rogers complained on 30 June 1863

---

115 See McIntyre, *Imperial Frontier,* esp. pp.3-9.
116 See J.M. Ward, *British Policy in the South Pacific* (Sydney: Australian Publishing Co., 1948), Ch. XVIII.
117 Mins. on Murdoch to Rogers, 16 June 1868. CO234/21; min. by Dealtry, 12 February 1870, on Notice of Questions for 18 February 1870. CO 201/560.
118 Rogers to Kinnaird, 30 March 1870. *PP* 1871, XLVIII [468].
119 Willmington, p.61.
120 Willmington, pp.82-83.
121 Parnaby, *Labor Trade*, p. vii.
122 Treasury to Colonial Office, 27 June 1863. CO 201/529.

about 'this bill, which has been asleep at the Treasury since 4 April 1862'[123] and, six weeks later, Dealtry referred to the Treasury objections to the proposed bill, commenting that 'the matter appears to be at a stand still'.[124]

The matter was still 'asleep' at the Treasury seven years later and an attempt by Kimberley, the new Secretary of State, to awaken it late in 1870 met with the same response.[125] Once again 'the refusal of the Treasury' made the bill 'impossible to proceed with'.[126] Ironically, H.C. Rothery, the Treasury's adviser on the slave trade, reported at this time that kidnapping from the Pacific islands was 'slave trading in the largest sense of the term'. But his comments were either ignored or overruled at the Treasury.[127]

When Robert Herbert, the former Premier of Queensland, arrived at the Colonial Office the following year as Rogers' successor, he minuted on 20 October that 'owing to the difficulties unfortunately raised as to paying of expenses of prosecutions the proposed imperial enactment ... for the punishment of kidnapping has not been passed and these kidnappers having consequently escaped with impunity, it may be expected that the trade will be carried on with increased vigour'.[128] But exactly one month earlier and unknown to Herbert as he wrote those words, Bishop Patteson had been murdered in the Santa Cruz Islands. The news of his death eventually reached London at the end of November 1871.

The news of the bishop's murder was greeted with an uproar in London and at last moral outrage overcame fiscal rectitude. 'It was only the shock of the murder of Bishop Patteson ... which broke through this Treasury opposition, and brought the Bill before Parliament in 1872.'[129] Knatchbull-Hugessen, the Parliamentary Under-Secretary at the Colonial Office, introduced the 'Bill for the prevention and punishment of criminal outrages upon natives of the islands in the Pacific Ocean' into the Commons on 15 February 1872. It was not without significance that the Bill's drafters gave it the short title of 'The Kidnapping Act, 1872'.[130] Knatchbull-Hugessen claimed Patteson as an old friend from Eton days and quoted the bishop's dictum that he advocated the

---

123 *Ibid.*, min. by Rogers 30 June 1863.
124 Min. by Dealtry, 17 August, on Young to Newcastle, 22 June 1863. CO 201/526.
125 Treasury to Colonial Office, 3 December 1870. CO 201/560.
126 *Ibid.*, Draft CO to FO, 29 December, 1870.
127 Report by Rothery, 15 October 1870, in FO to CO, 7 December 1870. CO 201/560, quoted in McIntyre, *Imperial Frontier*, p.243.
128 Min. by Herbert, 20 October 1871, on Belmore to Kimberley, 9 August 1871. CO201/564. Herbert was referring to the escape of 'Bully' Hayes, arrested by the British consul at Samoa at the instigation of LMS missionary Thomas Powell. But with the lack of any legal framework to support his action the Consul was unable to detain Hayes for long before he was able to escape. See Thomas Powell to Dr Mullens, 20 January 1870, and 5 August 1870 and Powell's Deposition of 6 January 1870, in LMS South Seas Letters, Box 32.
129 Parnaby, 'Aspects of British Policy in the Pacific', 55.
130 The Bill is printed in *PP* 1872, III.

regulation and not the suppression of the traffic. 'The bill was not intended to suppress the labour trade', he said, 'as some of the missionary societies and the Anti-Slavery Society desired, but to rid of abuse an essentially useful and good system of labour'. 'It was', said Knatchbull-Hugessen, 'impossible to deny that the importation of South Sea Islanders into our Australian colonies would be most advantageous if properly managed'.[131] Not everyone agreed, and Admiral Erskine complained that the bill did not go far enough. In the Committee Stage on 22 April he proposed an unsuccessful amendment to extend the provisions of the bill.[132] Erskine, Liberal Member for Stirlingshire, a supporter of both the Wesleyan Missionary Society and the Anti-Slavery Society, is a perfect example in his own person of how the missionary and humanitarian lobbies frequently overlapped, worked in harness, and are often impossible to disentangle.

The Bill's parliamentary progress was rapid and it had overwhelming support. At the second reading in the Lords on 3 May, Kimberley, too, claimed Patteson's friendship.[133] Patteson's former mentor Bishop Selwyn, having returned from New Zealand to become Bishop of Lichfield, also spoke in the debate and called for no retribution for the murder of Patteson, who was aware of the risks he was taking. Retribution, he said, should be left to God. Carnarvon, ill on 3 May, missed the debate, but four days later he appeared in the House and disagreed with Bishop Selwyn. 'Murder required punishment and he did not think it well that in such a case the State should do nothing, but leave the matter to the vengeance of God'.[134] The Lords gave the bill a third reading on 13 May and it received the Royal Assent on 27 June 1872, by which time the focus of attention had turned to Fiji.

The Decline and End of the Trade

The regulated labour trade reached its height in the early 1880s and then declined until its eventual abolition in Queensland in 1906. It has recently been calculated that a total of 62,000 South Sea islanders was recruited for Queensland, about 40,000 of whom came from the New Hebrides and 18,000 from the Solomon Islands.[135] By the early 1890s the missions were finally at work among the South Sea islanders on the Queensland plantations.[136] Long after the Act came into force, missionaries continued to report alleged kidnapping incidents and other irregularities. But even John Inglis, writing in

---

131 *Hansard*, Third Series, CCIX, cols 522-523.
132 *Ibid.*, cols 1615-1616.
133 *Hansard*, CCXI, cols 184-189.
134 *Ibid.*, cols 368-370.
135 Patricia Mercer, *White Australia Defied* (Townsville: James Cook University, 1995), quoted in Breward, p.223.
136 Scarr, 'Recruits and recruiters', 5 and 23.

1886 and complaining that, in his opinion, 'the spirit of the kidnapping Act has been largely evaded', conceded that 'the outrageous buccaneering character of the traffic has to a large extent disappeared'.[137] In that the worst abuses of the traffic were largely checked, the Act appeared, to all but its most hostile opponents, to be serving its purpose.

In conclusion, three points need to be considered concerning the labour trade: the experience of the labourers, the nature of the evidence and the role of the missionaries. The trade itself needs to be carefully distinguished from life on the plantations. Needless to say, the evidence of the treatment of labourers on the Queensland plantations is mixed and contradictory. Statements by J.P. Sunderland of the LMS (and a correspondent of the Aborigines Protection Society condemning plantation life as slavery,[138] and of the Acting Governor of Queensland stating that all is well on the plantations,[139] may be taken to cancel one another out. Indeed, Sunderland's attack on plantation treatment of South-Sea island labourers both in the Australian press and via LMS headquarters to the Colonial Office in London, was challenged by the Revd Edward Griffith of Brisbane, who wrote to Dr Mullens in London to complain of Sunderland's activities and especially his 'grave mistakes in unguarded speeches'. According to Griffith, Sunderland had surprisingly failed to accede to a request made two years previously to provide a native teacher for the islanders on the Queensland plantations. He had clearly failed to report this request to LMS headquarters in London as Dr Mullens offered to provide the same in his letter to Granville in April 1869.[140] Griffith reported that 'there are upwards of thirty [islanders] who are engaged sufficiently close to Brisbane who attend my service every Sabbath day – they are well dressed and very attentive although not understanding much...'.[141]

True, the mortality rate was unacceptably high,[142] but this in itself is no evidence of cruelty or maltreatment and it would seem to be due to a change in climate and diet and, most importantly, exposure to the diseases of 'civilisation' to which islanders had little or no immunity. Melanesian labourers in Queensland seem to have been treated as well as many rural labourers in Europe and probably much better than many manual workers in the mills and factories of British cities at that time.

Plantation life was one thing; how the labourers came to be there was quite another. F.A. Campbell, son of the Revd A.J. Campbell of Geelong, spent most

---

137 Inglis, p.208.
138 See Walcott to Rogers, 12 October 1869. *PP* 1871, XLVIII [468].
139 *Ibid.*, O'Connell to Kimberley, 21 March 1871.
140 Secretary of LMS to Granville, 6 April 1869. CO 234/23.
141 Griffith to Mullens, 10 June 1869. LMS Australian Correspondence Box 7. See also *ibid.*, Griffith's letter to the *Brisbane Courier*, 10 July 1869.
142 *Queensland Evangelical Standard*, 16 October 1885, quoted in Inglis, p.218. See also D.C. Gordon, *The Australian Frontier in New Guinea, 1870-1885* (New York: Columbia University Press, 1951), pp.154-155.

of the year 1872 in the New Hebrides and encountered the labour trade at first hand. In seeking to answer the question 'Why do natives leave their own islands?' he came to the following conclusions:

> 10% are taken by force.
> 20% are obtained by deceit ... by masters of labour vessels.
> 20% are bought from chiefs or relatives.
> 10% are defeated in war and driven off their land.
> 15% are returned labourers, who, finding their plantations destroyed, wives gone, etc., return in disgust.
> 5% accompany their chiefs when they go.
> 20% go from curiosity, or for a desire to get European goods.[143]

Though there is no indication as to whether this was based on a statistically significant sample or is merely a piece of guesswork, it is at least an interesting illustration of the diverse motives for emigration from the New Hebrides. Clearly Campbell was of the opinion that half the islanders who emigrated did so for reasons that could be legitimately described as 'kidnapping'. Peter Milne regarded the trade in 1872 as being 'in reality a modified slave-trade, so far as the obtaining of the natives is concerned'.[144] Bishop Patteson, as already noted, in his last, unfinished, letter, accused many of the labour traders of 'acting in the spirit of slavery'.

It is vital to understand the nature of the labour trade: labourers were often well cared for on the plantations, but were often brutally treated in order to get them there. Kidnapping was frequent and widespread, though by no means universal.[145] It was emotionally understandable but inaccurate and misleading of some missionaries to refer to slavery on the plantations. The disproportionately large number of Parliamentary Papers published on the subject of the labour trade indicates an intense interest, at least among Members of Parliament and those who lobbied them, in this subject. But a major problem in analysing the labour trade and missionary opposition to it is the difficulty of getting at the truth, for the tendency to see the issue from one side only and to exaggerate in order to score a debating point was almost overwhelming. It is very difficult to disentangle conflicting statements, for missionaries were not the only ones prone to painting a one-sided picture of the trade, as Knatchbull-Hugessen came to realise: 'Great caution is to be exercised in believing the statements either of the missionaries or those interested in the trade'.[146] The labour traders were well aware that, plying their trade far from any effective legal framework, they could

---

143 F.A. Campbell, *A Year in the New Hebrides*, quoted in Steel, p.407.
144 Don, p.34.
145 See Patteson to (cousin) Arthur, 6 August 1871. *Melanesian Mission Archives*. Bishop Patteson papers, Mel/M 2/8.
146 Min. by Knatchbull-Hugessen, 3 June 1871, on O'Connell to Kimberley, 20 March 1871. CO 234/26.

get away with most things other than outright atrocity. As they were often the only witnesses to their own illegalities there was clearly no incentive for them to tell the truth about their recruiting practices. Plantation owners, though generally treating their native labourers fairly and humanely, tended not to ask too many questions about the recruiting methods that had been employed on their behalf to get the labourers to Queensland in the first place.

From the Presbyterian quarter and particularly where John Paton was concerned, missionary 'evidence' of irregularities in the labour trade was often indistinguishable from propaganda. To them any form of indentured labour was tantamount to slavery. Royal Navy officers tended to endorse this view uncritically. The missionaries did their cause a disservice by a tendency to accept native accounts of native accounts of kidnapping and atrocity without troubling to establish the facts accurately. These highly coloured accounts were then reported to the authorities as if they represented the whole truth. The New Hebrides missionaries were not alone in this respect. J.P. Sunderland in Sydney was a tireless propagandist, and LMS headquarters in London often took his words at face value and recycled them uncritically.[147] The Colonial Office was well aware of exaggeration by the Presbyterian missionaries. Knatchbull-Hugessen, for example, in April 1871 wrote of 'making allowance for possible exaggeration' in missionary accounts of kidnapping, and the following month of the exaggerated form in which statements relating to native deportation are made by missionary or other enthusiasts'.[148]

In her recent study of the Pacific in this period Jane Samson, plays down the negative effects of the labour trade on island communities on the grounds that missionaries tended to exaggerate its deleterious effects. The missionaries, particularly the Presbyterians and especially John Paton did indeed often exaggerate in order to make a point – but there was undoubtedly a point to be made. Whether the end of destroying or reforming the trade justified the means of missionary exaggeration is, however, another matter. A vested interest in the destruction of the labour trade was indirectly acknowledged by John Inglis. When giving three reasons for urging the 'complete suppression' of the trade, Inglis candidly gives his primary reason as 'the injury that it is doing to missions'.[149] Clearly information of labour trade malpractice from the New Hebrides missionaries has to be seen more as part of a political campaign than as reliable evidence. Undoubtedly there was exaggeration by some missionaries, particularly by members of the Presbyterian New Hebrides Mission. But this must not be allowed to conceal the truth, frequently shocking but somewhat less lurid than it was often portrayed. The development in the thinking of Bishop

---

147 See, for example, Mullens to Granville, 6 April 1869. CO 234/23.
148 Min., 27 April, on Belmore to Kimberley, 14 February 1871, and min., 4 May, on Belmore to Kimberley, 27 February 1871. CO 201/563.
149 Inglis, p.208.

Patteson, who was always willing to sift the evidence and moderate his pronouncements until convinced otherwise, is particularly important for, unlike some others, Patteson had never mortgaged his credibility by 'crying wolf' on countless previous occasions. When Patteson spoke of kidnapping, or 'acting in the spirit of slavery', he was certainly near to the truth. Melanesian Mission evidence from Patteson or Codrington, makes Samson's view look less tenable.

Can the missionaries be said to have been solely instrumental in bringing pressure to bear on the Colonial Office to end the abuses in the labour trade? No. Opposition to the labour trade was clearly a *corporate* though not always orchestrated effort by both humanitarian and missionary movements. However, the missionaries, being the Europeans nearest to the injustices that were perpetrated in the islands, played an important part in bringing them to the attention of the authorities. Their supporters in Britain and particularly in Parliament used their considerable influence to keep the matter before the Colonial Office. But the most influential factor was the undesired death of the best known of the South Seas missionaries, Bishop J.C. Patteson, in September 1871. The reverberations caused by his murder cut through the discussions, the reports, the letters, the petitions and the despatches and brought him posthumous success in the shape of the imperial legislation to regulate the labour trade for which he had long called. Missionary humanitarianism prevailed – but at a high cost.

CHAPTER 3

Missionary Involvement in the Annexation of Fiji

In the early 1870s abuses in the Pacific labour trade drew the attention of the British Government to the Fiji islands: the plantations of Queensland were not the only destination of indentured labourers – whether kidnapped or freely engaged – from island groups such as the New Hebrides and the Solomons. Although the extirpation of the labour trade was ultimately to become a major factor in the annexation of Fiji by the British Crown, the islands had first come to the attention of the Colonial Office in London long before the labour traders began to transport islanders from the New Hebrides to work on the cotton plantations.

The Fiji or Viti Islands,[1] a group of 250 islands and islets, only a third of which were inhabited, cover a total area about the size of Wales and are situated about 1,400 miles north of New Zealand. In common with that of other island groups in the Pacific, the nineteenth-century development of Fiji fits broadly into three periods. First, the period of early settlement by traders, beachcombers and missionaries in the years up to 1850. Second, a period from 1850 to the mid-1870s when, having achieved sufficient strength and influence, and being the most powerful and most highly organised group of Europeans in the islands, the missionaries attempted to influence indigenous governments and to form future governments on European lines. Their influence, however, was undermined by unruly white settlers who were less easily overawed by missionary authority than were the native peoples. Third, and frequently as a result of white immigration, came the period of annexation and colonisation from the mid-1870s when European governments stepped in to take legal control of the islands.[2]

---

1 'Fiji' is the Tongan pronunciation of the native *Viti* and was adopted by the Methodist missionaries since it was from Tonga that they approached Fiji.

2 K.L.P. Martin, *Missionaries and Annexation in the Pacific* (Oxford: OUP, 1924).

The Establishment of the Wesleyan Methodist Mission in Fiji

Missionary work in Fiji began in 1830 when the London Missionary Society, from its Pacific base in Tahiti, landed two native teachers on Oneata, a small island in south-east Fiji. The Wesleyan Methodists, from their base in New Zealand, had also moved into Polynesia in 1822, setting up a mission in Tonga. With two missionary societies entering Polynesia, competition or duplication of work was a possible danger. To avoid this, the two societies entered into a comity agreement in 1836, whereby the Wesleyans gave up their interest in Samoa and concentrated on Fiji, while the London Mission concentrated their work in Samoa leaving Fiji to the Methodists.[3]

The first European missionaries landed on Lakeba in the Lau Group of eastern Fiji on 12 October 1835. William Cross and David Cargill[4] of the Wesleyan Methodist Missionary Society, with the help of Tongan native teachers, worked hard to establish the faith in Fiji, suffering much privation and hardship.[5] Their numerical success was slight, but like many pioneer missionaries they laid the foundations on which others were to build and, as more personnel arrived from Britain and Australia, new mission stations were established.

The Fiji Islands did not remain in obscurity for long. In a remarkable piece of early propaganda, the WMMS published in its *Missionary Notices*, 'An Appeal to the Sympathy of the Christian Public on behalf of the Cannibal Feejeeans',[6] written by a missionary in Tonga, James Watkin. The 'Pity Poor Feejee' appeal, as it became popularly known, first made the existence of the Fiji Islands and the practice of cannibalism[7] widely known in Britain. What is

---

3 WMMS *Annual Report* 1836, pp.26-27.
4 Not James Calvert, whom G.C. Henderson confused with Cargill in his unpublished *History of Government in Fiji, 1760-1875* (1941), I, p.131. Calvert did not arrive in Fiji until 1838. See R.A. Derrick, *A History of Fiji* (Suva, 1946), I, p.72 and another work by Henderson, *Fiji and the Fijians, 1835-1856* (Sydney: Angus and Robertson, 1931), p.104.
5 For the pioneering stage of the Fiji mission see John H. Darch, 'Missionaries to the Cannibals: the establishment of the first European mission in Fiji, 1835-1843, *Trivium*, 17 (1982), 103-117.
6 *Missionary Notices*, January 1838.
7 J.W. Burton, recounting oral evidence given to him by Fijians at the beginning of the 20th century, puts forward the view that although cannibalism was undoubtedly a Fijian custom, its roots lay in the sympathetic magic of devouring a fallen enemy and thus absorbing his strength and prowess. He blames the influx of Europeans and the consequent spread of firearms for greatly increasing the supply of human flesh and thereby increasing the incidence of cannibalism which so shocked the Victorian public. Burton, *Modern Missions in the South Pacific* (London: Livingstone Press, 1949), p.43. For a brief but thorough contemporary discussion of Fijian cannibalism, see Berthold Seemann, *Viti; an account of a Government Mission to the Vitian or Fijian Islands in the Years 1860-1* (Cambridge: Macmillan, 1862), pp.173-185. For a more recent

more, it was highly successful both in terms of publicity and of fund-raising and formed a model for subsequent appeals.[8] Though later deplored by Methodist stalwart J.E. Erskine,[9] this sensationalist approach of highlighting the depravity of a primitive society and, by way of contrast, the alleged instances of divine intervention to assist the missionaries, met with instant success and clearly struck a chord in the Victorian public consciousness. Fiji became known as the 'Cannibal Islands' and, as both interest and cash were easily generated by this kind of sensationalism, the WMMS continued to exploit it.[10]

As in both New Zealand and Tonga, the Methodist missionaries in Fiji, recognising that the Reformation principle of *cuius regio eius religio* obtained in Pacific island communities as much as it had done in sixteenth-century Germany, pursued a policy of seeking to convert the local chief or king in the hope that his people would follow his example and obey his authority.[11] The king of Lakeba, Tui Nayau, made the first missionaries welcome and provided accommodation for them. This may have been due as much to his wish to avoid offending the king of Tonga, who had sent an envoy with them, as to his desire to learn the new faith. Indeed Tui Nayau was only a minor chief on a small island far away from the centre of Fijian life and was unlikely to commit himself to *lotu*[12] ahead of a more powerful or influential chief. When pressed by the missionaries to convert, he habitually excused himself with the reply, 'when Tanoa becomes a Christian, I will follow him'.[13] Inevitably, the attention of the missionaries was drawn to the powerful kingdom of Bau and its king, Tanoa.[14] Tanoa, 'a little man of savage appearance', nicknamed 'Old Snuff ' by the Europeans, ruled with such brutality, even by Fijian standards, that he was driven into exile in 1832 after only three years on the throne of Bau.[15]

Seeking to extend the mission into the political centre of Fiji, William Cross arrived in Bau in January 1838, at an important juncture in the development of the islands. After a period of exile, the old king, Tanoa, had

---

assessment see Patrick Brantlinger, 'Missionaries and Cannibals in Nineteenth Century Fiji ,' *History and Anthropology*, 17:1 (2006), 21-38.
8 Findlay and Holdsworth, III, p.387.
9 J.E. Erskine, *Journal of a Cruise among the Islands of the Western Pacific* (London: Murray, 1853), pp.279-280.
10 See, for example, *Missionary Notices* for October 1839, p.152, and the *Quarterly Paper* No. LXXXVII.
11 Henderson, *History of Government in Fiji*, I, pp.133-134.
12 A Tongan word in use in Fiji. As a noun it meant 'Christianity', as a verb, 'to convert to Christianity'. In the south-west Pacific Methodism became known as the *lotu*, whereas the version of the Christian faith propagated by the LMS became known as the *lotu Tahiti*.
13 Cross and Cargill to Gen.Secs., 27 December 1837. *WMMS Archives*, Fiji Letters, 1837 file.
14 *Ibid*. Report of the Society at Lakeba for 1837, 10 October 1837.
15 Alan C. Burns, *Fiji* (London: HMSO, 1963), p.56.

recently been restored by the armed intervention of his son Seru. Seru, who took the name Cakobau,[16] was now clearly the power behind the throne and ruled in all but name until his father's death in 1852. Burns and Garrett agree that it was because Cakobau declared himself unable to guarantee the safety of the missionary that Cross remained only briefly in Bau and proceeded to set up the new mission station in the neighbouring kingdom of Rewa where the chief, Tui Dreketi, welcomed him and promised him protection.[17] The welcome was not surprising since Rewa was Bau's great rival for supremacy in that part of Fiji. Not for the first or last time did indigenous rulers seek to use missionaries in their own dynastic conflicts. But the evidence seems to indicate that Cross was so shocked by what he saw of the purge of Tanoa's enemies that he did not feel that there was anything to be gained at that stage by remaining in the midst of violent retribution and rampant cannibalism.[18]

In due course, missionary influence did begin to grow in Bau, particularly in the person of the shrewd Yorkshireman, James Calvert, who was always prepared to use his influence and personal connections to aid the extension of the British Empire as well as the kingdom of God. Calvert, who from 1838 served the mission in Fiji for over a quarter of a century, was for several years Superintendent Minister in the Ovalau circuit. As the missionary and the king came to know and to respect one another, there began a relationship between two forthright men that ultimately led to Cakobau's conversion, the conversion of Fiji, and the annexation of the islands to the British Crown. Captain Erskine noted the influence wielded by Calvert over Cakoabau during the visit to Fiji of HMS *Havannah* in 1849-50.[19] It was very much a personal authority. Following the death of Tanoa in 1852 Cakobau, observed by the Revd John Watsford, had taken a leading part in the strangulation of his father's widows. But in July the following year, when Cakobau was invested with the title *Vunivalu*,[20] so great was Calvert's moral authority that when he forbade the traditional cannibal feast Cakobau meekly complied.[21]

---

16 'Disturber of Bau'. For the best, albeit brief, study of Cakobau see Deryck Scarr, 'Cakobau and Ma'afu: contenders for pre-eminence in Fiji' in J.W. Davidson and Deryck Scarr, *Pacific Island Portraits* (Canberra: Australian National University Press, 1970), pp.95-126. William Cross noted that, 'although Tanoa was the greatest chief in Feejee, I think he has not much of greatness left but the name' and spoke of his interview with Cakobau, 'on whom the government chiefly devolves'. Cross to Gen. Secs, 9 January 1838. *WMMS Archives,* Fiji Letters, January to July 1838 file.
17 Burns, pp.57-58; Garrett, *Stars*, p.105.
18 'Four persons of the rebels had been just killed, two had been eaten and the other two were in the oven.' Cross to Gen. Secs, 9 January 1838. Fiji Letters, January to July 1838 file. See also Derrick, p.73.
19 Erskine, pp.188, 208.
20 'Root of war' – the traditional title of Bau's kings.
21 Findlay and Holdsworth, III, pp.453-456.

Calvert's patient influence eventually bore fruit in April 1854 when Cakobau renounced heathenism and announced his conversion to the *lotu*. The conversion of Fiji's premier chief was the culmination of the Wesleyan Mission's first twenty years in Fiji and, not unnaturally, historians have examined the king's motives. J.I. Brookes articulates the popularly accepted view that it was in essence a political decision where faith was subordinated to expediency.[22] It is true that Cakobau needed the military assistance of 'His Most Methodist Majesty', King George Tubou of Tonga. It is also true that after his conversion Cakobau received that assistance and as a result prevailed over his enemies at Kaba in 1855. However, it needs to be said that many genuine conversions, before and since, have taken place when worldly problems have been so overwhelming that an individual's only hope of improvement lay in reaching out into the spiritual realm. W.P. Morrell is more inclined to accept Cakobau's conversion at face value, stating that 'there is some reason to believe that Cakobau's declaration was a genuine act of faith'.[23] Ian Breward adds a further dimension to the discussion, suggesting that the sharp-witted Cakobau could see the way that the wind was blowing throughout the Pacific islands. It was, he argued, a strategic move to retain power for himself and to preserve as much of traditional Fiji as was consistent with Christianity.[24] Henceforth the increasingly powerful missions would be his allies. Nevertheless it is more than likely that both expediency and belief were entwined in Cakobau's decision – human motives are infinitely complex and faith is not infrequently a companion of circumstance.

In all events, Cakobau's new faith did in time come to have the hallmark of genuineness, since, even after his military victory and political dominance were complete, he underwent instruction leading to baptism in 1857 and adhered faithfully to the *lotu* throughout his life. But whatever Cakobau's motives for accepting the *lotu*, G.C. Henderson counsels caution in reading too much into Cakobau's conversion as far as the future of Fiji was concerned. It was not, he suggests, the conversion of one man, albeit the king, that induced the Fijian people to convert in droves but 'a conviction in the minds of the natives that Jehovah had proved that he was more powerful than their old gods, and that, therefore, it would be to their advantage to put their trust in him for the future...'.[25]

Certainly the missionaries were among the prime beneficiaries in this 'mighty change'[26] in Fijian religious practice. By 1860 the mission had sixteen missionaries in Fiji, aided by 200 local preachers, and claimed over 9,000

---

22 J.I. Brookes, *International Rivalry in the Pacific Islands, 1800-1875* (Berkeley and Los Angeles: University of California Press, 1941), p.232.
23 Morrell, *Pacific Islands*, p.127.
24 Breward, pp. 62-63.
25 Henderson, *History of Government in Fiji*, I, pp.134-135.
26 A phrase attributed to James Calvert.

members and 60,000 churchgoers.[27] This was just a beginning. Understandably, the missionaries could hardly believe the apparent flood of Fijian faith that had been unleashed. But any euphoria on their part caused by the mass conversions following the establishment of Bauan hegemony was misplaced. In due course the missionaries themselves came to realise this and a less triumphalist and more cautious approach received official sanction in the 1871 Annual Report:

> It must be remembered that the Christianity of a large number is only nominal. 'Such an event,' (the conversion of a chief followed by his people) writes the missionary in Rewa, 'is spoken of as the conversion of thousands in a day, whereas it is nothing more than the opening of a door which we may enter, and entering begin to teach the first principles of Christianity'.[28]

Nevertheless, the impact of Methodism in Fiji should not be underestimated and is best seen in the only indicator of the depth of spirituality that can be measured – the way in which the Fijians treated one another. The inhumane customs of the country – cannibalism, strangulation of widows, endemic inter-tribal warfare, burial alive – went into sharp decline, though it is probable that this owed as much to the strict paternalism of the missionaries as it did to the Fijians seeking to put the ethics of the New Testament into practice.

Missionary Involvement in Fijian Politics

In Cakobau's salvation lay the seeds of his downfall. His victory at Kaba in 1855 and the establishment of a fragile Bauan hegemony over most of Fiji (with the troublesome exception of the Lau Islands in the east where Ma'afu, a relative of the king of Tonga, held sway) led to an unfortunate *hubris*. After a makeshift 'election', Cakobau began to use the title *Tui Viti*.[29] This proved to be ultimately disastrous for him, arousing in others expectations of his power and authority which he was quite unable to justify, and was the cause of endless trouble and misunderstanding. This was discernible not just with hindsight: the missionary Lorimer Fison stated that in his opinion the assumption of the title of *Tui Viti* was at the root of all Cakobau's troubles.[30]

Cakobau's troubles began with a claim for compensation following the looting of the property of J.B. Williams, the United States Commercial Agent. In 1849 Williams had accidentally set his house on fire and the local people had looted it. Despite the fact that the incident did not take place in Cakobau's dominions and had taken place some six years before his victory at Kaba and

---

27 Revd W. Wilson to Dr Hoole, May 1860. *WMMS Archives*, Various Fiji Papers, 1858-60 file, quoted in McIntyre, *Imperial Frontier*, p.215.
28 WMMS *Annual Report* 1871, p.153.
29 'King of all Fiji'.
30 See Brookes, p.310.

therefore long before he had assumed the title of *Tui Viti*, he found himself at first pressed and then threatened by the captains of visiting American warships for the payment of compensation. By 1858 Cakobau had been browbeaten by an American officer to promise payment of $45,000 compensation within one year.[31] This predicament was the occasion that brought the problems of Fiji to the attention of the Colonial Office. Within a month of his arrival in Fiji in 1858, W.T. Pritchard, the first British Consul, was presented by Cakobau with an offer of the cession of the islands to the Crown.

The involvement of the missionaries in the 1858 cession has long been open to discussion. James Calvert had already been involved in private enterprise empire-building. In 1855, fearful of French influence,[32] he had instigated Tui Levuka's offer of the cession of the island of Ovalau to Captain Denham of HMS *Herald* and in the following year to Captain Fremantle.[33] Almost certainly Calvert's work behind the scenes had had its effect on Cakobau and when the 'final demand' from the Americans was closely followed by the arrival of Consul Pritchard, an official representative of the British government, the offer of cession was made.[34] In fact, it was a severely conditional offer and was clearly intended in Cakobau's mind to provide a powerful overlord who would protect him and relieve him of the American compensation claim.[35] Whatever Calvert's role may have been, he was not the only missionary involved in the offer of cession. John Fordham acted as translator and he and John Binner signed the document as witnesses. Without mentioning any individual names, K.L.P. Martin confidently attributes Cakobau's offer of cession to missionary influence. Although he is probably quite right, his sole authority for this seems to be Pritchard's memoirs.[36]

What is particularly interesting for this study is the reaction of the missionaries to Pritchard. J.D. Legge has suggested that missionaries and consul took opposite sides in the local power struggle in Fiji; that Pritchard supported

---

31 For full details of the various stages of the American claim see Morrell, *Pacific Islands*, pp.129-133.
32 Roman Catholic Marist priests had maintained a presence in Fiji since 1844. Though they posed no real threat to the position of the Wesleyan missionaries they were an irritant, increasingly so in the 1850s and in September 1858 a visiting French warship compelled Cakobau to grant them equal rights with the Methodists. See Thornley, 294-312.
33 Ward, p.184; Legge, p.27; Morrell, *Pacific Islands*, pp.130-131; Brookes, p.34.
34 For a full discussion of the offer of cession and its consideration by the Colonial Office see C.C. Eldridge, 'The Imperialism of the "Little England Era": the question of the annexation of the Fiji Islands, 1858-1861', *NZJH*, I, (1967), 171-184 and S.H. Farnsworth, *The Evolution of British Imperial Policy during the Mid-Nineteenth Century* (New York: Garland, 1992), pp.124-126.
35 Deed of Cession, 12 October 1858, enc. in Consul Pritchard to FO February 1859, enc. in FO to CO, 18 February 1859. *PP* 1862 XXXVI [2995].
36 Martin, p.49.

Cakobau whereas the missionaries supported Ma'afu.[37] It is certainly true that the missionaries were not averse to Tongan influence; after all, Tonga was their power-base in the south-west Pacific. Calvert feared that Cakobau's advisers might mislead him into seeking to rid Fiji of Tongans.[38] However, when Ma'afu overstepped himself and sought to claim that he was promoting the gospel rather than his own aggrandisement by his intrigues, he was duly ticked off.[39] But the scenario which Legge paints is extremely unlikely. Though the missionaries may well have attempted to maintain good relations with Ma'afu (he was, after all, the leading chief in the Lau Group) it is highly improbable that they would have backed him against Cakobau, a Christian convert recognised as *Tui Viti* by four fifths of the chiefs of Fiji and by the French and American governments.[40]

Taking the mission's self-interest alone as a factor requires another explanation. The real cause of missionary antipathy to Pritchard was much more straightforward. Unlike other non-missionary Europeans, who were regarded by the Fijians as figures of authority (naval officers, for example, who stayed only for a brief period and invariably upheld missionary influence), Pritchard was to be resident in Fiji and in the minds of the missionaries he immediately posed a threat to their influence. Bishop Stephen Neill is surely incorrect to suggest that the missionaries were opposed to the 1858 offer of cession [41] – what they were opposed to was Pritchard himself and to the way in which he appeared to be undermining their authority and arrogating to himself power and influence which they felt should rightfully be theirs.[42] Simple, old-fashioned jealousy was at the root of their dislike of Pritchard. This negative reaction of the missionaries to able Europeans surfaced once again with regard to a later consul, J.B.Thurston. In his memoirs Pritchard made the interesting suggestion that the missionaries turned against the offer of cession because he spelled out to them what this would mean in terms of their future influence:

> When I unwittingly stated that, in an interview with the late Duke of Newcastle, his Grace had asked me, "What will the Wesleyan missionaries do when they see a bishop accompanying the governor, for the Church always goes where the State

---

37 Legge, pp.40-41
38 Calvert To Gen.Secs., 1 January 1865. *WMMS Archives*, Box 532, Australasian Correspondence, Fiji 1858-1884 file.
39 See Revd J. Eggleston to Ma'afu quoted in Seemann, p.254 n.
40 Cakobau's 'election' as Tui Viti in May 1857 was reported as being by four-fifths of Fiji's chiefs. W.H. Drew to J.H. Drew 15 August 1869. *PP* 1871 XLVII [435].
41 S.C. Neill, *Colonialism and Christian Missions* (London: Lutterworth Press, 1966), p.254.
42 Revd J.S. Fordham to Gen. Secs., 19 November 1861. *WMMS Archives,* Box 532, Australasian Correspondence, Fiji 1858-1884 file. Legge, somewhat paradoxically, endorses this view in a footnote after having advocated the 'taking sides in native politics' view in his main text. See Legge, p.41n.

goes?" there was a sudden change. The cession was looked upon with suspicion – personal motives were imputed – and ultimately from cordial co-operation they passed to sullen opposition.[43]

But this account has always been regarded as somewhat suspect. Ward did not regard it as 'acceptable without some reservation',[44] Legge described it as 'an improbable story at best'[45] and Morrell concluded that 'there is singularly little evidence that the missionaries changed their views about the cession'.[46] It is more than probable that Pritchard, himself the son of a missionary,[47] somewhat disappointed with the attitude of the missionaries from whom he had expected support,[48] projected missionary dislike of him personally (arising from their jealousy of his influence) into opposition to 'his' cession.

The 'jealousy' theory is corroborated by the fact that the missionaries quickly established very cordial relations with Lt. Col. W.J. Smythe, who was sent out by the Colonial Office to report on the desirability or otherwise of accepting the cession. As a military man and one whose presence in Fiji would of necessity be brief,[49] Smythe posed no threat in the minds of the missionaries. If he seemed favourably disposed to the missionaries it is probably not surprising since, in his instructions to Smythe, the Secretary of State, the Duke of Newcastle, had reflected on the widespread beneficial effect that the Wesleyan missionaries had had upon Fiji in the quarter-century since their arrival:

> The missionaries ... have contended against the evil practices of the people ... and their efforts have been successful to a far greater extent than many would have expected. Mr Pritchard states that nearly one third of the population has embraced Christianity, nearly an equal number have renounced their heathenism,.... without ... attaching themselves to the Christian congregation. The services of these missionaries cannot be too highly appreciated; they have brought the truths of religion within the reach of this wild and distant people, they have abated human customs of a very inveterate power, and they have, in addition, secured an amount of safety and freedom previously unknown for the Europeans who traffic or settle amongst these islands ....[50]

---

43 Pritchard, *Polynesian Reminiscences* (London: Chapman & Hall, 1866), p.217.
44 Ward, pp.194-195.
45 Legge, p.41n.
46 Morrell, *Pacific Islands*, p.139
47 W.T. Pritchard was the son of the Revd George Pritchard, LMS missionary turned British Consul in Tahiti.
48 See W.T. Pritchard to Rev William Arthur, 2 August 1861. *WMMS Archives*, Box 532 Australasian Correspondence, Fiji 1858-1884 file.; Pritchard to FO, 28 March 1859. Enc. in FO to CO, 13 April 1859. *PP* 1862 XXXVI [2995].
49 Smythe arrived in Fiji on 5 July 1860 and completed his report on 1 May 1861.
50 Newcastle's Instructions to Smythe, 23 December 1859, enc. in Sir F. Rogers to Lord Wodehouse, 31 July 1860. CO 83/1.

But the duke tempered his approval of the missionaries' work with a warning to his commissioner:

> I must caution you not to suffer your sympathy with the Missionaries or your admiration of their achievements, to affect your judgment ... Her Majesty's Government must continue to entrust the Gospel in the distant parts of the earth ... to the piety and zeal of individuals. The hope of the conversion of a people to Christianity, however specious, must not be made a reason for increasing the British dominions.[51]

As they had done with Pritchard, the missionaries provided the translation facilities for Smythe, and the importance they attached to this – hardly surprising since it made them privy to all the information Smythe received – is shown by the fact that Joseph Waterhouse, the head of the mission, acted as Smythe's personal translator for most of the time he was in Fiji.[52]

Smythe's report, dated 1 May 1861 and received in London on 17 August that year,[53] recommended that the offer of cession should be refused. Cakobau, he had discovered, did not have the authority to make it and in his view the possession of the islands would not benefit Britain sufficiently to outweigh the extra cost and responsibility incurred. Nevertheless, Smythe spoke in glowing terms of the missionary contribution to the civilising and development of the Fijians. When he concluded that the best future for Fiji would be 'a native government aided by the counsels of respectable Europeans', it was clear to whom he was referring. Smythe's report has been the butt of much subsequent criticism, as indeed has his own suitability as a commissioner.[54] Whether these criticisms have validity is not at issue here, though one cannot help feeling that Smythe's critics have perhaps been wiser after the event, and viewed his rejection of annexation in 1861 against the subsequent reversal of policy and annexation of the islands in 1874.[55] What is of interest to this study is the criticism that Smythe 'sided with the missionaries' and that they 'influenced Smythe against recommending acceptance'.[56] Susan Farnsworth agrees that Smythe was 'sympathetic to the missionaries who opposed it [cession]'.[57]

---

51 *Ibid.*
52 Smythe to Rogers, 25 September 1860. *PP* 1862 XXXVI [2995].
53 Smythe's Report, 1 May 1861, enc. in Smythe to Newcastle 1 May 1861, CO 83/1.
54 See, for example, Ward, p.191-192 and Eldridge, 'Imperialism of the Little England Era', 177, 183-184.
55 Though it is only fair to note that Smythe rejected the expert opinions of both Captain John Washington, the Admiralty hydrographer and the botanist, Dr Berthold Seemann.
56 Ward, pp.191,195.
57 Farnsworth, p.125.

J.D. Legge has suggested that during his mission to Fiji in 1861 Smythe 'accepted, without serious question, the Wesleyan judgment on Fijian affairs'.[58] If that is indeed the case, then Smythe's report can just as easily be read as an example of his own robust independence of mind than as evidence that the missionaries had changed their minds about annexation and had thus influenced Smythe in this direction. There is, in fact, no evidence whatsoever that Methodist missionaries in Fiji ever turned against annexation.[59] The idea of missionary opposition is an assumption not a proven fact. The origin of this persistent myth[60] appears to be Pritchard's unreliable evidence that the missionaries opposed cession, which, as has already been argued, can be traced to missionary opposition to Pritchard, rather than a rejection of the idea of annexation. Indeed the WMMS Annual Report for 1862 deplored the fact that the opportunity for annexation had been lost[61] and there is no evidence that James Calvert ever wavered from his ardent annexationist views.

In advising his opposite number in the Foreign Office that Smythe's report was to be accepted and the offer of cession rejected, Sir Frederic Rogers, always supportive of the work of the missions, pointed to their role in Fiji's future: 'It would appear very uncertain whether the welfare of the natives would not be better consulted by leaving their civilization to be effected by causes which are already in operation'.[62] More succinctly, W.P. Morrell described the Smythe report as 'a report in favour of a missionary kingdom'.[63] J.M. Ward concludes that, 'when the British decision not to accept the offer was communicated to Fiji the missionaries regarded it as evidence that Great Britain deemed the responsibility for civilizing Fiji to be theirs alone and welcomed the trust'.[64] There is no doubt that the missionaries got on with the job and made the most of their opportunities in the power vacuum created by the rejection of British annexation especially after their hated rival, Consul Pritchard, was recalled to Britain in 1863.[65] Indeed, the missionaries induced Cakobau himself to write to WMMS headquarters in London to request more missionaries.[66] By 1870 the mission was a thriving enterprise with twelve white missionaries, 21 ordained and 23 lay native missionaries, 1,128 catechists and lay preachers, 277

---

58 Legge, p.42.
59 See Eldridge, 'Imperialism of the Little England Era', 180; Morrell, *Pacific Islands*, p.139.
60 So persistent that even Farnsworth uncritically recycles it. Farnsworth, p.125.
61 WMMS *Annual Report* 1862, quoted in Morrell, *Pacific Islands,* p.139.
62 Rogers to Hammond, 7 Sept 1861. Quoted in Ward, p.194.
63 Morrell, *Pacific Islands*, p.137.
64 Ward, p.195, referring to the Report of the Australian WMMS for 1862-3, pp.45-46.
65 For the numerical growth of Fijian Methodism, see the WMMS *Annual Reports* for the 1860s.
66 Cakobau to Gen. Secs., 10 June 1862. *WMMS Archives*, Box 532, Australasian Correspondence, Fiji 1858-1884 file. It is noticeable that Cakobau signs himself as *Vunivalu* and not *Tui Viti* in this letter.

places of worship, 107,771 worshippers, 17,401 members and 4,514 on trial for membership.[67] Some missionaries became financially as well as politically involved, like William Moore, Methodist Chairman in the 1860s, and John Horsley, who participated in the attempt of Messrs Evans and Brewer of Melbourne to set up a Polynesian Company which would receive land and privileges from Cakobau in return for settling his American debt.[68]

But as the 'missionary kingdom' received unofficial sanction from London, its days were already numbered. Although missionary influence was already paramount since Cakobau's victory at Kaba in 1855 and became firmly established after Smythe's report was accepted, it began to break down in the late 1860s and early 1870s as a result of the influx of Europeans into the islands.

Influx of Europeans

It was the growing number of white settlers free from any effective governmental control and living under what were for them conveniently anarchic conditions, which led to increasing pressure from those with an interest in stable government for Fiji to reopen the question of annexation. As in other 'frontier' situations, the Europeans (other than the missionaries) were not infrequently far from the best of their nationality.[69] The Smythe Report concluded: 'The great hindrance to the progress of civilization and Christianity among the inhabitants of the Pacific Islands is the conduct of the whites residing or roving among them',[70] a view endorsed by R.A. Derrick who described the early Europeans in Fiji as the 'derelict scourings of the ports of the Old World, among them some of the worst and lowest of their kind'.[71]

The increasing influx of Europeans, primarily to plant cotton,[72] had two direct results. It led to an extension of the labour trade and to the end of the 'missionary kingdom' which effectively existed in the late 1850s and 1860s. The missionaries exerted a degree of informal control over the Fijians but had

---

67 WMMS *Annual Report* 1870, pp.122-124.
68 See Revd William Moore to Thurston, May 1868 and Schedule, 23 May 1868; Revd John T. Horsley to Thurston, 28 May 1868. *PP* 1871 XLVII [435]. Moore was clearly much more than an 'interpreter' as Morrell regards him (Morrell, *Pacific Islands,* p.146) and Brookes refers to his 'large secular interests' (Brookes, p.306).
69 Jane Samson argues that missionaries, naval officers and consular officials were all prone to take a highly negative attitude, often rooted in social class distinctions, to white traders, beachcombers and others, invariably displaying their critical opinions in written despatches. See Samson, Ch. 2, 'White Savages'.
70 Smythe's Report, 1 May 1861, CO 83/1.
71 Derrick, p.37. See also Caroline Ralston, 'The Beach Communities', in Davidson and Scarr, pp.77-93.
72 See Evelyn Stokes, 'The Fiji Cotton Boom in the Eighteen-Sixties, *NZJH*, 2 (1968), 165-177.

little influence over the newly-arrived Europeans. The WMMS *Annual Report* for 1869, which noted 'the immigration of many hundreds of Europeans and other foreigners to some parts of this group' gloomily warned: 'whatever advantages may ultimately accrue to Fiji from the flowing of a European population to its shores ... viewing the matter in the light of past events and experience of other lands, New Zealand especially, we confess to the deepest anxiety for the future of our Mission in Fiji'.[73] Here the WMMS was being completely honest, for it had rightly come to realise that although missionaries in the field could acquire and maintain moral and sometimes even political sway over aboriginal peoples, the establishment of an alternative white society with little respect for the missionaries could only weaken and eventually undermine their authority in the eyes of the native peoples. In such a situation, unable any longer to keep the islanders safe in their paternalistic care the missionaries had to consider the option of lobbying for annexation. The WMMS *Annual Report* for 1869 concluded that only 'by the immediate introduction of righteous laws and authority, in connection with the work and influence of your missionaries, the evils so greatly dreaded may be averted, and the good ... realised'.[74] This fear was repeated in the Annual Reports for both 1871 and 1872, though by 1873 a positive side to the influx was noted – the presence of an English Methodist congregation in Levuka.[75]

In the summer of 1870, a plaintive despatch from Henry March, HM Consul in Fiji, painted a dismal picture of the kind of white settlers he had to contend with and to a large extent substantiated the misgivings of the mission:

> It is far from my intention to complain. Yet my position here is painful in the extreme. Apart from the utter isolation in which I live, in consequence of the want of any society which a gentleman – without being particular (if that be possible) can enter, I am in the midst of low adventurers, absconders from the colonies, and a class of men who are in a chronic state of excitement caused by continual indulgence in alcoholic drinks. I am at the mercy of any ruffian who chooses to walk into the office, abuse me and walk out again. I cannot well take the law into my own hands and I must bear the intrusion with patience. I am not even free from such visitors in my own private house. I have drunken men walking into the room at any time of night.[76]

---

73 WMMS *Annual Report* 1869, p.109-110.
74 *Ibid.*, p.110. This assessment was also, independently, made by the British Consul in Fiji. See Consul March's Report on the Fiji Islands, 27 March 1870. FO 58/118.
75 See *Annual Reports* for 1871 (p.153), 1872 (p.150) and 1873 (p.115). Though John Young regards the establishment of the white congregation as a backward step, a kind of spiritual apartheid which did nothing to foster inter-racial understanding. See Young, 'Evanescent Ascendancy', in Davidson and Scarr, p.160.
76 March to T.V. Lister, 2 July 1870. FO 58/118.

March did not request annexation – merely the building of a new consular residence – but his complaints give some indication of what life must have been like, at least in Levuka, in the years immediately preceding annexation. In a private letter, a copy of which quickly found its way via the missionary network to the Colonial Office, Lorimer Fison commented to his brother William on the problems of white immigration into Fiji. In a minute on this letter Robert Herbert was 'sorry to be obliged to agree with Mr Fison that there is great danger of a collision between the whites and the Fijians'.[77] Noting the impossibility of the situation, he feared that 'England will be blamed for this, as long as being the principal power in the islands, she does not govern' and mused:

> Would it be possible to make this letter a peg on which to hang a letter to the F.O. suggesting it might be to the credit of England ... if any diplomatic communications could result in the establishment of a friendly European government on these islands?

Herbert's comments are an indication that the Colonial Office was as yet unpersuaded of the value of Fiji to Britain. Annexation by another power was preferable to anarchy.

The Debate on Fiji's Future

When Alan Burns stated that [by 1873] 'power had ... passed from the hands of the Fijian chiefs into the hands of an alien minority',[78] he was chronicling in brief the net result of various experiments in government that had taken place in Fiji after Britain had declined to accept the cession. The Confederation of 1865, the Bau Constitution of 1867, the Amended Bau Constitution of 1869, and finally the Constitutional Monarchy of 1871 were a series of attempts to enable the *Tui Viti* to exercise the authority and responsibility that attached to his title.

Into this confused and fluid situation stepped in 1866 the figure of John Bates Thurston,[79] a man of considerable talent and ability who spent the rest of his life in the service of Fiji, eventually becoming governor of the Crown colony in 1888. Thurston had much in common with the missionaries, who were

---

77 Lorimer Fison to William Fison (copy) 27 August 1870, and min. by Herbert, 11 June 1871. CO 201/562.
78 Burns, *Fiji*, p.96.
79 For Thurston see Deryck Scarr, *The Majesty of Colour: a life of Sir John Bates Thurston,* 2 vols, (Canberra: Australian National University Press, 1973 and 1980). For his later life see also John Millington, 'The Career of Sir John Thurston, Governor of Fiji 1888-1897', unpublished MA thesis (London, 1947).

actually responsible for bringing him to Fiji in the first place.[80] Like them, he always sought to promote the interests of the native Fijians above those of the rapacious white settlers, who merely wished to exploit the Fijians and to maximise their own profits. When Consul Jones left Fiji in 1867, Thurston, then a coconut planter, stepped into his shoes as acting consul for a period of two years. He had great respect for the missionaries, recognising the enormous good they had done for the Fijian people.[81] But he was no sycophant, and when, in later years he felt that the mission was becoming lax, he had no hesitation in saying so.[82]

The missionaries came to regret having introduced Thurston to Fiji. Their peculiar jealousy of able and authoritative white men in Fiji has already been observed in their reaction to Pritchard. Thurston would have been doubly suspect in their eyes. Like Pritchard, he exercised authority and influence they would have preferred to exercise themselves, but, unlike Pritchard, he was not even in favour of ceding the islands to Britain – at least not until the very last minute. Worst of all, he wished to wean the Fijians away from being dependent on white men – including the missionaries. Although by the twentieth century, missionary societies themselves would subscribe to similar policies (Bishop Patteson was ahead of his time in this as in other areas, in advocating such self-denying policies),[83] this was certainly not on the Wesleyan agenda in the 1860s and 1870s. It may be that James Calvert felt a particular responsibility for Thurston's presence on the islands, and the records survive of a crude attempt by Calvert, using his extensive network of contacts, including William M'Arthur, Admiral Erskine and W.B. Boyce, to remove Thurston as acting British consul in 1869.[84] Certainly Thurston ceased to act as consul in December of that year, but whether this was due to Calvert's machinations is not known.

After a gap of ten years following the Smythe report, the attention of the British government was once again focused on Fiji because of the abuses of the labour trade as islanders were taken there to work on the growing number of cotton plantations. In 1869 the *Young Australian* and *Daphne* trials, though both in the Australian courts, had raised the question of Fiji, the destination of both vessels. The murder of Bishop Patteson in September 1871 led inexorably

---

80 Millington, p.72. Having been shipwrecked on Rotuma, he was conveyed to Levuka by James Calvert on the mission ship *John Wesley* in 1866.
81 Thurston to FO, 17 September 1867. FO 58/109. Quoted in Millington, p.9.
82 Millington, pp.92-93.
83 Patteson to ?, 11 November 1862. Quoted in S.M. Smythe, *Ten Months in the Fiji Islands* (Oxford: Parker, 1864), pp.277-278.
84 Calvert to W.B. Boyce, 4 March 1869 and encs. Calvert to Erskine (2 letters), 5 March 1869. *WMMS Archives*, Australasian Correspondence, Box 532, Fiji 1858-1884 file.

to the passage of the Pacific Islanders' Protection Act in 1872. But the *Carl*[85] massacre trial highlighted the fact that the Act applied only to British territory; consequently Fiji became an even more desirable base for unscrupulous cotton planters and labour recruiters alike. Indeed, only the month before his death, Bishop Patteson had recognised that as far as the labour trade was concerned, 'the demand creates the supply' in Fiji; a problem exacerbated by the cotton boom of 1870. Patteson had made contact with some of the white cotton planters and only his untimely death prevented him from visiting the Fiji Islands.[86]

Lord Kimberley, in his early months at the Colonial Office, tried to solve both the problem of lawlessness by British subjects in Fiji and the island's somewhat doubtful reputation with regard to the labour trade by encouraging New South Wales to annex the islands. The Legislative Assembly of that colony had, after all, on the motion of Alexander M'Arthur, voted an address to the Queen in support of the cession proposal of 1858.[87] But any such ideas had been cut short by the proclamation of the constitutional monarchy in Fiji in June 1871 and, by the autumn of that year, Kimberley had decided on the compromise plan of affording *de facto* recognition to the Fijian government under the Australian G.A. Woods, a decision subsequently endorsed by the Cabinet.[88] On 3 November 1871 a circular despatch to the Australian colonial governments instructed them to treat Cakobau's ministry as the *de facto* government of Fiji.

Susan Willmington has characterised the Colonial Office's attitude to Fiji at this period as one of 'indecisiveness' and 'confusion'.[89] But it should surely be remembered that this is not unusual in government departments at the best of times, let alone when in the throes of seeking to develop new policies to meet changing conditions. W.D. McIntyre is less critical, preferring to describe Kimberley's policy as 'flexible'.[90] Either way, Kimberley acquired breathing space on the matter of Fiji. Nevertheless, his policy continued to develop – or indecisiveness to prevail, dependent on the point of view – when in June 1872 he stated that any *de facto* recognition would be dependent on the Fijian government's attitude to the labour trade. In all probability this development was Kimberley's response to the increasing violence attendant upon the

---

85 For *Carl* see McIntyre, *Imperial Frontier,* p.351; and E.G. Blackmore, 'South Sea Slavery: Kidnapping and Murder' in *Macmillan's Magazine,* 27 (March 1873), 370-375.
86 See Patteson to Revd William Floyd, 26 May 1871; and Patteson to [Cousin] Arthur, 6 August 1871. *Melanesian Mission Archives,* Bishop Patteson Letters 2/8.
87 Seemann, p.vii.
88 See McIntyre, *Imperial Frontier,* pp.231-237 for the development of Kimberley's thinking.
89 Willmington, pp.99, 102 and 119.
90 McIntyre, *Imperial Frontier,* p.238.

kidnapping situation and to the pressure coming from the missionary and humanitarian lobbies.

When he was acting British consul, Thurston, who himself made use of legitimately-hired labour for his coconut plantation on Taveuni, had endeavoured to supervise and regulate the labour trade, on an unofficial basis, by interviewing indentured labourers as they landed in Fiji. Though disliked by both the missionaries and the white planters, his administrative ability and linguistic expertise marked him out for an indispensable role in the government of Fiji. In May 1872 Thurston took office as chief secretary in the Woods government, which had attempted to govern in Cakobau's name since the previous year. Thurston soon became the dominant member of the government in the rapidly deteriorating situation that was Fiji in the early 1870s.[91]

It is unlikely that the Fijian government had any inkling of the proviso now attached to Kimberley's *de facto* recognition when it put 'An Act to Regulate the Hiring and Service of Immigrant Polynesian Labourers' on its own statute book less than a month after the Pacific Islanders' Protection Act received the Royal Assent in London.[92] But, as in other areas too, the writ of Cakobau's government ran only so far as the white planters would allow, and lawlessness increased. Calls by the missionary and humanitarian lobbies for annexation multiplied as details of the *Carl* massacre, which had taken place in September 1871 (the same month as Bishop Patteson's murder), gradually came into the open though court cases in 1872 and early 1873, *after* the Pacific Islanders' Protection Act had become law in Britain. The Melanesian Mission's Annual Report in 1874 made it clear that the Act by itself was doing little to end the labour trade.[93] Writing in *Macmillan's Magazine* in March 1873, E.G. Blackmore, of the South Australia House of Assembly, echoed both John Paton and W.T. Pritchard:

> The only satisfactory regulation is total suppression. Total suppression is the duty of Great Britain, and there is only one way to do it – viz. to convert the Fiji Islands into a British colony .... Had she accepted the offer made her in 1859, the South Seas might have been spared the horrors and atrocities perpetrated by British man-stealers.[94]

The situation in Fiji continued to deteriorate, and early in 1873, Consul March, who had important links with the Aborigines Protection Society, suggested what

---

[91] For a sympathetic account of Thurston's part in the period leading up to annexation see Deryck Scarr, 'John Bates Thurston, Commodore Goodenough and Rampant Anglo-Saxons in Fiji', *HSANZ*, XI (1964), 361-382.

[92] Cakobau Rex No.34., 23 July 1872. Enc. in Thurston to Knatchbull-Hugessen, 11 September 1872. CO 83/2.

[93] Melanesian Mission *Annual Report* 1874.

[94] Blackmore, 375

Kimberley described as 'a clumsy kind of protectorate over British subjects'.[95] Thurston had already, on 19 October 1872, requested a firm statement of Britain's proposed policy towards the Fijian government. It was therefore inevitable that the Colonial Office, albeit reluctantly, should give serious attention to the enquiry made by Thurston in January 1873 as to whether the British government would view favourably a new offer of cession, if such were to be made.[96]

Pressure in Parliament: The Role of William M'Arthur

In order to have any influence at all in London, the missionaries in the field, however dedicated and well-informed, needed to have the right connections with the corridors of power. James Calvert recognised this fact, as his copious correspondence with influential contacts shows. The WMMS was fortunate indeed that among its leading supporters was Alderman William M'Arthur, Liberal MP for Lambeth from 1868 to 1885.[97] M'Arthur's connections were impressive, being a leading member of, *inter alia*, the WMMS, the Evangelical Alliance, the British and Foreign Bible Society, the Anti-Slavery Society and the Aborigines Protection Society. He had business interests in Australia and New Zealand. His brother Alexander, at one time a member of the New South Wales legislature, had married the daughter of W.B. Boyce (later WMMS joint general secretary) and after his return to Britain sat for Leicester in the 1874-80 Parliament. The two brothers and their families lived in cosy domesticity in adjoining properties adjacent to Brixton Hill. William was briefed in matters Fijian by James Calvert, who forwarded Fijian correspondence to him, as did W.B. Boyce from Australian contacts. Other correspondents included W.J. Smythe and Frederick Langham, the latter by the early 1870s head of the Methodist mission in Fiji. William M'Arthur proved to be the vital link between the mission and the government, the hinge between those with the knowledge and those with the power. Well might he be described by a fellow Member of Parliament as 'the patron saint of the Fiji Islander'.[98]

The growing co-operation between missionaries and humanitarians which has been observed in the campaign against the labour trade now began to focus on Fiji, where abuses in the trade were increasing. The Aborigines Protection

---

95 See encs in FO to CO, 9 May 1873, and min. by Kimberley, 15 May 1873. CO 83/4.
96 Thurston to Granville, 31 January 1873. FO 58/139. See David Routledge, 'The Negotiations Leading to the Cession of Fiji, 1874', *JICH*, 2 (1974), 283. Also Thurston to Calvert, 31 January 1873: 'the king has officially authorized me, as foreign minister, to put the question of cession directly to Her Britannic Majesty's government'. Quoted in T. M'Cullagh, *Sir William M'Arthur, KCMG* (London: Hodder & Stoughton, 1891), p.157. However, it should be noted that there is some disagreement among historians as to Thurston's precise motives in making this enquiry.
97 See M'Cullagh, for a thorough, if somewhat hagiographical, biography of M'Arthur.
98 Sir Wilfrid Lawson, 4 August 1874. *Hansard*, Third Series, CCXXI, col. 1296.

Society sent a deputation to Kimberley on 8 February 1872 to press for more vigorous measures for the suppression of kidnapping. Although under the Aborigines Protection Society banner, the deputation included M'Arthur and Kinnaird, both of whom held senior honorary positions in missionary societies. Also in the deputation were Dr Joseph Mullens, foreign secretary of the LMS, and John Kay, secretary of the Scottish Reformed Presbyterian Foreign Missions Committee. But even before the deputation waited upon Kimberley, concerted plans were clearly afoot to bring the matter of Fiji before Parliament[99] and on 6 March M'Arthur gave notice of his motion to be put before the House of Commons. The leadership of the missionary and humanitarian campaigns now coalesced. It was perhaps only natural that M'Arthur with his seat in Parliament, business interests and family connections in Australia, humanitarian sympathy and, most importantly, being a senior lay Methodist, should assume the leadership of the Fiji lobby.[100]

Before either March or Thurston had made their proposals for British involvement in Fiji, William M'Arthur moved a motion in the House of Commons on 24 June 1872. Seconded by another Methodist, Admiral J.E. Erskine, Liberal MP for Stirlingshire and a leading member of the Anti-Slavery Society, who as a naval captain had visited the islands and met Cakobau in 1849-50, the motion called for a British protectorate over Fiji and caused a debate lasting over three and a half hours.[101] Briefed by Calvert, 'a gentleman who knows more about Fiji than any other man living',[102] and drawing heavily on his missionary connections, M'Arthur presented the protectorate as the means to put down kidnapping where the 1872 Act had failed. Though the motion was lost by 135 votes to 84, M'Arthur was successful in putting Fiji firmly on the political agenda, exposing ambivalence at the Colonial Office[103] and extracting from Gladstone one of his most important statements on colonial policy.[104]

---

99 F.W. Chesson to Benjamin Millard, 13 January 1872, quoted in Willmington, p.116.
100 This was particularly important, as that other great campaigner, F.W. Chesson, of the Aborigines Protection Society, was incapacitated by illness for most of 1872.
101 Fiji debate, 25 June 1872. *Hansard*, Third Series, CCXII, cols 192-219.
102 It was fortunate that Calvert was in Britain in 1872, prior to his proceeding to a new posting in South Africa. From his base at Bromley in Kent he was in a convenient position to brief M'Arthur.
103 Knatchbull-Hugessen, replying for the Colonial Office, spoke in such ambivalent terms of a motion he was supposed to be opposing that *The Times* the following day compared him to the prophet Balaam in Numbers Ch.22-24: 'officially bound to curse he ended up by nearly blessing it altogether'. *Hansard*, Third Series, CCXII, cols 205-212; The Times, 26 June 1872, quoted in McIntyre, *Imperial Frontier*, p.250.
104 Gladstone, obliged to intervene because of Knatchbull-Hugessen's deliberate lack of clarity, declared that, 'So far as it was possible to lay down an abstract and general rule with regard to annexation, he was prepared to say that H.M.G. would not annex any territory, great or small, without the well-understood and expressed wish of the people

Subsequently M'Arthur maintained the pressure on the Government. On 7 February 1873 he put down another motion, this time for outright annexation of the islands. On 18 February 1873 M'Arthur enquired of the Foreign Office what reply had been given to a memorial from the Fijian government in 1870 requesting protection. The Under Secretary, Lord Enfield, was obliged to admit that no reply had ever been made.[105] Within a week a telegram arrived from Sir Hercules Robinson, Governor of New South Wales, giving advance warning that Thurston's telegraph of 31 January was on its way to London. To make sure that it would not be pigeon-holed by the authorities, Thurston had taken the precaution of sending details of the contents of his letter to Calvert, requesting that he should 'let Mr M'Arthur know this, and any other of your parliamentary friends'.[106]

In the Spring of 1873, with M'Arthur's motion down on the Commons' order paper for 13 May, decisions on Fiji were being made. The government's policy was becoming increasingly untenable. While Fiji lay outside British jurisdiction the Kidnapping Act by itself had little effect. To make matters worse, the Fiji cotton boom had collapsed by 1873 and conditions for indentured labourers were likely to deteriorate. Kimberley began to contemplate annexation as the best available option in the continued fight against the abuses in the labour trade. The day after Robinson's telegram arrived he shared his views with the Prime Minister:

> I have for some time been inclining to the opinion that we ought to accept the sovereignty of Fiji. We are and shall be at great expense in attempting to put down kidnapping in the South Sea Islands. If Fiji were under British rule, we should cut away the root of this evil which would disappear if we had control over the European settlers in Fiji.[107]

With the arrival in London of Thurston's request for a clear statement of how Britain would respond if a subsequent offer of cession were made, it seemed that Gladstone's condition, laid down in the first Fiji debate, was being met. At the very least a thorough investigation was required. Gladstone himself remained reluctant but Kimberley pressed him, knowing that the political tide was flowing in an annexationist direction and that M'Arthur and his supporters were unlikely to give up until Fiji was part of the British Empire. Gladstone continued to oppose annexation. Kimberley's master-stroke was to persuade the Prime Minister to consider a commission of enquiry. This had several advantages. It would delay a decision for months if not years; it would steal

---

to be annexed, freely and generously expressed, and authenticated by the best means the case would afford.' *Hansard,* Third Series, CCXII, col. 217.
105 *Hansard,* Third Series, CCXIV, col. 597.
106 Thurston to Calvert, 31 January 1873. Quoted in M'Cullagh, p.157.
107 Kimberley to Gladstone, 24 February 1873. Gladstone Papers, 44225/10, quoted in Willmington, p.132.

M'Arthur's thunder when his motion was debated: it did not actually commit the government to anything; and even made virtue out of necessity by appearing to be consistent with previous policy, both that of sending the Smythe commission in 1860 and with Gladstone's statement in the first Fiji debate. On 7 June, the week before the postponed debate was due, Kimberley's proposal for a commission was accepted by the Cabinet.[108]

As the pressure for annexation began to grow, the author of the 1861 report, which had led to the rejection of the Pritchard cession, announced his conversion to the cause of annexation. W.J. Smythe, now a major-general, indicated his change of heart to the Foreign Office in March 1873, stating that conditions had changed since his report twelve years previously and that, 'it would be better for the interests both of the natives and of this country that we should now take possession of the Fiji Islands'.[109] How Smythe arrived at this changed perception of the best interests of Fiji is not known, though he may have been stung by M'Arthur's description of him in the first Fiji debate as 'either unfit for his task or ... prejudice[d] against the proposal'. This, however, is unlikely since a month before his letter to the Foreign Office he had written privately to M'Arthur with the same information.[110] What is known is that James Calvert kept in touch with Smythe after the latter's mission to Fiji in 1861,[111] and it is probable that it was he who encouraged General Smythe to turn the other cheek to M'Arthur's apparent insult and, in the interests of Fiji, give the MP advance warning of his *volte face*.

M'Arthur's second motion on Fiji, postponed from May because of pressure on the parliamentary timetable, was debated on 13 June 1873.[112] M'Arthur claimed that Gladstone's condition had now been fulfilled. Further, General Smythe had changed his mind and the work of the missionaries now resulted in 107,250 attenders at Christian worship. Kidnapping would never be extirpated until Fiji was placed under the British flag. Admiral Sir Charles Wingfield of the Aborigines Protection Society seconded the motion and drew attention to the *Carl* massacre. Other contributors to the debate from the missionary movement included Kinnaird and Erskine. Giving Knatchbull-Hugessen no opportunity to stray from the party line, Gladstone replied for the government. He made no attempt to gainsay M'Arthur's humanitarian arguments but confessed frankly that accessions of territory did not excite him. Though unable to resist a sarcastic comment that if M'Arthur's figures were

---

108 For the details of the formation of policy by the Colonial Office and the Cabinet, see McIntyre, *Imperial Frontier,* pp.253-257 and Ethel Drus, 'The Colonial Office and the annexation of Fiji', *TRHS,* XXXII (1950), 101-103.
109 Smythe to Under Secretary, FO, 1 March 1873, enc. in FO to CO, 26 March 1873. CO 83/3.
110 Smythe to M'Arthur, 12 February 1873, quoted in M'Cullagh, pp.158-159.
111 See, for example, Calvert to Smythe, 3 December 1863. *WMMS Archives.* Australasian Correspondence, Box 532, Fiji 1835-1884 file.
112 *Hansard,* Third Series, CCXVI, cols 934-958.

correct, 'the Fiji Islands furnished a larger proportion of attendants upon Divine Worship than any country in Christendom', he announced the appointment of two commissioners to proceed to Fiji to enquire and report. He was satisfied with the outcome of the debate. Once again M'Arthur lost the vote, the government's procedural amendment to his motion being carried by 36 votes.

In fact, no special commissioners were actually appointed for Fiji. Instead, two government servants, recently appointed to south Pacific posts, were given an extra brief and the expense and publicity of a special commission was avoided. The men selected were Edgar L. Layard, the new British Consul in Fiji in succession to Henry March, and Commodore James G. Goodenough, who was about to take over command of the Australasian squadron from Commodore Stirling. Goodenough's appointment was calculated to please the missions and their supporters. A committed Anglican, the son of the Dean of Wells, Goodenough took the trouble to visit the WMMS headquarters in Bishopsgate Street before proceeding to the Pacific. This would doubtless have endeared him to the missionary interest. Indeed, McIntyre hints that here he may well have come under M'Arthur's influence.[113]

It was as well that Goodenough took the trouble to acquaint himself with the missionary world. Thirteen years earlier Newcastle's instructions to Smythe had painted in glowing colours the achievements of the missionaries in Fiji. No such panegyric was contained in Kimberley's instructions to Goodenough and Layard.[114] It may have been that Kimberley did not regard the contribution of the Methodist missionaries as relevant to the mission of Goodenough and Layard. Alternatively, the fact that despatches were now drafted by Robert Herbert and not the more sympathetic Rogers may well have been the reason for the lack of any reference to the work of the Wesleyan mission.

The British Annexation of Fiji

As Goodenough and Layard proceeded slowly to Fiji, further orchestration of the campaign to extend British sovereignty to those islands was in evidence in Britain. A small group of parliamentary supporters of annexation, owing allegiance to the missionary societies, to the Aborigines Protection Society, to

---

113 McIntyre, *Imperial Frontier*, p.322.
114 Instructions to Commodore Goodenough. Final draft after FO to CO 5 August 1873. CO 83/4. Instructions to Layard, 15 August 1873. *PP* 1874 XLV [C.983]. In essence they were asked to decide between four possible options: magisterial power for the British consul, *de jure* recognition of the existing Fijian government, a British protectorate and outright annexation.

the Royal Colonial Institute, or to a combination of them, began to make their presence felt.[115]

The campaign had been begun when a group, aiming to create a favourable reception for M'Arthur's forthcoming motion, presented a memorial to Kimberley on 12 May 1873. In fact, the deputation consisted of two distinct groups with separate memorials, the Aborigines Protection Society and the Royal Colonial Institute. Kinnaird took the lead on this occasion. The members of the deputation were much pleased with their reception and felt that Kimberley was now fully aware of the issues which concerned them. Indeed, C.W. Eddy, secretary of the Royal Colonial Institute, prophesied with uncanny precision that, '[Kimberley] ... will now be obliged to do something. I suspect that something will be to send out a commission to report in order to gain time and perhaps leave the question on the hands of their successors'.[116]

After the second Fiji debate and following in the path of the May deputation, a more formal 'Fiji Committee' was organised to lobby for annexation. With M'Arthur as chairman and F.W. Chesson as secretary, the committee was formed under the auspices of the Aborigines Protection Society and the Royal Colonial Institute, though the latter soon withdrew and the former continued, this time in partnership with the WMMS. As well as M'Arthur and Chesson, the committee's membership included Alexander M'Arthur and Arthur Kinnaird, Admirals Wingfield and Erskine and the Revds William Arthur and W.B. Boyce. Here was the classic combination of humanitarian and missionary supporters, in some cases the same people, making common cause. But by the time the committee was fully constituted and operational, the Liberal government had been defeated and in February 1874 Lord Carnarvon replaced Lord Kimberley at the Colonial Office.

Having made their separate ways to Fiji, Commodore Goodenough and Consul Layard met on the island of Kadavu on 29 December 1873. In their instructions from Lord Kimberley, the commissioners had been given a choice of four options to consider. These were conferring magisterial power on the British consul, recognising *de jure* the Fijian government, establishing a protectorate over the islands, or annexing them outright.[117]

The head of the Methodist mission in Fiji, the Revd Frederick Langham, who acted as translator in meetings with Cakobau, expressed his approval of the commissioners:

> Unquestionably they are the gentlemen for the work to which they have been designated, and I am satisfied that they will win the confidence of the entire

---

115 For brief discussions of the Fiji Committee and its antecedents see C.C. Eldrid· *England's Mission: the Imperial Idea in the Age of Gladstone and Disraeli, 1868-1880* (London: Macmillan, 1973), pp.153-154; and Willmington, p.129-132.
116 Quoted in Willmington, p.132.
117 See n.114, above.

community. Separately and unitedly, they are gaining golden opinions wherever they go, and whatever the nature of their report may be, I am sure their visit will be of incalculable service to the country.... We missionaries of course are delighted with the attention which he [Layard] is already giving to the labour traffic.[118]

W.D. McIntyre has suggested that Langham was, unlike his colleagues, 'not an annexationist'.[119] It was certainly true that annexationist views were paramount among the Wesleyan missionaries in Fiji at this time; there always had been, whatever W.T. Pritchard may have felt. But this description of Langham is at best ambiguous and at worst misleading; closer inspection is needed.

After the debate on M'Arthur's first motion, a different picture emerges. Langham regarded the Woods/Thurston government as 'the best ministry that can be got out of the materials available', but conceded that 'it cannot stand long'. He also wrote of his puzzlement as to why the 1870 memorial requesting a protectorate had gone unanswered, expressed 'regret that it [M'Arthur's motion] was not carried', and requested Calvert to forward his letter to M'Arthur.[120] While it is true that Langham did not sign the congratulatory address on annexation sent by several senior missionaries to Sir Hercules Robinson on 18 October 1874,[121] this can be accounted for by reasons more probable than opposition to annexation: first the poor state of communications between the islands; secondly, the existence of two factions within the group of white missionaries in Fiji led by Langham and Waterhouse (if this was the case, then the fact that Waterhouse was one of the three signatories would have meant that Langham was either not invited to sign or, if invited, refused to do so).[122]

The third possibility is that Langham, as Chairman of the District, felt that such a sycophantic memorial to a government official, albeit the Governor of New South Wales, was beneath the dignity of his office. It is known that Langham had a high opinion of himself and after the Crown colony was established, the young men of Sir Arthur Gordon's staff nicknamed him 'the Cardinal'.[123] Whatever may have been the case, in February 1874 Langham wrote to M'Arthur in a very supportive manner.[124] Though frankly admitting that 'for myself I should prefer a national government' and realistically seeing problems as well as advantages in annexation, he nevertheless believed that annexation was the only solution to the abuses in the labour trade, a matter on

---

118 Langham to M'Arthur, 13 February 1874. Enc. in Chesson to Carnarvon, 8 May 1874. CO 83/5.
119 McIntyre, *Imperial Frontier*, p.322
120 Langham to Calvert, 14 October 1872. Quoted in M'Cullagh, pp.156-157.
121 Waterhouse, Brooks and Wylie to Robinson, enc. in Robinson to Carnarvon, 18 October 1874. *PP* 1875 LII [C.1114].
122 Legge, p.211.
123 Morrell, *Pacific Islands*, p.376.
124 Langham to M'Arthur, 13 February 1874. Enc. in Chesson to Carnarvon, 8 May 1874. CO 83/5.

which he had strong views and which clearly overrode any possible reservations. He gave M'Arthur his outright support: 'I say go on and prosper in your endeavours to secure annexation for us and may your next speech gain over a majority to your views'. The following month he was again in touch with M'Arthur, this time accusing members of the (white) Fijian government of seeking to influence the chiefs against annexation for their own pecuniary interest.[125] Finally, after the cession had taken place Langham thanked M'Arthur for his efforts on behalf of Fiji. By this time he was effusive in his descriptions of the benefits to the island of imperial rule. As regards the labour trade, he viewed 'the annexation of this country to Great Britain ... as the most effectual blow aimed at that most degrading thing ...'.[126]

There is no evidence that Langham was at any time disingenuous in his views and there was no reason for him to hide any anti-annexationist opinions. Certainly, when he wished to make a point forcefully he had no hesitation in doing so.[127] It would be true to characterise his views as less doctrinairely annexationist than those of his colleagues, but to suggest, as McIntyre does, that he was against annexation is simply not the case. And by the time of annexation in October 1874 any reservations he may have had appear to have been resolved. He saw it as the only way to bring the labour trade under effective control. Though annexation would not perhaps have been Langham's preferred option for the future development of Fiji, he was realistic enough to see its inevitability and was happy to accept and support it.

What influence, then, did the missionaries have on the commissioners? Colonel Smythe, in his mission to Fiji in 1860-61, allegedly came under their influence. (Whether they influenced his eventual recommendation is much more open to doubt.) Was this also to be the case with Goodenough and Layard in 1873-74? Certainly Goodenough, the more dominant of the two, had credentials to recommend him to the missionaries, and his visit to their headquarters before embarking for Fiji could only have enhanced his reputation in their eyes. As Smythe had done before them, Goodenough and Layard made use of the services of Methodist missionaries as translators. What is more, Goodenough quickly fell out with Thurston, to the extent of a 'virulent personal hatred' in Deryck Scarr's judgment, which can only have improved his standing in the estimation of the missionaries.[128]

---

125 Langham to M'Arthur, 18 March 1874. Enc. in M'Arthur to Carnarvon, 22 May 1874. CO83/5.
126 Langham to M'Arthur, 20 November 1874. Quoted in M'Cullagh, pp.182-183.
127 See two letters on the subject of the labour trade and a dispute with Thurston over missionary reaction to it: Langham to Thurston, 12 February 1874. Sub-enc. in Chesson to Carnarvon, 8 May 1874. CO 83/5. Also Langham to Editor of *Fiji Times*, published 7 October 1874, enc. in Robinson to Carnarvon, 16 October 1874. *PP* 1875 LII [C.1114].
128 Scarr, 'Rampant Anglo-Saxons', 363. Scarr is perhaps excessively protective of Thurston's reputation. See also Goodenough and Layard to Kimberley, 19 March 1874. CO 83/5; Goodenough's Journal, II, 26 November 1873, quoted in W.D. McIntyre,

If Langham took his time and carefully considered all the available options for Fiji's future before supporting annexation, it would appear that Goodenough and Layard did not. Whether Goodenough was influenced by the missionaries it is impossible to say but it would appear that, ever the naval officer used to making quick decisions, he soon settled on one of Kimberley's four options as the most desirable. Having identified his objective he proceeded with military efficiency to achieve it. Within six weeks of the commencement of their work the commissioners were writing to Kimberley, that 'even at this early period of our enquiry, the surest and best mode' of proceeding was 'the formation of the Fiji group into a Crown colony ...'.[129]

The tortuous turns and manoeuvres in the negotiations by the commissioners, the Fijian chiefs, Thurston's government and the Colonial Office are ably chronicled and analysed in some detail elsewhere.[130] The part played in them by the missionaries on the spot, however, was small, except in their invaluable role as translators and possessors of local knowledge. Far, far more important was the part played by the missionary lobby, led by William M'Arthur, in London. Goodenough and Layard knew full well that the House of Commons would have to have its say. It may be that this knowledge was instrumental in concentrating the commissioners' minds in favour of the annexation option, knowing this was the preferred option of the most organised and outspoken group of MPs at Westminster. It is also quite possible that, in a private interview with Goodenough before he departed for Fiji, Kimberley may have communicated his preference for the annexation option. Equally, it may be that Goodenough and Layard, with or without Kimberley's prompting, speedily came to a realisation that only one of the four options was really viable.

Goodenough and Layard's predisposition to favour the annexation option did not go unnoticed by their new political masters in Downing Street. James Lowther, who replaced Knatchbull-Hugessen as Parliamentary Under-Secretary, commented with disfavour on the

> strong bias in favour of annexation displayed by the Commissioners in their letter [which] must not be forgotten when we come to deal with their report, the value of which is not unlikely to be seriously diminished by the manner in which they have set about their enquiries.[131]

'New Light on Commodore Goodenough's Mission to Fiji, 1873-74', *HSANZ*, X (1962), 279.
129 Goodenough and Layard to Kimberley, 13 February (also 20 March) 1874. CO 83/5.
130 See McIntyre, 'New light', 270-288; Drus, 87-110; Scarr, 'Rampant Anglo-Saxons', 361-382; Routledge, 278-293.
131 Min. by Lowther, 10 March 1874, on Aborigines Protection Society to Carnarvon, 7 March 1874. CO 83/5.

The pressure was kept up on the new administration in London. On 7 March 1874 the Aborigines Protection Society sent a deputation (including Kinnaird and both the M'Arthurs) to Lord Carnarvon to present an address of congratulation to the new Secretary of State.[132] William M'Arthur also wrote to Carnarvon on 22 May to urge annexation, enclosing both a letter from Langham to support this view and a copy of his own speech from the second Commons Fiji debate.[133] On 3 July, a three-fold deputation, from the Fiji Committee, WMMS and Aborigines Protection Society waited upon Lord Carnarvon. Along with Lord Belmore, Kinnaird (who held senior honorary positions in both the LMS and the CMS) and M'Arthur, Drs Osborn and Jobson and the Revd W.B. Boyce were the Wesleyan representatives. They 'reminded his Lordship that the missionary had preceded the trader, and made the settlement of a white population possible and safe in what were once cannibal islands'.[134]

In the meantime Goodenough and Layard had obtained, on 20 March 1874, an offer of cession from Cakobau and the chiefs. But the offer was flawed and unacceptable to Britain since it was not unconditional: 'We offer to Her Majesty the Queen the Government of the Islands, but not the soil or the Fijian people, and we trust to her generosity in dealing with us and our children'.[135] In their report, Goodenough and Layard acknowledged the assistance of the missionaries, especially of Langham, and commented favourably on the contribution of the Methodist mission to the development of Fijian civilization.[136] Nevertheless, despite exceeding their instructions and causing embarrassment to the Colonial Office, they had failed to obtain an unconditional cession.

On 17 July 1874, Lord Carnarvon presented Goodenough and Layard's report to the House of Lords. He was not greatly impressed:

> I do not mean to say that the report of the commissioners is ... an altogether satisfactory one. I do not think the calculations of the commissioners are so reliable that we can trust them on all important points, and I do not think that the mode in which the cession is proposed is one to which your Lordships would be disposed to accede.[137]

Referring to Britain's 'indirect duty' to assume responsibility for islands whose problems were largely caused by British citizens, he announced that he was sending Sir Hercules Robinson, Governor of New South Wales, to conclude what Goodenough and Layard had failed to finish. A genuine unconditional

---

132 Address of Congratulation accompanying deputation of Aborigines Protection Society, 7 March 1874. CO 83/5.
133 M'Arthur to Carnarvon, and encs., 22 May 1874. CO 83/5.
134 M'Cullagh, p.177.
135 Goodenough and Layard to Kimberley, 20 March 1874. CO 83/5.
136 Goodenough and Layard's report, 13 April 1874. *PP* 1874 XLV [C.1011].
137 *Hansard*, Third Series, CCXVIII, cols 179-187.

offer of cession would not be declined and he suggested that the best future for Fiji was a Crown colony 'of a rather severe type'. He had intended to share the responsibility for the final decision on Fiji with his Cabinet colleagues, but the Prime Minister would not allow the Cabinet to meet.

Fiji was not the only political hot potato in 1874. The Cabinet was split over the Public Worship Regulation Bill, designed to check the spread of ritualism in the Church of England.[138] The House of Lords had, on 4 August 1874, rejected Commons' amendments to the Bill, and Salisbury and Carnarvon had spoken and voted against it. For Carnarvon the Bill had opened the issue of personal trust between himself and Disraeli. Carnarvon had served on the Ritual Commission from 1868 to 1870, and though deploring ritualism he had differed from the rest of the commission members on the best way to tackle it, refused to sign their report, and issued a minority report of his own. Consequently in 1874, when he was offered a Cabinet place by Disraeli:

> Lord Carnarvon alluded to the possibility of some aggressive measure against the ritualists being urged, and said, that although he had no sympathy with them, he should object to legislation being directed against them, and he trusted that Mr Disraeli would not sanction it. Mr Disraeli entirely assented....[139]

So from Carnarvon's point of view this was neither a difference of opinion nor a matter of religious scruple, but a breach of trust by the Prime Minister affecting the very basis of his agreement to serve in the government. This, he felt, entirely justified his action in joining Salisbury in the Not Content lobby.[140]

It was not, therefore, just the temporary estrangement from Carnarvon and Salisbury, but the whole hornets' nest of the Public Worship Regulation Bill that made Disraeli unwilling to risk a Cabinet at which further fault lines might emerge. Carnarvon's protest against the postponement of the Cabinet and his request that the vital matter of settling the Fijian question should be left in his hands drew a reply from Disraeli. After complaining about the action Carnarvon and Salisbury had taken, he changed his tune, adopting an unconvincingly flattering tone to his errant Colonial Secretary:

> I must leave the matter entirely to your discretion. There is none of my colleagues in whom I have more confidence than yourself, and I always say that your

---

138 Owen Chadwick, *The Victorian Church*, 2 vols, (London: A. & C. Black, 1966, 1970), II, pp.322-325, 348-352, 361-362.
139 A. Hardinge, *Life of Henry Howard Molyneaux Herbert, Fourth Earl of Carnarvon, 1831-90* 3 vols (London: OUP, 1925), II, p.62.
140 With regard to Carnarvon's temperament, it should be remembered that in 1867 Carnarvon had resigned from the previous Conservative ministry over the Reform Bill and that he would resign again in 1878 over the Eastern Question.

administration of your office is most able. I believe too, that is the public opinion.[141]

Whether taken in by the Prime Minister's flattery or not, Carnarvon now had a free hand to conclude the Fijian drama, and the final act was not to be a long one. On 10 August Robinson was telegraphed to proceed to Fiji and to obtain an unconditional offer of cession from the chiefs.[142]

With victory virtually within his grasp, and in order to keep Fiji in the forefront of public attention during the period of hiatus while Sir Hercules Robinson made his way to the islands, M'Arthur moved another motion in the House of Commons on 4 August 1874 calling for annexation of the islands.[143] The empire enthusiast Alexander Baillie-Cochrane, who seconded the motion, took the opportunity to praise the work of the missionaries, without whom the cession would not now be imminent: 'Nothing the Wesleyans might have done in this country in the past century could surpass the remarkable results of their efforts in Fiji'.

It was left to Gladstone to strike a sour note and he claimed that any talk of unanimity among the Fijians on this subject was 'a mockery'. Describing the report of the commissioners he had sent to Fiji as 'one of the most chaotic documents I ever read in my life', he warned of increased expenditure and the possibility of native wars as being the price that might have to be paid for Fiji. Turning to M'Arthur he paid grudging tribute to 'the real but sadly deluded philanthropy of my hon. friend'. M'Arthur, who could afford to be magnanimous in his hour of victory, concluded by expressing his confidence in the government and withdrew his motion.

Sir Hercules Robinson arrived in Fiji on 23 September 1874. Within six weeks he obtained an unconditional offer of cession from Cakobau, had it ratified by the other chiefs, proclaimed Fiji to be British territory, hoisted the Union Jack and formed a caretaker government under Consul Layard.[144] In the midst of this flurry of activity Fiji became a British dependency on 10 October 1874. To the annoyance of the missionaries and to the irritation of Robert Herbert in London, Thurston was included in the caretaker government as colonial secretary.[145] This was partly because he was the most able, experienced European in Fiji and virtually indispensable to effective government there; and partly, no doubt, because Cakobau, who had seen Fiji exploited by so many

---

141 Disraeli to Carnarvon, 8 August 1874. Quoted in Hardinge, II, p.74.
142 Summary of telegrams from Carnarvon to Robinson. *PP* 1875 LII [C.1114].
143 *Hansard*, Third Series, CCXXI, cols 1264-1301.
144 See Robinson to Carnarvon, 3/11/16/17 October and 5 November 1874. CO 83/5.
145 'I cannot help wishing that he could have disposed with Mr Thurston; but I presume he felt that if he discharged the Head Keeper he would at once become a most dangerous poacher'. Min. by Herbert on Robinson to Carnarvon (telegram), 5 November 1874. CO 83/5.

white men, knowing whom he could trust to give a high priority to the interests of the native Fijians, put in a good word for him with Robinson:

> I wish your Excellency to lend no ear to people, whoever they may be – missionaries or others – who may seek to set you against Mr Thurston. He has a good many enemies who will not hesitate to say all bad things of him, but I wish to say that he is a good man, and has been a faithful servant to me, and to Fiji and my people. He is the one man whom I trust before anyone else, and the chiefs repose entire confidence in him.[146]

And so it was Thurston, as colonial secretary, who issued the proclamation which extended the scope of the 1868 Queensland Polynesian Labourers Act to Fiji.[147]

Fiji under British Rule

The first governor of the new Crown colony, Sir Arthur Gordon, son of former Prime Minister, Lord Aberdeen, and a friend and former secretary of Gladstone, arrived in Fiji on 24 June 1875. In fact, the new governor had not been allowed to leave London without a visit from Fiji's 'patron saint'. M'Arthur not only saw Gordon twice in one day as a member of two separate deputations, representing the WMMS and the Aborigines Protection Society, but also 'had, in the interval between the two, some private conversation with Sir Arthur'.[148]

Gordon's first impressions of Fiji were entirely favourable. Commenting to Lord Carnarvon on the Wesleyan missionary organisation he found in place on his arrival, Gordon wrote with admiration of the 'political significance ...[of] ... the really wonderful organization of the Wesleyan body here'. He continued:

> I know nothing equal to it except the Jesuits. In every village there is a *lotu* teacher. The different kinds of superior administration are admirably fitted on to one another and finally the Head at Navoloa has at his command a perfect machinery which enables him to know down to the minutest detail all that is doing in every part of the islands. His statistics and information are far greater than those which the government can obtain....[149]

---

146 Notes of a conversation between Robinson and Cakobau on HMS *Dido*, 25 September 1874, enc. in Robinson to Carnarvon, 3 October 1874. *PP* 1875 LII [C.1114]. See also Goodenough and Layard to Carnarvon (Confidential), 13 April 1874. Confidential Print Australian No.41. CO 881/4.
147 Extract from *Fiji Government Gazette*, 14 October 1874, enc. in Robinson to Carnarvon, 16 October 1874. *PP* 1875 LII [C.1114]. In 1875 the Imperial Parliament extended the Pacific Islanders' Protection Act to Fiji.
148 Extract from M'Arthur's diary for 17 March 1875. Quoted in M'Cullagh, p.190.
149 Gordon to Carnarvon, 21 August 1875, Carnarvon papers, PRO 30/6/39, quoted in Legge, p.25 n.1.

Writing privately to Gladstone the following year, he still had, 'nothing but good to report of the Wesleyan mission. If they have made some mistakes they are but trifles compared with the great work they have accomplished and the beneficial influence they daily exercise'. Once again he spoke of their organisational machinery which had clearly made a great impression on him, and concluded, 'fortunately, the missionaries and I are on the best of terms. They would be very formidable opponents for any government to deal with'.[150]

Although Sir Arthur Gordon endeavoured to maintain good relations with the Wesleyan mission, inevitably they clashed, initially over the missionaries' method of collecting money from the people, and later over land questions and the validity of native (ie non-Methodist) marriages. 'Leave nothing undone on your part to soothe and please them,' he told his subordinate, W.S. Carew. 'Bear in mind that I think their support so important and their enmity so dangerous, that I would sacrifice a great deal to conciliate them'.[151] It was not Gordon's nature to pick a fight with the missionaries, but neither would he shirk one if a matter of good government and lawful authority was involved. The honeymoon period quickly deteriorated into cold war. As with Pritchard and Thurston before him, Sir Arthur Gordon found himself up against the resentment and opposition which the missionaries reserved for able Europeans in positions of authority which they themselves coveted. According to Gordon, Langham began to behave as virtual leader of the opposition, 'his chief effort was to regain his lost ascendancy or, failing that, to destroy what had superseded it'.[152] This time, however, the missionaries could not win. Langham met his match in Gordon, 'an aristocrat by birth and an autocrat by inclination'.[153] The annexation by Britain for which the missionaries had so long prayed, worked, lobbied and manoeuvred meant, ironically, the end of their authority in the non-spiritual realm in Fiji. It was to take time before the missionaries gradually became reconciled to their change of circumstances. Several months after Gordon's tenure of office had ended, Thurston wrote to his former chief lamenting that 'the chief drag upon the progress of the Native Coach is the presence in Fiji of the great political and trading concern of John Wesley and Co.'[154] The observation of the Comaroffs regarding Nonconformist missionaries' attitudes to working under a colonial government in southern

---

150 Gordon to Gladstone, 22 March and 7 June 1876. Quoted in P. Knaplund, 'Sir Arthur Gordon and Fiji: some Gordon – Gladstone Letters', *HSANZ* 8 (1958), 291.
151 Gordon to Carew, 4 November 1878. Carew MSS, quoted in Morell, *Pacific Islands*, p.377.
152 Lord Stanmore, *Fiji: Records of Private and of Public Life, 1875-80* (Edinburgh, 1897), II, p.250, quoted in Morrell, *Pacific Islands*, p.377.
153 Deryck Scarr, *Fragments of Empire* (Canberra: Australian National University Press, 1968), p.24.
154 Thurston to Gordon, 21 March 1881. Stanmore papers 49204, quoted in J.K. Chapman, *Arthur Hamilton Gordon, first Lord Stanmore* (Toronto: University of Toronto Press, 1964), p.198.

Africa, might appropriately be applied to the Fijian context. While such a government 'might give security and support to missionaries, it also curbed their freedom to minister to an unfettered spiritual sovereignty.'[155] But the essential difference was that in Fiji it severely circumscribed the temporal rather than spiritual power they had accrued and exercised in the islands.[156]

Fiji was annexed by Great Britain in October 1874 not because of the desire of the missionaries for colonial status but because of the lawlessness caused by the presence of other Europeans, particularly their involvement with the labour trade. Lord Carnarvon made this clear in his speech to the House of Lords on 17 July 1874, when he described Fiji as,

> a place into which English capital has overflowed, in which English settlers are resident, in which, it must be added, English lawlessness is going on and in which the establishment of English institutions has been unsuccessfully attempted....[157]

Nevertheless, the Methodist missionaries in Fiji played an important role in the development of Fiji as a focus of European and Australian interest. By bringing the situation in the islands to the attention of the British government through their supporters at home, by correspondence, deputations and parliamentary action, they created an irresistible pressure for annexation which convinced two successive Colonial Secretaries that this was the only way to proceed.

The main missionary contribution was their civilising effect on the people of Fiji. The spread of Christianity had an adverse effect on the traditional 'customs' of the Fijians. Cannibalism, and other inhumane practices began to die out as the missionaries increased their influence and authority over the Fijian people. But in this development of civilised values lay the seeds of destruction of Fijian independence. Once they were less likely to be killed and eaten, Europeans began to regard Fiji as an altogether more desirable place for trading and plantation culture. G.C. Henderson has commented that the missionaries 'deserve more credit than has generally been conceded to them for making residence in and travel across the country less dangerous for settlers and traders'.[158] Noting that the very first white visitors to Fiji – sailors, whalers, sandalwood and *bêche-de-mer* traders – had often ill-treated the islanders, he points out that the conduct of the missionaries and their relations with the natives had the opposite effect; for every one of them had the welfare of the natives, as they conceived it, at heart. The natives knew it, respected and liked

---

155 Comaroff and Comaroff, I, p.78.
156 For a brief analysis of the Methodist role in the 1874 annexation see John H. Darch, 'Methodist involvement in the British annexation of Fiji, 1874', *Proceedings of the Wesley Historical Society* 55:5 (2006), 189-196.
157 *Hansard,* Third Series, CCXVIII, col.185.
158 Henderson, *History of Government in Fiji*, I, p.141. The Duke of Newcastle referred to this fact in his instructions to Colonel Smythe, 23 December 1859. Enc. in Sir F. Rogers to Lord Wodehouse, 31 July 1860. CO 83/1.

them for it, and consequently were disposed to treat other white men in the same spirit.[159]

The second role of the missionaries was to make Fiji known to the outside world. The 'Pity Poor Feejee' appeal and countless articles in missionary publications in Britain and Australia raised the profile of these hitherto unknown islands in European consciousness. It can be argued, however, that this subsequently proved to be very much a mixed blessing.

Their third role was to provide information and evidence of the lawlessness of white residents and traders and the inhumanities inflicted upon Fijians and indentured labourers from other Pacific islands. Without this information, the campaign against the labour trade and in favour of annexation could not have been so effectively prosecuted. James Calvert, who acted for many years as the link between the mission in Fiji and influential supporters in Britain, was of particular importance in maintaining contacts even at times when annexation was not on the political agenda. Furthermore, the missionaries were able to assist, by means of their local knowledge and contacts and ability to speak the Fijian language and its dialects, successive commissioners – Smythe, Goodenough and Layard and Robinson – sent by the British government to Fiji.

The Duke of Newcastle's alleged suggestion to W.T. Pritchard in 1859 that it was the Established Church the Methodist missionaries would have to fear in the event of annexation proved to be groundless. It was, in fact, the colonial administration itself which eclipsed any remaining political power and influence the missionaries may have had, and restricted them to a purely educational and spiritual role. The Wesleyan missionaries had been among the foremost proponents of annexation. Ironically, after it had taken place they realised that their informal influence over Cakobau and the chiefs had been replaced by the formal influence and authority of a governor who was less susceptible to their influence and whom they quickly and foolishly alienated despite the initial respect he had for them.

Though the missionary movement as a whole could claim much credit for the civilising and development of Fiji and its absorption into the British empire, it must be said that it was the influential supporters of the missionary movement in Britain, rather than the missionaries in the field, who successfully pressed the government to annex the Fiji Islands to the Crown. In the last analysis, the real influence in bringing about annexation was exerted by William M'Arthur and the alliance of missionary supporters and humanitarians who, well briefed by the missionaries on the ground (with James Calvert as the vital link), were able to use the parliamentary forum to bring pressure to bear on the government to effect in 1874 the annexation which the missionaries had favoured since the 1850s. Ironically, elsewhere in the Pacific, in the eastern half of the vast island of New Guinea, only a comparatively short period of time elapsed between the

---

159 Henderson, *History of Government in Fiji*, I, p.141.

advent of the missionaries and the subsequent arrival of British colonial officials.

CHAPTER 4

The Role of Missionaries in the Events Leading to the Establishment of a British Protectorate in Papua New Guinea

After Greenland, New Guinea, is the second largest island in the world, being 1,500 miles in length and 450 miles wide at its broadest point. It was first sighted by the Portuguese in the early sixteenth century, and named 'New Guinea' by the Spaniard, de Retes, in 1545. Later, some of its coasts were explored by the Dutch who, finding it less inviting and less commercially advantageous than the neighbouring East Indies, largely ignored it until the early nineteenth century. In 1828 the Dutch took formal possession of the southern coast of the western half of the island, apparently to forestall any possible British use of the island which would have adversely affected Dutch control over the trade in spices and other exotic products of the East Indies. Twenty years later the Dutch confirmed their sovereignty over all the island west of longitude 141 degrees East.[1]

Papua, the eastern, non-Dutch part of New Guinea received several visits from the Royal Navy. In 1842-46 HMS *Fly* under Captain Blackwood surveyed the Gulf of Papua, and in 1846-50 Captain Owen Stanley explored the south-east coast of the island and the Louisiade Archipelago in HMS *Rattlesnake*. Indeed, a proclamation of British sovereignty of the non-Dutch part of the island was made by Lt. Yule of HMS *Bramble* in 1846, though this was never ratified by the British government.[2]

By far the most important voyage of discovery, however, was made by Captain John Moresby in HMS *Basilisk* in the years 1871 to 1874.[3] Moresby explored and charted large areas of the south-east coast of Papua and the adjacent islands to the east. It was he who discovered and charted the China Strait and then moved north-westwards along the north coast. As he was the first European to view a large number of hitherto unknown physical features, it

---

1 For a brief summary of this early period of European exploration see Morrell, *Pacific Islands,* pp.238-240. More detail is given in Gordon, Ch.1 and 2.
2 Admiralty to CO, 14 October 1873. CO 309/111.
3 See Moresby, *Discoveries and Surveys* (London: J. Murray, 1876).

fell to Moresby to give them European names and so the map of Papua New Guinea became littered with the names of Victorian politicians, colonial governors and naval officers. Thus, Ward Hunt Straits separate Cape Vogel from Goodenough Island; Goschen Straits separate Normanby Island from the mainland; and Cape Nelson separates Collingwood Bay from Dyke Ackland Bay. The most auspicious were the 11,000 feet twin peaks of Mount Gladstone and Mount Disraeli in the Finisterre range.[4] But from the point of view of both missionary and imperial expansion Moresby's greatest contribution was his discovery on 20 February 1873 of Port Moresby.[5] This site was to be the key to the opening up of New Guinea. Within nine months four Polynesian teachers of the LMS had been located there and before the following year was out the first white missionary on the mainland of New Guinea was in residence at Port Moresby.[6] Moresby not only explored, charted and named important parts of Papua, but on 24 April 1873 he took 'formal possession of our discoveries in the name of Her Majesty. Such a course secured postponement of occupation by any Power till our Government could consider its own interests...'.[7] The Colonial Office concurred with this action, Robert Herbert minuting:

> Capt. Moresby would appear ... to have done rightly in claiming for this country the territory.... Otherwise another power might have stepped in and taken the part most valuable and nearest to Australia.[8]

Herbert, a former Premier of Queensland, entirely understood the colonial mind with regard to the future of New Guinea. He was instrumental in forming

---

4 When Moresby wrote to the two party leaders to ask their permission to use their names, Gladstone replied with all due seriousness. Disraeli, however, commented on Moresby's choice of 'a godfather so distinguished for the peak which faces Mount Disraeli' and remarked that 'I hope we shall agree better in New Guinea than we do in the House of Commons'. Disraeli to Moresby, 17 April 1874. Quoted in John Moresby, *Two Admirals* (London: J. Murray, 1909), pp.368-369.

5 This natural harbour with a couple of small villages is today the capital of the independent state of Papua New Guinea, with a population of 155,000. Most commentators assume that Moresby reserved his own name for his greatest discovery, but he makes it clear that it is named after his father, Admiral of the Fleet Sir Fairfax Moresby (1786-1877). Moresby, *Two Admirals*, pp.302-303. See also Ian Stuart, *Port Moresby, Yesterday and Today* (Sydney: Pacific Publications, 1970), Ch.1.

6 Morrell, p.241; Lawes to Mullens, 4 December 1874. LMS Papua Correspondence, 1/2/C.

7 Moresby, *Discoveries and Surveys*, pp.207-208. Paul Knaplund clearly misunderstood the nature of Moresby's action and is misleading when he states that 'this act was disavowed by the imperial authorities'. Knaplund, *Gladstone's Foreign Policy* (New York: Harper & Bros, 1935), p.100.

8 Min. by Herbert, 15 October 1873 on Admiralty to CO, 14 October 1873. CO 309/111.

opinions on the subject in the Colonial Office and his concern that 'another power' might steal a march on Britain in an area where Australia's vital interests were allegedly at risk was to be a constant refrain in the years leading up to Britain's establishment of a protectorate over, and then the formal annexation of, Papua New Guinea, the south-eastern part of the island.

Certainly Moresby's explorations and the publicity attendant upon them together with the ensuing establishment of a mission base at Port Moresby by the London Missionary Society, served to generate interest about this large undeveloped island, in both Britain and Australia. And while the Royal Navy continued surveying the coasts and offshore islands of Papua, it was the missionaries of the LMS who, without outside assistance, set about the work of opening up the interior. Earlier French and Italian Roman Catholic missionaries who established short-lived mission stations on Woodlark (Murua) and Rooke Islands in the east, between 1847 and 1855, had left the mainland well alone.[9] The location and fate of two German missionaries who apparently went to New Guinea in 1855, is unknown.[10]

According to both W.P. Morrell and the Revd Joseph King (the biographer of W.G. Lawes) the idea of a New Guinea mission by the LMS had first been mooted by the Revd John Jones in 1870.[11] King suggests the source of inspiration was one Captain Banner of the *Blue Belle* who called on Jones in the Loyalty Islands in 1866 and offered the use of his vessel if the LMS decided to open up a mission field in the islands of the Torres Straits. Subsequently on furlough in England in 1870, Jones suggested New Guinea to Dr Mullens, the Society's Foreign Secretary, as an alternative location for a colleague, Samuel McFarlane, whose position on Lifu was becoming increasingly untenable in the face of French opposition. Accurate as this scenario may be, others had already considered the possibility of a New Guinea mission. Richard Lovett, the official historian of the LMS, states that 'the project had long been before the mind of the Directors at home, and on the hearts of many of the missionaries in Western Polynesia'.[12] Certainly J.P. Sunderland, the Society's representative in Australia, had mentioned New Guinea as a potential mission field to Dr Mullens in both 1869 and 1870.[13] Although the letter is no longer extant, it is known

---

9 Morrell, *Pacific Islands*, pp.240-241.
10 M.E. Townsend, *Origins of Modern German Colonialism, 1871-1885* (New York: Columbia University, 1921), pp.34-35.
11 Morrell, p.241; J. King, *W.G. Lawes of Savage Island and New Guinea* (London: Religious Tract Society, 1909), pp.48-50.
12 Lovett, *History of LMS*, I, p.431.
13 Sunderland to Mullens, 26 March 1869 and 25 February 1870. LMS Australian Correspondence, Box 7.

from the published reply that Samuel McFarlane had also written to Bishop Patteson on the subject of a mission to New Guinea.[14]

For McFarlane, stationed at Lifu in the Loyalty Islands since 1859, the arrival of French troops in 1864 had presented problems.[15] The intolerant attitude of the French commandant and the reciprocal stubbornness of the missionary resulted in conflict and, by 1869, a French demand for his removal. Despite much correspondence between British and French governments, the directors of the LMS bowed to the inevitable and removed McFarlane from Lifu.[16] Thus McFarlane, with A.W. Murray, boarded the *Surprise*, 'to make a prospective voyage to New Guinea before proceeding to England, so that upon my arrival in the old country I might be in a position to lay before the directors such information as would enable them to mature their plans'.[17]

After the conclusion of the voyage of the *Surprise*, McFarlane returned to England on furlough and Murray, on returning to the Loyalty Islands, was instructed to take charge of the embryonic New Guinea mission.[18] Meanwhile, in London, Samuel McFarlane presented his proposals for the mission to the LMS Directors on 23 December 1872. They resolved to establish the mission's initial headquarters on Cape York, to appoint at least three English missionaries to the field, and to service the mission with a small steam vessel.[19]

In fact, during the voyage of the *Surprise* McFarlane and Murray had not merely carried out a reconnaissance of the Torres Straits islands and the southern coast of Papua, they had also landed Polynesian Christians, the so-called 'native teachers' (from the training institution on Lifu), on Darnley and other islands in July 1871 to begin the work of evangelisation. Further Polynesian teachers, this time from Rarotonga as well as Lifu, were placed on both the Torres Straits islands and on the mainland of New Guinea in the autumn of 1872.[20]

The role of Polynesian 'native' teachers in missionary strategy in the South Seas has already been discussed.[21] In New Guinea the strategy was not without human cost – the native teachers perhaps suffered more than elsewhere and the

---

14 See Patteson to McFarlane, 12 April 1871, marked 'not sent' and printed as Appendix III in Yonge, II, p.591. See also Chapter XXVII of McFarlane's *The Story of the Lifu Mission* (London: J. Nisbet, 1873).
15 For missionary accounts of the French landing and the effect on the mission see S.M. Creagh to LMS, 13 June 1864, James Sleigh to LMS, 7 July 1864, and Samuel McFarlane to LMS, 20 June (continued 22 August) 1864. LMS South Seas Letters, Box 30.
16 McFarlane, Chs XI to XXI.
17 McFarlane, p.345. For the voyage of the Surprise see 'Journal of a Missionary Voyage to New Guinea', in McFarlane, pp.355-386.
18 Lovett, *History of LMS*, I, p.440.
19 King, pp.59-60.
20 Lovett, *History of LMS*, I, 437-438, 442-446.
21 See Chapter 1, above.

mission was criticised by observers for leaving the teachers in such a hostile environment, inadequately provided for and without effective means of communication. Captain Moresby of HMS *Basilisk* gained a closer view than most of the condition of the Polynesian teachers, some dead, some having fled from their posts, some starving and some just managing to survive. He was able to rescue those who survived providing either food or transport back to Murray's headquarters at Somerset on Cape York. Though conscious of the 'vast benefits [that] have resulted from missionary enterprise in the South Seas', he was strongly critical of the mission (and especially Murray) for 'a culpable want of foresight ... in occupying so large a field of mission labour by native teachers without any properly organised system for their due support'.[22] Lovett suggests the cause of this neglect of the Polynesian teachers was that at this initial stage of the mission there was no mission vessel, and that Murray was reliant on being able to charter a small ship whenever he required one. But during the first half of 1873, a critical time for the native teachers and also the time when the *Basilisk* was in the area, all vessels had been required by the Queensland government to proceed to Brisbane in order to be licensed in compliance with the Pacific Islanders' Protection Act.[23]

The absence of ships from the Torres Straits for a few months in 1873 does not entirely absolve the LMS for the conditions endured by its Polynesian teachers. The arrival in November 1874 of the *Ellengowan*, the 36 ton mission steamer, however, radically improved communications and made the strategy of scattered mission settlements more viable.[24] Nevertheless, as late as 1878 Henry Chester, the Queensland police magistrate in the Torres Straits islands, wrote a critical letter to the *Sydney Morning Herald*. He criticised the mission's treatment of its native teachers, 'dropped here and there along an unhealthy coast with £15 p.a. living expenses'.[25]

James Chalmers, in turn both the heroic figure and later the martyr of the New Guinea Mission, was conscious of the drawbacks of using Polynesian teachers. He was also aware of the mission's shortcomings with regard to its treatment and use of the teachers as cheap missionary labour. After the Kalo massacre in March 1881 when ten Polynesian teachers were murdered, he commented:

---

22 See Moresby, *Discoveries and Surveys*, pp.33-5, 163-165. Also Moresby to Murray, 20 March 1873. LMS Papua Correspondence 1/1/B. Murray's attitude to Moresby was ambivalent. Cf. Murray to Mullens, 27 January 1873 with Murray to Mullens, 11 March 1873. LMS Papua Correspondence 1/1/A.
23 Lovett, *History of LMS*, I, p.445.
24 See McFarlane's article on the Ellengowan in the LMS *Chronicle*, January 1880, pp.3-5.
25 Chester to *Sydney Morning Herald*, published 24 September 1878. Quoted in Morrell, p.245. Chester's criticism is all the more likely to be accurate since he was a good friend of the missionaries and especially of Chalmers. See Lawes to Whitehouse, 7 April 1883. LMS Papua Correspondence 3/2/C.

> I fear we are not altogether free from blame; the teachers are often very indiscreet in their dealings with the natives and not over-careful in what they say; there has also perhaps sometimes been a niggard regard to expense on our part. A very few pounds spent at a station like Kalo in the first years would, I believe, prevent much trouble, and probably murder.[26]

British Government Awareness of New Guinea

Lord Carnarvon had been Colonial Secretary for only a month when a letter concerning New Guinea arrived on his desk. In contrast with the decisions which were being made about the imperial frontier elsewhere in the tropics – in Fiji, in Malaya and in West Africa – the future of New Guinea did not seem particularly important. The Colonial Office, after all, received a regular flow of correspondence from individuals who had personal interests which rarely coincided with the national interest. Unlike most such letters, this one – from Francis P. de Labilliere, an Australian barrister resident in London – merited some attention. He argued for British annexation of New Guinea in the interests of the Australian colonies (strategic importance), the Papuan peoples ('to leave the Papuans would be their certain destruction – Fiji is a warning against that') and the imperial exchequer (any expenditure would soon be recouped by the value of trade and of natural resources). He concluded:

> Only three things can happen to New Guinea: it may be left as it is, or be annexed by a foreign power, or by Great Britain. The first is out of the question ... the second would be the most undesirable for us; and that, therefore, the third remains our only alternative.[27]

The timing of Labilliere's letter is interesting. It is probable that he was representing interested parties in Australia by his letter, yet it contained no information not available the previous year. Had Labilliere waited for the advent of a Conservative ministry, imagining that Carnarvon would be more sympathetic to his request than his Liberal predecessor?

Certainly the initial response by the Colonial Office was not unfavourable. Robert Herbert, Permanent Under-Secretary, minuted with obvious enthusiasm:

> This is a much more important question to the Australian colonies and to the Empire than that of the annexation of Fiji. The great wealth and extent of New Guinea and its proximity to Australia render the question of its ownership a

---

26 J. Chalmers and W.W. Gill, *Work and Adventure in New Guinea* (London: Religious Tract Society, 1885), p.209. For an account of the massacre see T. Beswick to Wardlaw Thompson, 24 March 1881. LMS Papua Correspondence 2/5/A.
27 Labilliere to Carnarvon, 26 March 1874. Confidential Print Australian No.47. CO 881/4.

somewhat pressing one.... I do not at all anticipate that the occupation of New Guinea if judiciously entered upon need be very costly. If a settlement ... were made on the South Eastern and healthy part of the coast and our ships were employed to control and regulate trading operations we should probably spend much less than by letting matters drift until we have to interfere, and probably fight, on a large scale.[28]

Indeed, throughout the deliberations on New Guinea (ten years elapsed between the receipt of Labilliere's letter and the proclamation of the British Protectorate), Herbert showed a clear interest in acquiring Papua New Guinea for Britain. His experience as an Australian colonial premier clearly gave him sympathy for the views of the Australians, but he nevertheless was able to rise above the narrow confines of Australian opinion and take an imperial over-view of the subject.

Lord Carnarvon was sufficiently impressed either by Labilliere's arguments or Herbert's advocacy of the case, or with both, to send, within a month, a circular despatch to the governors of the Australian colonies, with a copy of Labilliere's letter, inviting their observations on the matter.[29] The response from Sir Hercules Robinson of New South Wales contained another letter which indicated that Labilliere was not the first person to advocate British involvement in New Guinea. The enclosure was a letter received by G.A. Lloyd, the Treasurer of New South Wales, from W. Wyatt Gill, LMS missionary on Rarotonga in the Cook Islands, who had been involved in supplying Polynesian teachers for the New Guinea mission. Gill's letter, dated 28 January 1873, fourteen months before Labilliere's and presumably pigeon-holed and almost forgotten in Sydney, might never have come to light had not Carnarvon sent the circular despatch to the Australian governors. Gill's concern was for the future development of the island and that, 'should New Guinea fall into hostile hands, the key of the Torres Straits would be lost ...'. He continued:

I do trust that the eyes of the Colonies and of distant Imperial Government will be open to watch the movements of German and of other expeditions. At any cost (save the dire curse of war) let not the rich prize fall into other hands. All I desire at present for New Guinea is that she may be kept free from any power alien to Britain

---

28 Min. by Herbert, 3 April 1874, on Labilliere to Carnarvon, 26 March 1874. CO 234/34. See also Herbert to Carnarvon, 10 April 1874, British Library Add. Mss. 60791; quoted in Bruce Knox, 'The Earl of Carnarvon, Empire, and Imperialism, 1855–90,' *JICH*, 26 (1998), 48–66.
29 Circular to Governors of Australian Colonies, 17 April 1874. *PP* 1876 LIV [C.1566].

and Australia. Meantime we hope gradually, by means of missionary and commercial enterprise, to open up this vast, unknown country.[30]

Gill claimed to write, 'as an individual and not representing any religious society whatever'. The views he expressed were more imperialistic than those normally associated with LMS missionaries, who usually adopted an isolationist, anti-imperialist stance, opposing annexation of any kind in the interests of the aboriginal people (but where annexation was impossible to avoid, preferred Britain as the colonial power). Where it existed – as in New Guinea – missionary paternalism of native peoples was a forerunner of the principle of trusteeship that was to be of such importance in parts of the British Empire in later years. Despite the provisions of the Pacific Islanders' Protection Act, the labour trade had not abated and kidnapping was still taking place in parts of the south-west Pacific.[31] Thus, humanitarian groups, frequently allies of the missionaries, were not slow to take an interest in New Guinea as increased publicity (not to mention its proximity to Queensland) made it vulnerable to the attentions of the labour ships.[32]

This process was hastened by a paper given to the Royal Colonial Institute on 'Great Britain and New Guinea' on 16 March 1875 by Archibald Michie, Agent-General of Victoria,[33] which was also indicative of the growing Australian interest in New Guinea in the aftermath of Moresby's voyage and its attendant publicity. In the discussion which followed this paper, speakers included Captain Moresby, Sir George Bowen, the Governor of Victoria, Francis de Labilliere and, from the missionary movement, Dr Joseph Mullens and Arthur Kinnaird. Michie's plea for early annexation was treated cautiously by Moresby, Kinnaird and especially Mullens, who expressed concern for the welfare of the native Papuans. But this was clearly a minority view, and in the following month the Institute's deputation to Lord Carnarvon (which included Labilliere, F.W. Chesson and William M'Arthur) requested that 'the authority of the British government should without delay be extended' to non-Dutch New Guinea.[34]

What also exercised the humanitarians was the threat of commercial expeditions to New Guinea which would, in their view, be highly detrimental to

---

30 W.W. Gill to G.A. Lloyd, 28 July 1873. Enc. in Lloyd to Robinson, 31 July 1874. Confidential Print Australian No. 47. CO 881/4.31
31 See, for example, Herbert's comments on 'the really great disgrace which is brought upon the flag by the unchecked barbarities of British subjects'. Min., 3 April 1874, on Labilliere to Carnarvon, 26 March 1874. CO 234/34.
32 See Docker, Ch.8.
33 *PRCI*, VI (1874-5), 120-40. Michie's paper was not the first given to a learned society on the subject of New Guinea. On 24 November 1873 W. Wyatt Gill had given his paper, 'Three Visits to New Guinea', to the Royal Geographical Society. *JRGS*, 44 (1874), 15-30.
34 R.C.I. to Carnarvon and Deputation, 21 April 1875. *PP* 1876 LIV [C.1566].

the welfare of the Papuans. A New Guinea Company had been formed in Sydney as far back as 1867. Its approach to the New South Wales government had been unsuccessful, as was a subsequent approach to the Colonial Office and the project never got off the ground. C.B. Adderley, the Conservative Parliamentary Under-Secretary, minuted on 5 August 1867: 'decline to have anything to do with it'. His advice was followed by his superior, the Duke of Buckingham. In the draft reply, the project was refused any official approval, and its advocates told not to 'look for aid or protection from the National Forces'. They were also informed that the title to any land acquired would not be recognised. But, with remarkable prescience, Buckingham deleted this last part from the draft, commenting 'I think the last paragraph goes a little too far if twenty years hence this country colonises it ...'. His timescale was almost perfect: New Guinea became a British protectorate seventeen years after he wrote, and was annexed to the Crown a further four years after that.[35]

Another expedition, ill equipped and ill-fated, and calling itself the New Guinea Prospecting Association, left Sydney in 1872 on board the *Maria,* but its rapid failure left Moresby to rescue the survivors.[36] In the autumn of 1875, a body calling itself the New Guinea Colonizing Association, led by one R.H. Armit, attempted, unsuccessfully, to solicit support from the Colonial Office.[37] This last proposed expedition was the catalyst for a request from the Anti-Slavery Society to be allowed to send a deputation to Lord Carnarvon to 'present ... to your Lordship an address in reference to the expedition now being fitted out for New Guinea, especially to the proposed seizure of one thousand square miles of the island, for allotment among the adventurers, without reference to the rights of the natives'.[38] The deputation which waited upon the Colonial Secretary on 17 November 1875 had a strong representation from the LMS, including Dr Joseph Mullens, the Society's foreign secretary, and A.W. Murray who had left New Guinea the previous year. An important link between the LMS and the Anti-Slavery Society was the secretary of the latter, the Revd Aaron Buzacott, himself the son and namesake of a highly respected LMS missionary, who had served for many years at Rarotonga in the Cook Islands. This deputation was indicative of the relationship between missionaries and humanitarians as far as New Guinea was concerned. Unlike Fiji, where there had been collaboration and concerted action, here we see no more than a common interest, an overlap between the two groups as both sought to protect the Papuan people from the worst excesses of white exploitation.

---

35 Sir John Young to Duke of Buckingham, 31 May 1867, and encs. and mins. Buckingham to Young (draft), 14 September 1867. CO 201/542. See also Gordon, pp.82-83.
36 *Ibid.,* pp.83-87. Moresby, Discoveries and Surveys, pp.38-48.
37 See New Guinea Colonizing Association to Carnarvon, 9 October and 3 November 1875, and replies. Confidential Print Australian No.52. CO 881/4.
38 Anti-Slavery Society to Carnarvon, 11 November 1875. *PP* 1876 LIV [C.1566].

In the summer of 1875, between the visits of the two deputations, the Colonial Office was moving towards a decision on New Guinea with the New Guinea Colonizing Association's proposed quasi-military expedition giving the matter added urgency in the autumn. Communications to both the Foreign Office (6 August) and the Admiralty (21 August) indicated how far Carnarvon was prepared to go while keeping an open mind on the subject. The Admiralty was requested to survey the coast of New Guinea immediately opposite to Cape York in order to have a suitable site for a possible settlement prepared should the need arise.[39] Much more revealing, however, was the letter to the Foreign Office dated 6 August. In a remarkably frank communication from one government department to another, and one which was requested to 'be brought under the special attention of Lord Derby', Herbert was candid about Britain's possible choices with regard to New Guinea:

> Lord Carnarvon is disposed to think that it may be desirable to request the Admiralty to instruct one of their officers to proceed forthwith to the southern coast of New Guinea adjacent to Queensland, and to formally hoist the British flag, and proclaim Her Majesty's sovereignty over such parts of New Guinea and, so far as it is not claimed by the Dutch, at the place or places affording the greatest advantages for shipping, commercial and other purposes of colonisation.
>
> Such declaration of sovereignty need not involve any further immediate action.... It is clear that this district *must ultimately be possessed by Great Britain* [my italics], and if through delay it falls into the hands of some other Power very grave complaints will be made. It may be necessary to purchase it (if possible) at whatever cost.[40]

In the meantime, W.R. Malcolm of the Colonial Office investigated the advantages and disadvantages of possible annexation of New Guinea. His memorandum on the subject appeared in October 1875. Malcolm was clearly unimpressed with any urgency or desirability to annex New Guinea, and concluded:

> It would seem then,
> 1. that as a place for colonization New Guinea is useless.
> 2. that the command of the Torres Straits is already in the hands of England.
> 3. that Capt. Moresby's new route has not hitherto shown to be of any use.
> 4. that there is no reason to suppose any foreign power contemplates annexing New Guinea.[41]

---

39 CO to Admiralty, 21 August 1875. Confidential Print Australian No.53. CO 881/4.
40 *Ibid.*, CO to FO, 6 August 1875.
41 W.R. Malcolm, Memorandum on the Question of the Annexation of New Guinea, October 1875. Confidential Print Australian No.51. CO 881/4.

Between the measured enthusiasm of Herbert and the scepticism of Malcolm, Carnarvon was able to assert that, whatever the long-term desirability of acquiring New Guinea, the time for annexation had not yet come. By 8 December 1875 his decision to leave New Guinea well alone for the present time was communicated to the Australian colonies in a despatch to Sir Hercules Robinson.[42] Carnarvon discounted the Australian arguments for annexation, especially their claim that the annexation of New Guinea would benefit the empire as a whole, frankly admitting that 'it is simply impossible either for me to admit ... or to persuade the English people that the Australian colonies have no special interest in New Guinea'. But it is significant that he undertook to keep the matter under review and did not rule out future annexation when circumstances might make it appropriate.

Development of the LMS Mission

So, for the time being, the flag did not follow the mission and the pioneer LMS missionaries were left undisturbed in New Guinea. However, as the mission began to prosper and to grow, the increase in mission personnel led to important differences of opinion concerning the strategy of the mission. Samuel McFarlane served in New Guinea from 1871 until 1885, but he was a missionary of the old school; New Guinea was his last overseas posting, and he had a highly contentious temperament.[43] One can only guess at how much his temperament was a contributory factor in the dispute with the French in Lifu. After the retirement of Murray in 1874, McFarlane was next in seniority, but Murray's replacement was one of a younger breed of missionaries, with different ideas about mission work.

W.G. Lawes, though only thirty-five when he arrived in New Guinea in December 1874, was already a highly experienced missionary. He had served for ten years on the Pacific island of Niue ('Savage Island') and was the first white missionary to reside on the mainland of New Guinea.[44] At first the magnitude of the task nearly overwhelmed him,[45] and he quickly learned that Murray's assessment of the mission's initial success was wildly over-optimistic.[46] Lawes' self-imposed motto was 'preach, teach, translate' and those three imperatives were the keynote of his ministry in Papua. His gift for

---

42 Carnarvon to Robinson, 8 December 1875. Confidential Print Australian, No.53. CO 881/4.
43 One such example was his falling out with the other passengers on board the ship Mermerus in Australian waters in 1874. See McFarlane to Whitehouse, 23 June 1874. LMS Papua Correspondence 1/2/A.
44 King, *op. cit.*, is a detailed biography of Lawes.
45 'I feel already how utterly powerless we are, how unable to reach the hearts of this people'. Lawes to Mullens, 30 December 1874. LMS Papua Correspondence 1/2/C.
46 Lawes to Mullens, 12 January 1875. LMS Papua Correspondence 1/3/A.

languages was of paramount importance to the mission. Within four months he was able to read a prepared sermon in the indigenous language; within seven months he could 'now preach to the people with some freedom'.[47] Lawes tackled the task of reducing the Papuan languages to writing and then to print. His correspondence with LMS headquarters in London contains selections of this printing, of which he was clearly proud. His educational work, training the Papuan native teachers at the Port Moresby Institute, did much for the indigenization of Christianity in New Guinea. As soon as was practicably possible, the Christian faith was to become the religion of New Guinea and not the 'white man's religion'. Lawes' ministry, over a forty-year period, was the backbone of the LMS mission to New Guinea.

In October 1877, Lawes was joined by James Chalmers who came to New Guinea direct from Rarotonga in the Cook Islands, where he had served since 1867. His task was to superintend the extension of the mission in the south east of the island and to penetrate the interior. Chalmers was a born pioneer, an affable, warm-hearted Scot, who later achieved unsought fame in New Guinea and became the mission's first European martyr.[48] His colleague Wyatt Gill described him as 'the Livingstone of New Guinea'.[49] Near the end of his life, at a gathering in Edinburgh to celebrate the centenary of the LMS, Sir William MacGregor, first Governor of British New Guinea, lauded Chalmers as 'the greatest explorer of the LMS, the discoverer of the Purari river, the Apostle of the Papuan gulf'.[50] Chalmers was an unconventional missionary, describing himself with some relish to his future second wife as 'a very unclerical bronzed wayfarer'.[51] Hugh Romilly, Sir Arthur Gordon's deputy in the Western Pacific High Commission, concurred, describing Chalmers as 'a capital fellow [but] utterly unlike a missionary'. By way of supporting evidence he continued, 'I overhauled his wardrobe by force the other day, and found that he had not even got a black coat and tie'.[52] In the late Victorian period Chalmers came to be lauded in church circles as the 'missionary hero' of New Guinea. Indeed, D.C. Gordon, from a non-partisan stance, regarded him as 'the dominating personality there for many years'.[53] Through deputation speaking and addresses

---

47 Lawes to Mullens, 5 July 1875. LMS Papua Correspondence 1/3/C. Even three years later, Lawes was alone among Europeans in understanding the aboriginal languages. See Mullens to Hicks Beach, 3 June 1878. *PP* 1883 XLVIII [C.3617].
48 Several biographies of Chalmers suffer from the fact that he was a legend in his own lifetime and even more of one after his martyrdom. Lovett is by far the best of these early ones since it is based on Chalmers' own writings. More recently, Langmore's *Tamate* avoids the hagiographical streak of earlier writers, but is limited to the period of his life in New Guinea.
49 Lovett, *Chalmers*, p.166.
50 *Ibid.*, p.420.
51 *Ibid.*, p.231.
52 *Ibid.*, p.243.
53 Gordon, p.66.

to learned societies when he was in Britain on rare furloughs[54] and through the publication of articles and books, Chalmers unintentionally became something of a celebrity and his name came to be inextricably linked with New Guinea in the same way as David Livingstone is with central Africa, Hudson Taylor with China, Robert Moffat with southern Africa and Bishop Patteson with Melanesia.

In this period, other mission personnel arrived in Papua New Guinea, but also departed with alarming rapidity. In the eleven years from 1874 to 1885, eight missionaries were appointed to the field, but none lasted more than three years, with the exception of Lawes and Chalmers, who remained at their posts until the twentieth century dawned.[55] Of the quick turn round of the others – some could not cope with the climate, others could not cope with McFarlane, still others had family tragedies or difficulties – only Lawes and Chalmers survived and thrived, in Papua New Guinea. The two formed a remarkable partnership, each complementing the other in their skills and characteristics. If the LMS mission to New Guinea in the last quarter of the nineteenth century is viewed in cricketing metaphor, then Chalmers was the gifted, adventurous, flowing stroke-player, Lawes the solid, equally gifted batsman who was content to play the reliable sheet-anchor role, quietly and without fuss, accumulating runs in business-like fashion, while his companion grabbed the headlines by scoring in flamboyant fours and sixes.

It was understandable that these two younger missionaries would have their disagreements with McFarlane and that a debate on mission strategy would develop. Of course, the standard mission strategy of seeking the permission and protection of friendly chiefs was employed, but Papuan society was inchoate on a Melanesian rather than a Polynesian model. A chiefdom would often be no more than one village. There were no paramount chiefs over large areas as in Fiji and no-one like Cakobau claiming, albeit unconvincingly, overall authority.[56] In New Guinea the conversion of a chief was no guarantee of any further conversions.

Two differing views developed on the strategy which the mission should adopt.[57] The first was that favoured by McFarlane as it had been by Murray. From headquarters in the Torres Straits, first Darnley Island then from 1877 Murray Island, the evangelisation of the mainland was to take place.

---

54 Chalmers dreaded the thought of deputation speaking and even asked to be excused it, until he discovered that he was actually an extremely effective deputation speaker and that large congregations in Britain hung upon his every word. See Chalmers to Whitehouse, 9 January 1883. LMS Papua Correspondence 3/2/B; and Basil Matthews, *Dr Ralph Wardlaw Thompson* (London: Religious Tract Society, 1917), p.127. Most notable of his addresses to learned societies were those given to the Royal Colonial Institute and to the Royal Geographical Society in 1887.
55 Lovett, *History of LMS*, I, Appendix I, p.797.
56 See Lawes to Sir Arthur Gordon, 20 January 1878. Quoted in King, p.168.
57 *Lovett, History of LMS*, I, pp.447-49.

McFarlane's admiration and respect for Bishop Patteson and his methods led him to desire to imitate, on Murray Island, the Melanesian Mission's use of Norfolk Island as a training centre for Papuan youths, who would then return to the mainland as trained Christian teachers.[58] To this end the Papuan Gulf Native College was inaugurated in 1879. This strategy, which was highly effective over the countless scattered islands of the Anglican Diocese of Melanesia did not transplant so successfully to New Guinea. As late as 1899 the official history of the LMS confessed that 'the results have not yet vindicated the Murray Island scheme'.[59]

An alternative strategy was favoured by Lawes and Chalmers: rather than seeking to run the mission at a distance from an off-shore island, they favoured a more 'hands-on' approach. Their view was that missionary work in New Guinea could be done effectively only by living among and with the people. As with the McFarlane strategy, native teachers were the key to effective mission work, but they should be supported and encouraged by regular visits and even longer stays by the white missionaries. Instead of taking likely youths away from their heathen environment to Murray Island for education and training, Lawes and Chalmers wished to train at Port Moresby only those natives already influenced by Christianity and who were trying to understand it more deeply. In this strategy Lawes was to be the trainer at Port Moresby, while Chalmers, in addition to his exploration and church planting, engaged in a peripatetic apostolic ministry linking the increasing number of mission stations in southeast New Guinea.

But the debate, though conducted in gentlemanly fashion, was clearly far from amicable. McFarlane was not only highly contentious but also critical of his colleagues. As well as clashing over mission strategy, he disagreed with his colleagues over the use of tobacco, which Lawes and Chalmers maintained was a strategic matter. Lawes, though a non-smoker himself, defended and even advocated the use of tobacco as a currency and a means of influence:

> Each teacher uses about 120lbs of tobacco a year – it really is the currency here. Houses and churches are built with it, boats are pulled by it, gardens and fences made with it .... It is the sign of peace and friendship, the key which opens the door for better things, and (as I so often stated in England) the shortest way to a New Guinean's heart is through his tobacco pipe.[60]

---

58 McFarlane to Mullens, 22 May 1879. LMS Papua Correspondence 2/3/C.
59 Lovett, History of LMS, p.448. Chalmers commented, somewhat tartly, 'Mac stands at the portals and only occasionally looks in'. Chalmers to J.L. Green, 29 March 1884. LMS Papua Personal, Box 1.
60 Lawes to Whitehouse, 6 February 1883. LMS Papua Correspondence 3/2/B. See also Lovett, Chalmers, pp.214-218.

The gregarious Chalmers, who enjoyed a tot of whisky as well as his pipe, frequently smoked with native peoples in order to win their confidence and trust. Disagreements, in typical missionary fashion, were aired in their despatches to their headquarters in London.

McFarlane was also unpopular because of his authoritarian manner and lack of consideration for his colleagues, whom he treated with scant respect.[61] One clear example has survived in Lawes' complaint to Dr Mullens of 8 October 1877.[62] At issue appears to have been the treatment afforded to Lawes and William Turner and his wife after they retired from Port Moresby to McFarlane's residence in Somerset, Queensland to recover from an attack of fever. Mrs Turner died and her husband left the mission field, though whether her death was from the effects of fever or of her concurrent pregnancy is not clear. What is clear is that Lawes' sympathy was firmly on the side of the Turners. He accused McFarlane of accommodating Mrs Turner in a bedroom unfit for a lady near her confinement, of a clear lack of welcome or sympathy with their plight and of 'Mr McFarlane's treatment of Mr Turner [which] seemed to me to be harsh and overbearing in the extreme – assuming the tone of a superior officer to his subordinate'. Whatever the veracity of Lawes' accusations, they are indicative of a clear breakdown of relations between brother missionaries.[63] Since no consensus, or even a friendly agreement to differ, was ever achieved, the district committee of the New Guinea mission hardly ever met and, despite constant chiding from LMS headquarters, the two parts of the mission drifted apart and ran virtually separately until McFarlane's return to Britain in 1885.[64]

Britain's Interest Develops

Lord Carnarvon's decision in December 1875 to proceed no further with any request from Australia to annex New Guinea was certainly not the end of the matter and is best understood as no more than an interim decision. That the Colonial Office continued to keep the matter under review in keeping with

---

61 Extract from Fanny Lawes' diary, quoted in Diane Langmore, *Missionary Lives: Papua, 1874-1914* (Honolulu: University of Hawaii Press, 1989), pp.189-190. See also Langmore, *Tamate*, pp.32-33.
62 Lawes to Mullens, 8 October 1877. LMS Papua Correspondence 2/1/D. This was clearly part of a lengthy dispute since Lawes refers to earlier contributions by Turner and McFarlane.
63 Lest the disagreement be construed as a personal one between McFarlane and Lawes, see also Chalmers to Whitehouse, 14 February 1883. *Ibid.*, 3/2/B.
64 Mullens' successor, Ralph Wardlaw Thompson, constantly chided the New Guinea missionaries for their lack of committee meetings, but to no avail. Chalmers explained: 'The real reason for our not having committee meetings is that they are useless, our work is so different although all for the same Master'. *Ibid.* 3/3/C.

Carnarvon's commitment of December 1875 is clear from its records. Once again, most of the serious thinking came from Herbert, who agonised in his minutes over the best way to proceed. Within seven months of Carnarvon's decision he expressed the dilemma:

> It is very difficult to decide what course to take. If we delay annexation the serious risk is that(?) of an almost immediate collision with Australia. If we are too hasty in annexing, we stimulate a rush of people to an almost inhospitable country, and saddle this government with heavy expense.[65]

He continued, 'I do not think we can afford to postpone the annexation of the shore nearest to Australia'. A year later, the pendulum had swung: 'I think that neither the Cabinet, nor Parliament, nor the public are prepared for the annexation of New Guinea'. Nevertheless, Herbert looked ahead to a possible change in policy by Queensland: 'Lord Carnarvon has pretty well committed himself to the theory that this policy cannot be supported by him unless the Australasian colonies bear a full share.... The next and more difficult question to consider is whether we should annex the country if the colonies propose to bear the cost'.[66] Lord Carnarvon confessed, 'It is altogether a very difficult question'.[67] But he left office long before a final decision had to be made. That was made by his successor-but-two.

Following the early, unsuccessful, attempts to exploit New Guinea commercially in the 1860s and 1870s, leading to Carnarvon's decision not to annex any part of the island in 1875, the next potential crisis was the 'gold rush' of 1878. Ironically, the gold had actually been discovered by Lawes and the British trader Andrew Goldie on a joint expedition inland of Port Moresby.[68] Realising the damage a gold rush could to mission work in Papua, Lawes kept the discovery as quiet as possible and even after it had become known, tried to damp down 'gold fever' by exhibiting the poor quality of the gold ore in Sydney on his way back to Britain.[69] McFarlane was not so circumspect, though he too recognised the damage that could be done to the mission and drew annexationist conclusions:

> Mr Lawes will tell you about some of the specimens of gold found by some of the natives who accompanied him and Mr Goldie in their expedition inland. An account of the discovery is to be published in the Sydney papers. Should there be a

---

65 Min. by Herbert, 24 July 1876, on FO to CO (Confidential), 21 July 1876. CO 201/562.
66 Min. by Herbert, 30 August 1876, on FO to CO, 19 August 1876. CO 201/562.
67 *Ibid.*, Min. by Carnarvon, 31 August 1876, on FO to CO, 19 August 1876.
68 See Lawes' Journal, 28 October 1877. Quoted in King, p.159.
69 Lawes to Mullens, 21 January 1878. LMS Papua Correspondence. 2/2/A.

rush, the interests of the mission may require that we now go strongly for annexation .... I fear our work may be seriously affected. [70]

Though he received this information in March 1878, Dr Mullens the LMS Foreign Secretary, waited nearly three months before communicating the news to the Colonial Office.[71] In all probability he shrank from being the agent of publicising the discovery of gold and only after the information was clearly in the public domain did he share his concern with the authorities. Clearly concerned about the potential breakdown in law and order if a gold rush developed as feared, the Colonial Office replied to the LMS in July 1878 that a naval vessel would be dispatched to Port Moresby, to 'be stationed in the neighbourhood of the principal assemblage of diggers until it can be seen whether the rush to New Guinea is of more than temporary duration'.[72] As the Western Pacific High Commissioner, Sir Arthur Gordon, was shortly due to arrive in Britain he would be consulted as to the most appropriate measures to take.

Ten days before Gordon replied to the Colonial Office's request for advice, he received a letter from W.G. Lawes, now at home on furlough and resident in Reading. Gordon enclosed a copy of this letter to the Colonial Office in his reply.[73] Lawes wrote of the fear of the disorder the gold prospectors would bring and that 'there is no local native government capable of dealing with the difficulties which are sure to arise from the presence of a number of white men'. Though nowhere did Lawes explicitly request annexation, he concluded that 'foreign residents themselves are anxious to have British authority established and would gladly submit to it'. It can, of course, be argued that 'British authority' could be established by means other than outright annexation. What is clear is that Lawes saw the future of New Guinea in some way bound up with that of Britain. Gordon clearly assented to this view and advised Hicks Beach accordingly,[74] but no action needed to be taken since the 'gold rush' proved to be literally no more than a flash in the pan; the prospectors returned to Australia and ideas of annexation were once again shelved.

---

70 McFarlane to Mullens, 14 December 1877. LMS Papua Correspondence 2/1/D.
71 Mullens to Hicks Beach, 3 June 1878. *PP* 1883 XLVII [C.3617]. Henry Chester, the Queensland police magistrate in the Torres Straits islands was also concerned with the influx of Europeans into his jurisdiction even before news of the gold discovery was known. *Ibid.*, Chester to Colonial Secretary Queensland, 23 November 1877, enc. in Governor Kennedy to Western Pacific High Commissioner, 19 December 1877.
72 *Ibid.*, CO to LMS, 13 July 1878; CO to Sir Arthur Gordon, 5 October 1878.
73 *Ibid.,* Lawes to Gordon, 21 January 1879, enc. in Gordon to CO, 31 January 1879. King, pp.166-169, also prints the former, incorrectly dating it as 20 January 1878.
74 See also D.C. Gordon, p.168. Before returning to Britain, Sir Arthur Gordon took the precaution of appointing the Queensland police magistrate in the Torres Straits islands as a deputy commissioner of the Western Pacific High Commission. *Ibid.,* p.118.

Australian Intervention

Following the return of the Liberals to office in the aftermath of the 'Midlothian' election of April 1880, Hicks Beach was succeeded by Lord Kimberley, who returned to the Colonial Office which he had vacated six years previously. He did not however remain at the Office throughout Gladstone's second ministry. Following the humiliation of Majuba Hill in February 1881, internal divisions in the government became apparent. An alliance of Radicals and Irish members was able to outvote the Whigs, ultimately restoring self-government to the Transvaal. A casualty of the crisis was Kimberley, who was eventually unseated at the Colonial Office. He was replaced in December 1882 by the 15th Earl of Derby. Derby, following the precedent of his ancestor at Bosworth Field, had changed sides in the political battle and crossed the floor of the House of Lords after leaving Disraeli's Cabinet, with Carnarvon, over the Eastern Question in 1878. Hardly an expert on colonial matters, Derby was perhaps best remembered for his remark, often held against him, that the British Empire had 'black savages enough'. Ronald Robinson characterized him as a 'Gladstonian non-interventionist' as far as imperial matters were concerned.[75] Yet, paradoxically, it was to be Derby who was responsible for the extension of British authority over Papua New Guinea.

As Derby was moving into the Colonial Office, a letter arrived, addressed to Kimberley, from Francis de Labilliere.[76] Just as Labilliere's first letter (to Carnarvon some eight years previously) had drawn the territory to the attention of the Colonial Office, so this one was to begin, though not to cause, the final phase in Britain's doomed attempt to avoid responsibility for Papua New Guinea. Though the Colonial Office sent a negative reply to Labilliere – 'the question is one which Her Majesty's Government is not prepared at present to re-open'[77] – developments on the far side of the globe were soon to force New Guinea back on to the political agenda. These factors were an increase in commercial activity (including kidnapping), a growing fear of foreign intervention and a growing impatience in Queensland.

Moresby's survey work in the early 1870s had charted most of the coasts, islands and straits of Papua New Guinea and thus made them more accessible. Pearling had begun in the Torres Straits islands as far back as 1868 and by 1881 about 120 vessels were operating on a regular basis.[78] The abortive gold rush showed the accessibility of New Guinea from Australia; once it was established that there was commercial profit to be made in the island, it would be impossible to stop speculators and, without legal jurisdiction, difficult to regulate and control their activities. This lack of supervision or regulation also made New Guinea and the island groups around it desirable territory for the

---

75 *CHBE*, III, p.138.
76 Labilliere to Kimberley, 11 December 1882. *PP* 1883 XLVII [C.3617].
77 *Ibid.*, CO to Labilliere, 28 December 1882.
78 D.C. Gordon, p.98.

labour traders. Largely deprived of human cargoes elsewhere, they began to prey on the Papuans, with the same cycle of violence that has been observed elsewhere in the Pacific.[79] As further proposals for commercial exploitation were made, missionary concern once again expressed itself. James Chalmers and the Russian explorer and anthropologist, Count de Miklouho Maclay, wrote to the Colonial Office specifically to request assurances on no alienation of native land, a prohibition of the labour trade and a ban on the importation of alcohol into New Guinea.[80] These requests, however, presupposed an extension of British jurisdiction in some form. Lawes contacted George Palmer, an MP who was also a member of the Aborigines Protection Society, to engage his support against proposed speculation in native land.[81]

As far back as November 1874 Robert Herbert had reflected on the dangerous possibility of 'a foreign flag [being] hoisted twenty miles from Queensland'.[82] At that time such a scenario appeared far-fetched, but by the early 1880s it seemed far less improbable. Such rumours were, naturally, more prevalent in Australia than in Britain,[83] but in December 1882 the Royal Colonial Institute drew the attention of the Foreign Secretary, Lord Granville, to an article of the previous month in the *Allgemeine Zeitung* of Augsburg encouraging the German government to annex and colonise New Guinea. The Institute's Council urged Granville to consider 'the annexation of the eastern portion of New Guinea, in order to prevent any action on the part of a foreign power which would be so seriously detrimental to the interests of the British Empire'.[84] The communication was passed to Lord Derby who remained unmoved. It was undoubtedly true that German interest in the area was

---

79 See, for example a letter in the *Brisbane Courier*, 6 October 1880, from the missionaries Chalmers and Beswick, describing the murder of seven Chinese *bêche-de-mer* traders by natives, probably in retaliation for a kidnapping raid. Quoted in Wawn, p.209. Lawes wrote on 15 September 1884 to the editor of The Times to complain about kidnapping in eastern New Guinea, but by the time his letter was published on 5 December the British Protectorate had already been proclaimed.

80 Maclay and Chalmers to CO, 1 June 1883. *PP* 1884 LV [C.3863].

81 *Ibid.*, Lawes to Palmer, 21 December 1883. Enc. in Palmer to CO, 11 December 1883.

82 Min., 21 November 1874, on Robinson to Carnarvon, 7 September 1874. CO 201/577.

83 D.C. Gordon commented: 'With the nations of the world entering a new period of imperialist expansion, and with Papua one of the largest unappropriated areas in the world, it was not unnatural that rumours of foreign annexation of eastern New Guinea periodically created excitement in the Australian colonies, and that these rumours were met with more credulity than sound appraisal'. Gordon, p.122.

84 R.C.I. to Granville 9 December 1822 enc. in FO to CO, 18 December 1882. *PP* 1883 XLVII [C.3617].

increasing,[85] though whether annexation was a serious possibility which Britain needed to forestall or whether eventual German annexation of the north coast was merely a response to Britain's protectorate in the south is more problematic.

In June 1879 the Queensland government had officially extended its territory northwards to take in the islands of the Torres Straits as their response to the increase in commercial activity. A small vessel was purchased for the use of the police magistrate, Henry Chester, already stationed on Thursday Island. Increasingly fearful of rumours of foreign interest, the Queensland premier, Sir Thomas McIlwraith ('a stubborn, good, honest Scotchman', according to Chalmers),[86] requested permission from London to forestall any foreign threat by annexing New Guinea in the Queen's name.[87] He did not, however, wait for a reply before acting. Possibly panicked by the departure of the small German warship *Carola* from Sydney, on 18 March 1883, McIlwraith sent immediate instructions to Henry Chester to take formal possession of New Guinea and adjacent islands east of the Dutch border. W.G. Lawes, an eye-witness and participant, relayed to LMS headquarters the events of 4 April 1883:

> Long before you receive this you will receive telegraphic news of the annexation of New Guinea. The account of the ceremony is as follows. On Wednesday morning at 10 o'clock Mr Chester hoisted the Union Jack at *our* flag-staff and it was saluted by the two ... guns of the 'Pearl'. After the ceremony Mr Chester made a present to the natives and we explained to them as best we could the nature of the proceedings.[88]

The Queensland annexation of New Guinea, caught the Colonial Office off guard. Though technically illegal, the annexation was of sufficient popularity, and near enough to possible imperial action, to cause severe embarrassment and it left Lord Derby initially at a loss as to how best to respond. He asserted to the Queen's Private Secretary on 16 April that the government was quite 'free to sanction or annul the act as we may think expedient', but he was much more concerned that 'to undo what the colonists have done would create a bad feeling locally'.[89] On 16 April 1883, Parliamentary Under-Secretary Evelyn Ashley, in response to a question by Sir John Hay, merely quoted to the Commons from

---

85 See, for example, Morrell, *Pacific Islands*, pp.247-248; Deane, Ch.XIV; M.G. Jacobs, 'Bismarck and the Annexation of New Guinea', *HSANZ*, 5 (1951), 16-19.
86 Chalmers to ?, 25 June 1883, quoted in Lovett, *Chalmers*, p.240.
87 The Governor of Queensland's telegram requesting permission for the proposed annexation was delivered to the Colonial Office on 28 February 1883, by Thomas Archer, Queensland's Agent General. He had a personal interview with Derby the following day. Gordon, p.155.
88 Lawes to Whitehouse, 7 April 1883. LMS Papua Correspondence, 3/2/C. See also King, pp.203-204; Chester to Colonial Secretary of Queensland, 7 April 1883. *PP* 1883 XLVII [C.3691].
89 Derby to Ponsonby, 16 April 1883, quoted in Gordon, p.157 n.15.

the Governor of Queensland's telegram.[90] A rougher ride was reserved for Derby in the Lords four days later. Carnarvon asked if Britain was a consenting party to the annexation, remarked that Derby was once much opposed to it, and reminded him of his 'blacks enough' remarks.[91] But the government seemed in no hurry to reach a decision. Despite regular questioning in both Houses from, *inter alia*, Carnarvon and Hicks Beach,[92] it was not until 2 July that Derby announced the government's decision – a rejection of the annexation.[93]

The reason for the delay, officially blamed by ministers on having to wait for the arrival of despatches,[94] was that the government was in confusion over having to formulate a policy where there was none, and, in a cabinet riven with such dissension as Gladstone's second, any agreement on new policy was difficult to come by. Gladstone himself was opposed to annexation, as was habitually his practice, and he was supported (in a private correspondence) by Sir Arthur Gordon, who had changed his mind since he was consulted on the matter by Hicks Beach in 1879.[95] This time he opposed annexation, considering Queensland 'specially unfit to exercise dominion over native races'. But a few months later conceded that, 'strongly as I am opposed to annexation, I am bound to admit that some more efficient steps than have yet been taken for the control of British subjects in the Pacific & also for their protection, appear to be inevitable'.[96]

The Colonial Office, on the other hand, was not nearly so hostile to the annexation as was Gladstone. Herbert, as has been noted, was a long-standing advocate of annexation, when the circumstances permitted – his consistent and patient advocacy of New Guinea's value was not lost on his political masters. Evelyn Ashley consistently failed to condemn the annexation in the House of Commons and, as with Knatchbull-Hugessen over Fiji, this was left to Gladstone; though it is significant that even he, possibly because of weight of opinion in the Cabinet, did not rule out a future imperial annexation and merely contented himself with attacking Queensland's action and her suitability as a

---

90 *Hansard*, Third Series, CCLXXVIII, 16 April 1883, col. 324.
91 *Ibid.*, 20 April 1883, cols 724-728.
92 It was left to Sir George Campbell to point out, to Gladstone himself, the inconsistency of abandoning the Transvaal while at the same time acquiring fresh responsibilities in New Guinea. *Ibid.*, 20 April 1883, col.748.
93 *Ibid.*, CCLXXXI, cols 14-19.
94 Ashley, 19 April 1883, *Hansard*, Third Series, CCLXXVII, col.626. Derby, 25 May 1883, *ibid.*, CCLXXIX, col.881; Ashley, 31 May 1883, *ibid.*, col.1335. D.C. Gordon accepts this reason at face value, Gordon, p.156, but fails to explain why the government still prevaricated for over a fortnight after the necessary despatch had been received before announcing a decision. See Ashley, 15 June 1883, *Hansard*, Third Series, CCLXXX, col.692.
95 See P. Knaplund, 'Sir Arthur Gordon and the New Guinea Question, 1883', *HSANZ*, VII (1956), 328-333.
96 *Ibid.*, Gordon to Gladstone, 20 April 1883; Gordon to Gladstone, 8 October 1883.

colonizing power.[97] The Colonial Office was not short of unsolicited advice on the matter. The Royal Colonial Institute argued in favour of annexation, both in a memorial of 22 May and a deputation of 1 June 1883.[98] The Aborigines Protection Society, writing to Derby on 14 May, was prepared to accept annexation, but only if it were undertaken by Britain, regarding annexation by Queensland as 'particularly undesirable', and fearing that 'if the administration of New Guinea were placed in its hands, the temptation to extend the labour trade to that country would prove irresistible'.[99] The Australian colonies, needless to say, strongly supported the annexation.[100] Derby was acutely aware of this support and feared for the relationship between Britain and Australia if the annexation were disallowed.[101]

As Lord Derby was preparing to make his announcement to the Lords of the Government's repudiation of the Queensland annexation, he wrote to Lord Granville:

> Do you see any harm in my saying that 'We consider the eastern part of New Guinea as lying within the sphere of British interests – and that it would be an unfriendly act on the part of any foreign power to establish a settlement there?'[102]

This proviso, agreed bilaterally by Colonial Secretary and Foreign Secretary, and without reference to Prime Minister or Cabinet, was included in Derby's statement to the Lords, and effectively kept alive British interests in New Guinea and kept open the door for future annexation.

Missionary Reaction to the Queensland 'Annexation'

How did the New Guinea missionaries feel about the abortive Queensland annexation and its disallowance by London? Certainly there was no love for Queensland in the missionary fraternity – the excesses of the labour trade for which Queensland was blamed saw to that. It was feared that annexation by Queensland was merely an attempt to acquire a vast pool of labour which could be exploited at will.[103] Traditionally, LMS missionaries had been far less imperialistic than other missionaries in the Pacific. Unlike the Wesleyans, who had middle class pretensions, and unlike the Scottish missionaries, who operated in a different social *milieu*, the LMS, though technically non-

---

97 *Ibid.*, CCLXXXI, cols 55-56, 2 July 1883.
98 Memorial of Council of R.C.I. to Derby, 22 May 1883. *PP* 1883 XLVII [C.3691].
99 Aborigines Protection Society to Derby, 14 May 1883. *PP* 1883 XLVII [C.3617].
100 See, for example, Kennedy to Derby, 26 April 1883. *Ibid.*, [C.3691]; Loftus to Derby, 19 February 1883. *Ibid.*, [C.3617].
101 Derby to Ponsonby, 16 April 1883, quoted in Gordon, p.157 n.15.
102 Derby to Granville, 2 July 1883. Granville Papers, PRO 30/29/120.
103 See McFarlane to ?, 8 April 1883. Quoted in Lovett, *Chalmers*, p.237.

denominational, in practice represented the Congregational churches, largely artisan or lower middle class in membership and with limited access to, or support from, the ruling classes of the day.[104] The extension of the British empire was not on their agenda: the protection of indigenous peoples was. They took seriously their responsibility to foster the welfare of native races – what to a later generation would be known as 'trusteeship' – and, provided the natives were not exploited, but educated and helped gradually into civilised ways, they held no strong opinions on the type of government that should be employed, and could work happily under any form.

As has been noted, W. Wyatt Gill, who replaced Chalmers at Rarotonga, and who had made three preliminary visits to New Guinea in 1872 to place Polynesian teachers, had expressed his personal view in favour of annexation well before Labilliere's first letter had reached the Colonial Office. Gill had made no secret of his annexationist views despite the LMS's official neutrality on the matter. After the Queensland annexation was rejected he commented, with a rich mixture of themes – humanitarian, nationalistic and financial:

> although at present the imperial government through Lord Derby has given its decision against annexation, yet the whole matter must, no doubt, be reconsidered and the island be eventually annexed. It is to be hoped that the country is not to become part of the Australian colonies .... Annex New Guinea, and save it from another power, who might harass our Australian colonies; administer it for the natives, and the whole machinery of government can be maintained by New Guinea, and allow a large overplus.[105]

W.G. Lawes, by contrast, was far less imperialistic. His views, as expressed in his letter to Sir Arthur Gordon in 1879, have already been noted.[106] Though he expressed his fears about the detrimental effects on the Papuans of a clash of cultures, it is important to note that he was expressing the view of foreign residents (not necessarily his own) and that he spoke of British authority not sovereignty. To state, as Garrett does, that Lawes 'lobbied the imperial government' in favour of a protectorate is over-stating the case.[107] It is most probable (since he was actually writing to the High Commissioner) that his preferred solution would have been an extension of the Western Pacific High Commission to New Guinea and not annexation or a protectorate. After his factual account of Henry Chester's annexation of New Guinea, Lawes added his

---

104 There were exceptions. In addition to senior role in the CMS, Arthur Kinnaird was also treasurer of the LMS until 1875. See LMS Home Secretary to Kinnaird, 31 March 1875; Kinnaird to LMS Home Secretary, 2 April 1875. LMS Home Office Papers, Box 12.
105 Chalmers and Gill, pp.16-17.
106 See n.73. For a discussion of Lawes' views see also King, pp.211-213.
107 Garrett, *Stars*, p.213.

personal interpretation of the event and its significance, the last sentence being a classic statement of LMS views:

> Annexation we were in a measure prepared for, although we did not wish it, but that an Australian colony should be allowed to do it to us is most surprising. Here is the largest island in the world ... annexed by a Police Magistrate in a little tub of a cutter! There must be some mistake somewhere. We would much rather not be annexed by any body, but if there was any probability of a foreign power taking possession then let us have British rule but as a Crown colony not as an appendage to Queensland.[108]

He would not promote annexation, neither would he work towards it, but if it was inevitable then Britain, and not Queensland, with her reputation sullied by the labour trade, should be the colonial power.

Niel Gunson has described James Chalmers as being 'patriotic as any Wesleyan' and notes his 'strong reservations about colonial rule. Protection and trusteeship were his only pleas...'. Chalmers' writings largely justify this assessment. A few months later, after Britain's repudiation of the Queensland annexation, Chalmers commented:

> The whole matter must, I have no doubt, be reconsidered and the island be eventually annexed. It is to be hoped the country is not to become part of the Australian colonies – a labour land and a land where loose money in the hands of a few capitalists is to enter in and make enormous fortunes, sacrificing the natives and everything else....[109]

But as he continued, the 'philanthropy plus five per cent' argument came to stand alongside the humanitarian:

> Let Britain ... annex, and from the day of annexation New Guinea will pay all her own expenses; the expenses of the first three years to be paid with compound interest at the end of that term. Let us begin by recognising all native rights, and letting it be distinctly understood that we govern for the native races, not the white men; that we are determined to civilise and raise to a higher level of humanity those whom we govern; that our aim will be to do all to defend them and save them from extermination by just humanitarian laws – not the laws of the British nation – but the laws suited for them.[110]

Yet he was using the word 'annexation' in its very widest sense. For him, the protectorate (as established in 1884) was ideal: it gave Britain a responsibility

---

108 Lawes to Whitehouse, 7 April 1883. LMS Papua Correspondence, 3/2/C.
109 Quoted in Lennox, p.126.
110 *Ibid.*, pp.126-127.

and duty to protect the Papuan people from their exploiters – both actual and potential – without Britain acquiring sovereignty and thus being able to treat the land and the people as it wished.[111]

It is clear from their comments that the missionaries did not want a colonial government controlled from Brisbane. But they increasingly came to the conclusion that only some form of British control would save the Papuan people from Queensland, from a foreign power, or in the absence of either, from commercial exploitation, anarchy and bloodshed.

Britain Proclaims a Protectorate

But if the British government was against annexation in July 1883, why was it in favour of a protectorate only fifteen months later? The answer would appear to be threefold. First, despite reservations by some, government feeling was *not* against annexation – what it was against was an unauthorised act by a colony, albeit one possessing responsible government, which could create a precedent and store up trouble for the future. Thus, Gladstone declared to Derby on 19 May 1883, 'I hope we may find ourselves in a condition utterly to squash this annexation effected by Queensland on her sole authority'.[112] The government's opposition, therefore, was to the agent of the annexation — not necessarily to the principle itself. There was unity in condemning Queensland's action but there the agreement ended. It is clear from a note by Gladstone, written at the Cabinet meeting on 5 July 1884, a year *after* Derby had disallowed the Queensland annexation, both that the matter was still very much on the agenda and that only he, Selbourne and Harcourt now opposed annexation *per se*.[113]

A second factor was that British (as opposed to Australian) fear of foreign intervention in New Guinea was much greater in the summer and autumn of 1884 than it had been in the spring of 1883. In April 1884, Bismarck declared a German protectorate over Angra Pequeña in south-west Africa, where the German trading firm of Lüderitz was operating. The fact that this part of Africa was adjacent to Cape Colony immediately made Germany into a threat – and the parallel with the south-west Pacific was clear. Thus the imperial government was now more disposed to agree that Australia's concerns may not have been so far-fetched as had been thought. The fact that Germany had strong trading links with the islands to the north of New Guinea was an uncomfortable reminder that the Australians may not have been 'crying wolf' all along. A constant refrain in Robert Herbert's many minutes on New Guinea was his concern about 'another

---

111 See also Niel Gunson, 'British Expansion in the South Pacific', *JRH*, III (1965), 308.
112 Gladstone to Derby, 19 May 1883, quoted in Knaplund, *Gladstone's Foreign Policy*, p.104.
113 Notes taken at Cabinet meeting 5 July 1884, original MS, Gladstone Papers, quoted in *ibid.*, p.110.

power' stealing a march on Britain and annexing a territory as strategically important as New Guinea.

This was also a highly important factor in missionary concerns for the future of New Guinea. Though annexation by Britain was not necessarily their preferred option, it was always regarded as preferable either to annexation by Queensland or by a foreign power. Although the missionaries are thought of as having mainly humanitarian interests where they supported annexation, a nationalistic strain runs through a significantly large number of missionary writings on the subject. The LMS was indeed apolitical, but its humanitarian concerns resulted in a significant emphasis by LMS missionaries in the field on Britain being the only acceptable colonial power in New Guinea.[114] Concerns about German intentions appeared entirely justified in that only two days after the Cabinet had agreed on the principle of proclaiming a protectorate over New Guinea, the German ambassador, Count Munster, informed Granville that his government had decided to afford protection to German trading interests in the south-west Pacific and intended to colonise the northern coast of New Guinea.[115]

A third factor influencing the British government's thinking on New Guinea was that the Australian colonies began to present a united front, and at last agreed to make a financial contribution to a colonial government in New Guinea as first suggested by Lord Carnarvon in 1875 and repeated by Lord Derby in May 1884.[116] This was largely as a result of an Australian Intercolonial Convention, proposed by McIlwraith,[117] which met in Sydney in November 1883. The Convention resolved that further acquisitions of territory south of the equator by any foreign power would be highly detrimental to the safety and well-being of Australia and urged the immediate incorporation of non-Dutch New Guinea in the empire.[118] Bismarck referred contemptuously to this as an Australian 'Monroe Doctrine in the South Pacific'.[119] The details of the somewhat tortuous discussions between the Australian colonial governments and London are described elsewhere.[120] Basically, discussion through 1884 brought both parties closer together, initially over an extension of the High Commission to New Guinea, but eventually, assisted by the German catalyst,

---

114 See, for example, Chalmers' assertion to the R.C.I.: 'As Britons, we may be pardoned for wishing to see the influence of Britain supreme rather than that of any other Power'. *PRCI*, XVIII (1876-7), 102.
115 Knaplund, *Gladstone's Foreign Policy*, p.111.
116 Derby to Governors of Australian Colonies, 9 May 1884. CO Confidential Print, Australian No.103. CO 881/6.
117 McIlwraith himself had fallen from power before the convention was able to meet and Queensland was now governed by the more moderate Sir Samuel Griffith.
118 For details of the conference see Gordon, pp.174-197.
119 Quoted in Morrell, *Pacific Islands*, p.254.
120 Jacobs, 115-116; Morrell, pp.253-254; Gordon, pp.219-231.

the assurance of Australian funds[121] made a British protectorate over Papua the mutually agreed solution.[122] Derby recommended a protectorate to the Cabinet on 5 July, but a decision was postponed until 6 August 1884.[123] In fact continuing changes of view and disagreement over the details meant that the final decision to go ahead was not made until 6 October, as Lord Derby noted:

> The Cabinet has agreed in the matter of New Guinea that the declaration of a Protectorate along the whole of the southern coast, including the islands contiguous to it, shall be made forthwith. This is to be done without prejudice to any territorial question beyond the limit. This decision to be communicated to the German government simultaneously with its execution.[124]

Missionary Reaction to the British Protectorate

The decision to declare a protectorate over south-eastern New Guinea may have been a long drawn out affair, but the proclamation itself contained elements of farce, not high drama. This was largely because Deputy Commissioner Hugh Romilly misunderstood his instructions and jumped the gun by making an official proclamation of the protectorate on 23 October 1884. Consequently the whole ceremony had to be repeated on 6 November upon the arrival of Commodore Erskine, to the bemusement of the Papuans and to the amusement of Lawes.[125]

If there were any reservations in the minds of the missionaries with regard to the new protectorate, these were quickly overcome by the courteous and respectful treatment they received from the official representatives of Britain. Indeed, the advice of the missionaries was much sought after, but this was hardly surprising since they alone possessed the local knowledge of New Guinea which the new colonial authorities desperately needed to acquire. Lawes, who among the missionaries had the least time for imperial expansion, was offered and accepted a passage to Sydney in the Commodore's flagship,

---

121 £15,000 p.a.
122 Colonial Office thinking on the matter is admirably summarised in a Confidential Print (Australian No.103) 'Annexation or Protection of New Guinea and other islands in the Western Pacific' of 28 June 1884. CO 881/6. Official nervousness over German intentions is clearly apparent.
123 Morrell, *Pacific Islands*, p.254.
124 Memorandum: Derby to Granville (copy), 6 October 1884. Granville Papers, PRO 30/29/120. The idea of notifying Bismarck was Granville's, agreed bilaterally with Derby, and not a Cabinet decision. *Ibid.*, Derby to Granville, 16 September 1884. See also CO to Admiralty, 8 October 1884. *PP* 1884-1885 LIV [C.4217].
125 Lawes to Thompson, 30 October 1884, with post script 11 November 1884. LMS Papua Correspondence, 3/4/C. See also King, pp.214-219.

Nelson.[126] But his opinions were not softened by imperial hospitality and remained unswervingly constant:

> I considered I was doing the best service to the people of New Guinea by assisting the Commodore.... He asked our help. We gave it willingly and he has repeatedly acknowledged it. With the desirability or otherwise, of the annexation (for such it will become), we have nothing to do. I have never by letter or word of mouth sought to bring it about. It would have been better for our work and for the people if they could have been left alone, but as this was impossible it is far better to have an English government than any other.[127]

Chalmers, whose knowledge of the country was second to none, was courted both by Erskine and, after his arrival in 1885, by the Special Commissioner for the Protectorate, Major General Sir Peter Scratchley.[128] Both men sought and relied heavily on his advice, and that of Lawes, much to the disgust of the small group of European traders, who regarded the mission's aims as antipathetic to theirs and referred disparagingly to 'mission rule'.[129] Though he never lost sight of the principles of trusteeship which, he believed, underpinned British rule and gave Britain its moral authority to govern New Guinea,[130] Chalmers, unpredictable and unconventional to the last, became almost an establishment figure in New Guinea. On furlough in Britain in November 1886, he was interviewed by Robert Herbert at the Colonial Office and, before his return in 1887, the Parliamentary Under-Secretary, Lord Onslow, sounded him out for a position in the government of the territory.[131] Chalmers refused any official position but remained in close touch with the colonial government and, after formal annexation in October 1888, became a close friend of the first governor of the Crown colony, Sir William MacGregor.

But, as Diane Langmore has pointed out,[132] because Chalmers' concern was for the protection of the Papuan people and not the expansion of empire, he was satisfied with protectorate status for New Guinea and the declared principles which underpinned it. She is somewhat misleading, however, when she goes on to suggest that Chalmers opposed the subsequent change of status from protectorate to colony. In fact he had an open mind on the subject, as he told the Royal Colonial Institute on 11 January 1887, at a time when the British protectorate was well-established and there was a debate on whether or not to

---

126 Lawes to Thompson, 30 October 1884. LMS Papua Correspondence, 3/4/C.
127 Lawes to Thompson, 8 May 1885. LMS Papua Correspondence, 3/5/A.
128 Chalmers to Thompson, 10 February and 13 November 1885. LMS Papua Correspondence, 3/5/A and 3/5/C.
129 Langmore, *Tamate*, p.51.
130 Chalmers to Thompson, 1 December 1884. LMS Papua Correspondence, 3/4/C.
131 Lovett, *Chalmers*, pp.270-271.
132 Langmore, *Missionary Lives*, p.214.

go a step further and formally annex New Guinea as a Crown colony. From this paper in which Chalmers was weighing up the pros and cons of annexation, Langmore, in her more recent book, takes one sentence out of context in an attempt to show that 'he opposed the transformation of the protectorate into a colony': 'Annexation would, I fear, render just treatment almost impossible: ... the young, pushing, daring Anglo-Saxon colonist would look upon the "nigger" as something to be got rid of'. But she fails to quote from just a few lines earlier in Chalmers' paper, when he states that, 'If, on the other hand, annexation would be a benefit to the natives, and a necessity to Australia, I would support the proposal to annex the country'.[133] Neither does she consider his words of just over a year earlier when he wrote to LMS headquarters that 'sincerely do I hope that we shall be annexed and for ever remain a Crown colony...'.[134] Nevertheless it would be as much a mistake to seek to pin down Chalmers' views on the basis of these two quotations as Langmore has done on one. There were as many rough edges and inconsistencies in Chalmers' opinions as there were in his character. As long as the aboriginal peoples were given primary consideration, the minutiae of governmental arrangements were of secondary importance to him.

Analysis

W.P. Morrell suggested that the establishment of the British protectorate over Papua New Guinea was unusual in the annals of British imperialism in that it was 'the outcome of external pressures rather than of the condition of New Guinea itself'.[135] In conclusion, then, it would appear to be appropriate to summarise these 'external pressures' and to evaluate their responsibility for Britain's assumption of authority in New Guinea in 1884. The relevant external pressures were: missionary activity, Australian pressure, foreign intervention or fear of it, and the presence of Robert Herbert at the Colonial Office.

The presence of the missionaries in Papua New Guinea was of primary importance. The LMS missionaries really put the island on the map – both figuratively and literally. It was they, and particularly Chalmers, who did the inland exploration and pioneering analogous to that of Moresby on the coast. Sir William MacGregor, first governor of British New Guinea as a Crown colony, greatly respected the work of the mission, and stated that 'It was more through it than by any other means that the way was prepared for the founding

---

133 *PRCI*, XVIII (1886-1887), 104. It should, however, be noted that in her earlier book, Langmore was less dogmatic on this point, also quoted this sentence and admitted that Chalmers 'refrained from whole-hearted opposition to annexation'. Langmore, *Tamate*, p.53.
134 Chalmers to Thompson, 13 November 1885. LMS Papua Correspondence 3/5/C.
135 Morrell, *Pacific Islands*, p.400.

of the colony'.[136] Certainly the mission role was not limited to exploration but to fostering education, Christianity, freedom from cruel and superstitious practices and, inevitably and more dubiously, European values and making New Guinea known to those who did not share their high moral outlook. For, as D.C. Gordon has rightly pointed out, 'the missionaries were frontiersmen of forces they could not control. By their work they contributed to the interest in New Guinea in distant lands, and such interest was not confined to the godly'.[137] It should be noted, however, that LMS missionaries were far less inclined to impose Western values as being analogous with Christian values than were, say, WMMS missionaries. Yet, however hard they tried (and Chalmers tried particularly hard – even to the controversial lengths of approving of nudity and other native modes of dress),[138] it was impossible for the missionaries not to impart Western ideas (albeit unintentionally) and equally impossible for the Papuans not to absorb such ideas. Nevertheless, in taking a humanitarian, not imperialistic, attitude to the Papuan people and steadfastly supporting and defending them against exploiters, real and imagined, and acting as a moral watchdog when New Guinea came under British authority, the missionary movement ensured that trusteeship would be high on the agenda of the colonial government.

Yet it is doubtful whether missionary involvement alone would have brought the British government to the point of annexing New Guinea. The catalyst for this was the pressure exerted by the Australian colonies.[139] Though there was a tendency at the time, by the missionaries as well as others, to regard pressure from Queensland as a cynical attempt to acquire an inexhaustible source of plantation labour, this was really a red herring. Even Australian colonies that had nothing to gain from the labour trade wanted to see the British flag flying over Papua, and the reason was far more fundamental – colonial security. Although the McIlwraith annexation was disallowed by the imperial government, it was instrumental in forcing the Colonial Office to review its somewhat ambivalent attitude to New Guinea and make a decision as to Britain's part in the island's future.

The fear of foreign intervention was, in many ways, the unifying factor which held the others together. It began in Australia, where there was a near paranoid attitude to other nations' interest in the south-west Pacific, and was accepted and adopted by the missionaries to the extent of almost undermining their policy of neutrality on annexation. It finally arrived in the Colonial Office in time to influence its decisions on the future of New Guinea. There was a degree of irony, at least as far as the missions were concerned, over this factor.

---

136 Quoted in Koskinen, pp.224-225. As John Garrett tersely put it, 'Missions helped him; he helped missions'. Garrett, *Stars*, pp. 230-231.
137 Gordon, p.73.
138 Lovett, *Chalmers*, p.257.
139 Gordon, p.13.

The LMS missionaries feared that annexation by a foreign power would adversely affect their work – they had the French occupation of the Loyalty Islands in mind as a clear recent example. Yet when, in December 1884, a large part of the northern coast of eastern New Guinea, together with the adjacent islands – New Britain and New Ireland – were annexed by Germany, the Australian Wesleyan mission under George Brown and Benjamin Danks found the new colonial power courteous and helpful and disinclined to interfere in the mission's business or to place restrictions on it. Under German rule, that mission continued to grow and prosper.[140]

For a number of years Robert Herbert had clearly seen the advantages of a British New Guinea, not surprisingly in view of his deeper understanding of the Australian situation derived from his period as premier of Queensland. As far back as November 1874, he minuted on a despatch of Sir Hercules Robinson, critical of annexation:

> Sir H. Robinson does not sufficiently appreciate the end that will probably result from some European power claiming and annexing all of non-Dutch New Guinea.... The outcry will be loud when a foreign flag is hoisted twenty miles from Queensland. To hoist that of England need not be costly.[141]

However, Herbert was not fanatical about the matter, being critical of Australian politicians who advocated annexation in a selfish fashion. For example, in April 1875 he minuted on a letter from the Governor of Queensland:

> The prevailing idea of Australian statesmen appears to be that their country must perish if any foreign power hoists its flag within a week's steaming of the shores of the great island continent; and that it is the duty of the British taxpayer to defray all the charges of the premature occupation of a country unsuited for white labourers, while the Australian taxpayer, who is much better able to pay, reaps the commercial profit of the enterprise.[142]

Herbert shared the Australians' concerns about foreign intervention in New Guinea and he was instrumental in persuading Lord Derby of this danger.[143] To have in a position of great influence at the Colonial Office, a senior official sympathetic to the Australian view of New Guinea (though not always to their arguments or methods) was of incalculable importance in the eleven years between Labilliere's first letter and the establishment of the protectorate.

---

140 Deane, Ch. XIV.
141 Min., 21 Nov 1874, on Robinson to Carnarvon, 7 September 1874. CO 201/577.
142 Min., 26 April 1875, on Cairns to Carnarvon, 22 Feb 1875. CO 234/35.
143 Jacobs, 106-118.

In the last analysis, these four factors – missionary influence, Australian pressure, fear of foreign intervention and the presence of a sympathetic and influential permanent official at the Colonial Office – worked together to bring about the proclamation of the British protectorate over south-eastern New Guinea (followed in 1888 by the annexation of the protectorate as a Crown colony). But without the primary pioneering work of the LMS missionaries, the subsequent history of Papua New Guinea would have been totally different. The work of the missionaries may not have been paramount but it was fundamental.

Indeed, these three case studies in the south-west Pacific have demonstrated the links between missionary involvement and the development of the empire in all their complexity. While the missionaries in the field, and more frequently their supporters at home, were often in the forefront of those calling for an extension of British authority, formal annexation was not always their objective. Nevertheless, the very presence of missionaries in an area was of fundamental importance. But could they be equally influential when it came to resisting the British government's desire to withdraw from existing areas of colonial rule? Turning now to West Africa, the next case study deals with one of the very rare occasions in the second half of the nineteenth century when the abandonment of an existing colony was a real possibility.

CHAPTER 5

The Proposed Cession of The Gambia to France

The present-day republic of the Gambia, which achieved independence within the Commonwealth in 1965, is a narrow strip of land, never more than twenty-five miles wide, following the course of the River Gambia 200 miles inland from its estuary into the Atlantic Ocean. First discovered by the Portuguese in 1455 and explored a considerable distance up-river three years later, the river proved to be one of the main waterways of the continent. In the whole of West Africa it is comparable only to the Niger, and is navigable for 500 miles from the Atlantic coast.[1]

British interest in the commercial potential of the waterway began in Elizabethan times, when the Queen granted a patent to Exeter merchants to trade in the Gambia. Interest greatly increased in the seventeenth century (including a voyage by Prince Rupert in 1652) culminating in the granting of trading charters to a series of English companies. The Royal Adventurers, the Gambia Adventurers, the Royal African Company, the Company of Merchants Trading in Africa successively held monopoly rights for the Gambia trade. For a brief period during and after the Seven Years' War, the Company of Merchants relinquished control and a Crown colony was established. The Gambia was used for the transportation of convicts in this period between the loss of the American colonies in 1776 and the acquisition of New South Wales in 1788.[2] In 1783 colonial status was abandoned and the company once again resumed control. This remained the *status quo* at the turn of the nineteenth century.[3]

The subsequent expansion of British interest was linked with the abolition of the slave trade. Fearful that the River Gambia was being used to evade the provisions of the 1807 Act because there was no British presence to deter slave

---

1 The early period of European exploration and exploitation of the Gambia is discussed in greatest detail in J.M. Gray, *A History of the Gambia* [1940] (London: Frank Cass, 1966), pp.1-29. See also H.A. Gailey, *A History of the Gambia* (London: Routledge & Kegan Paul, 1965), pp.18-34.
2 See T.R. Reese, *The History of the Royal Commonwealth Society, 1868-1968* (London: OUP, 1968), p.4.
3 See J.M. Gray, pp.30-293.

traders, Colonel Charles McCarthy, the governor-in-chief of the West African territories, sent Captain Alexander Grant with a detachment of the Africa Corps from Goree to the Gambia. In April 1816 Grant occupied the island of Banjul (subsequently renamed St Mary's Island) at the mouth of the river. Here, on this island of thirty square miles, the settlement of Bathurst was built. In 1823 the small strategic island of Lemaine, 160 miles up-river and renamed McCarthy's Island in honour of the governor, was added to the tiny colony, which had come under the control of the governor-in-chief in Sierra Leone in 1821.[4]

The Start of Missionary Activity

The first British Protestant missionaries in the Gambia were a group of Quakers, eager to work among freed slaves. Led by Hannah Kilham their short-lived mission lasted from 1821 to 1824.[5] They were not long alone, however, as the same year saw the arrival of both a Roman Catholic mission in the shape of the Sisters of St Joseph of Cluny and the first Wesleyan Methodists who quickly established themselves as the prime mission in the Gambia.[6] Already at work further down the coast in Sierra Leone they had become concerned at the lack of spiritual oversight for the new community of merchants and liberated slaves that was developing at Bathurst. As a result, the governor-in-chief at Freetown, Sir Charles McCarthy, suggested to the Revd John Baker of the Sierra Leone mission that the Wesleyans should extend their mission field into the Gambia. This suggestion was endorsed at the Methodist Conference of 1820 and the Revd John Morgan was appointed to begin the new mission.[7]

He was briefed at Bathurst by John Baker, *en route* from Freetown for his next posting in the West Indies. In a memorandum to the General Secretaries of the WMMS, Baker outlined his views on the future shape of the Gambia mission, based on his own considerable experience of West Africa: the centre of the mission should be St Mary's Island (Bathurst) where a stone mission house should be built with accommodation for a married man and a young single missionary; no missionary should be alone on a mission station; language study should be of prime importance (the Wolof language should be studied as the

---

4 *Ibid.*, pp.306-336.
5 For a long-term perspective of the role of the Christian faith in the Gambia see Martha T. Frederiks, *We have Toiled all Night: Christianity in the Gambia, 1456-2000* (Zoetermeer: Uitgeverij Boekencentrum, 2003).
6 See Findlay and Holdsworth, pp.118-146.
7 *Ibid.*, p.121. While briefly in England in 1820 McCarthy had taken the opportunity to visit the London headquarters of the WMMS in Bishopsgate Street and argued strongly for the Society to initiate a Gambia mission. J.M. Gray, p.311. But as Frederiks points out (pp.183-184), this was far from an exclusive invitation.

most potentially useful) and industry (especially agriculture) should be the chief feature of up-country mission stations.⁸

Education was, in Martha Frederiks' view, 'the Methodists' most important contribution to Gambian Society'. In fact, much of the mission's work was in the educational sphere, with the clear encouragement of the colonial government.⁹ One twentieth-century authority, H.A. Gailey, even accused the government of abdicating any responsibility for education by simply relying on what the mission could provide.¹⁰ This, presumably, is an example of what David Hilliard meant, in a rather different context, of 'the imperial utility of Christian missions'. ¹¹

On the spiritual level the mission was initially successful in gathering a congregation but thereafter had no spectacular success. In 1836 it registered a membership of 535. Between that date and 1860, when 812 members were recorded, its membership showed an apparent increase of 50%. But this is somewhat misleading being almost certainly accounted for by the beginning of a new mission station by Robert MacBrair at McCarthy's Island in 1836. Indeed, of the 812 members recorded in 1860, 600 were residents of the capital.¹² In the 1870s, the period of particular interest for this study, the membership of the mission remained virtually static. Indeed the marginal increases and decreases indicate a slight underlying decline.¹³

As in Fiji, the Wesleyan Methodists were the majority Christian community in the Gambia. For individual missionaries, the Gambia was a hard and unhealthy posting. More than one missionary succumbed to the climate shortly after arriving in the territory,¹⁴ and the WMMS archives contain numerous 'sick notes' for missionaries suffering from tropical diseases who needed leave from the Gambia in order to recover their health.¹⁵ It was thus not surprising that

---

8 Baker to Gen. Secs., WMMS, n.d., quoted in Findlay and Holdsworth, IV, pp.125-126.
9 Frederiks, p.200. Col. Ord reported in 1865 that 'an allowance of £100 per annum is made to the Wesleyan mission and the same to the Roman Catholic, in aid of general education...'. See *PP* 1865 XXVII [170]. By 1870 this had increased to £128.16s. See Revd H.J. Quilter to Acting Gen. Sec. Perks, 13 May 1870. *WMMS Archives*, West Africa Correspondence, Box 295.
10 Gailey, p.69.
11 Hilliard, *God's Gentlemen*, p.134.
12 See the WMMS *Annual Reports* for these years.
13 *Ibid.* 1870 - 705; 1872 - 741 1873 - 704; 1874 - 639; 1875 - 694; 1876 - 695; 1877 - numbers not given; 1878 - 675.
14 Tregaskis to Perks, 20 December 1874. *WMMS Archives*, Gambia Correspondence – West Africa Box 295. Sir Arthur Kennedy, Governor of the West African Settlements, referred to the four months' rainy season as the 'funeral season'. Kennedy to Kimberley, 20 July 1870. CO 87/97.
15 See, for example, Thomas Spilsby to ?, 28 December 1872; Thomas Spilsby to ?, 19 September 1873; certificate by Assistant Colonial Surgeon, 16 June 1874. *WMMS*

alongside a native population estimated in 1870 at 8,000 there were no more than forty or fifty Europeans in the whole of the colony.[16]

The Development of French Interest in The Gambia

In addition to the development of missionary activity, three other factors provide a backcloth to the exchange proposals of the late 1860s and early 1870s: French imperialism, Gambia's trade and its public finances, and unrest among the native population.

The very word, 'imperialism', which was described by Lord Carnarvon in 1878 as 'a new word ... which has crept in among us',[17] and which came to be used as an unflattering description of Disraeli's so-called 'forward policies' of the late 1870s, was in fact a product of the second French Empire, when Napoleon III sought to recreate the Napoleonic myth, though more in style than in substance.[18] The governorship of Louis Faidherbe in Senegal between 1854 and 1861, and again between 1863 and 1865, brought a renewed vision of dynamic French colonial power – a foretaste of the attitudes of the 1880s and 1890s. Thus there arose a French imperialism, both consolidationist and expansionist, which began to see the British Gambia territory, an anomalous riverbank colony surrounded by French Senegal, as a prize for France at small expense, if Britain was prepared to exchange the dubious advantages of the Gambia for other potentially more lucrative territories further down the coast. The Gambia was a block to French expansionist aspirations since it lay between Senegal and the so-called 'Northern Rivers' where France had considerable trading interests. In French theory, exchange could be beneficial to countries.[19]

French desire to acquire the Gambia stemmed partly from its domination of the trade of the area. From the 1840s cultivation of the groundnut became a major economic activity in the coastal region and along the rivers between Senegal and Sierra Leone.[20] Despite the nationality to which individual traders or their companies belonged, France was the principal market for the Gambian groundnut crop. In the absence of any other viable alternative the groundnut

---

Archives, Gambia Correspondence West Africa Box 295. See also Findlay and Holdsworth, IV, p.139.
16 Population estimate by Administrator Bravo. Bravo to Granville, 13 May 1870. CO 87/96.
17 'Imperial Administration', *Fortnightly Review*, XXIV (December 1878), 760.
18 See R. Koebner and H.D. Schmidt, *Imperialism: the story and significance of a political word, 1840-1960* (Cambridge: CUP, 1964), esp. pp.1-26.
19 See J.D. Hargreaves, *Prelude to the Partition of West Africa* (London: Macmillan, 1963), pp.91-144.
20 For an overview of the role of the groundnut and other crops in the wider West African economic context see A.G. Hopkins, *An Economic History of West Africa* (London: Longman, 1973), esp. pp.124-143.

increasingly became the agricultural *raison d'être* of the Gambia. By 1860, 10,000 tons per annum were being exported and by 1889 this was nearly 20,000 tons.[21] Before 1871, most of the trade was in the hands of English trading houses; 1871 saw equilibrium, and from 1872 onwards French trading houses had the majority of the groundnut trade. Indeed, in the period 1870-1873 France received four times the volume of exports from the Gambia (mainly groundnuts) than did Britain.[22]

As French trade was so successful in the Gambia without the cost of colonial administration, one is left to guess why the French desired this extra financial burden, and the only possible answers are imperialistic – consolidation of existing territories and the potential for expansion inland by means of the River Gambia and south beyond that river. Certainly it would not be a financially profitable acquisition since the colonial finances were hard pressed to break even. Indeed, the doubtful financial benefits of the Gambia colony meant that Britain would not be averse to considering exchange proposals since, as J.D. Hargreaves has pointed out, a central principle of British colonial policy – *the* central principle, in the opinion of the Gladstonian Treasury, which during the 1860s was greatly tightening its control over departmental policies – was that every colony ought to meet the cost of its own administration.[23] Governor Kennedy, admittedly hostile to the continuance of the Gambia as a British colony and thus likely to exaggerate its difficulties, was nevertheless not wildly inaccurate when he declared that 'the whole value of imports and exports do not equal the amount taken over the counter of a haberdasher's shop in the London season'.[24]

But if the groundnut was a staple crop for the Gambia, it was one of doubtful reliability and value. It was frequently at the mercy both of climatic factors and of the political and social instability caused by 'native' wars. Unrest amongst the indigenous population, occasioned by the rise of militant Islam, proved to be detrimental to the peace and prosperity of the Gambia. Followers of the fundamentalist Muslim leader Màbba, known to the British as 'Marabouts', clashed with the more nominal Muslims who were referred to as 'Soninkes'.[25] These clashes spilled over from the French territory of Senegal and took place over a period of half a century from 1850 to 1900. Trade was disrupted, lives threatened and the settlements at Bathurst and McCarthy's Island were at times almost engulfed in the violence. The unrest saw the end of traditional tribal rule in the Gambia valley and the creation of a power vacuum

---

21 Gailey, p.72.
22 Trade statistics contained in Administrator Kortright to Carnarvon, 19 June 1874. *PP* 1876, LII [C.1409].
23 Hargreaves, *Prelude*, p.106.
24 Kennedy to Kimberley, 26 August 1870. CO 87/97.
25 For Màbba see James F. Searing, *'God Alone is King': Islam and Emancipation in Senegal* (Oxford: James Currey, 2002), pp. 42-48.

which led to further instability. This led to the deployment from time to time of West Indian troops to bolster the British position in Bathurst and McCarthy's Island. The expense of such military deployment with apparently little to show for it was not unnoticed at the Colonial Office. Because the Combo territory, from which much of the unrest emanated, straddled Gambia's southern border with French territory, to have unified the administration of both parts of Combo under one colonial power would clearly have been greatly advantageous in the maintenance of law and order.[26]

British Reconsideration of The Gambia's Value

The Gambia was not Britain's only involvement in West Africa. There were also interests, in varying degrees, in Sierra Leone, the Gold Coast and the port of Lagos, and it was a conflict in one of these – the Gold Coast – that became the catalyst for a reassessment of Britain's presence in the region and led to the Gambia exchange project. In 1863 the powerful African state of Ashanti invaded the so-called 'protectorate', inland of Britain's Gold Coast forts. This was an area of British paramountcy rather than a legal protectorate. A moral obligation existed to protect the tribes against Ashanti and on a purely practical level it represented a buffer between Britain's coastal forts and a powerful and warlike inland kingdom which could easily disrupt British trade.[27] The fall-out of the military debacle which followed Britain's response to the Ashanti invasion soon reached London and Palmerston's government found itself on the receiving end of what in effect was a motion of censure in the House of Commons.[28] Though the government escaped defeat by the narrow margin of seven votes, Edward Cardwell, the new Colonial Secretary, well aware that he had inherited a policy vacuum with regard to West Africa, decided on a review of Britain's commitments in the area. He had cancelled military operations even before the debate took place and on the day following, let it be known that he would be sending a commissioner to enquire into Britain's involvement in West Africa.

When the matter came up for discussion again the following month C.B. Adderley, the Conservative colonial reformer, made it clear that he would use the first opportunity in the next session of Parliament to move for a Committee of Enquiry into Britain's role in West Africa.[29] Cardwell's chosen commissioner Colonel Harry Ord, Governor of Bermuda, carried out his commission in late 1864 and early 1865. Unlike Captain Andrew Clarke, a Royal Engineers officer who, having survived the ravages of the Ashanti War, had penned a

---

26 For a detailed discussion of the 'native' disturbances, see Gailey, pp.39-60.
27 See C.C. Eldridge, `Newcastle and the Ashanti war of 1863-64: a failure of the policy of "Anti-Imperialism"', *Renaissance and Modern Studies*, XII (1968), 68-90.
28 *Hansard*, Third Series, CLXXV, 17 June 1864, col.1962ff.
29 *Hansard*, Third Series, CLXXVI, 18 July 1864, cols 1670-1674.

memorandum advocating a drastic reduction of territory (since, in his understandably jaundiced view, the West African territories were a 'costly and profitless experiment'),[30] Ord's report of March 1865 proved to be much more optimistic.[31] In his view, British settlements assisted commerce and prevented a revival of the slave trade. As far as the Gambia was concerned he rejected the abandonment of McCarthy's Island, but recommended withdrawing the garrison. To improve the administration of the West African settlements he recommended unifying the four colonies, on the West Indian model, under a single governor-in-chief based in Sierra Leone.

Before Ord's report was completed, however, Adderley successfully moved his motion for the establishment of a Commons' Select Committee on 21 February 1865.[32] The committee's membership, included such well-known names as Cardwell, Fortescue (Cardwell's Parliamentary Under-Secretary), Hartington, Lord Stanley, Lord Alfred Churchill, Sir John Hay, Arthur Mills, W.E. Forster and Adderley (who acquired the chairmanship for himself). Only one member could be regarded as representative of the missionary interest – Sir Francis Baring, 'a high-principled Anglican',[33] who was a member of the Church Missionary Society with an interest in West Africa.[34]

The report of the '1865 Committee',[35] described by McIntyre as 'the most quoted document in the history of the West African settlements',[36] ruled out immediate withdrawal from any of the West African settlements. In the Gambia it recommended withdrawing from McCarthy's Island and concentrating the settlement on the mouth of the river. With the dual aims of increased efficiency and reduced expenditure, a central government based in Sierra Leone was recommended for the four settlements. The committee sought to encourage the growth of African civilisation through, wherever possible, self-governing African states rather than British colonies. No new settlements were to be made and Africans were to be led to exercise 'those qualities which may render it possible for us more and more to transfer to them the administration of all the Governments with a view to our ultimate withdrawal from all, except, probably, Sierra Leone'.[37] Robinson and Gallagher suggest that 'the Committee

---

30 Andrew Clarke, Confidential memo; 'British possessions on the West Coast of Africa', June 1864, WO 33/13/1387, p.69, quoted in McIntyre, *Imperial Frontier* p.97.
31 *PP* 1865, XXXVII [170].
32 *Hansard* Third Series, CCLXXVII, 21 February 1865, cols.535-559.
33 Hargreaves, *Prelude*, p.74.
34 See *Hansard* Third Series, CCLXXVII, col.559 for the full membership of the committee.
35 *PP* 1865, V [412].
36 McIntyre, *Imperial Frontier*, p.100.
37 *PP* 1865, V [412]. For a discussion of the 1865 Select Committee Report see Hargreaves, *Prelude*, pp.64-78.

genuflected towards the humanitarians by consenting to stay in Freetown',[38] but there is no evidence for this and Hargreaves is probably right to point to the naval, financial and commercial advantages of Sierra Leone in general, and Freetown in particular, for this decision.[39] An important proviso was included in the report, apparently at Cardwell's behest:

> That this policy of non-extension admits of no exception, as regards new settlements, but cannot amount to an absolute prohibition of measures which, in peculiar cases, may be necessary for the more efficient and economical administration of the settlements we already possess.[40]

This loophole proved, in due course, to be the ruin of the Select Committee's recommendations.

The wide diversity in opinion on the value and usefulness of the Gambia to Britain was coincidentally highlighted in Parliament on 15 July 1870.[41] In the Commons Sir John Hay referred to 'an extremely valuable possession: within ten days' steam of England and white men could live there happily and healthily for eight months of the year'. By contrast, in the Lords, the Colonial Secretary, Earl Granville, described the Gambia as 'an absolute burden without any redeeming characteristics'. They might have been referring to different British possessions.

The idea of seeking an exchange of territory for the Gambia is said to have originated with Faidherbe. It was suggested to the Colonial Office in 1861 by the Gambia's governor, George D'Arcy, having first been put to him by the French. The proposal was formally conveyed to Britain by the French government in March 1866.[42] Hargreaves considers that initially 'the Colonial Office ... regarded the problem as being less the negotiation of an even bargain than the decision whether a unilateral cession of the Gambia would be politically expedient'[43] and quotes Assistant Under-Secretary T.F. Elliot's minute that:

> The only use of an exchange with the French would be to preclude any mistaken annoyance of public opinion at a pure cession of territory to them. Otherwise it appears certain that anything we accept from them will be a loss and not a gain.

---

38 R. Robinson and J. Gallagher with A. Denny, *Africa and the Victorians* (London: Macmillan, 1961), p.30.
39 Hargreaves, *Prelude*, p.77, n.1.
40 *PP* 1865, V [412].
41 *Hansard*, Third Series, CCIII, 15 July 1870, cols 341-342, 351-355.
42 FO to CO, 10 March 1866, encl. Tour d'Auvergne to Clarendon, 2 March 1866. CO 87/86.
43 Hargreaves, *Prelude*, p.138 and min. by Elliott on FO to CO, 10 March 1866. CO 87/86.

At this early stage it was the sharp insight of an experienced civil servant which penetrated to the root of the issue – the problem of weighing the desirability of being rid of a politically unstable and economically unviable colony against the potential for public disquiet at such a move – especially if the arrangement proved to be a cession of territory to the old enemy, France. Against this background discussions and negotiations took place in a desultory fashion over several years, for until the advent of Lord Carnarvon there was little impetus or direction from the British side. The minutiae of these proposals, counter-proposals and negotiations are ably chronicled by Hargreaves.[44]

Based in Freetown, over 500 miles away from the Gambia, the Governor-in-chief of the West African Settlements, Sir Arthur Kennedy,[45] was an enthusiastic supporter of the exchange proposals. With some justification he regarded Sierra Leone as the most important part of his jurisdiction and the Gambia as a problematic insolvent territory on the frontier of empire.[46] When the French put forward the Mellacourie region (adjacent to Sierra Leone and, in Kennedy's view, part of its natural commercial hinterland)[47] as a possible exchange for the Gambia, he needed no convincing. He explained his support for the exchange project to the Colonial Office on the following grounds:

1. The expense of maintaining troops in the settlement, about 20,000*l.* a year, which I believe to exceed the ... mercantile profits of the place.
2. The hopelessness of extending civilization among the population.
3. The precarious nature of the revenue.
4. That the trade is almost exclusively French and will become more so yearly.
5. Its utter uselessness as a military post and its unimportance to Britain as a mercantile settlement.
6. The probability, if not certainty, of frequent collisions with the surrounding native tribes.
7. The responsibility of maintaining the settlement without any result or prospective advantage.[48]

Kennedy used the influence of his office to highlight both the Gambia's problems and the consequent desirability of cession.[49] He certainly cannot be regarded as an unbiased and objective observer of the Gambia's situation. Despite the fact that he was instructed to report on the possible reaction of

---

44 See Hargreaves, *Prelude*, pp.136-165.
45 As a result of the 1865 report, the four West African Settlements (Sierra Leone, the Gold Coast, Lagos and the Gambia) had been united under a single governor-in-chief based in Freetown. Under him, in the three territories in which he was not resident, was an 'Administrator'.
46 For a gloomy view of the Gambia's financial viability and prospects see memo. by Henry Fowler, Acting Collector and Treasurer, 12 March 1870. *PP* 1870, L [444].
47 Hargreaves, *Prelude*, p.151.
48 Kennedy to Monsell, 23 September 1869. *PP* 1870, L [444].
49 See, for example, *ibid.*, Kennedy to Granville, 29 March 1870 and 19 April 1870.

native Gambians to an exchange,[50] Kennedy dismissed them with the patronising comment that 'the natives are docile and would be easily influenced if their rights and property were previously guaranteed'.[51] When they actually demonstrated their lack of docility by producing two petitions in two months against the proposals,[52] Kennedy sought to undermine their credibility by casting aspersions on their personal integrity and social standing.[53] His hostility to the petitions and his dismissal of the importance of African opinion was not shared by the Gambia's Administrator, Major Alexander Bravo: 'with regard to the native population I fear the representations I have made of the advisability of the measure has met with little response, and any efforts made to convince them to approve the transfer can only, I feel sure, result in failure'.[54]

Kennedy's many despatches reveal an almost pathological dislike for the Gambia and his advocacy of Britain's exchange of territory with France developed a missionary zeal about it. Since the Gambia was one of the most unpopular postings in the colonial service and very difficult to fill, it is hardly surprising that it had few if any supporters among its officials.[55] But what of other sections of the British expatriate community in the Gambia – the missionaries and merchants?

Missionary Response

The response of the Wesleyan missionaries to the proposals did not initially show more than a passing interest: they were more concerned with preserving the rights and privileges which had accrued to the mission as the majority Christian community than with campaigning against the exchange proposals. When the news of the negotiations first came to their attention Henry Quilter, senior missionary in the Gambia, merely expressed his concern about its implications for the educational grant the mission received and Benjamin

---

50 Granville to Kennedy, 21 February 1870. CO 87/98A. This had been insisted upon by Lord Clarendon, now Foreign Secretary. See FO to CO, 22 January 1870. CO 87/98.
51 Kennedy to Granville, 29 March 1870. *PP* 1870, L [444].
52 *Ibid*. Petitions of April and 6 May 1870 enc. in Kennedy to Granville, 30 April 1870 and Kennedy to Granville, 10 May 1870.
53 Kennedy claimed that only ten out of the 517 signatories of the first petition were property owners and denigrated Harry Finden, the native storekeeper who organised the petition, as the proprietor of a 'grog shop'. Kennedy to Granville, 30 April 1870. CO 87/96.
54 Bravo to Granville, 13 May 1870. CO 87/96.
55 It seems certain that this reference to 'those non-residents so deeply committed to the advocacy of transfer' in the minutes of the 1871 Gambia District Synod is a clear reference to the lack of impartiality in the matter by Governor Kennedy. *WMMS Archives*. Gambia Synod Minutes 1842-1910. West Africa Box 297.

Tregaskis, chairman of the District, wrote from Freetown of the need to preserve missionary privileges.[56]

The following January, when Tregaskis presided over the Synod of the Gambian mission, the minutes recorded somewhat pompously that 'the ministers in charge of the Wesleyan mission on the Gambia feel a very solemn responsibility resting upon them regarding the proposed transfer of the settlement to the French government'.[57] It stated that as neither the Roman Catholic priests nor the Anglican colonial chaplain could be expected to oppose the exchange, the responsibility to do so rested with the Methodists. The minute continued: 'The Annual Meeting therefore respectfully but earnestly requests the Wesleyan Missionary Committee to use its influence in aid of those measures which have been taken, so laboriously, and at much sacrifice of time and money, in remonstrances to the Colonial Office and in recent Parliamentary movements'.

J.D. Hargreaves suggests that the merchant Thomas Brown may have been behind this request to the WMMS in London, though he adduces no evidence. From the WMMS Gambia correspondence file it is clear that Brown was in touch with the missionaries.[58] In fact it would have been surprising if this was not the case as there were only about fifty Europeans in the territory. Indeed, the exchange proposals must have been a constant topic of conversation among the white residents of this otherwise sleepy imperial backwater. Of course Brown must have discussed the exchange with the missionaries and in such conversations it is highly unlikely that he would not have tried to win them round to his point of view. The amount of influence, if any, which he was able to exert on the missionaries, remains unknown. The missionary committee in London was not, however, greatly moved by this request, nor by a subsequent appeal by Tregaskis,[59] but merely contented itself with a brief note in the 1871 *Annual Report* to the effect that:

> This settlement has been much agitated during the year by the report of a proposed cession of its Government and territory to France – a measure which has excited the alarm and indignation of all classes and which is specially deprecated by our missionaries.[60]

---

56 Quilter to Perks, 13 May 1870. *WMMS Archives.* Gambia Correspondence; West Africa Box 295. Tregaskis to WMMS, 11 May 1870, quoted in Hargreaves, *Prelude,* p.160.
57 Gambia Synod Minutes, January 1871. *WMMS Archives.* Gambia Correspondence; West Africa Box 297.
58 See, for example, Brown to Tregaskis, 19 May 1873. *WMMS Archives.* Gambia Correspondence; West Africa Box 297.
59 Ibid. Tregaskis to Gen.Secs., WMMS, 3 February 1871.
60 WMMS *Annual Report* 1871, pp.82-83.

In fact there is no evidence at any point in the controversy over the Gambia exchange proposals that the Wesleyan Methodist Missionary Society in London took any active steps to oppose the transfer. Any opposition that emerged came from individual missionaries in the Gambia or from individual influential Methodists at home.

Opposition from the Business Community

If, despite their initial disquiet, the missionaries were less than fanatical in their opposition to the exchange proposals and largely contented themselves with the writing of letters and minutes rather than any more vigorous action, this certainly could not be said of the British merchant community in the Gambia. The latter, though small in number, pursued their cause with vigour and terrier-like determination. They were easily able to take the moral high ground, both as those who stood to lose their livelihoods if the Gambia became French and also as the supposed defenders of the integrity of the British empire when it was perceived to be under threat. T.F. Elliot of the Colonial Office recognised the built-in disadvantage of the government case in 1868 when he minuted his concern 'whether general opinion would be offended by a cession of British Territory for which the public mind is not prepared ... [and] which would very probably be generally condemned by the outer Public who are unacquainted with the subject'.[61] The Permanent Under-Secretary, Sir Frederic Rogers, was equally aware of the problem:

> The difficulty is that if once these merchants determine to thwart the transfer, it is hardly conceivable that they would find any difficulty in getting up such a black opposition as could be paraded in Parliament, and it is not very easy for the English Government to counter-work such a movement.[62]

Thus the campaign of opposition to the transfer proposals came primarily from the British merchants based in the Gambia, who feared a loss of livelihood if transfer of sovereignty took place. The largest British firm in the Gambia, Forster & Smith, had been involved there since the 1820s, but the recent death of both the senior partner and the local agent meant that in 1870 they were to cease trading in the Gambia and transfer their business elsewhere. They were thus in no position to give a lead to the commercial community in the Gambia in opposing the proposed change of status, though in common with the other traders they wrote to the Colonial Office and, using their contacts in the City, were instrumental in sending a memorial to the Colonial Office signed by forty-one other firms.[63] Indeed, at this time the Colonial Office was in receipt of a

---

61 Min. by Elliot, 7 May 1868, on FO to CO, 5 May 1868. CO 87/90.
62 Min. by Rogers, 25 January 1870, on FO to CO, 22 January 1870. CO 87/98.
63 Forster and Smith to Granville, 18 June and 4 July 1870. *PP* 1870, L [444]. Memorial of London Merchants, 14 July 1870. CO87/98. Willmington suggests that

flurry of memorials from interested commercial organisations.[64] Three smaller firms headed by Thomas Brown, T.C. Chown and T.F. Quin, provided the main opposition, and of these Brown was by far the most active and influential.[65]

Quin's letter of 12 January 1870 to the Colonial Office elicited from Rogers the reply that parliamentary consent would have to be obtained before a transfer could take place.[66] This may have been intended as an emollient reply by Rogers but was surely a misjudgement since opponents to the transfer now knew that the Colonial Office was not the final court of appeal in the matter and so opposition increased rather than died down. In addition to letters and petitions, questions were now asked in Parliament. Little wonder that the Methodist missionaries to the Gambia, in their Synod minute of January 1871, referred to 'remonstrances to the Colonial Office and ... recent Parliamentary movements'.[67]

From June 1870 Government intentions concerning the Gambia came into the public domain. In the Commons on 10 June R.N. Fowler, treasurer of the Aborigines Protection Society, asked Monsell to confirm or deny that negotiations had taken place. When Monsell confirmed this, Sir John Hay enquired if a transfer could be effected without parliamentary consent. Gladstone himself intervened, repeating the opinion given by Rogers to Quin that such consent would be necessary and went further by stating that 'there never had been the slightest intention of taking any proceedings of the kind without the consent of Parliament'.[68] Thus, with the death of Lord Clarendon and Granville's translation to the Foreign Office, the new Secretary of State, Lord Kimberley, who took up the Seals of the Colonial Office on 7 July 1870, unexpectedly found himself at the receiving end of the growing campaign against the cession of the Gambia. The Manchester Chamber of Commerce had called at the Colonial Office on 4 July; London 'Merchants Manufactures and Traders', including the Manchester MP Thomas Bazley, followed on 14 July, as did Forster (of Forster & Smith) and Brown, Chown and Quin. On 27 July 1870 a delegation from the Aborigines Protection Society waited upon the new

---

Forster and Smith 'were not averse to coming under French rule as long as their property was protected, and parity, between French and English merchants was protected as in the (sic) Senegal'. Willmington, p.150.
64 See memorials of Manchester Chamber of Commerce, 4 July 1870, and Bristol Chamber of Commerce, 30 July 1870. CO 87/98.
65 That these merchants had previously collaborated to oppose government policy which they regarded as being hostile to their interests can be seen in their opposition to the abandonment of McCarthy's Island following the 1865 Report. See Quin, Goddard, Chown and Brown to Governor D'Arcy, 16 April 1866. CO Confidential Print African No.23, 1866. CO 87/93.
66 T.F. Quin to Granville, 12 January 1870; CO to Quin, 3 February 1870. CO 87/98.
67 WMMS *Annual Report* 1871, pp.82-83.
68 *Hansard*, Third Series, CCI, 10 June 1870, cols.1842-1843.

Secretary of State and the Bristol Chamber of Commerce followed three days later.[69]

Questions on the Gambia were asked in both Houses of Parliament on 15 July. In the Lords, the Duke of Manchester, president of the Royal Colonial Institute, knowing that Kimberley would at this stage know little of the preceding events, asked Granville for an account of the Gambia negotiations. Leaving no room for doubt as to where his sympathies lay, Granville sarcastically dismissed the significance of the petition. He repeated Kennedy's slur against Harry Finden as being 'a very respectable man who keeps a grog shop', described the Gambia as 'an absolute burden without any redeeming characteristics', but nevertheless endorsed the commitment to obtaining parliamentary consent to any exchange.[70] By contrast, in the Commons, Sir John Hay presented the Gambia in the best possible light.[71] He complained about the visit of a French admiral the previous month to inspect the public buildings and rejected the use of the 1865 Committee's report as a justification for the transfer of the Gambia's sovereignty to France. From the Opposition front bench Adderley alone spoke in favour of the exchange. A promise of compensation to merchants who suffered financially by the exchange was then made by Monsell, almost certainly a response to the plethora of commercial deputations which the Colonial Office had recently received, including a letter from Thomas Brown two days beforehand.

Thomas Brown, the first of the three Gambia merchants to come to England, had been active in speaking and making contacts since his arrival. Though Brown was in contact with the Wesleyan missionaries in the Gambia, there is no evidence that he approached the parent society whilst in Britain – he clearly found commercial contacts more useful. Indeed, the agitation against the Gambia exchange began in late June 1870, coinciding exactly with Brown's arrival in England. His letter of 12 July no doubt exaggerated both the extent of his interest in the Gambia and his probable losses (estimated between 15% and 66% of his existing trade) if the transfer went ahead.[72] Nevertheless, Brown spoke up for the Anglicised Africans who would perhaps be the greatest losers if the Gambia became French. He also pressed for substantial compensation for merchants – 'the imperial purse and not the private property of individuals should be called upon to make the sacrifice' – so much so that Hargreaves discusses the possibility that a desire for compensation was Brown's real motive in opposing the exchange.[73] Herbert regarded his letter as 'intelligent and

---

69 Memorial of Manchester Chamber of Commerce, 4 July 1870; memorial of London Merchants to Kimberley, 14 July 1870; memorial of Bristol Chamber of Commerce, 30 July 1870. CO 87/98; Willmington, pp.152-153.
70 *Hansard,* Third Series, CCIII, 15 July 1870, cols 339-342.
71 *Ibid.,* cols 351-367.
72 Brown to Kimberley, 12 July 1870. CO 87/98.
73 Hargreaves, *Prelude,* p.159.

temperate' and Kimberley minuted on a letter from the Chowns, dated 30 July, that 'The statement is a good one and deserves consideration, I am much disposed to think they are probably right in apprehending that the British merchants will suffer'.[74] Clearly under Kimberley the Colonial Office was to be much more open to discussion on the Gambia that it had been under Granville.

In a debate on the British West African Settlements on 9 June 1871, William M'Arthur, in a wide-ranging speech, took the opportunity of stressing 'the importance of relieving the minds of British subjects at the Gambia from the apprehension of their transference to a foreign power'.[75] M'Arthur was, of course, a leading lay Methodist, and through his membership of that church and his contacts with James Calvert and others played a leading part in the campaign to annex Fiji. However, it should be borne in mind that his evangelical and humanitarian interests and contacts were far wider than just the missionary movement . In fact, there is ample evidence to suggest that in the case of the Gambia it was his membership of the Aborigines Protection Society that was the vital motivating factor rather than his involvement with the WMMS.[76] In order to dampen the agitation, Knatchbull-Hugessen, in reply to M'Arthur, reminded the House that the outbreak of the Franco-Prussian War had put an end to discussions with France and 'it was not the intention of the Government to propose any renewal of the negotiations'.[77]

When, two months later, the French proposed a resumption of negotiations, Kimberley rejected this,[78] and the Gambia exchange project remained a dead letter during his tenure of the Colonial Office. Susan Willmington, the historian of the Aborigines Protection Society, recognised the 'cumulative effect' of opposition to the exchange on Kimberley, and conceded that that Society's 'voice was only one among many which opposed the cession of the Gambia...'.[79] The voice of the missionaries cannot be said to have been particularly loud either. The first exchange attempt was foiled largely by commercial interests, and Thomas Brown, with support from Chown and Quin, was undoubtedly the project's most effective opponent.

---

74 Min. by Herbert, 14 July, on Brown to Kimberley, 12 July 1870. CO 87/98. *Ibid.* T. Chown and T.C. Chown to CO, 30 July 1870 and min. by Kimberley, 4 August 1870.
75 *Hansard*, Third Series, CCVI, cols 1806-1813. See also M'Cullagh, p.137.
76 M'Arthur was, in fact, the Aborigines Protection Society's parliamentary spokesman on the Gold Coast. His remarks on the Gambia were very much in the nature of an aside in a longer speech. Willmington, p.172.
77 *Hansard*, Third Series, CCVI, cols 1814ff. He nevertheless reserved the right to abandon McCarthy's Island in line with the 1865 report.
78 Min. by Kimberley on FO to CO, 14 August 1871, and Kimberley to Quin, 15 September 1871. CO 87/101.
79 Willmington, p.153.

The Exchange Proposals Renewed

Within two months of Disraeli's election victory in February 1874, the French revived the Gambia exchange proposals in the hope that they would now be more favourably received.[80] Unlike his predecessor, who had been battered by the opposition to exchange during his formative first month in office and who came to doubt the moral justification for the proposal, the new Colonial Secretary, Lord Carnarvon, was more enthusiastic. In May 1874 he announced to the Administrator of the Gambia that, 'There are reasons which would induce me to look favourably on [an exchange]',[81] and three months later, writing to the Foreign Secretary, Lord Derby, he confided that, 'My leaning is ... in favour of the exchange being attempted'. The reasons he gave to Derby were that an exchange of the Gambia would simplify government on the Gold Coast and probably increase its revenue, while avoiding further 'native trouble' in the Gambia (he feared 'another West African war there'). He felt that 'recent annexationist policy at Fiji' gave his party better imperial credentials than those of the late government and this would 'save us from the suspicions which our predecessors would have had to meet...'.[82] The problem of opposition could be solved by 'a question of a mere few thousand pounds' compensation'.[83] This optimism was to survive for less than two years.

Though Lord Carnarvon was confident about being able to deal with any opposition, his confidence was built on somewhat shaky foundations. An almost complete change of personnel in the African and Mediterranean Department of the Colonial Office had taken place in the four years since the matter was last fully discussed. Of the officials who had encountered the previous hostility to exchange, only Henry Holland, the Legal Adviser, remained. With only Holland sounding a cautious note based on his previous experience,[84] Carnarvon saw no

---

80 Derby to Lord Lyons, 11 April 1874, enc. in FO to CO, 27 April 1874. *PP* 1876, LII [C.1409]. The French were now proposing to exchange their Ivory Coast forts at Assinie and Grand Bassam, as well as the Mellacourie, in return for the Gambia. Territorial amendments to these proposals, increasing British control to the south, are outlined in Willmington, p.157; Hargreaves, *Prelude*, pp.177-178.
81 Carnarvon to Administrator Kortright (Confidential), 21 May 1874. *PP* 1876, LII [C.1409].
82 Carnarvon to Derby, 31 August 1874, quoted in Hardinge, II, p.142. It should be noted that the motives for exchange were now somewhat different from the earlier proposal, the emphasis having shifted from the possible benefits of the Northern Rivers to those which would consolidate the Gold Coast following the investment of both money and human life in the 1873-74 Ashanti War. The Gold Coast, which had been administratively combined with Lagos in August 1874, had a new prominence in the official mind. The Gambia remained an unwelcome encumbrance.
83 *Ibid.* Carnarvon to Derby, 12 December 1874.
84 Mins. By Holland and Carnarvon, 2 and 3 May, on FO to CO, 27 April 1874. CO 87/107, quoted in Willmington, p.155. Administrator Kortright also contributed to

need to rush the matter. This lack of urgency, which was compounded by his withdrawal from the active business of the Office at the beginning of 1875 because of Lady Carnarvon's illness and subsequent death,[85] gave ample time for an opposition to emerge and organise.

Negotiations with the French having been satisfactorily completed by the end of June 1875 only the hurdle of Parliament remained to be surmounted and here the actions of Carnarvon and Disraeli are open to different interpretations. C.C. Eldridge describes Carnarvon at this stage as still 'unperturbed and unhurried' and W.D. McIntyre places the blame for delay at this vital moment on Disraeli, who reacted adversely to the political hornets' nest stirred up by Samuel Plimsoll's tantrum on the floor of the House of Commons on 22 July 1875. As 'the Prime Minister did not want to risk a controversial Gambia Cession Bill in the same parliamentary session, the matter was postponed [and] Disraeli's delay wrecked the project'.[86] Susan Willmington offers a different interpretation. She suggests that it was Carnarvon, not Disraeli, who panicked,[87] because of a report from Captain Cooper, the Acting Administrator of the Gambia predicting an imminent outbreak of war amongst the native population. This resulted in Carnarvon attempting to rush the project through before matters became worse and the French had second thoughts. She also maintains that McIntyre is incorrect in that Carnarvon had already abandoned the idea of a parliamentary bill to give effect to the cession and that Disraeli was fully aware of his plans.[88] Indeed Carnarvon had minuted as far back as 6 July that when the exchange proposals were presented to the French,[89] 'the words "with the consent of Parlt." must come out'.[90] As Hargreaves commented:

Carnarvon's false sense of security by belittling (in the Kennedy tradition) any possible Gambian opposition. See Kortright to Carnarvon (Confidential), 19 June 1874. *PP* 1876, LII [C.1409].

85 Hardinge, II, pp.80-81.

86 Eldridge, *England's Mission*, p.60; McIntyre, *Imperial Frontier*, p.287. Delay did not, however, spare the government embarrassment. A report on 29 July in the French newspaper *Le Moniteur* announcing completion of the negotiations led Knatchbull-Hugessen to raise the matter in the Commons. His successor, Lowther, was obliged to deny the report and, three days later, assured the House that parliamentary discussion would take place before any action was taken. *Hansard*, Third Series, CCXXVI, 30 July 1875, col.222 and 3 August, col.444.

87 Willmington, p.158. A state of alarm by Carnarvon, if correct, would be in line with the nickname Disraeli used for him (though never to his face, to which he exuded charm and flattery) – 'Twitters'. The strained relationship between Disraeli and Carnarvon has already been referred to in Chapter 3 above.

88 Carnarvon to Disraeli, 28 July 1875. Copy in Carnarvon Papers, PRO 30/6/11, No.40, quoted in Willmington, p.158.

89 They received the British proposals on 23 July – less than three weeks before Parliament was due to rise for the summer recess.

90 Min., 6 July, by Carnarvon on FO to CO, 25 June 1875. CO 87/108.

Carnarvon still hoped to complete negotiations and put the agreement through in a hurry. Reflection had convinced him that there was no need for legislation, or even a vote in the House of Commons, in order to effect a transfer of territory; formal consultation would suffice. His intention was, if France accepted the offered terms, to make a brief announcement of the government's decision, trusting that no effective opposition could be organised before the adjournment of the House.[91]

It is quite possible that the deteriorating spiral of relations between Carnarvon and the Prime Minister, noted in the chapter on Fiji, took a downward turn at this time leading towards Carnarvon's resignation in 1878. Certainly, a few months later, in November 1875, Disraeli offered the Viceroyalty of India to Carnarvon and, less than a fortnight later after this offer had been declined, offered him the Admiralty.[92] One explanation is that Disraeli, after disagreeing with Carnarvon, first over Fiji and then over the Gambia, felt the wisdom of moving him from a potentially controversial department where he might find himself in circumstances which might, once again, lead him to contemplate resignation. The evidence, however, is not conclusive and it may even have been kindness on the Prime Minister's part to offer the recently bereaved Carnarvon a new and potentially less stressful post. Whatever the truth of the matter, Disraeli fell back on his normally effective expedient of flattery, and retained Carnarvon in the Cabinet and at the Colonial Office until the Eastern Question occasioned his resignation in 1878. And Carnarvon bore no grudges. In a memorandum written in 1879 on the subject of his time in government and the events leading to his second resignation, Carnarvon reflected that 'I am bound as a matter of justice to place on record that Disraeli was not really unfair to me. He manoeuvred of course for his own ends ... and up to the end of my tenure of office I believe that he sincerely desired to retain me in the Cabinet'.[93]

Whatever the reasons, when Carnarvon addressed the Lords on 3 August 1875 he sought to allay current fears concerning the proposals.[94] After praising the post-war opportunities of the Gold Coast he turned to the division of Anglo-French jurisdiction along the West African coast and put forward the Gambia exchange project as a way of rationalising the demarcation of colonial jurisdiction. He sought to distance the current proposals from those which had foundered previously. This time he did not even promise consultation with Parliament, he simply stated that 'nothing final or conclusive shall be done in this matter until the meeting of Parliament next year'. Finally, a note of exasperation crept in as he spoke of a mere 'handful' (he used the word three times) of British citizens who were, in his view, responsible for delaying this undoubtedly beneficial exchange.

---

91 Hargreaves, *Prelude*, p.179.
92 Hardinge, pp.94-95.
93 Quoted in *ibid.*, p.377.
94 *Hansard*, Third Series, CCXXVI, 3 August 1875, cols 436-438.

Renewed Opposition

The opposition to the second exchange proposal was somewhat different to that which foiled the first. Whereas those who had protested against the first exchange had the appearance of a group of individuals largely persuaded and briefed by Thomas Brown, the second exchange proposal experienced much more organised opposition. The probable reason for this was the recent success of the campaign for the annexation of Fiji. A network of humanitarians, missionaries and empire enthusiasts had been established. With little additional effort this support was tapped and mobilised for the retention of the Gambia, the parliamentary delay, from July 1875 to February 1876, giving the opposition ample time to prepare and present their campaign.

Did the Wesleyan missionaries figure any more largely in the opposition to the second exchange proposals than they had in the first? Though better organised and with more influential support, opponents of the exchange once again had only marginal support from the Gambia missionaries. Since 1871 there had been a complete change in the ranks of the Wesleyan mission in the Gambia. Tregaskis had left West Africa in 1875 to be replaced as District Chairman by the Revd Charles Knight, who, being new to his post when the second exchange proposal became public knowledge, stayed put in Sierra Leone and gave no indication of any opposition to (or, indeed, support for) the exchange. George Adcock was the senior mis   ry at Bathurst. He was joined by James Fieldhouse from Sierra Leone after the death of the unfortunate J.W. Bell who survived only two months in the Gambia's unhealthy climate at a time of much fever and sickness in the colony.[95] During 1875 John Badcock joined them in Bathurst to increase the mission staff in the Gambia and on 29 June 1875 the three missionaries wrote to the WMMS general secretaries in London urging official opposition to the exchange proposals, a plan which would be 'destructive to the commercial. civil and religious privileges of its inhabitants'.[96] Indeed, George Adcock went further and was one of only two Europeans who signed a petition against the exchange.[97] However, Hargreaves described Adcock as 'unstable'[98] and, more telling than the presence of his signature – clearly more of a gesture than a policy – is the absence of those of his colleagues. Were they all *really* serious about the matter, or were they reacting as they felt it was proper for missionaries to do under the circumstances or, indeed, merely responding to the persuasive lobbying of Thomas Brown?

---

95 Tregaskis to Perks, 20 December 1874. *WMMS Archives*, West Africa – Gambia Correspondence, Box 295. See also WMMS *Annual Report* for 1875, p.123.

96 *Ibid* for 1876, p.113. Babcock, Adcock and Fieldhouse to WMMS, 29 June 1875. *WMMS Archives*, West Africa – Gambia Correspondence, Box 295.

97 Petition from Joshua Richards and 151 others, 7 October 1875, enc. in Officer Administering the Government to Carnarvon, 23 November 1875. *PP* 1877, LX [C.1827].

98 Hargreaves, *Prelude*, p.183.

Except for one possible factor – the presence of W.B. Boyce, on the emergent 'Gambia Committee' – there is no evidence that the WMMS headquarters in London responded any more favourably to the letter from Babcock, Adcock and Fieldhouse in 1875 than they had done to Tregaskis's request in 1871. Yet only the previous year the WMMS had been prepared to expend considerable energy and influence in order to persuade the government to annex the Fiji islands. Despite the absence of any documentary evidence on this lack of interest in the Gambia exchange, the reason for the disparity is not hard to fathom. Fiji was a territory where Methodism had taken root in a remarkable way and which had considerable commercial prospects. The same could not be said for the Gambia. Though a British possession for many years and though Methodism was the majority faith there, the Gambia was never going to be more than a political and commercial backwater, and the work of the missionaries though tireless and faithful in their efforts was never likely to have the same effect as it had in Fiji. The missionaries in the Gambia might feel strongly about the matter, but they found it impossible to persuade their headquarters in London to oppose the exchange in anything more than a perfunctory fashion.

The opposition to the Gambia exchange crystallized in the long parliamentary recess of 1875-76 and emerged in January 1876 as the 'Gambia Committee'.[99] Like the Fiji Committee before it, it operated from rooms in the Canada Government Building in London. Admiral Sir Charles Wingfield was the chairman and the joint secretaries were Captain Charles Fitzgerald, an army officer with Gambia experience, and F.W. Chesson of the Aborigines Protection Society. Chesson was the real driving force behind the committee. The parliamentary delay was critical and once the Gambia Committee was up and running, the future of the exchange proposals was in jeopardy.

A *prima facie* examination of the committee's members would indicate that the missionary movement was well represented since it included William and Alexander M'Arthur, Admiral James Erskine, also a Methodist, W.B. Boyce, shortly to retire as one of the WMMS's general secretaries, and Robert Moffat of the LMS. It would be misleading to put too much weight upon numbers, however. Boyce and Moffat clearly represented the WMMS and LMS respectively, but this was in all probability a token representation. Certainly Boyce and Moffat took part in the deputation to Lord Carnarvon on 1 February 1876 and Boyce and his fellow WMMS general secretary, Dr Morley Punshon, received an unctuous letter of thanks from Thomas Brown and thirty three others in the Gambia.[100] Boyce's commitment to opposing the exchange has to

---

99 For the Gambia Committee see Eldridge, *England's Mission*, pp.161-162; Willmington, pp.159-164.
100 Thomas Brown *et al.* to Boyce and Punshon, 24 February 1876. *WMMS Archives*, West Africa – Gambia Correspondence, Box 295. Hargreaves describes this document

be held in question, however, in view of comments made six years earlier. Writing to Dr James Rigg of the WMMS Committee, who had received a communication concerning West Africa from the Foreign Office, Boyce had replied:

> I fear the French are on the whole better administrators than we are for colonies like ours in West Africa; [despite their] arbitrary acts. ... the community gains the benefit of having only one master and matters are quickly settled .... good national government in which the rulers *'bear not the sword in vain'* but are *'a terror to evil doers'* (Rom.13) is equally an ordinance of God – and in this I think we fail in West Africa.[101]

Certainly each of the lay missionary supporters on the committee wore more than one hat. Both M'Arthur brothers belonged to the Aborigines Protection Society and Erskine the Anti-Slavery Society, though, as with the Fiji Committee, it is impossible to say which 'hat' any of them was wearing at one particular time. This is, indeed, a false dichotomy since they themselves would not have made a distinction between their spiritual and humanitarian interests, seeing both as integral parts of their Christian faith. Nevertheless, having said that, there is clear evidence from his correspondence with Chesson that William M'Arthur, the most influential of the three, approached the Gambia from the angle of his humanitarian contacts. It is of course possible, even probable, that Boyce spoke with M'Arthur on the subject – they were, after all, related by marriage.[102] But far more important in this instance was M'Arthur's membership of the Aborigines Protection Society and his close contact with the society's secretary, F.W. Chesson.

It has already been noted that M'Arthur spoke on West African matters in the Commons on behalf of the Aborigines Protection Society. It was Chesson, now recovered from the illness which had kept him out of the Fiji campaign, who was the leading light in the Gambia Committee. His society's concern was for the native Gambians who, it was felt, would suffer from an exchange of sovereignty.[103] He worked closely with M'Arthur who was able to advise on strategy: 'The proper time for taking action in the case of the Gambia will be

---

as a 'sanctimonious round robin'. Hargreaves, *Prelude*, p.183. Hargreaves has confused Dr Punshon with his predecessor, Dr Bunting.
101 W.B. Boyce to Dr J.H. Rigg, 17 September 1869. CO 87/98B.
102 William M'Arthur's brother, Alexander, MP for Leicester, was married to Boyce's daughter. When William M'Arthur spoke in the Commons on 2 May 1876, he quoted from an (undated) letter from George Adcock, which clearly must have been supplied by Boyce. *Hansard*, Third Series, CCXXVIII, cols 1998-2004.
103 *Aborigines Friend*, November 1875, p.234, quoted in Willmington, p.160.

just before the meeting of Parliament'. He proposed 'a strong deputation to Lord Carnarvon on the subject'.[104]

As well as those already mentioned, the Gambia Committee included a number of merchants including Chown and Thomas Brown's son, David. Though by its very nature an umbrella organisation, the Gambia committee was not a global umbrella. Others with legitimate interest in the Gambia chose to stay outside its shelter and to work independently along parallel lines. These were the Royal Colonial Institute and the Manchester Chamber of Commerce. As far as the Institute was concerned, it would seem that having established a committee of its own to look at the Gambia question in October 1875 it was then reluctant to throw in its lot with the Gambia Committee when that body later emerged under Chesson's supervision.[105] This duplication of effort caused untidiness rather than hostility or rivalry. The leaders of the three groups remained on good terms and often shared information. Yet all three ventured into print[106] and the unfortunate Lord Carnarvon was obliged to receive three deputations on the Gambia within two days.[107] This cannot have been without significance in convincing the government of the increasing opposition to their proposals. When this opposition began to surface in Parliament, Carnarvon's chances of gaining support for the exchange began to slip away.[108]

On 17 February, after a battering from three deputations and with their several publications fresh off the presses, Carnarvon rose in the Lords to give the statement on the Gambia which had been postponed from the previous July. This delay, far from gaining breathing space for the government, had intensified the criticism of the exchange and Carnarvon now appeared more defensive.

---

104 M'Arthur to Chesson, 20 November 1875, A.S.C. C141/151. Quoted in Willmington, p.160.
105 Reese, p.46. Here Reese describes the R.C.I.'s campaign as a 'useful supplement to the pressure being applied ... by other interested bodies'. For full details of the Institute's involvement see Reese, pp.46-47 and Avaline Folsom, *The Royal Empire Society* (London: George Allen and Unwin, 1933), pp.215-216, 228-229.
106 The Gambia Committee spawned *The Gambia and its proposed cession to France* by Charles Fitzgerald (London, 1875), the Royal Colonial Institute's secretary produced a 'Report on the Gambia Question', PRCI, VII (1875-76), 68-85. J.F. Hutton of the Manchester Chamber of Commerce wrote *The Proposed Cession of the Gambia to France* (Manchester, 1876).
107 Manchester Chamber of Commerce on 31 January, Royal Colonial Institute and Gambia Committee on 1 February 1876. The third deputation expressed missionary concerns of possible French ill-treatment of Protestant converts, but this appears to be peripheral rather than central to their argument. See Fitzgerald.
108 To give the Colonial Office further pause for thought there came a letter from Thomas Chown, clearly representative of the Gambia Committee (Chown to CO, 9 February 1876. CO 87/109). Chown painted a bleak picture of the hardships to the native Gambians that exchange would cause, to set alongside the benefits Britain would allegedly accrue. Nevertheless as much as the content it was the timing of his letter, at a time when the government's resolve was weakening, that was important.

Even a *Times* leader a fortnight earlier had questioned the desirability of the exchange.[109] Despite support from Hemming within the Colonial Office and Lord Derby without,[110] a heavy cold meant that Carnarvon was not at his best in the chamber on a crucial occasion that required a masterly performance from the Colonial Secretary.

Carnarvon's political weakness, compounded by a physical one, was made even worse by telling the House at the outset that he was not presenting a resolution for them to debate, merely a 'short statement' for their information. To the opposition this no doubt smacked of either uncertainty or an attempt to by-pass parliamentary approval. He surveyed the history of the exchange proposals (emphasising that an exchange *not* a cession was the object) and stated that the need to consolidate the new Gold Coast colony had brought a new situation in which the confusion of sovereignty along the West African coast was highly undesirable: 'we should be making the territory that belongs to us more compact and more consolidated, and therefore more manageable for political purposes'. He outlined the precise territorial details of the exchange which, in essence, gave Britain a free hand between Sierra Leone and Lagos and exclusive rights at the mouth of the Niger. All this in exchange for the Gambia.[111]

Lord Granville responded first for the Liberals. Though personally happy to be rid of the Gambia he observed Carnarvon's weakness and twisted his knife in the wound:

> What I rather gather is this, that the government have not quite made up their minds, although a short time ago they thought they had made up their minds, and that they think it better to ventilate the subject and see how the cat jumps....[112]

Lord Blachford, formerly Sir Frederic Rogers, also spoke in favour, but the remainder of the speakers, including the Duke of Manchester, President of the Royal Colonial Institute, were opposed. Kimberley, though not hostile, felt that the government had not made a sufficiently convincing case for the exchange.[113] Predictably, Carnarvon failed to win over the House by means of his statement. He no doubt reflected that to have adopted a bold course and pursued the matter as planned the previous summer could not have been worse than the present situation, caused largely by effective campaigning in the intervening months. To put the matter to an immediate parliamentary vote would now clearly be unwise.

The government's loss of the initiative on the Gambia was clearly illustrated two days later by its presence on the Cabinet agenda. Perhaps not

---

109 *The Times*, 2 February 1876.
110 Derby to Carnarvon, 1 February 1876. PRO 30/6/8. Memo. by Hemming,
7 February 1876. CO 806/60.
111 *Hansard*, Third Series, CCXXVII, 17 February 1876, cols 374-378.
112 *Ibid.*, cols 385-387.
113 *Ibid*, cols 388-396.

surprisingly they were 'as usual adverse to a bold course', wrote Carnarvon[114] The Cabinet, now in full retreat, attempted to buy time by the time-honoured expedient of a Select Committee of the House of Commons, announced by Disraeli, in response to a question by M'Arthur on 21 February. This change of policy was a clear reflection of the government's lack of confidence that the exchange would secure parliamentary approval. Despite continued questioning in the Commons by Arthur Mills on 22 February[115] and Alexander M'Arthur on 9 March[116] the final blow to the exchange project was dealt, not by the Gambia Committee or its supporters, but by the French. The precise details of the minor misunderstanding which caused the Gambia exchange to be buried are given elsewhere.[117] In essence a French request for clarification of some of the details of the exchange, possibly because a translation error had caused some confusion, was inflated into a larger disagreement between the two governments and also highlighted communications lapses between the Foreign and Colonial Offices: Carnarvon's Lords statement on 17 February had been made without his knowledge of a French note of 11 February which the Foreign Office had failed to forward. It was a minor disagreement – far greater ones had been overcome at previous stages in the negotiations – but the political will to reach a mutually acceptable agreement had disappeared. After holding out for so long against a well-organised and highly-motivated opposition, Carnarvon had finally run out of steam. Fearing he may have inadvertently misled the Lords on the 17 February because he was not in full possession of the facts on the current French position, he now took the line of least resistance and allowed the negotiations to lapse.

Whether this was a loss of nerve by Carnarvon or simply the last straw which broke the camel's back is a moot point. In the view of Lord Blachford (formerly Sir Frederic Rogers, the Permanent Under-Secretary) Carnarvon had 'a disposition to be caught in showy schemes'.[118] As the author of the successful British North America Act of 1867, Carnarvon perhaps had a greater confidence in his subsequent projects than was necessarily warranted. Certainly his desire for South African confederation was pushed further than was wise and Britain became embroiled in a highly complex and dangerous situation there. Indeed, his confederation policy in the Windward Islands was running into trouble at the very time the Gambia exchange project was coming to an end.[119] Although he continued to support the Gambia exchange project beyond

---

114 Hardinge, II, p.144.
115 *Hansard*, Third Series, CCXXVII, 22 February 1876, cols 682-84.
116 *Hansard*, Third Series, CCXXVII, 9 March, 1876, col.710.
117 McIntyre, *Imperial Frontier*, pp.288-289; Hargreaves, *Prelude*, pp.190-194.
118 G.E. Marindin, *Letters of Frederic, Lord Blachford, Under-Secretary of State for the Colonies, 1860-1871* (London: John Murray, 1896), p.263.
119 The end of the Gambia exchange project brought no respite for Carnarvon, The following month saw his Windward Island confederation policy in tatters after rioting in

any reasonable hope of its being effected, he came to accept that he was beaten and on 20 March 1876, in response to a question by Lord Cottesloe Carnarvon rose in the Lords to bury any hope of exchanging the Gambia. Clearly with more than a tinge of regret for what he had regarded as a good deal for Britain, yet glad to be rid of what had become a politically inexpedient incubus, and thankful that he could now blame the French and not Cabinet faint-heartedness or effective opposition winning the argument, Carnarvon stated:

> it now appeared that the French government were unwilling to give up to them that entire and exclusive control of the coast which Her Majesty's Government expected, and upon which, of course, the articles of agreement were based. Under these circumstances they had no option but to abandon the negotiations.[120]

Assessment

Who then, was responsible for defeat of the Gambia exchange project, frustrating the wills of both British and French governments over a period of ten years? The British government themselves were of course to blame for ineptitude in their handling of the matter at vital moments. But defeat of the exchange proposals can under no circumstances be claimed as a victory for the missionary movement. The first defeat of the exchange in 1869-71 seems to have been the result of a successful campaign mounted by local commercial interests (especially Thomas Brown) who harnessed the support of both commercial interests and humanitarian groups in England. The Gambia missionaries did little apart from passing resolutions at their synods and writing to their headquarters.

Admittedly, the second campaign, in 1875-76 was different. This time organised opposition in Britain was the critical factor. The Royal Colonial Institute was clearly of the opinion that the retention of the Gambia was in no small way due to their intervention and this view is perpetuated by both its official historians. Trevor Reese describes the conclusion of 'the Gambia affair' as being:

> a victory for the Royal Colonial Institute, the Manchester Chamber of Commerce, and other interests which by public pressure at Westminster, in Whitehall, and in the press had contributed to the government's hesitancy in pursuing the offer from the French government.[121]

Barbados. See W.B. Hamilton, *Barbados and the Confederation Question, 1871-1885* (London: Crown Agents, 1956).

120 *Hansard*, Third Series, CCXXVIII, cols 264-265.

121 Reese, p.47. The Institute's triumphalism over the Gambia is probably due to the fact that of the three causes which the Institute's council had espoused in the 1870s (the other two being New Guinea and Newfoundland fisheries) the Gambia was the only one that came to a successful conclusion at that time and so the Institute may be forgiven for

Hargreaves rightly disagrees with such an interpretation: 'these "new Imperialists" would hardly have taken up the Gambia question unprompted; but for the merchants' campaign, the transfer might have been quietly and speedily effected'.[122] While the Institute, and the Manchester Chamber of Commerce both lent weight to the argument against exchange, by far the most influential and effective body opposing the 1875-76 exchange was the specially convened Gambia Committee.[123]

Finally, however, it is interesting to consider whether the second exchange proposal was ever really viable. Was it a real possibility or merely Carnarvon's single-mindedness which beguiled many into thinking it so? There is reason to believe that the lapse of the first exchange proposal in 1871 was decisive and that the second was always doomed to failure. The words of those in office at the time certainly tend to point in that direction. Lord Kimberley commented, 'when we tried to get rid of it [the Gambia] with what a clamour we were met',[124] and Knatchbull-Hugessen asserted, 'In the present tone and temper of the British mind, no abandonment of territory would, in my view, be permitted by Parliament, or sanctioned by public opinion'.[125] The importance of the failure to exchange the Gambia with France was not just, as Hargreaves and McIntyre contend, the loss of a potential single, united, British West Africa but rather that it may well have marked a watershed of attitudes with regard to the integrity of the empire. In 1862 and 1863 it had been perfectly possible to relinquish unwanted territories[126] and, even as late as 1869, the Liberal Foreign Secretary Lord Clarendon could assert that 'there is no care in this country for our West African possessions – I believe that an announcement of intention to get rid of them would be popular'.[127] Yet by 1870 and certainly by 1876, 'not

---

patting itself, albeit with very little justification, on the back. See also Folsom, pp. 215, 224, 228.

122 Hargreaves, *Prelude*, p.158.

123 Andrew Porter emphasises the role of Chesson in bringing together the Gambia Committee in the summer of 1875. Andrew Porter (ed.), *OHBE*, III (Oxford: OUP, 1999), 215. The missionary contribution to the committee, in the person of W.B. Boyce, was minimal.

124 Min. by Kimberley, 23 September 1873, on Cooper to Administrator-in-Chief, 29 July 1873. CO 87/105.

125 Min. by Knatchbull-Hugessen, 18 February 1873, on M'Arthur's motion for publication of correspondence about the Gold Coast, 17 February 1873. CO 96/104.

126 The Bay Islands had been ceded to Honduras in 1862 and the Ionian Islands to Greece the following year. See C.C. Eldridge, 'The Myth of Mid-Victorian "Separatism": the Cession of the Bay Islands and the Ionian Islands in the early 1860s', *Victorian Studies*, XXI (1969), 331-346.

127 Clarendon to Admiral Harris, 21 October 1869, Granville papers, PRO 30/29/55, quoted in Peter J. Durrans, 'The House of Commons and the British Empire, 1868-1880', *Canadian Journal of History*, IX (1974), 25. Indeed, the period 1868-70, during Lord Granville's tenure as Colonial Secretary, has been dubbed the 'climax of anti-

even a colony as futile and minute as the Gambia could be jettisoned'.[128] Was the failure of the Gambia exchange merely a piece of effective campaigning by interested parties and pressure groups in a manner which had become well established in nineteenth-century Britain as the growth of parliamentary democracy gave greater opportunity? Could the commotion surrounding the proposed abandonment of this small West African colony have marked a stage in the development of a concept of empire from a diverse and unrelated collection of colonies into a wider vision of an empire with a corporate integrity marked by some kind of 'Britishness' and which it was now becoming unthinkable to alienate?

If the second exchange project of 1875-76 was never really a viable proposition then Thomas Brown deserves the credit for keeping the Gambia British. If it was, and if there really was a window of opportunity in the summer of 1875 before Carnarvon, Disraeli and Samuel Plimsoll together closed it, then the credit should be shared between Brown, F.W. Chesson and William M'Arthur. Brown brought the Gambia's plight to public attention in Britain, Chesson created an organised network of opposition and M'Arthur led the parliamentary challenge. These three played the leading roles in the drama of the defeat of the Gambia exchange – the Methodist missionaries merely formed part of the chorus. Steven Maughan's perceptive phrase, 'marginal actors in empire' (regarding the treatment of missionaries by the dominant forms of imperial history), accurately sums up the role of the Methodist missionaries in the Gambia affair.[129]

What emerges from this case study as far as missionary involvement in imperialism is concerned adds to the view that there were enormous variations in missionary attitudes to the empire. Brian Stanley has suggested that the relationship between missions and the forces of imperialism was a 'complex and ambiguous' one.[130] Missionary involvement in the opposition to the Gambia exchange would seem to bear this out. Even the WMMS, often regarded as having a very positive attitude towards imperial expansion, notably in successfully lobbying for the annexation of Fiji, seem to have had little enthusiasm for maintaining British control of the Gambia.

---

imperialism' as many links with a number of colonies were relaxed or cut and there were fears that Britain was about to shed the last vestiges of her empire. See Eldridge, *England's Mission*, Ch. 3, pp.53-91. Thus the timing of the Gambia exchange project was unfortunate, encountering as it did the reaction to this perceived official hostility to the empire.
128 Robinson and Gallagher, p.30.
129 Steven Maughan, 'Imperial Christianity? Bishop Montgomery and the Foreign Missions of the Church of England', in Andrew Porter (ed.), *The Imperial Horizons of British Protestant Missions, 1880-1914* (Grand Rapids and Cambridge: Eerdmans, 2003) p.34.
130 Stanley, *The Bible and the Flag*, p.184.

But what of the other West African settlements where missionaries were more firmly established and had played a part in the initial development of British colonial rule? The annexation of Lagos and missionary work among the Egba is an obvious case for investigation. Unhappily, missionaries and British government did not always see eye-to-eye elsewhere on the West African coast.

CHAPTER 6

Missions and the Growth of British Power in Lagos and Yorubaland

In the period under review, official British jurisdiction in what was to become Nigeria[1] was limited to the island and environs of Lagos on its south-west coast. Lagos, which as will be seen, was acquired by Britain in 1861 – not without missionary involvement – formed one of the four West African Settlements which had come under the microscope of Adderley's 1865 Select Committee. The Gambia was not the only West African territory that could have been abandoned by Britain in response to the Select Committee's report.[2] Yorubaland, where missionary interest was initially directed, formed the commercial hinterland of Lagos. It was an area bounded to the north and east by the River Niger, with the Bight of Benin to the south and Dahomey to the west.[3]

Just as disquiet about the Pacific labour trade was to be the trigger for British involvement in Fiji and other Pacific islands, so the Atlantic slave trade focused British attention on West Africa. Though slavery had been abolished in the British territory in 1807 and the trade itself declared illegal in 1833,[4] it

---

1 The part of West Africa today known as Nigeria, is a creation of the colonial age. The name, reputedly coined by Lady Lugard, wife of the pro-consul, did not achieve official status until 1 January 1900, when the Protectorates of Northern Nigeria and Southern Nigeria came into being. They were united into a single colony in 1914. A.C. Burns, *History of Nigeria* (London: Allen & Unwin, 1929, 7th edn., 1969), p.182.
2 *PP* 1865, V [412].
3 'This part of the country in which Lagos in the Bight of Benin is the seaport, is generally known as the Yoruba country, extending from the Bight to the banks of the Niger. This country comprises many tribes governed by their own chiefs and having their own laws'. Revd Samuel Crowther to Edward Hutchinson, 10 September 1856. CMS Yoruba Mission papers, CA2/031(a).
4 It should be noted that the 'founding fathers' of the Church Missionary Society were closely linked to, and in the case of Wilberforce and John Venn identical with, the Clapham evangelicals and their supporters who lobbied tirelessly for the abolition of

remained highly profitable, and evasion of the Preventive Squadron off the West African coast was rife.

Discovered by Mungo Park in 1796 and charted by Richard Lander in 1830, the basin of the River Niger became the focus of the aspirations of the second generation of humanitarians who wished to complete the work of Wilberforce and his friends. In his seminal work, *The African Slave Trade and its Remedy*, Thomas Fowell Buxton propounded his vision of saving Africa by 'calling out her own resources'. Buxton envisaged the regeneration of Africa being effected by a combination of what he called 'the Bible and the plough'. At headline-grabbing meetings at Exeter Hall in 1839 and 1840, with a glittering array of bishops and peers on the platform (not to mention Gladstone and Prince Albert), the new 'Society for the Civilization of Africa' was formed. Described in the Victorian *Church Missionary Atlas* as 'one universal den of desolation, misery and crime',[5] Africa was thus a sitting target for philanthropic action. The initial practical response to Buxton's challenge was an expedition up the River Niger in 1841, the Church Missionary Society sending two of its members, J.F. Schön and Samuel Adjai Crowther,[6] as part of the expedition. Though the expedition itself failed to fulfil expectations, J.F.A. Ajayi suggests it nevertheless marked 'the beginning of new missionary enterprise in Nigeria' since 'for a crucial period, the initiative passed from the government, even from the anti-slavery movement ... to the missions'.[7]

The high death toll of the white expedition members did not deter the missions. Rather, it helped them to formulate future strategy, as did the publication of the journals of Schön and Crowther.[8] The principal lesson learned, and quickly accepted by the CMS, was that the high mortality rate of Europeans on the expedition indicated that the main body of future mission personnel in the region would have to be African. But the implementation of the decision was to be painfully slow. The vision of an indigenous church leadership was tempered with realism and the pioneer missionaries were warned, before they even set off, that any African who was ordained:

---

slavery and the slave trade. See E.M. Howse, *Saints in Politics: the 'Clapham Sect' and the Growth of Freedom* (Toronto: University of Toronto Press, 1952).
5 Quoted in Stock, I, p.45.
6 Schön, a German, was a CMS missionary in Sierra Leone. Crowther, here near the beginning of his distinguished career in West African missions, was himself a freed slave, being landed by HMS *Myrmidon* in Sierra Leone in 1822. Currently, the only biography of Crowther is Jesse Page, *The Black Bishop* (London: S.W. Partridge, 1908).
7 J.F.A. Ajayi, *Christian Missions*, p.13.
8 Forty-two out of 150 white men died in two months. Stock, I, p.455. For further details see also J. Gallagher, 'Fowell Buxton and the New African Policy, 1838-1842', *Cambridge Historical Journal*, X (1950), 36-58; H. Temperley, *White Dreams, Black Africa; the Antislavery Expedition to the Niger, 1841-1842* (New Haven and London: Yale University Press, 1991); Yates, pp.140-141.

should not be highly raised above his countrymen in his habits and mode of living... it is important that the social state of a people should steadily advance as Christianity advances. The missionary must therefore always be a little ahead of the civilization and lead it forward.[9]

The native pastorate was not launched until 1875.

CMS, the Yoruba Mission and Henry Venn

A possible source of African mission personnel came from the liberated slaves taken by the Royal Navy to Sierra Leone. Many had accepted the Christian faith there and by the late 1830s increasing numbers returned to Yorubaland from whence they had been taken. By 1842 over five hundred returned slaves had settled in the Egba city of Abeokuta where mission work was, not surprisingly, initially concentrated.[10] The WMMS was the first missionary society to establish a mission in Yorubaland with the arrival in 1842 of T.B. Freeman, himself of mixed race, from the Gold Coast. Freeman landed at Badagry and erected mission premises there, but finding that many of the emigrants from Sierra Leone to whom he wished to minister had moved from the coast inland to Abeokuta, he set off in pursuit.[11] The Anglicans, who were quickly to become the dominant mission in Yorubaland,[12] were not far behind – the CMS Yoruba Mission being founded in 1845.[13] However desirable the CMS may have regarded indigenous missionary personnel, there were no others at this stage of the calibre, or even the training, of Samuel Crowther. So the pioneers of the Yoruba mission were Crowther, a veteran of the Niger expedition who had been ordained in 1843, and Henry Townsend, a CMS lay teacher in Sierra Leone, who had been summoned back to England in 1844 for ordination and to report on his preliminary visit to Yorubaland.[14] The third member was Charles Gollmer, another of the considerable number of Germans in the employ of the CMS. Arriving in Badagry in 1845, they were held up there for eighteen months, during which time Gollmer's wife, Eliza, became the first of many mission personnel to perish in the inhospitable climate of Yorubaland. Gollmer

---

9 CMS Secretaries to Gollmer, Townsend and Crowther, 22 October 1844. CMS Yoruba Mission papers, CA2/L1.
10 *Ibid.*, p.143. Venn commented, 'The Committee regard this hiving-off of the liberated Africans from Sierra Leone to the countries whence they have been "carried away captive" as full of promise for Africa'. CMS *Proceedings* 1844, p.40; quoted in W.O. Ajayi, p.38.
11 Findlay and Holdsworth, IV, Ch. 3.
12 Michael Crowder emphasises the political pre-eminence of the CMS. See Crowder, *The Story of Nigeria* (London: Faber and Faber, 1962), pp.144-145.
13 For the early days of the Yoruba mission see Stock, I, p.458; II, pp.103-119.
14 Christopher Lloyd incorrectly described Townsend as 'a Wesleyan missionary'. *The Navy and the Slave Trade* (London: Longmans, Green, 1949), p.156.

was left in Badagry to supervise the new mission station as Crowther and Townsend moved on to Abeokuta in August 1846.

If Abeokuta was the 'sunrise in the tropics',[15] then much of the reflected glory shone on Henry Townsend. As secretary of the CMS local committee, Townsend was the nominal leader of the Yoruba mission. Though he served at Abeokuta with breaks from 1846 to 1876, his considerable prestige was in many respects greater in the early years. To a large extent this was due to the successful repulse of the attack made on the city by King Gezo of Dahomey in March 1851.[16] The defeat of Dahomey's supposedly invincible 15,000 strong army followed earnest prayer by the Christians in the city and was attributed by many to this prayerful intercession. Needless to say, it considerably enhanced the reputation of the missionaries and Townsend's influence increased.

It is important to note that Townsend was a highly political animal and his influence in Abeokuta was as much political as spiritual. Over a period of ten years, for example, he served as secretary to the *Alake*, the titular head of the Egba. He came to develop a taste for the exercise of power. Near the end of this period, William McCoskry, then the British agent in Lagos, observed that Townsend 'has been so long in directing the affairs of Abeokuta, that he would not brook any interference'.[17] Townsend regarded the growing influence of Lagos and, in due course, its resident governor, as a threat to Abeokuta and, indeed, to himself, for he felt that the survival and growth of the Christian gospel in Yorubaland was to a large degree dependent on the Egba winning the continuous struggle for power among the Yoruba tribes and cities.[18] Little wonder that what started as a niggling dispute with the British traders developed into a full-scale disagreement with the colonial government after Governor Glover backed Ibadan against the Egba in the long-running Yoruba wars.[19]

But far more influential than those who laboured in the field for the CMS was the Society's 'Honorary Clerical Secretary' in London, Henry Venn. Born at Clapham Rectory, the son of Wilberforce's friend and colleague, Henry Venn inherited his father's evangelical faith and social conscience. A disciple of T.F. Buxton, Venn shared his vision for the regeneration of Africa by the Bible and the plough. For thirty-one years (1841-72) Venn presided at CMS headquarters in Salisbury Square. He was a missionary strategist of the first order and his long tenure of office provided stability and continuity to the missionary lobby over this period. Cousin of Sir James Stephen, Permanent Under-Secretary at

---

15 A description popularised by a contemporary book by one Miss Tucker: *Abbeokuta, or Sunrise within the Tropics* (1853).
16 See Stock, II, pp.108ff.
17 McCoskry to Earl Russell, 2 December 1861. CO 147/2.
18 J.F.A. Ajayi, *Christian Missions*, p.79.
19 For the missionaries' relationship with Glover and others see John H. Darch, 'The Church Missionary Society and the governors of Lagos, 1862-72', *JEH*, 52 (2001), 313-333.

the Colonial Office from 1836 to 1847, his parliamentary and government contacts were an enviable entrée into the corridors of power, which he exploited tirelessly for the good of missions and those races among whom they worked.

Venn's representations to those in office soon paid dividends, for it was what C.W. Newbury describes as 'the Buxton thesis of encouraging legitimate trade which was urged on the Foreign Office by the Church Missionary Society' that turned the attention of Lord Palmerston towards Lagos and Yorubaland as a centre of African regeneration and a route to the Niger.[20] Indeed, many of the Society's representations to the government concerned the destruction of the slave trade. When in London, both Townsend and Gollmer gave evidence to the Hutt Select Committee (1847-48) and after the committee failed to recommend the retention of the West Africa squadron, delegations were launched at those in authority – to Palmerston and to the Third Earl Grey in December 1849 and again to Palmerston in March 1850. In the latter month a petition was sent to the Commons, timed to arrive just before the crucial vote. This lobbying was successful; the squadron was retained and the appointment of a consul, which was in fact already in hand, was jointly agreed.[21]

Official British Involvement

Lord Palmerston appointed Captain John Beecroft as the first 'British Consul for the Bights of Biafra and Benin'.[22] It should be noted that despite the wide regional area of his official title, Beecroft was regarded very much by the missionaries as the consul in Abeokuta, which was where he was to be based. The appointment of the consul was for the best humanitarian and commercial reasons: here was an area where the vestiges of the slave trade needed to be rooted out and replaced with legitimate trade, and from which Britain stood to make commercial gain. Indeed, representations from the Church Missionary Society emphasised this point[23] and missionaries in the field lost no opportunity to lobby for annexation[24] especially of the strategic port of Lagos on the coast

---

20 C.W. Newbury, *British Policy towards West Africa: Select Documents, 1786-1874* (Oxford: Clarendon Press, 1965), I, p.338.

21 Stock suggested that the appointment of the consul was in response to a promise given by Palmerston to the CMS deputation of 4 December 1849. His evidence appears to be Venn's private journal, but the wording, if correct, is somewhat ambiguous. Stock, II, pp.106-108.

22 See Palmerston to Beecroft, 30 June 1849. *PP* LIV, 1852 [1455].

23 *Ibid*. 'A deputation from the CMS waited upon me, and represented ... that the establishment of commercial relations with the interior of Africa through the Yoruba tribe, would materially contribute to the suppression of the slave trade.' Palmerston to Beecroft, 25 February 1850.

24 See, for example, *ibid.*, Revd Charles Gollmer to Revd Henry Venn, 3 January 1851, in which abolition is held out as the ultimate prize if Lagos, 'that dreadful den of iniquity', is annexed.

of Yorubaland, where the slave trade continued to flourish in the midst of a disputed succession. When Charles Gollmer wrote to London of 'often long[ing] to see unmistakable signs of God's work here', it is to be considered just how much he identified the divine work with the establishment of British authority.[25] Since Gollmer was a German it is reasonable to assume that he was not so much motivated by nationalism as by equating civilisation with British authority – under which he no doubt felt that the mission would have much more settled conditions in which to prosper. During his visit to Britain in 1851, Samuel Crowther, in an audience at Windsor Castle, told the Queen that 'the slave trade on that part of the African coast would be at an end if Lagos, the stronghold of its greatest supporter, was destroyed'.[26]

In February 1851 Palmerston instructed Consul Beecroft to negotiate a treaty with King Kosoko of Lagos for the suppression of the slave trade and its replacement with legitimate trade. Palmerston did not trouble to couch his intentions in diplomatic language; little doubt was to be left in Kosoko's mind as to the consequences of a refusal to cooperate with the overwhelming might of Britain. Beecroft was instructed to warn him:

> Great Britain is a strong power both by sea and land; that her friendship is worth having; and that her displeasure is well to avoid. That the friendship of Great Britain is to be obtained by the chiefs of Africa only on condition that they abandon [the] slave trade and expel the slave traders, and that those chiefs who refuse to do these things will surely incur the displeasure of the British government. If the chief shows a disposition to refuse compliance, you should beg him to remember that Lagos is near to the sea, and that on the sea are the ships and the cannons of England; and also to bear in mind that he does not hold his authority without a competitor.[27]

Therefore when Beecroft, accompanied by three naval officers, conferred with Kosoko in November 1851 and the latter failed to be intimidated,[28] Beecroft resorted to a show of force. Again, he underestimated his opponent who put up stout resistance, which Beecroft, not unnaturally for a British envoy who was not used to being crossed by a local ruler, felt he had to crush. Consequently on 28 December 1851, Commodore Bruce bombarded Lagos and made a successful landing with a much stronger force.[29] If a pretext of legitimacy was

---

25 *Ibid*.
26 Quoted in Burns, *Nigeria*, p.116.
27 Palmerston to Beecroft, 21 February 1851. Beecroft performed Palmerston's bidding in imitation of his master – his persuasion of Kosoko is described by J.F.A. Ajayi as 'a veritable cocktail of imperialistic gin and philanthropic tonic'. J.F.A. Ajayi, *Christian Missions*, p.71.
28 Kosoko's obduracy is recounted in Beecroft to Palmerston, 28 November 1851. *PP* LIV, 1852 [1455].
29 *Ibid*. The details are recorded in Beecroft to Palmerston, 3 January 1852.

needed to underpin British intervention, it was provided by Akitoye, deposed King of Lagos. In exile at Badagry, Akitoye had, in an exercise repeated many times elsewhere in seeking foreign support for domestic disputes, already petitioned Consul Beecroft for British intervention:

> My humble prayer to you is that you would take Lagos under your protection, that you would plant the English flag there and that you would re-establish me on my rightful throne at Lagos and protect me under my flag; and with your help I promise to enter into a treaty with England to abolish the slave trade at Lagos and carry on lawful trade, especially with the English merchants.[30]

This invitation to intervene in Lagos was, in fact, penned by Akitoye's adviser, none other than Charles Gollmer of the CMS, and Michael Crowder suggests that the willingness of the CMS missionaries to back the deposition of Kosoko and the reinstatement of Akitoye was because the former's continued involvement in the slave trade was prejudicial to the development of legitimate trade to which the missionaries were committed as to an article of faith.[31]

The installation of a compliant ruler, largely at the behest of the consul and the resident missionaries, resulted in Britain taking sides in a local dynastic dispute. From this point onwards, not only was the king of Lagos a British puppet, but Britain, for reasons of credibility and prestige, had to maintain him in power,[32] a situation which continued until Lagos was annexed to the British Crown in 1861. But had Britain intervened in Lagos for purely humanitarian reasons? Certainly Commodore Bruce, sympathetic to the missionaries, tried to give them that impression: 'I am not without hope that the measures I have carried out may be the means, under God's blessing, of contributing in some degree to the success of the most important undertaking which devolves upon you'.[33] Indeed, the treaty which the restored Akitoye was required to sign contained, in its eighth article, 'complete protection' and 'encouragement' for missionaries and Christian ministers of whatever nation, together with land to be provided for Christian burial.[34]

J.F.A. Ajayi suggests that Britain's altruistic motives were 'at best only a half-truth'. He proposes an additional economic motive: the rivalry of various European powers to control the trade of important areas in West Africa. In addition to any philanthropic desire to destroy slave-trading activities, there was

---

30 Gollmer's journal, 9 December 1850. CMS Yoruba Mission papers, CA2/043.
31 Crowder, p.145. He also notes the irony that the re-emergence of the slave trade was caused by the spectacular growth of legitimate trade (especially palm oil) which created an even greater demand for labour. *Ibid.* p.152.
32 This early involvement in the affairs of Lagos is discussed in J.F.A. Ajayi, 'The British Occupation of Lagos, 1851-1861: a critical review', *Nigeria Magazine*, 69 (August 1961), 96-105.
33 Quoted in W.O. Ajayi, p.79.
34 Treaty with the King and Chiefs of Lagos, 1 January 1852. *PP* LXI, 1852 [2982].

an 'economic desire to control the trade of Lagos from which [Britain] had been excluded and from where they hoped to exploit the resources of the vast country stretching to and beyond the Niger'.[35]

But who was using whom? If Britain harboured self-interest alongside her more philanthropic motives, could it be that she was not alone in this and that what might be described as a mutual exploitation of convenience was going on? E.A. Ayandele suggests that 'political thinking ... was the primary motive of the ... chiefs who invited the missionaries to their country. Neither the Egba nor the Efik chiefs had the least interest in the white man's creed *per se*'. He continues: 'from 1846 to 1860 missionary propaganda played well the part expected of it by the Egba: it kept Dahomey at bay without manifesting any imperialist intention ... the missionaries were conferring material prosperity on the Egba as part of their programme to make Abeokuta a "sunrise within the tropics"'.[36] As a result, Egba states came to look upon the presence of missionaries as a matter of prestige and in the 1850s the mission expanded to areas such as Ijaye, Oyo, and Ilesha.

The Yoruba Mission Expands

The CMS took immediate advantage of Britain's new position, recognising the strategic importance of Lagos for the Yoruba mission. Within ten days of Akitoye signing the treaty with Britain, an African CMS catechist had arrived in Lagos and preached before the king. Not surprisingly, Charles Gollmer soon moved his field of mission from Badagry to Lagos, having acquired land for mission premises there. In Lagos King Akitoye continued to depend on Gollmer's advice in both religious and political matters.[37] Indeed when Benjamin Campbell was appointed as the first British consul to Lagos in 1853, it was Gollmer who acted as his guide and host. In the meantime, however, Akitoye had died, reputedly by poison, and was succeeded by his son Dosumu.[38]

In the CMS *Proceedings* for 1852, Henry Venn enthused over the 'vast field opening before us', the 'new responsibilities' and the 'boundless facilities'. A firm believer in the 'Bible and plough' approach, he used his influence to encourage commerce both as the positive means to destroy the vestiges of the slave trade and as a means of promoting the evangelization and the ultimate self-support of the Yoruba church. To achieve this, Venn encouraged the missionaries to send samples of African produce (e.g. cotton, palm oil, arrowroot, ivory, ginger) to England where experts could judge their quality and commercial potential. But Venn was aware of the possible pitfalls and was

---

35 J.F.A. Ajayi, 'British Occupation', 69 (August 1961), 96-105.
36 Ayandele, *Missionary Impact*, pp.8-10.
37 See, for example, Gollmer's Journal for 11 April 1853, quoted in W.O. Ajayi, p.92.
38 Also spelled Docemo.

careful not to turn the missionaries into traders, keeping commercial experiments entirely separate.[39]

The growing size of the church at Abeokuta is given in the annual letters of report which Townsend sent to London.[40] The mission also grew on the European side, with the arrival in 1853 of two further German recruits, David Hinderer who started a mission at Ibadan[41] and Adolphus Mann who began work at Ijaye. They were each to spend several decades serving the Yoruba mission. By contrast, from Britain came Richard Paley, a Cambridge graduate who had been inspired to offer for missionary service by hearing Crowther preach during his visit to England. He lasted but three months before fever took him, and his young wife died on the return voyage. Growth in personnel, however, was not without its problems. The abrasive nature of Henry Townsend, the senior missionary in the Yoruba mission, was brought to the fore when the German missionaries, Gollmer and Mann, complained of his overbearing manner towards them, an issue which involved London and led Henry Venn to intervene. Townsend responded by criticising Venn for having regard for Gollmer's judgement and even recommended Gollmer's removal from the mission.[42] Townsend was also hostile to Crowther.[43]

Though this hostility might have been expected to die down after Crowther moved to Onitsha in 1857 to found the Niger Mission,[44] it became even more pronounced after Venn's minute on the 'Extension of the Episcopate'[45] in 1858. Townsend came to realise that the identity of the proposed missionary bishop whom Venn had in mind for Yorubaland was not himself but Crowther.

---

39 W.O. Ajayi, p.105; S.O. Biobaku, *The Ebga and their Neighbours, 1842-1872* (Oxford: OUP, 1957), pp.57-58. J.F.A. Ajayi noted the displeasure of the CMS with much of the palm-oil trade which was replacing the slave-trade on the coast, apparently in tune with their stated policy. Their hostility was caused, he suggested, because 'it was conducted in a way that did not lead to the emergence of a middle class and so left African society unchanged'. J.F.A. Ajayi, *Christian Missions*, p.19.
40 Unfortunately his figures are not consistent. From 1861 to 1863 he gives the number of 'native Christians', presumably adults, which are in 1861 - 639; 1862 - 637; 1863 - 745. In 1870 he gives the figure for communicants - 128; and in 1871- 126, but another figure of 761, presumably all adult members. In 1875 the figure is 2,000 for the 'total number of Christians connected with the congregation'. CMS Yoruba Mission papers, CA2/085.
41 Hinderer, a linguist, had been appointed to study the Hausa language in preparation for a northern extension of the mission. But an opening in the north never came, and he and his English wife Anna remained in Ibadan for seventeen years and suffered greatly during the long 'siege' of that town.
42 Townsend to Major Straith, 6 March 1854; Townsend to Venn, 2 May 1854. CMS Yoruba Mission papers, CA2/085.
43 *Ibid.*, Townsend to Venn, 28 March 1856.
44 See K.O. Dike, *Origins of the Niger Mission, 1841-1891* (Ibadan: Ibadan University Press, 1962), pp.13-15.
45 *Church Missionary Intelligencer*, 1858, pp.36-39, 169-172.

Thus began a bitter rearguard action by Townsend to deny a bishopric to Crowther, including an accusation that he had engaged in 'improper conversation with a young female'.[46] It was no mere personality clash that led Townsend to oppose Crowther's consecration. He was fundamentally at odds with Henry Venn's policy of advancing indigenous clergy into office, preferring to see white men in positions of authority in the church as the logical accompaniment to colonial government. To give weight to his argument Townsend sought to use the name of Bishop Weeks of Sierra Leone, reporting back to London that 'I asked him to give me his opinion whether it would be good to appoint a coloured person as bishop ... and he strongly expressed his opinion that it would be most undesirable'.[47] All this was ultimately unsuccessful and Crowther was consecrated, according to the Letters Patent, 'Bishop of the United Church of England and Ireland, in the said countries of Western Africa beyond the limits of our dominions', in Canterbury Cathedral on 29 June 1864. But such was the hostile feeling that Townsend had stirred up, mainly on racial lines, that the CMS committee found it expedient to go to the ridiculous lengths of excluding the European missionaries at Abeokuta and Ibadan from Crowther's jurisdiction, keeping them under the Bishop of Sierra Leone until they themselves should choose to come under Crowther's episcopal care.[48] To his credit, the supremely humble Crowther made no complaint about this farcical arrangement.

As well as being a missionary strategist *par excellence*, Henry Venn was a visionary, and his ideas of the future of the indigenous church growing out of a missionary culture and leadership anticipated the (unacceptably progressive) views of the 1865 Committee on the gradual transfer of authority to educated Africans. In three remarkable minutes, written in 1851, 1861 and 1866, Venn advocated the establishment of a 'native pastorate'. This required the European missionaries, who had established a mission, which had subsequently grown into a church, to move on to the evangelism of new territory. They would leave behind them trained indigenous clergy – the native pastorate – to administer the

---

46 Lithographed Circular Letter from Henry Venn, 19 April 1861. CMS Yoruba Mission papers. CA2/L3. J.F.A. Ajayi asserts that Venn was 'constantly on guard to resist his [Townsend's] ambition to become head of the Yoruba mission'. Ajayi, *Christian Missions*, p.182.

47 Townsend to Venn, 30 June 1859. CMS Yoruba Mission papers. CA2/O85(a). Ajayi suggests that Townsend wanted the bishopric for himself, and that he bore a grudge against both Crowther and Venn since Venn's policy 'deprived him of the office to which his achievements entitled him and in which his abilities would have full scope'. Thus 'he remained an ambitious but frustrated leader of the opposition'. Ajayi, *Christian Missions*, p.182.

48 Venn has been criticised by his twentieth century successor, Max Warren, for failing to support Crowther sufficiently strongly, so that after Venn's death Crowther became subject to hostile criticism both from white missionaries and, indeed, from Salisbury Square. Max Warren, *To Apply the Gospel* (Grand Rapids: Eerdmans, 1971), p.30.

infant church, which was to be, according to Venn's visionary strategy, self-governing, self-supporting and self-propagating.[49]

Lord Palmerston took a personal interest in the work of the mission, no doubt more because of its humanitarian and commercial effects than its spiritual ones, writing to Samuel Crowther in 1851, 'Her Majesty's Government take a lively interest in the welfare of the Egba nation, and of the community settled at Abeokuta, which town seems destined to be a centre from which the lights of Christianity and of civilization may be spread over the neighbouring countries'.[50] Resolved to defend the principal missionary settlement of Abeokuta, fifty miles inland from Lagos, against the powerful, slave-trading kingdom of Dahomey, Palmerston sought to do this by strengthening British authority at Lagos, and in 1853 he appointed a separate British consul for Lagos. The effect of this appointment was to tilt the balance of British interests from the missionaries at Abeokuta to the traders at Lagos. As British influence increased in Lagos, that of the native ruler rapidly declined as Lagos had now become what Palmerston described as an 'anomalous quasi-protectorate'.[51] This anomaly was soon rectified, however, in August 1861 when Dosumu was glad enough to cede what remained of his sovereignty to Britain in return for a pension.[52] The Colonial Office was less than enthusiastic about the new colony which it would be required to administer, described by Sir George Barrow, of the African section, as 'a deadly gift from the Foreign Office'.[53]

Rumbling on in the background in Yorubaland at the time of the cession, was the so-called Ijaye war, which had started in the previous year. It was one of the seemingly interminable series of Yoruba wars in the nineteenth century. Henry Townsend had encouraged the Egba to check the power of Ibadan on the grounds that 'the Egbas are the power that represent progress and advancing civilization and it is to be feared if they should be conquered our cause, or rather that of God, would suffer'.[54] Not surprisingly, David Hinderer, who headed the mission in Ibadan, did not share Townsend's point of view. Hinderer and his wife, Anna, suffered great hardship during the war, being trapped in Ibadan for a period of five years.[55] Nevertheless Townsend clearly felt vindicated by results in terms of numerical conversions, conveniently ignoring death and destruction, since after the fall of Ijaye in March 1862 when the refugees fled to Abeokuta, more than ninety conversions ensued, more in one year than in the nine years of Adolphus Mann's patient ministry in Ijaye.[56] But

---

49 Printed as Appendix I in Shenk, *Missionary Statesman*, pp.118-129.
50 *Ibid*. Palmerston to Crowther, 18 December 1851.
51 Quoted in Hargreaves, *Prelude*, p.56.
52 The treaty is printed in J.F.A. Ajayi, 'British Occupation', 100-101.
53 Min., by Barrow, 22 April 1864, on Governor of Lagos to Duke of Newcastle, 9 March 1864. CO 147/6.
54 Townsend to Venn, 4 October 1860. CMS Yoruba Mission papers. CA2/085.
55 Hinderer to Knight, 21 June 1860. CMS Yoruba Mission papers. CA2/049.
56 CMS *Proceedings*, 1863, p.48. Quoted in W.O. Ajayi, p.174.

the annexation of Lagos resulted in suspicion developing among the interior tribes, especially the Egba. They now became somewhat wary of Britain since the annexation marked the end of a policy stretching back twenty years of official British involvement in Yorubaland only at arm's length. From being an interested spectator, Britain, it seemed, had ceased to shout advice from the terraces and had run on to the pitch, becoming a player in its own right in the unstable game of Yoruba politics.[57]

With the annexation of Lagos came a period of expansion for the Yoruba mission. Only in time would the disadvantages of the new political situation become apparent to the missionaries. W.D. McIntyre has suggested that the beginning of the decline of missionary influence goes back as far as the appointment of the Lagos consul in 1853.[58] Nevertheless, as long as Palmerston remained at the helm in London, the missionaries felt that as their final court of appeal they had a man who was sympathetic, even paternalistic, to their cause. Henry Venn expressed this feeling after Palmerston's death in 1865 when he commented darkly that: 'now that Lord Palmerston is gone we may be more than ever at the mercy of certain officials who view everything under strong prejudices *for* the government and *against* the mission'.[59]

The support given to missionaries by British naval officers has been noted in the chapter on the Pacific labour trade. This same advantage helped the Yoruba mission and, as in the Pacific, came from a common unity in the face of the slave trade. C.P. Groves may have been correct when he spoke of 'an attitude of genuine regard in the British squadron for the missionaries and their work', but goes rather too far in turning what was no doubt the feelings of *some* into a generalisation about *all* naval personnel:

> Officers and men, in their detestation of the slave trade and concern for African welfare, shared with them [the missionaries] a certain community of purpose and regarded their own work as clearing the ground of evil that the positive contribution of Christian mission might be made.[60]

To attribute such lofty thoughts to the mind of the average Able Seaman of the Royal Navy serving in the West Africa Squadron would appear to be overstating the case. There is, however, no doubt that some of the officers did have sincere humanitarian and evangelical sympathies. In his treaty with the reinstated Akitoye, Commodore Bruce made sure that the missionaries and their work were explicitly safeguarded. Later, in 1853, Dr Edward Irving RN, who had served for nine years in the naval squadron was seconded, on his own initiative, to work in the Yoruba mission and formed a living link between the

---

57 See McIntyre, *Imperial Frontier*, p. 90; W.O. Ajayi, p.165.
58 McIntyre, *Imperial Frontier*, pp.89-90.
59 Venn to Townsend, 23 November 1865. CMS Yoruba Mission papers, CA2/L3.
60 C.P. Groves, *The Planting of Christianity in Africa*, (London: Lutterworth, 1954), II, p.52.

Royal Navy and the mission (albeit a short-lived one, since he succumbed to dysentery within eighteen months).[61]

However, it was undoubtedly true that what Cardwell's Parliamentary Under-Secretary, Chichester Fortescue, later called the 'Foreign Office policy of "petting" the Abeokutans and their missionaries'[62] gave rise to unrealistic expectations of support from British officials, for it was inevitable that once Lagos formally became a British possession it would eclipse and supersede in importance any informal imperialism that had been exercised from Abeokuta by the missionaries. Indeed, it was only a matter of time before the interests shared by British officials at Lagos and the Anglican missionaries at Abeokuta diverged. The missionaries could then no longer rely on the automatic support of British authority they had received when they and the traders were the only British presence in Yorubaland. In time the missionaries came to question whether their advocacy of the annexation of Lagos had in fact been in their own best interest.[63]

Governor Freeman and Missionary Opposition

Appointed as the first governor of the new colony was Henry Stanhope Freeman, who served from 1862 to 1864.[64] It was not long before he fell foul of the missionaries who used their parent society in London to apply sustained pressure on the government in an attempt to outwit the governor and isolate him from his masters in London. Freeman's ill-judged attempt to impose a vice-consul on Abeokuta, without the elementary step of first obtaining the permission of the chiefs, provides one such example. After the rejected vice-consul, Thomas Taylor, stated that 'he regarded his refusal by the chiefs as in some degree attributable to Mr Townsend's influence', Venn was quick to write to the Foreign Secretary, Earl Russell, pointing out that, 'the letters of the other missionaries also concur in proving that the displeasure of ... Abeokuta was so much excited by what they regarded as an unwarrantable assumption of power over the town by the Governor of Lagos'.[65]

When the next King of Dahomey, Gelele, threatened Abeokuta at the end of 1862, the ensuing stand-off was not just between Dahomey and the Egba but

---

61 Irving's appointment received the approval of the Foreign Secretary. See Clarendon to CMS, 11 June 1853. CMS Yoruba Mission papers. CA2/L1.

62 Min. by Fortescue, 17 September, on Freeman to Cardwell, 15 August 1864. CO 147/7.

63 Cf. the feelings of the Wesleyan missionaries in Fiji after annexation when Sir Arthur Gordon's government increasingly exercised authority in areas which they had previously regarded as their own preserve.

64 Newcastle to Freeman (draft), 16 December 1861. CO 147/1.

65 Venn to Russell, 1 December 1862. *PP* XXXVIII, 1863 [3212]. See also the enclosure, from Townsend to Venn.

also between the CMS and the colonial authorities. First, Governor Freeman instructed the missionaries to leave Abeokuta for their own safety. Then Commodore Wilmot (after visiting Abomey and failing to persuade King Gelele to call off his attack) bluntly informed them that if they did not comply with the governor's instructions they risked losing naval protection. The missionaries, however, realised that to leave the Christian Egba to their fate would destroy the mission and the work of the past seventeen years. The CMS strongly supported their stand: it was felt the governor had exceeded his lawful authority in requiring the missionaries to leave.[66] British officials should have been protecting Abeokuta not evacuating European missionaries.[67]

In London, Henry Venn responded to the threat with a combination of prayer and political action. Prayer meetings were held in Britain and overseas by CMS supporters to entreat divine aid for Abeokuta. On a more pragmatic level the lobbying of government, parliamentary and naval personnel gave great impetus to the campaign of support for Abeokuta.[68] A deputation of the CMS waited upon the Colonial Secretary, the Duke of Newcastle, in March 1863 and presented a memorial highly critical of the governor. After pointing out that CMS missionaries had resided in Abeokuta for seventeen years, they complained that:

> Governor Freeman has reversed the policy of Her Majesty's Government, as expounded by Lord Palmerston in 1851, and which has been acted upon for the last ten years; ... he has weakened the confidence of African chiefs in the faith and justice of Great Britain; has encouraged Dahomey; and has imperilled the existence of Abeokuta and the lives of the missionaries who were successfully engaged in civilizing and Christianizing the native tribes.[69]

In conclusion, they requested a check on Freeman's policy and, more revealingly, a reassurance that the missionaries 'shall receive such moral competence and support as they have heretofore received'. The missionary tail clearly resented being unable to wag the official dog. They did have some success, in that Newcastle reminded Freeman that the 'chiefs of Abeokuta ... may always look to Her Majesty's Government for moral support, so long as their conduct shall justify it'.[70] Yet this success was bound to be limited since even the Colonial Office found it increasingly difficult to control headstrong

---

66 Venn to Freeman, 20 October 1863, CA2/L3.
67 See also W.O. Ajayi, pp.180-183.
68 See Stock, II, pp.437-438. The lifting of the siege after sixteen days was accompanied by great rejoicing and the drawing of obvious biblical parallels with the lifting of the siege of Jerusalem by the Assyrian king Sennacherib in II Kings Ch.19.
69 Memorial of the CMS to Duke of Newcastle, 17 March 1863. *PP* XXVIII, 1863 [512].
70 *Ibid*. Newcastle to Freeman, 20 March 1863.

governors and administrators of Lagos (the official title was to change) of the stamp of Freeman and, later, Glover.

Representations made by the CMS committee the following year to Newcastle's successor, Edward Cardwell, were even more vitriolic in their criticism of Governor Freeman and are indicative of the declining influence the missionaries felt they exercised. Yet far from being a crude attack, it was a detailed eighteen-point critique of Freeman's policy, as one might expect from the incisive pen of Henry Venn.[71] Having imposed 'strict injunctions' on their missionaries to cease from 'all interference with political questions, to uphold respect due to British authority' and 'to abstain from any public stricture', the CMS claimed to be able to 'represent to Her Majesty's Government the general dissatisfaction the native tribes in the neighbourhood of the colony of Lagos have expressed at the policy of the Governor of Lagos'. Among the criticisms of Freeman's policy were: disturbing trade, making 'warlike preparations', being 'seen to advocate and favour the cause of Ibadan', acquisitions of territory which 'have led to two disastrous collisions with the natives', and 'arbitrary acts' against educated Africans. CMS alleged that, having lost the respect of the people and having had his impartiality called into question, the governor was no longer in a position to mediate between the inland tribes or to promote legitimate commerce 'as the only effective remedy for the ... slave trade'.[72]

Freeman took Venn's criticisms personally, claiming that 'a body of the power and influence of the Church Missionary Society, whose members, numbering tens of thousands of Englishmen, naturally believe the reports of their agents and above all of their Committee, [has made] a deliberate and persistent attack on me'. Referring to the CMS deputation to the Duke of Newcastle of the previous year as the 'first attack on me', he proceeded to complain that 'the Duke of Newcastle's reply ... was twisted into a condemnation of my policy and the missionaries at Abeokuta openly declared that my conduct has been disapproved'. It was a robust response but damage had nonetheless been done to the governor's reputation. Venn appeared to have very effectively raised doubts in the minds of Freeman's superiors in London. For instance, Fortescue minuted: 'it is difficult not to believe that a governor possessed of more judgment and less irritable and self-sufficient than Mr Freeman could have maintained better relations with natives and missionaries'.[73]

A major issue of contention was the extension of territory which Venn had raised in paragraph eleven of his letter to Cardwell. Venn claimed that it was the acquisition of further territory, such as Badagry, by the Lagos government that was at the root of Egba suspicions. These could be removed only by publicly

---

71 W.O. Ajayi, p.62, described Venn as 'an expert in the gentle art of pressure'.
72 Venn to Cardwell (copy), 17 May 1864. CO 147/7.
73 *Ibid.* Min., 17 September, by Fortescue.

disavowing further expansion.[74] Even Governor Freeman acknowledged the apprehension caused by his policies: 'This Government is, in fact, an object of suspicion and mistrust to all the surrounding country ... the general fear is that the territory of Lagos will gradually extend itself until it swallows up all the neighbouring states'.[75] But though recognising this fear in Lagos' neighbours, Freeman had done little to allay it. As S.O. Biobaku noted, 'the full implication of the annexation of Lagos in 1861 was that the authority of the Lagos government would inevitably extend unless the circumjacent governments were strong enough to maintain law and order and were sufficiently enlightened to promote commerce and stamp out evil practices'.[76] According to A.A.B. Aderibigbe it was 'the attempt of Governor Freeman to embark on the difficult path to financial self sufficiency that first set the colony on the easy road to expansion'.[77] It was a matter of 'customs house imperialism'. With an inexorable logic, financial self-sufficiency required the imposition of customs dues, which in turn required the extension of British sovereignty over any nearby ports to which traders might be tempted to resort in order to evade the payment of customs duty. Indeed, it was for this very purpose that, before his first gubernatorial year was out, Freeman extended British control (and the colonial tariff) to the nearby port of Badagry, and shortly afterwards to Palma and Leke,[78] justifying his action by a loophole in the somewhat imprecise wording of the treaty of cession.[79] Perceptively, it was the Assistant Under-Secretary at the Colonial Office, T.F. Elliot, who minuted, not disapprovingly:

> I do not think that it is at all a good policy to multiply our stations on the coast of Africa. But if we do choose to create a new station it seems to me necessary to take sufficient territory to make it self-supporting by admitting of the successful collection of a customs revenue to give us elbow room relatively [sic] to other European powers. [80]

At this stage the Colonial Office did not share Henry Venn's concern about minor territorial expansion. However, the situation became considerably more fraught after Freeman's death in 1865, a year of some significance in West African history.

---

74 Venn to Cardwell (copy), 17 May 1864. CO 147/7. Ayandele describes the colony of Lagos from this time onwards as 'a constant source of fear and irritation'. Ayandele, *Missionary Impact*, p.15.
75 Freeman to Newcastle, 4 June 1862, quoted in Ayandele, *Missionary Impact*, p.13.
76 Biobaku , p.98
77 A.A.B. Aderibigbe, 'Expansion of the Lagos Protectorate, 1863-1900'. Unpublished PhD thesis (London, 1959), p.11.
78 There are various spellings for this port.
79 Freeman to Newcastle, 9 October 1862. CO 147/1. See also Aderibigbe, p.11.
80 Min. by Elliot on Glover to Newcastle, 6 April 1863. CO 147/4.

As discussed in the previous chapter, the report of the 1865 Select Committee ruled out immediate withdrawal from any of the West African settlements. With the dual aims of increased efficiency and reduced expenditure, a central government, based in Sierra Leone, was recommended for the four settlements. The committee sought to encourage the growth of African civilisation through, wherever possible, self-governing African states rather than British colonies. No new settlements were to be made and Africans were to be led to exercise 'those qualities which may render it possible for us more and more to transfer to them the administration of all the Governments with a view to our ultimate withdrawal from all, except, probably, Sierra Leone'.[81]

Significantly, in a despatch to Henry Townsend in the summer of 1865, Henry Venn reflected on the situation with regard to the threatened expansion of Lagos in the light of the recommendations of the 1865 Select Committee (which were partly due to his own intense lobbying):

> We have little hope of any satisfactory solution under the present authorities being sustained for any length of time. I have every confidence in the present Secretary of State [Cardwell]. But during the [1865] Committee I saw so much of the influence and interference of subordinate parties *as to check my hopes of an effectual control over a strong-willed governor as long as he appears to be successful in his policy.*[my italics] The minds of several members of the [1865] Committee have been opened to the real state of missions and the positive Resolution that the natives are to be trained for ultimate self-government is an important principle on our side.[82]

In this important analysis Venn notes that, in effect, the end of Palmerston's supportive influence meant an unsettled period for missions when their fortunes would depend on whoever held the seals of the Colonial Office. Perceptively, he also understood what was to be a common phenomenon in this period — the paramount influence of the 'man on the spot' in imperial expansion, operating virtually unchecked and almost always endorsed by the home government, as long as his policy was successful. Conversely, encouraged that Select Committee members had understood his advocacy of the role of missions, Venn was unduly optimistic in believing that the Committee's principle that 'natives are to be trained for ultimate self-government', would rapidly be put into effect.

---

81 For discussions of the 1865 Select Committee Report see Hargreaves, *Prelude*, pp.64-78, and Farnsworth, pp.214-217. The important proviso which was included in the report should also be noted: 'That this policy of non-extension admits of no exception, as regards new settlements, but cannot amount to an absolute prohibition of measures which, in peculiar cases, may be necessary for the more efficient and economical administration of the settlements we already possess'. *PP* 1865, V [412].

82 Venn to Townsend, 22 August 1865. CMS Yoruba Mission papers, CA2/L3.

Glover and the Egba

It is undoubtedly the case that before the advent of Frederick Lugard in the late nineteenth century, the British official most responsible for the development of the Lagos Protectorate was John Hawley Glover.[83] Glover served as Lieutenant-Governor of Lagos from 1864 to 1866, and Administrator from 1866 to 1872. The son of an Anglican clergyman who had himself served in the military in West Africa before ordination, Glover entered the Royal Navy as a cadet at the age of twelve, and after a wide-ranging naval career he volunteered for service on the second Niger expedition, led by Dr Baikie in 1857. 'A sincerely religious man',[84] Glover revelled, albeit in a somewhat mystical fashion, in the spiritual significance of the expedition (during which Samuel Crowther founded the Niger Mission) even to the highly unorthodox extent of acting as the expedition's unofficial chaplain with the aid of a portable communion set.[85]

One might have expected such a man as Glover to be a close ally of the missionaries, especially after he took service under the new colonial government in Lagos (initially as harbour master) in 1861. Though he often tried hard to help them, as he rose in rank in the colonial service of the colony he increasingly found that he did not see eye to eye with all the missionaries all the time. One cause of friction was his almost paranoid dislike of the Egba, whom the missionaries (and, indeed, the existing colonial government) regarded as the most enlightened tribe in Yorubaland, through whom they thought they could best work and who were to be supported against their enemies. The real reason for this dislike may never be known though McIntyre hints, presumably in the absence of any hard evidence, at 'unfortunate, if rather obscure, experiences at the hands of the Egba' during Glover's overland journeys necessitated by the wreck of the second Niger expedition in October 1867.[86] Rather more prosaically, J.D. Hargreaves suggests that Glover, like Freeman before him, was persuaded by the arguments of Lagos merchants (notably William McCoskry) who were reluctant to become exclusively dependent on the Egba for the expansion of trade and commerce.[87] Certainly, when he was in charge of the colonial government in Lagos, first deputising for Freeman, then in his own right, Glover pursued an aggressive expansionist policy. Aggressive, because he had no liking for the Egba, expansionist, because he appeared to follow in Freeman's footsteps believing that the best way for Lagos to survive

---

83 The only biography of Glover, *Life of Sir John Hawley Glover, RN, GCMG* (London: Smith and Elder, 1897), by Lady E.R. Glover and Sir R. Temple contains the main events of his life and career but lacks any real analysis. More useful for present purposes is the biographical detail contained in W.D. McIntyre's article, 'Commander Glover and the Colony of Lagos, 1861-73', *JAH*, IV (1963), 57-79.
84 Groves, I, p.75.
85 McIntyre, 'Commander Glover', 58.
86 McIntyre, *Imperial Frontier*, p.92.
87 Hargreaves, *Prelude*, p.57.

was to expand. Aderibigbe described Glover's frontier policy as 'a *realpolitik* which exploited the mutual animosities of neighbouring states'.[88]

At home on leave in March 1864, Glover sought to use his influence to advance the expansionist policy of Governor Freeman, a policy with which he wholly concurred and which he was to make his own. He wrote to both Foreign and Colonial Offices and paid the latter a visit. Writing to Earl Russell, the Foreign Secretary, Glover complained that 'the opposition of the Egbas was fostered (apparently) by the advise [sic] of the Church Missionary Society's agents in Abeokuta'. He also advocated British intervention to prevent the Egba taking the strategic town of Ikorudu.[89] Writing to the Colonial Secretary, the Duke of Newcastle, Glover unambiguously expressed his support for Ibadan and his dislike and distrust of the Egba, claiming that the latter were hostile to trade, to the suppression of slavery and to peace. Finally, the letter ended with an appeal that came perilously close to an attempt at moral blackmail:

> Under these circumstances, my Lord, it is for Her Majesty's Government to consider ... whether Lagos shall be allowed to become a self-supporting settlement independent of the Imperial revenue, a prosperous emporium of commerce, and the future Liverpool of Africa, or a deplorable failure like all our other forts and settlements on the Gold Coast, and a continual drain on the Imperial Treasury.[90]

Sir Frederic Rogers, who sat in on an interview Glover had with Fortescue, the Parliamentary Under-Secretary, commented that Glover exhibited 'a certain impatience of obstacles and rather too lofty a tone in speaking of other powers and interests'.[91]

On his return to Lagos, now as lieutenant governor, Glover reported the Egba annexation of Ikorudu which had effectively cut the trade route from Ibadan to Lagos and expressed his preference to 'render effective assistance' to Ikorudu, i.e. to drive the Egba out.[92] If the missionaries had felt that Governor Freeman was hostile to the Egba, Glover appeared even more so. To Glover, the well-being of Lagos and its trade was paramount. If that trade was disrupted by warfare among the Yoruba tribes then Lagos would be the loser. He regarded it as his duty to counteract this perceived threat to Lagos by whatever means were necessary – by military action or by opening new roads not susceptible to Egba interference.[93] If, as Aderibigbe claims, 'Glover's solution to the problems arising from the annexation of Lagos appeared to be one of unlimited

---

88 Aderibigbe, pp.63-64.
89 Glover to Russell, 9 March 1864, enc. in FO to CO, 16 March 1864. CO 147/7.
90 Glover to Newcastle, March 1864. Quoted in Glover and Temple, pp.98-100
91 Min., 17 March, on Glover to Russell, 9 March 1864; enc. in FO to CO, 16 March 1864. CO 147/7.
92 Glover to Cardwell, 5 April 1865. CO 147/8.
93 See Glover to Russell, 9 March 1864, CO 147/8.

expansion',[94] his period in sole charge of Lagos seems to provide ample evidence. After his return from leave, Porto Novo, in the west, came under his consideration as a means of countering both the power and slave-trading of Dahomey and he recommended its annexation to the Secretary of State, Cardwell.[95] But the architect of the 1865 Committee's policy of qualified restraint was the last man to sanction extensions of the frontier:

> I lose no time in informing you that the annexation to Lagos of the town of Porto Novo ... is not likely to receive the sanction of Her Majesty's Government ... and would moreover be opposed to the opinion expressed by the Select Committee on the West Coast of Africa against any further extension of territory on that coast.[96]

When Glover tried to resurrect the suggestion two years later, Buckingham, the Conservative Secretary of State, gave it equally short shrift:

> I disapprove of Commander Glover's having attempted to enlarge the Lagos territory and jurisdiction, entirely on his own motion, without leave, and contrary to what he must well know to be the policy of Her Majesty's Government. I regret to say that I am compelled to view the whole of Commander Glover's proceedings with great dissatisfaction.[97]

A potential check on Glover's actions was the arrival, at the end of 1865, of Samuel Blackall as Governor-in-chief of the West African Settlements.[98] He brought news of the Cardwell policy following the 1865 Report, and although Lagos was not to be abandoned immediately, he instructed Glover to refrain from intervention outside the colony. For a short time it seemed as if the new policy might prevail as Blackall visited Lagos and listened to representations from the missionaries. He even repealed Glover's restrictions on trade with Abeokuta and attempted to normalise relations with the Egba. During the few months in 1866 when Admiral Patey held the post of Administrator in Lagos, trade with Abeokuta began to flourish, but in November of that year Patey was transferred to the Gambia and Glover became Administrator in his own right, a post he was to hold until 1872. The weakness of the reorganisation of the West African settlements soon became apparent: the governor-in-chief was responsible for four territories, but he could not be in more than one at a time and the time spent at sea travelling between the territories made regular

---

94 Aderibigbe, p.11
95 Glover to Cardwell, 7 September 1865. CO147/9, quoted in Newbury, p.359ff.
96 Cardwell to Glover, 23 October 1865. CO 147/9, quoted in Newbury p.363.
97 Buckingham to Blackall, 23 November 1867. Quoted in Newbury, p.366.
98 This amalgamation of the four West African territories was one result of the 1865 Report. The Governor of Sierra Leone became governor-in-chief and the governors of the Gambia, Lagos and the Gold Coast became 'Administrators' responsible to the governor-in-chief.

communication even more difficult – a determined subordinate in any of the territories could easily manipulate his chief and evade his control.

It was to Blackall that Glover first proposed the building of new roads 'to assist civilization and to strengthen the hands of the Lagos government'.[99] A detailed map showing several options accompanied his proposals.[100] In effect, he wished to evade the stranglehold which the Egba could exert on Lagos's overland trade. The new Secretary of State in 1871, Lord Kimberley, recognised this and expressed approval:

> It is evident that the opening of road number five will effectively turn the flank of the Egbas. The Administrator seems to be pursuing a wise policy – approve him and say I shall learn with satisfaction that he has succeeded in establishing secure communications with the interior free from the interference of the Egbas.[101]

Robert Herbert, the new Permanent Under-Secretary, was not so sure, minuting that:

> the native tribes are as adverse to opening roads through their country as some English landowners were to the introduction of railroads through their property fifty years ago. Time and patience are the only remedies in this case and our principal object should be to avoid being drawn into difficulties or in any way compromising neutrality [in] these native squabbles.[102]

These concerns were not shared by Glover who continued to pursue his own agenda. Thus, when Glover again raised the subject of the annexation of Porto Novo in 1871 and Herbert and Knatchbull-Hugessen both gave it qualified approval, this was too much for Kimberley, who minuted bluntly: 'I am altogether against Captain Glover's proposal. On similar grounds of philanthropy we might be called upon to annex Dahomey, Ashantee, Abbeokuta and for anything I see ... the greater part of Africa'.[103]

---

99 Glover to Blackall, 17 January 1868, enc. in Blackall to Buckingham, 30 January 1868. CO 147/14.
100 A simplified copy of the map is shown in McIntyre, *Imperial Frontier*, p.91.
101 Min., 15 November 1871 on Glover to Administrator-in-Chief, 7 September 1871. CO 147/21.
102 *Ibid*. Min., 1 December 1871 on Glover to Kennedy, 18 October 1871.
103 Minutes by Herbert, 6 December, Knatchbull-Hugessen, 9 December, and Kimberley, 11 December, on Glover to Kennedy, 1 November 1871 enclosed in Kennedy to Kimberley, 15 November 1871. CO 147/21. Knatchbull-Hugessen took the opportunity to complain that 'we refused Fiji; which to my mind was a stronger case than Porto Novo'. Porto Novo was at first ignored by the Colonial Office, then included in the bargaining for the abortive Gambia cession negotiations, and eventually annexed by France in 1883.

Glover, the Missionaries and the *Ifole*

What was the reaction of the missionaries to Glover and the policies he pursued, virtually independently of the Colonial Office? Glover's relations with the missionaries, whom he respected as individuals and for their work in spreading the Christian gospel, was inevitably going to founder on tribal allegiance. For it was a *sine qua non* of missionary policy to work through the Egba, the Yoruba tribe who were the first to embrace Christianity in significant numbers. Glover, however, held a very different opinion regarding the Egba as obstacles to peace and to trade; in other words, a real threat to the stability and commercial viability of the Lagos colony. It was not without significance that the missionaries with whom he had the closest ties were David and Anna Hinderer, who ministered not to the Egba but to the Ibadan, whom he regarded as 'the flower of the Yoruba people'[104] and a counterbalance to the Egba. He did his best to provide help for David Hinderer and his wife during the lengthy siege of Ibadan in the early 1860s. Glover was himself held in high esteem by the Hinderers. They felt trapped and alone and possibly even abandoned by their fellow missionaries in Egba territory who failed to get relief supplies through to them, and regarded Glover as a very real friend who had not forgotten their plight.[105] In April 1865 when rescue eventually came after five years and two months, it was their 'kind friend, the Governor of Lagos' who got through to Ibadan.[106]

It was perhaps inevitable that two such strong personalities as Townsend and Glover would clash at some time, and in the CMS Yoruba Mission papers there is a remarkable correspondence between them which took place throughout the year 1865.[107] The Ijaye war was at its height and Glover's blockade of the Egba was presenting a serious problem to the missionaries both in terms of disrupting the work of the mission and also the inevitable backlash they, as white men, feared at the hands of the Egba. Glover must clearly have regarded the conversion of Townsend to his cause as a prize worth the expenditure of much time and ink in his patient efforts to explain the reasons for his policy and why the missionaries should support it. He had initially tried an aggressive tack, but when this failed to move Townsend,[108] he tried a more conciliatory approach stating that 'I am activated by no hostile feeling to the

---

104 Quoted in McIntyre, *Imperial Frontier*, p.92
105 'Captain Glover, RN, was unwearied in his attempts to relieve them, and three times was on the point of penetrating to Ibadan itself; but he was absolutely refused permission to pass through the Ijebu country'. Hinderer, p.270-271.
106 *Ibid.*, pp.279-280.
107 CMS Yoruba Mission papers, CA2/04/33ff.
108 *Ibid*. 'It is only in a policy of peace and good will I can take part, it is not right for me to become an agent for uttering threats...'. Townsend to Glover, 20 February 1865. CMS Yoruba Mission papers, CA2/04/33.

Egbas. I do not wish to see harm come to Abeokuta'.[109] Once again, Townsend failed to respond positively, seeing a certain incompatibility between Glover's soft words and tough actions.

> I don't know how to represent your good feelings and intentions towards the Egbas with the events that are taking place – I should do evil and not good to the cause of peace by attempting it. I am not moved by any other than a desire to promote peace in refusing to be the medium of expressing hostile intentions. I hope the time will come when the country will be opened up as it was before these unhappy wars commenced.[110]

The only practical result of this correspondence which Glover had initiated was a memorial from the missionaries to Cardwell, in their by now traditional fashion of complaining about the governor direct to the Colonial Office. It ended:

> We therefore most respectfully beg you to grant us that freedom of which the Governor and Government of Lagos deprive us, for our efforts for the advancement of Christianity and Christian laws are seriously interfered with, and we fear the heathen governments around us will be too ready to adopt a repressive policy against us with the example of the Government of Lagos before them.[111]

It is perhaps an indication that Glover either felt some sympathy for the missionaries or that he recognised their considerable influence in that he was prepared to bandy words with Townsend in such a detailed and lengthy correspondence. Equally significant is the fact that when the chips were down the missionaries preferred to side with their Egba converts than with their fellow countrymen in the Lagos government. The dream of British colonial authority easing the path of the gospel among the Yoruba tribes had already turned sour. Inexplicably to the missionaries, the colonial governor had now turned against the very tribe whom they had wished to use as the vehicle of both trade and Christianity. It seemed as if the ploughshares which were to accompany the Bible in Buxton's vision of a renewed Africa had been beaten into swords to be used against the leading Christian tribe. Little wonder there was disillusionment with colonial policy and confusion as to how this could ever have happened.

Henry Townsend relayed all the information he acquired back to Salisbury Square where it was analysed by Henry Venn, but it would be a mistake to suppose that Venn unthinkingly accepted all that Townsend told him about Glover's activities without engaging his own not inconsiderable critical

---

109 See, for example, Glover to Townsend, 6 March 1865. CMS Yoruba Mission papers, CA2/04/33.
110 Townsend to Glover, 9 March 1865. CMS Yoruba Mission papers, CA2/04/33.
111 Missionaries in Abeokuta to Cardwell, 2 December 1865. CMS Yoruba Mission Papers, CA2/04/38.

faculties. In an important letter to Townsend of 24 April 1865 Venn reflected on the information he had received concerning 'the change of policy on the part of Governor Glover' and reported back on his official contacts. Referring to Glover's 'impulsive' character, he regretted that in his recent visit to Lagos Colonel Ord, the commissioner sent out by the Colonial Office to gather information for the Select Committee, had apparently failed to impress upon Glover 'that the home government could never support a policy of hostile intimidation'. He noted with some surprise that Glover 'had given his own complexion to the affair as one of simple self-defence for Lagos!'[112] But Venn was a realist and he did not hold out false hope to Townsend. He wrote in August of his confidence in Cardwell but regretted the 'interference of subordinate parties' which would prevent any 'effectual control over a strong-willed governor as long as he appears to be successful in his policy'.[113] In October he confessed that 'it is difficult to discover in the governor's policy what is mere blundering and what is deep design'.[114] Within a few months Venn's estimate of Glover plumbed the depths as he lamented that 'it is dreadful to contemplate the evils which might arise from the changeable and short-sighted policy of the governor of Lagos'.[115]

The answer to Venn's rhetorical fear came less than two years later, when on 13 October 1867, an *ifole* (outbreak) of violence against the European missionaries in Abeokuta took place: services were forbidden, churches and mission property were attacked and looted and the missionaries were ordered to leave.[116] Thankful there was no bloodshed, they departed quietly and headed for Lagos, though whether this would have been the case had Henry Townsend not been on leave in England at the time, one can only speculate. This was a bitter humiliation for the CMS, mitigated only by the lack of bloodshed, and Glover was undoubtedly seen as bearing responsibility. Indeed, later that month, George W. Johnson, secretary of the Egba United Board of Management, the body of educated Africans that had emerged to fill the power vacuum as Townsend's personal influence waned during the Ijaye war, wrote to the governor to point out that the *ifole* was the effective result of his policy: 'Alas your excellency must remember, that the Word of God which has been planted for more than twenty-one years in Abeokuta, is now closed up, on account of a

---

112 *Ibid.* Venn to Townsend, 24 April 1865. CA2/L3. Venn acquired the information regarding Glover's gloss on the affair by calling in at the Colonial Office to hand his letter personally to Sir George Barrow – a clear example of the ease with which Venn could enter government offices and was accepted within official circles.
113 Venn to Townsend, 23 August 1865. CA2/L3
114 *Ibid.* Venn to Townsend, 23 October 1865.
115 *Ibid.* Venn to Townsend, 23 November 1865.
116 See the unsigned and unaddressed letter written from Abeokuta on 16 October 1867 for a first-hand account. CMS Yoruba Mission papers, CA2/011/35. T.E. Yates stresses that the *ifole* was directed at the missionaries 'not as Christians, but as Europeans'. Yates, p.145.

few constables whom you have stationed in the Egba territory'.[117] The events in Abeokuta necessitated a reorganisation of the Yoruba mission: for the next twelve years white CMS missionaries excluded from Abeokuta had to make their headquarters in Lagos.[118]

The Governorship of John Pope Hennessy

It is unlikely that the missionaries prayed for retribution on Glover after the *ifole* and yet nearly five years later his nemesis arrived in the unlikely shape of an Irish Roman Catholic layman, who succeeded Sir Arthur Kennedy as governor-in-chief. John Pope Hennessy was a highly controversial colonial governor later characterised by his grandson as a man of humanitarian beliefs, volatile judgements and autocratic behaviour.[119] Hargreaves regarded him as having 'strong claims to be the worst colonial governor of the century'.[120] Eugene Stock, the historian of the CMS, referred to Disraeli's 'unfortunate choice' in first giving him a colonial governorship, complained about the 'mischief' he did in West Africa and regarded him as a 'most troublesome governor' in his subsequent appointments.[121] Indeed, in his previous appointment (Labuan), he had suspended from duty his own father-in-law, and in his next appointment (Barbados) his policies led to rioting. Pope Hennessy was a combative champion of what he presumed to be the oppressed native peoples of the colonies and had a temperamental dislike of those in the colonial service who lorded it over them,[122] though Piers Brendon regards him as 'more eccentric than progressive'.[123]

Pope Hennessy breezed into Lagos in April 1872 and within a few days had begun the process of reversing much of Glover's policy. Pope Hennessy's temperament is one key to understanding his actions. Another is the fact that he was a close friend and ally of Sir Charles Adderley, chairman of the 1865

---

117 George W. Johnson to Glover, 31 October 1867. CMS Yoruba Mission Papers, CA2/06. It would seem that the occasion for the *ifole* (which was an outburst of long-standing and deep-seated resentment) was Glover's mobilisation of both troops and police following the murder of several messengers passing through Egba territory.
118 Stock, II, p.443.
119 James Pope Hennessy, p.21.
120 Hargreaves, *Prelude*, p.168.
121 Stock, II, p.449. It should be noted that Stock is not entirely objective, appearing to display here a certain anti-Catholic bias.
122 'Glover was a perfect example of the type of adventurous imperialist which John Pope Hennessy least liked.' Pope Hennessy, p.135.
123 Piers Brendon, *The Decline and fall of the British Empire 1781-1997* (London: Jonathan Cape, 2007), p.638.

committee, and a convinced supporter of his policy.[124] Between Pope Hennessy's arrival on 24 April and his final departure on 9 July,[125] a sea-change took place in the colony's policy towards the surrounding tribes. The writing was on the wall for Glover: even before he took up office, Pope Hennessy had told Kimberley that 'Glover has so far failed to obey instructions in withdrawing the *Eyo* [the warship he had sent] from Porto Novo'.[126] Though shortly after his arrival he was writing that although 'it is impossible not to see that Capt. Glover is a zealous officer who has devoted his energies to the improvement of the place', he reported ominously that 'white merchants were annoyed with Capt. Glover because the trade was stopped'. He concluded that 'I am disposed to attribute the stoppage of trade to some extent to the unfortunate relations that have for so long existed between the Administrator and the Egbas.'.[127] Within a short time, the blockade of Porto Novo was called off, Egba grievances were listened to, Glover's actions were disavowed, and Pope Hennessy was convinced that he had come to a friendly understanding with them which would lead to normalisation of relations. By June, Glover had been dismissed.[128]

The reaction of the missionaries can be gauged from a letter from Lancelot Nicholson, secretary of the Yoruba Mission:

> Great changes ... have taken place in Lagos. Capt. Glover has left for England and is not to return to Lagos. The Governor-in-Chief Mr Pope Hennessy will, I trust, be able to come to a good understanding with the Egbas, if so the roads will be opened and I trust the way for the white man to go to Abeokuta.

A follow-up letter continued the impression of breathless change:

> Mr Pope Hennessy arrived here on June 12 and Capt. Glover...left June 15th. There is now a complete change in the policy, in future the Administrator is not to meddle with the interior tribes but to confine his attention to Lagos .... It is now widely spread abroad that the Lagos government is not to acquire fresh territory.

---

124 'Probably the only enthusiastic supporter of the Cardwell policy to receive an official appointment in West Africa during the period when it might have been tried.' McIntyre, *Imperial Frontier*, p.117.
125 Pope Hennessy was not continuously resident in Lagos during this period, leaving and returning on at least one occasion.
126 Pope Hennessy to Kimberley, 10 April 1872. CO 147/23.
127 *Ibid*. Pope Hennessy to Kimberley, 27 April 1872.
128 For Glover's side of the dispute between the two men see Glover and Temple, pp.132-143. Interestingly, Glover's biographers maintain that Pope Hennessy was erroneous in his ideas that 'Glover entertained a personal hatred of the Egbas, and that they were a down-trodden and oppressed people'. Glover and Temple, p.133.

In a most revealing comment, Nicholson accurately indicated the attitude of the missionaries to Glover, illustrating perfectly the clear dichotomy between their opinions of the man and of his policies: 'as far as I am concerned personally I am sorry Capt. Glover has gone. He was very kind to us personally, all the missionaries will say this. But none of us can agree with his policy with respect to the interior'.[129] Indeed some years later when mission and colonial government were again in dispute, J.B. Wood, who had taken over Townsend's role as the leading white missionary, lamented Glover's departure from Lagos and even advocated his return.[130]

Initially the Colonial Office endorsed the *volte face* in policy brought about by Pope Hennessy. Within nine months of approvingly referring to Glover's 'wise policy' in seeking to open new roads, Kimberley had changed his mind. Realising the negative effect on relations with the coastal tribes through whose territory Glover was seeking to open and maintain roads, Kimberley minuted, 'Captain Glover's policy has been too ambitious'.[131] Then, in early November Glover wrote to Kimberley expressing his disagreement with the reversal of his policy and attacked Pope Hennessy personally, referring to his 'vanity and culpable weakness'.[132] As well as Glover's letter and minutes from Knatchbull-Hugessen hostile to Pope Hennessy and supportive of what Glover had tried to do,[133] Kimberley also received a letter from Hinderer, on leave from Ibadan, repaying his debt to Glover for his support during the siege.[134]

By the end of November, although Kimberley still felt that Glover had erred, he had lost his confidence in Pope Hennessy, referring in a despatch to his 'grave doubts whether you have acted prudently in suddenly reversing Capt. Glover's policy, and whether you have not been misled by persons at Lagos, acting exclusively in the interests of the Egbas and Jebus'.[135] C.W. Newbury

---

129 Nicholson to Edward Hutchinson, 19 June 1872. CMS Yoruba Mission papers, CA2/O3/406. Nicholson to Secs. of CMS, n.d. CMS Yoruba Mission papers, CA2/O3/408.
130 See, Wood to Hutchinson, 11 December 1880, G3/A2/01 and Wood to Sec. of CMS, 14 December 1881, G3/A2/02. CMS Yoruba Mission papers.
131 Min., 6 August 1872, on Pope Hennessy to Kimberley, n.d. CO 147/23, quoted in Newbury, p.370.
132 *Ibid.* Glover to Kimberley, 7 November 1872. CO 147/23.
133 Knatchbull-Hugessen was not impartial in the matter. It should be remembered that Pope Hennessy was a close friend and political ally of Adderley, Knatchbull-Hugessen's *bête noir*. Kimberley countered his subordinate's forceful advocacy of 'combat with native habits, ignorance and prejudices' by confessing that 'I am ... less combative than Mr Hugessen, and am not prepared for a crusade in W. Africa on behalf of trade, civilization and Christianity'. Mins., by Knatchbull-Hugessen, 10 October and Kimberley, 12 October, on Charles Leigh Clare to Kimberley, 3 October 1872. CO 147/26, quoted in McIntyre, *Imperial Frontier*, p.119.
134 Hinderer to Kimberley, 1 November 1872. CO 147/26.
135 *Ibid.* Kimberley to Pope Hennessy, 28 November 1872.

Lagos and Yorubaland 199

regards Glover's policy as a failure since his coercive methods neither improved relations with the Yoruba peoples nor guaranteed open roads.[136] Despite all his efforts Lagos remained economically dependent on the region which Glover had failed to control.[137] But Pope Hennessy, for all his ostentatious efforts, had done no better. That Kimberley could criticise first Glover then Pope Hennessy was symptomatic of the fact that neither man seemed able to please the Colonial Office. But was this really their fault? The Colonial Office had signally failed to make up its mind about the future of Lagos – failing to engage either first gear or reverse, it had been cruising in neutral with no real sense of direction. Was the Cardwell policy to be endorsed and followed, or had it now been abandoned? A decision was urgently needed.

Political Decision Making

No decision on the future of Lagos (or the other West African territories) had been made. In effect, Kimberley had chosen to work within the discretion provided by Cardwell's loophole in the 1865 Committee Report – what Susan Farnsworth has dubbed the 'margin of flexibility'[138] This situation continued until the issue was finally forced by Pope Hennessy's rashness. By February 1873 Kimberley had made up his mind:

> I put out of the question retirement from Lagos, the place must be held by force if necessary. I would keep generally within the lines laid down by Mr Cardwell in 1864, that is, I would only hold under British sovereignty Lagos, Badagry, Palma and Leckie ... the rest of the territory should be 'protected'.[139]

But the question must be asked – why did Kimberley come to this decision? W.D. McIntyre suggests that it was the reasoned arguments of Knatchbull-Hugessen which won the Secretary of State round to his point of view. McIntyre regards Edward Knatchbull-Hugessen as 'the most important of the parliamentary under-secretaries in the mid-Victorian era'.[140] Such generalisations are notoriously difficult to justify, but he goes on to attribute to Knatchbull-Hugessen the credit for persuading Kimberley to agree to the retention of Lagos in particular and to the abandonment of the '1865 policy' of

---

136 It was not until July 1874, two years after his departure from Lagos, that the roads were finally opened to all trade and traffic.
137 Newbury, p.35.
138 Farnsworth, p.328.
139 Min. by Kimberley, 25 February 1873, on Pope Hennessy to Kimberley, 30 December 1872. CO 147/24.
140 McIntyre, *Imperial Frontier*, p.59.

qualified restraint in general.[141] It is not totally impossible that this may be the case, particularly in view of an important minute, written on 23 February 1873:

> Natives ... have been left ... uncertain of our intentions towards them – even doubtful whether we desire or intend to keep Lagos.... They look upon attempts to open roads as something conceived in the interests of the Foreign occupiers of Lagos rather than as that which cannot fail to be one of the greatest benefit to their own country, and their whole position as regards British occupation is uncertain and unsatisfactory. To this state of things the report of 'Sir Charles Adderley's Committee' contributed not a little and I am at a loss to conceive how the half-and-half policy of Great Britain – occupying territory as if she was ashamed of it and felt she had no business there – c(ing one day and threatening the next – can have been expected to produce anything but confusion and disaster. Why did we ever occupy Lagos? To put down slavery and to extend Christian civilization. Are these still considered objects worthy of your attention? If not – the sooner the withdrawal the better, and if English opinion will endure our withdrawal no doubt a certain amount of expenditure will be saved and we shall be spared some trouble. But if these are still objects to be aimed at, and if, as I think, a great country which has undertaken certain responsibilities of this kind cannot evade or abandon them without loss of Honour and Character, then surely some definite course of action should be adopted....[142]

It should be noted, however, that in more recent research, Knatchbull-Hugessen's role has been questioned. In her unpublished thesis on 'Edward Knatchbull-Hugessen ... and the British Empire', Judith Rowbotham has cast considerable doubt on the reality of Knatchbull-Hugessen's status and influence at the Colonial Office, which McIntyre takes for granted.[143] There is no doubt that Knatchbull-Hugessen's minutes tended to be long and forceful, but quantity was no substitute for quality. His literary experience was not in the field of concise minute-writing but that of writing fairy stories[144] and contributing to the contemporary gossip-sheet, *The Owl*, a fact which seems to have been held against him by Gladstone. If, as Rowbotham asserts,[145] he had been demoted

---

141 *Ibid.*, p.121.
142 Min. by Knatchbull-Hugessen, 23 February 1873, on Pope Hennessy to Kimberley, 30 December 1872. CO 847/24, quoted in McIntyre, *JAH*, 75.
143 Judith D. Rowbotham, 'Edward Knatchbull-Hugessen, first Lord Brabourne, and the British Empire', unpublished PhD thesis (Wales: Lampeter, 1982).
144 An entry in his journal only a few months after the Lagos discussions has Knatchbull-Hugessen writing fairy stories (many of which were published) in Colonial Office time and using William Baillie Hamilton, one of the clerks, as his amanuensis. The fact that such an activity could hardly have been kept secret in the close confines of the Colonial Office, and that there is no record of any reprimand, would seem to indicate that Knatchbull-Hugessen's peculiarities were resignedly tolerated in the Colonial Office precisely because he was not taken seriously by the other staff.
145 Rowbotham, p.221.

rather than promoted to the Colonial Office, a fact which his natural vanity had completely failed to grasp, and if his colleagues and superiors failed to take his contributions seriously, no amount of forceful minutes would turn the head of the diligent Kimberley. In fact it is possible to read many of Kimberley's minutes referring to his deputy's views in an ironic sense.

Rowbotham has demonstrated that Knatchbull-Hugessen was frequently not sent papers until after decisions had been taken, a fact about which he complained and which may have indicated an official conspiracy to keep him as far away from decision-making as was practicable. Certainly, one of Knatchbull-Hugessen's longer and better-argued minutes, a document which McIntyre regards as 'most revealing' and which 'bears extensive quotation', was written two days before Kimberley's decision, minuted on the same despatch, to 'put out of the question retirement from Lagos. The place must be held, by force if necessary'. *Post hoc ergo propter hoc* is, however, a misleading deduction. It is more than probable that Kimberley read Knatchbull-Hugessen's minute. It is, however, less than probable that the views of an unreliable subordinate would have influenced such an important decision.

To assert, as McIntyre does, that 'Knatchbull-Hugessen inaugurated a serious review of Lagos policy' is based on a misunderstanding of his influence in the Colonial Office. It is certainly true that he opposed the abandonment of any West African territory as advocated by the 1865 Select Committee,[146] though his personal dislike of Adderley is difficult to disentangle from political differences. McIntyre is right to draw attention to the length and the consistency of Knatchbull-Hugessen's minutes on Britain's apparent inability to make a clear choice between withdrawal from or expansion of the imperial frontier in the tropics. He is even correct in asserting that 'eventually Kimberley accepted Knatchbull-Hugessen's view',[147] though it would make for greater clarity to describe it as 'the view already held by Knatchbull-Hugessen'. He fails however to demonstrate that Knatchbull-Hugessen was in any way instrumental in influencing that change of view in the Secretary of State. The weight of evidence is that Kimberley paid scant attention to the views of his Parliamentary Under-Secretary. In short, after Rowbotham's researches, any suggestion that Knatchbull-Hugessen was instrumental in changing Kimberley's mind must be treated as not only not proven, but as highly suspect.

Susan Farnsworth suggests that as a result of the abortive Gambia negotiations Kimberley had decided that a literal enactment of the 1865 Committee's recommendations was in fact unworkable. Certainly Kimberley had taken the decision, eighteen months earlier, to end the Gambia exchange negotiations with France. If the Gambia was to be retained (he of course was not to know that Lord Carnarvon would later re-open the negotiations), it was

---

146 See for example, min., 3 October 1872, on Pope Hennessy to Kimberley, 1 September 1872. CO 236/316.
147 McIntyre, *Imperial Frontier*, p.65.

logical also to retain Lagos. But much more important than the Gambia in influencing Kimberley's decisions on Lagos was the nearer West African territory, the Gold Coast. For running concurrently with the problems which were forcing a decision in Lagos were much greater problems in the Gold Coast, where the Fante confederation movement in the 'Protectorate', just outside Britain's legal jurisdiction, was looking to Britain for official recognition and also for protection from their warlike neighbours in Ashanti. It needs to be understood that Kimberley made a virtually identical decision to remain in the Gold Coast a month *before* he made the same decision on Lagos.[148] After rejecting abandonment of both the Gambia and the Gold Coast, the decision to retain Lagos was hardly surprising; it was entirely consistent with Kimberley's effective abandonment of the vestiges of the Cardwell policy.

With the Liberals going out of office in February 1874, it fell to Lord Carnarvon to bury the Cardwell policy in a speech to the Lords on 12 May 1874. As was his wont he clothed practicalities with grandiose language:

> A great nation like ours must sometimes be prepared to discharge disagreeable duties; she must consent to bear burdens which are inseparable from her greatness ... it is certainly not a desire of selfish interests or the ambition of larger empire which bids us remain on the West Coast of Africa; it is simply and solely a sense of obligations to be redeemed and duties to be performed.[149]

He now treated Lagos and the Gold Coast as a single entity, and from 1874 to 1886 the governments of the two territories were combined in a single Crown colony.[150]

Lagos and Yorubaland from 1874

The post-retention period was not an auspicious time in the history of Lagos; in practical terms there were few changes. E.A. Ayandele has described Lagos in this period as being in the 'doldrums' because of its weak administration which, going to opposite extremes from the Freeman/Glover policy, 'withdrew to the shell of Lagos island'.[151] J.E. Flint agrees and goes further: 'By the 1880s the

---

148 'For all present practical purposes therefore we may dismiss the question of retiring from the [Gold] coast.' Min. by Kimberley, 20 January 1873, on M'Arthur's question. CO 96/106, quoted in McIntyre, *Imperial Frontier*, p.138.
149 *Hansard*, Third Series. CCXIX, 12 May 1874, cols 157-168,
150 Aderibigbe regards this union of the two territories 'the culmination of sustained efforts on the part of Lord Kimberley...to pursue a policy of limited financial liability on the West coast of Africa. Aderibigbe, p.66.
151 Ayandele, *Missionary Impact*, p.36. He quotes a complaint from John Maser, the local mission secretary that the colonial government had failed to put a stop to 'war and robbery within twenty miles of Lagos. 'Which is, if I remember correctly,' he tartly reminded the Administrator 'the zone allowed by the English government within which

morale of the British in Nigeria had reached its lowest ebb ...'. He also criticises the missionaries: 'The white missionaries were, by this time, usually men of limited vision, with petty obsessions, much concerned with questions of Sunday observance, opposition to the liquor trade, and personal rivalries.[152]

The crucial word in the foregoing sentence is *white*, for it was in this period that the African missionaries began to supersede the Europeans in terms of energy and ability and to assume positions of authority in the hierarchy of the growing church (though it should be noted that there were exceptions, and that racism was far from dead). It was the educated Africans, both ordained and lay, whom the 1865 Committee had adjudged to be those to whom power could be gradually transferred and whom Henry Venn wished to elevate, who began to make the running in the life of the Yoruba mission and the CMS found itself becoming reactive rather than proactive as far as the future of the mission was concerned.

Foremost among the educated Africans was James 'Holy' Johnson, a Sierra Leonean by birth, who was transferred to Lagos in 1874 by the CMS, anxious to head off a nationalist movement within the Yoruba church which aimed at the complete exclusion of Europeans. Faced with a more extreme threat the CMS reluctantly adopted Henry Venn's scheme for a native pastorate which he had been advocating for the last twenty years of his life. Johnson was brought in to initiate it and the white missionary at the Breadfruit Church, (the most important in Lagos) was obliged to move aside to make room for him. The following year the native pastorate was launched, starting with just one church, another joining in 1878. In 1881 the prestigious Breadfruit Church joined the scheme and by the end of the decade all but one church in Lagos came under the pastorate. This had the effect of widening the rift between black and white missionaries. By 1882 the pastorate had became a missionary body in its own right with outstations away from Lagos. Eventually, in 1891, it seceded from the Church Missionary Society. But although this displeased the white missionaries, the far-seeing Henry Venn would have regarded it as entirely consistent with the growing-up process of the mission developing into a fully fledged independent church under indigenous leadership.

James Johnson's appointment, in 1876, to the novel post of 'superintendent' of the Yoruba Mission was very much a political accommodation. In May 1875 David Hinderer wrote to Venn's successor, Henry Wright, confessing that he had changed his views since 1864 and that he felt that the time was now right to extend Crowther's episcopal jurisdiction over the Yoruba mission: 'there is now ... no ground why we should not have him as

---

the administration may bring crime to its due punishment'. Maser to Maloney, 2 October 1878. CMS Yoruba Mission papers, CA2/04.
152 J.E. Flint, 'Nigeria: the Colonial Experience from 1880 to 1914', in L.H. Gann and P. Duignan (eds), *Colonialism in Africa, 1870-1960*, (Cambridge: CUP, 1969-70), I, p.221.

our bishop now, but much in favour of the change...'. Significantly, he referred in passing to the racist attitudes of some of the younger white missionaries, and in a following letter inconsistently advocated Abeokuta remaining outside Crowther's jurisdiction and under a white colonial bishop on the peculiar grounds that 'English protection will come upon it sooner or later'.[153] Townsend countered this proposal with a suggestion that James Johnson be created bishop instead. Whether this was a last-ditch attempt to deny Crowther authority over the Yoruba mission or a genuine conversion to the idea of an indigenous bishop – but with a younger man – cannot be known, though Townsend did refer to the success of the Egba United Board of Management that he had witnessed while in Abeokuta and wondered if the same thing might be successful in the church.[154] The Committee accepted the proposals, and Johnson was sent to Abeokuta in 1877 to head the whole Yoruba Mission (except Lagos and Ondo), but on Bishop Cheetham's advice he was initially given the title of 'Superintendent' with a view to making him bishop if all went smoothly.[155] All did not go smoothly, however, and Johnson soon ran into difficulties over the issues of finance and domestic slavery. Finance was hardly his fault since it was the CMS who had reduced expenditure on the Yoruba mission by 5%, in keeping with the policy of transferring more responsibility to the fledgling church. Johnson sought to make up the shortfall by increasing weekly class fees. When this aroused opposition he high-handedly excluded non-payers from church membership. His authority was further undermined when Bishop Cheetham declined to back him up.

Domestic slavery was even more of a hornets' nest.[156] In an otherwise favourable report on Johnson's leadership, Bishop Cheetham had chided those missionaries and mission supporters who held domestic slaves. The CMS in London endorsed this with a minute on domestic slavery which effectively banned the practice for CMS members and supporters:

> It has been with much sorrow that the Committee of the Church Missionary Society have heard that there still prevails among the members of the Christian church in the Yoruba country, as among their heathen and Mohammedan neighbours, the practice of holding property in their fellow creatures as slaves or pawns, and this custom is not confined to those who held slaves or pawns before they became

---

153 Hinderer to Wright, May 1875, and 10 September 1875. CMS Yoruba Mission papers, CA2/049.
154 Townsend to Wright, 25 November 1875. CMS Yoruba Mission papers, CA2/085.
155 See Cheetham to Wright, 2 March 1876. CA1/025, quoted in J.F.A. Ajayi, *Christian Missions*, p.232. Ironically, Henry Townsend was offered a suffragan bishopric at Lagos, but the preferment had come too late for him – he declined the post and retired on health grounds in March 1876.
156 Fortescue, in a minute written over fifteen years earlier, had referred to 'the perplexing subject of slavery'. Min., 16 December 1863, on Glover to Newcastle, 10 November 1863. CO 147/4. It had become no less perplexing over that period.

Christians, but is found also among those who have acquired them since they became Christians, and, in some cases, since they were called to the ministry of the Word of God.

No one in the employment of the Society shall hold man, woman or child, or have personally any connection with the practice.... After the 1st of January [1880] no Agent of the Society either in the Yoruba or Niger Missions or in any mission of the Society, shall be permitted to hold either slave or pawn, and that any one so doing shall *ipso facto* cease to be connected with the Society.[157]

Johnson sought to enforce this ruling with his customary enthusiasm and zeal – 'almost too much zeal', according the official historian of the CMS[158] – and found himself in trouble both with the authorities of Abeokuta who took umbrage at his criticisms of their social institutions and the mission agents, both white and black, who found domestic slavery a very convenient arrangement for themselves and resented anyone who tried to deprive them of their servants. The Yoruba Mission Papers contain the minutes of a conference on the subject held at Lagos over several days in September 1879. The 'conference' consists largely of complaints against James Johnson and has all the hallmarks of a kangaroo court.[159] The CMS also failed to back up their man and took swift action to remove Johnson. He registered an 'earnest protest' against this injustice, but obeyed, leaving Abeokuta in February 1880. Ayandele is probably right in adducing a racist motive for the removal of Johnson, while Johnson himself was no doubt right in suggesting that not even a white missionary could have dealt with domestic slavery without a backlash.[160] The undoubted fact was, however, that a white missionary would have experienced *less* of a backlash.

One real difference in style of government, which was maintained until the days of the 'scramble', was a steadfast refusal by the Lagos authorities to get involved beyond British territorial boundaries and it adopted a 'hands-off' approach to the continuing Yoruba wars. Indeed, in 1881, no doubt in reaction to the policies of Glover ten years earlier and fearful of being dragged into the minefield of Yoruba politics, Kimberley (back at the Colonial Office in Gladstone's second ministry) chided the governor for even suggesting that he should offer mediation and prohibited direct interference with the tribes outside British jurisdiction. 'Such a course would not fail to involve the Colonial Government in dangerous complications, and would entail on this country an extension of responsibilities which Her Majesty's Government are not prepared to undertake.'[161]

---

157 Minute on Domestic Slavery, 1879. CMS Yoruba Mission papers, CA2/L4.
158 Stock, III, p.83.
159 CMS Yoruba Mission papers, CA2/O2/16.
160 Ayandele, *Missionary Impact*, pp.195-196; Johnson to Maser, 9 February 1880. CMS Yoruba Mission papers, CA2/O56.
161 Kimberley to Governor of Gold Coast and Lagos, 26 August 1881. *PP* 1887, LX [C.4957].

By 1886, however, with this latest phase of the Yoruba wars having dragged on for nine years, Administrator Alfred Moloney[162] was able to make use of the Yoruba mission to effect mediation between the warring tribes. Having first satisfied himself 'that there still existed a desire for peace', he told Foreign Secretary Lord Granville, 'I ... obtained the co-operation of Archdeacon Hamilton, head of the Church Missionary Society here ... to place ... at my disposal the services of two native clergymen, the Rev S. Johnson and the Rev. C. Phillips'.[163] The accounts of Samuel Johnson and Charles Phillips engaging in what by the late twentieth century would become known as 'shuttle diplomacy' are contained in two Parliamentary Papers.[164] The fact that they were trusted to mediate between the complex web of tribal alliances and their success in brokering a peaceful resolution to decades of war was a tribute, not just to their own considerable abilities,[165] but to the fact that the missionaries were respected and trusted by all tribes involved. The significance of their being *black* missionaries cannot be too highly stressed. The fact that they were chosen to mediate (whether by Moloney or by Hamilton is not clear) was an indication that by this time only African clergy would be accepted in such a role of trust and integrity.

Assessment

Though the extirpation of the slave trade was the reason for Britain's involvement in Lagos, it was the CMS missionaries who were instrumental in drawing official attention to Lagos. J.F.A. Ajayi describes the missionaries' 'great success' as coming 'at the end of 1851 when they got the British government to order the bombardment and occupation of Lagos'.[166] If they rejoiced at that point they could little have foreseen how events would turn sour for them within just a few years. If they had encouraged intervention in order to destroy the vestiges of slavery and to develop legitimate trade, then it succeeded. But if they had an additional motive of protecting, raising up and working through the Egba, a tribe over whom in the 1840s, 1850s and early 1860s they had a very strong influence, then British intervention was a disaster. With the establishment of a full-blown colonial government in 1862, not only did the balance of power move away from them, but the Egba, far from being exalted as the example their fellow Africans should follow, both in faith and in

---

162 Later in 1886 the administration of Lagos was separated from the Gold Coast and Moloney became full governor.
163 Moloney to Granville, 25 March 1886. *PP* 1887, LX [C.4957].
164 *PP* 1887, LX [C.4957] and [C.5144].
165 Phillips, who had worked first in Ijaye, then in Ondo, became Assistant Bishop of Western Equatorial Africa in 1893. Samuel Johnson wrote the standard *History of the Yorubas* (Lagos, 1937).
166 J.F.A. Ajayi, *Christian Missions*, p. xv.

trade, were execrated as disturbers of the peace and disrupters of trade and commerce.

Unlike both Fiji and the Gambia no pressure group emerged to promote the interest of Lagos and Yorubaland in Westminster and Whitehall. And unlike Fiji or the Gambia there are hardly any column inches in *Hansard* concerning this territory. However, Yorubaland had the advantage of the CMS to look after its interests and most important of all, until 1872, Henry Venn guiding the not inconsiderable power and influence at the disposal of the largest missionary society of the Established Church. If William M'Arthur was said to be 'the patron saint of the Fiji islander' then the same could certainly be said for Venn with regard to the Yoruba tribes in general and the Egba in particular. Whereas M'Arthur and the Fiji and Gambia Committees with whom he worked, relied on a balanced programme of parliamentary questions and lobbying ministers, Venn relied almost exclusively on the latter. But he also relied on prayer and, in particular, organised prayer.[167] He had at his disposal the Church Missionary Society and its world wide contacts to be used in this capacity. The response to the Dahomian siege of Abeokuta in 1863 was just one example of highly-organised prayer across the world.[168] As well as lobbying government ministers, Venn put much effort into the organised lobbying of the Almighty.

The role of the missionaries was greater in the initial annexation of Lagos. As time progressed, their influence waned, particularly when they clashed with colonial governors over expansion and official hostility to the Egba. The retirement of Henry Venn in 1872 was also very significant. Never again was there a 'missionary statesman', to use Wilbert Shenk's phrase, with such easy access to the corridors of power. By the end of our period the emergence of an indigenous leadership, both within and without the native pastorate, was the mark of a church coming of age. Henry Venn had distinguished between a mission and a church – the Yoruba mission was rapidly turning into the Yoruba church.

It was in the influence of the 'educated Africans' in whom Venn had so much confidence and hope for the future, that missionary success can be seen in the long term. Because of its role in raising up Africans of ability through mission schools, 'the church became the cradle of Nigerian nationalism'.[169] Dr Nnamdi Azikiwe, the father of twentieth-century Nigerian nationalism, was the product of a missionary education. Herbert Macaulay, whom Michael Crowder describes as 'the father of all Nigerian nationalism', was an ordained Anglican and actually a member of Bishop Crowther's family.[170] Yet significantly it is a

---

167 This is not to suggest that William M'Arthur was not a man of prayer, but Venn had a missionary society with all its members and supporters under his influence. He was always ready to organise them to pray.
168 Stock, II, pp.437-438.
169 Ayandele, *Missionary Impact,* p.175.
170 Crowder, p.226.

Nigerian historian E.A. Ayandele who states that, 'If any individual is to be credited with originating Nigerian nationalism ideologically, then that individual is unquestionably the Revd Henry Venn'.[171]

The missionaries brought Lagos to the attention of the British government so that it was informally controlled from 1851 and annexed in 1861, and thereafter sought to make the colonial government pursue humane policies which did not disadvantage the Egba. Nevertheless, it was not until the advent of Lugard and the incorporation of Lagos into the larger state of Nigeria that it became a place of importance in West Africa. As Robinson and Gallagher remind us, 'on the eve of the scramble [for Africa] Lagos was still regarded as a liability'.[172]

Lagos, however, was not the only 'liability' the British government possessed in Africa. For just as the need to put down the Atlantic slave trade had drawn Britain to the west coast of Africa, so the Arab slave trade led to British involvement in East Africa. And, once again, the missionaries were to be found in the vanguard.

---

171 Ayandele, *Missionary Impact*, p.180.
172 R.E. Robinson and J. Gallagher, with A. Denny, *African and the Victorians* (London: Macmillan, 1961), p.40.

CHAPTER 7

The Aftermath of Slavery in East and Central Africa

On 2 January 1851, nearly twelve months before the British bombardment and occupation of Lagos, Henry Venn prophesied, 'If Africa is to be penetrated by European missionaries, it must be from the East Coast'.[1]

In this period a number of missions were involved in the vast area that is East Africa, and although reference will be made to several of the missions involved, including the LMS and the newly-founded Universities' Mission to Central Africa, not to mention the commanding figure of David Livingstone, the main focus of this chapter will be on the involvement of the CMS, the first British mission in the region. CMS missions developed in four distinct phases: the initial pioneering stage by Ludwig Krapf, continued by Johannes Rebmann; the attack on the slave trade culminating in the 1871 Select Committee and the outworking of its report; the establishment of Frere Town as a settlement for freed slaves; and the establishment of the Nyanza Mission and the inland extension of missionary work to Buganda.

The Pioneer Missionaries in East Africa

The occasion on which Henry Venn made his prophecy was a valedictory service in Islington for Ludwig Krapf prior to his return to East Africa in 1851. In 1844 Krapf had established a mission station at Rabai, near Mombasa, an area in which British interests had already been in evidence, to the extent of a temporary Protectorate in the years 1824-26. The death of his wife on arrival (his first despatch from his new mission field recorded her death)[2] was to Krapf a challenge rather than a setback. The subsequent arrival of Johannes Rebmann

---

1 Quoted in Stock, II, p.124.
2 Krapf to Dandeson Coates, 13 August 1844. CMS East African Mission papers, CA5/016. For a first-hand account of the pioneering period of the mission see J.L. Krapf, *Travels, Researches and Missionary Labours* (London: Trübner and Co., 1860). See also Stock, II, 124-129.

in Mombasa in June 1846 was almost immediately followed by permission from the chiefs of the Wanika to establish a mission on the mainland at Rabai.[3] For ten years this first mission on the East African mainland was run by these two German-speaking CMS missionaries. Their wide-ranging journeys of exploration did much to aid geographical knowledge of the region long before Livingstone arrived on the scene.[4] Indeed, it was Rebmann who was the first European to set eyes on the snow-capped peak of Mount Kilimanjaro, and Krapf the first to see Mount Kenya.[5] Rebmann produced the first sketch map of the region in 1848 and heard and reported stories of a great inland sea which acted as a spur to later explorers – Speke, Burton and Livingstone.

Krapf retired in 1855, returning to his native Wurtemburg, from where he continued his intelligent and prayerful interest in missions, bombarding Salisbury Square with letters right up until his death in 1881.[6] Rebmann remained at Rabai for a further twenty years during which period the mission can hardly be said to have flourished. From time to time incursions by Masai warriors compelled Rebmann to take refuge in Mombasa, but he always returned to Rabai to continue his work of exploration, translation and pastoring his tiny flock. During the 1860s he had a succession of colleagues, but none stayed for long in this missionary backwater. Norman Bennett is critical of Rebmann for allowing the mission to decay and for having 'given up to trying to convert' the local people, and he quotes a letter of 1865 from Henry Venn to the consul in Zanzibar, Colonel Pelly, to suggest that Rebmann was only left in post because of his work on the native language.[7] But Venn's words can equally be read without a critical slant. Venn, after all, knew that missionaries were primarily called to be faithful, success depended entirely on God's providence. Rebmann was nothing if not faithful, stubborn and tenacious. Even in 1874, when the mission was once again flourishing, he remained at his post long after his eyesight had failed.[8] However, this could equally be viewed as stubbornness

---

3 Krapf to Venn, 20 September 1846. CMS East African Mission papers, CA5/016.
4 For a brief survey of exploration in this region see Roy C. Bridges, 'The Historical Role of British Explorers in East Africa', *Terrae Incognitae*, 14 (1982), 1-21.
5 When scientific journals in Europe failed to believe that a mountain in equatorial latitudes could possibly have snow on it and consequently patronised Rebmann and claimed that he was mistaken, Rebmann replied that someone like himself who had been brought up in Switzerland was unlikely to be mistaken when identifying a snow-covered peak! Stock, II, p.127.
6 Having served in Abyssinia before Mombasa, he was briefly brought out of retirement in 1867 as interpreter to General Napier on the Abyssinian expedition. Krapf's voluminous correspondence is contained in the CMS CA5/016 file.
7 Venn to Pelly, 24 May 1865, E-46 in Zanzibar Archives, quoted in Norman R. Bennett, 'The Church Missionary Society at Mombasa, 1873-1894', *Boston University Papers on African History* (Boston, 1964), 160.
8 See William Chancellor to CMS, 7 July and 29 September 1874. CMS East Africa Mission papers, CA5/05.

and a refusal to allow younger and more able men to take over the mission and it is certainly the case that Rebmann had been left too long in an isolated situation thus allowing progress to cease and any originality to atrophy. Bennett notes succinctly that 'events had passed Rebmann by'.[9] It would appear that Rebmann's vision failed in more ways than one.

Roland Oliver pointed out the irony that 'it was Livingstone the individual and not the CMS missionaries with their twelve years' start and their powerful society behind them, who set in motion the missionary invasion of East Africa'. Yet it was their linguistic work and initial work of exploration that 'laid a solid foundation for all who came after'.[10]

Confronting the East African Slave Trade

If the Atlantic slave trade had been the reason for British involvement on the west coast of Africa then the Arab slave trade in the east, a less well-known but equally brutal and more tenacious trade, proved to be the lure of British involvement on the east coast.[11] If, as has been noted in Chapter 2, there was some genuine doubt among both officials and missionaries as to whether the transportation of indentured labour in the Pacific was actually *slavery,* there was no room for doubt in East Africa and the Indian Ocean. The Arab slave trade had been restricted first by the Moresby Treaty of 1822, then by the Hammerton Treaty of 1847, both with the Sultan of Zanzibar. Though their purpose was to limit the trade, these treaties had, in the view of missionaries and humanitarians, the adverse effect of giving recognition to the trade without having sufficient teeth to make much of an impact on it.

The 1860s witnessed an expansion in the Arab slave trade in East Africa despite the preventative measures of the Royal Navy. Indeed R.J. Gavin has suggested that the political will was slackening and the naval squadron had neither the resources nor the necessary pressure from the government to do more than make a small dent in the trade.[12] In this climate of official apathy it was the CMS that took the lead in seeking to move East Africa from the political back-burner and bring it back to the boil. Coupland and Lloyd are of the opinion that it was the interest aroused by the Zambesi expedition, and the information disseminated by Livingstone's writings that the slave trade was still alive and well in East Africa, that captured popular interest and gave new

---

9 Bennett, 163.
10 Oliver, p.7.
11 For a survey of the Arab Slave Trade see R. Coupland, *Exploitation*, pp.134-151 and *The British Anti-Slavery Movement* (London: Thornton Butterworth, 1933), pp.189-208; Christopher Lloyd, *The Navy and the Slave Trade* (London, Longmans, Green, 1949); Raymond Howell, *The Royal Navy and the Slave Trade* (London: Croom Helm, 1987).
12 R.J. Gavin, 'The Bartle Frere Mission to Zanzibar, 1873', *Historical Journal,* V (1962), 132-133.

impetus to the flagging abolitionist movement. Oliver, however, suggests that it was Lincoln's Emancipation proclamation, with anti-slavery attention now shifting from the Atlantic to the Indian Ocean, that provided the inspiration for the CMS to take up this cause.[13] It is important to remember that East Africa, very much a backwater of the world unknown and unheard of by most British people until Livingstone began to publicise its problems, was suddenly thrust into the mainstream of world trade routes by the opening, in November 1869, of the Suez Canal which cut two thousand miles off the sea journey to East Africa and made it more accessible to commercial enterprise as well as to missions.

Roland Oliver noted that from 1869 the CMS had 'encouraged its political friends to press for a Select Committee'.[14] Events had, however, been moving in this direction since 1867 when Bishop Ryan of Mauritius appealed to the CMS to make representations in Britain against the trade.[15] This resulted in a deputation to the India Office (through which relations with Zanzibar were normally conducted) in February 1869. The deputation called for 'measures to effectively terminate this remaining relic of that infamous traffic which it is the pride of England to have swept from the Atlantic'.[16]

The opportunity came in the House of Commons on 30 June 1871 when Gilpin proposed, Kinnaird seconded and Viscount Enfield of the Foreign Office conceded, a Select Committee.[17] Peter J. Durrans detects a change in the national mood which made such a committee congenial to public opinion, attributing this mainly to the 'publicity given to the exploits and exposure of the missionary and explorer David Livingstone'.[18]

Among the committee's fifteen members were the Quaker Russell Gurney in the chair, John Kennaway, president of the CMS, Sir Robert Fowler of the Aborigines Protection Society, Sir John Hay, who had sat on the 1865 West Africa Select Committee, and Arthur Kinnaird, who represented both CMS and LMS. Considering it was the consummation of two years' efforts, the Committee met, did its business and dispersed with considerable not to say astonishing rapidity, its first meeting being held on 10 July 1871 and its report being dated 4 August. Among those who gave evidence were Sir Bartle Frere, H.C. Rothery, the Treasury's adviser on the slave trade, Edward Steere, Charles Allington and Horace Waller of the UMCA and Edward Hutchinson of the CMS.

---

13 Coupland, *The British Anti-Slavery Movement*, p.210; Lloyd, p.258; Oliver, pp.18-19.
14 Oliver, p.19. In fact a joint departmental committee of the Foreign, Colonial and India Offices and Admiralty had been convened by Lord Clarendon in 1869 to look into the matter, but proposals were nullified by the Chancellor, Robert Lowe, who refused to provide any additional finance. Gavin, 133-135.
15 Stock, III, pp.73-74.
16 Quoted in Shenk, *Missionary Statesman*, p.77.
17 *Hansard,* Third Series, CCVII cols 952-957.
18 Durrans, 'House of Commons and the British Empire', 25.

The committee's report made a series of recommendations to put into effect their opinion 'that all legitimate means should be used to put an end altogether to the East African slave trade'.[19] In essence these were: coercion of the Sultan into a new treaty to put an end to the slave trade, increasing the British consular staff in Zanzibar, providing the naval squadron with interpreters in order to examine boarded dhows and their crews and cargoes more effectively, recommending acceptance of the CMS offer to care for and educate liberated slave children in the Seychelles, making permanent Dr John Kirk's temporary appointment as consul and political agent at Zanzibar and engaging the assistance of other nations (Germany, France, USA, Portugal) in the elimination of the slave trade.

Peter J. Durrans gives positive approval of the Committee's work, regarding its report as 'strongly-worded', whereas R.J. Gavin takes a much more critical stance seeing the report as 'a loose amalgam of definite and indefinite proposals mixed with quotations of suggestions put forward by witnesses without comment by the committee itself'.[20] Eugene Stock commented on what seemed to him the main omission of the report: that 'it fell short of recommending the real remedy, viz., to apply to East Africa the method that had been so successful in West Africa, that is, to annex a bit of territory on the East Coast, upon which, being British, the slave would at once become a free man'.[21]

The mere publication of the Select Committee's report, however, was not enough to ensure government action. The year that followed saw a sustained campaign by the missionary and humanitarian lobbies working together to achieve intervention in the Arab slave trade by the British government. A series of articles by Edward Hutchinson seemed to be making little headway when, at the end of November 1871, the news of Bishop Patteson's death in Melanesia once again focused public opinion on the dire effects of the slave trade. A series of public meetings was sponsored by the Anti-Slavery Society in the spring and summer of 1872, during and after the passage of the Pacific Islanders' Protection Act. These meetings grew in size and prestige, starting out at Surrey Chapel in March and ending up at the Mansion House in July. John Kirk kept up the pressure from Zanzibar, bombarding Lord Granville with a series of despatches spelling out the increase of the slave trade and graphically describing its ill effects on East Africa and its population.[22] The agitation

---

19 Report from the Select Committee on Slave Trade (East Coast of Africa), *PP* 1871, XII [420].
20 *Ibid*; Gavin, 137.
21 Stock, III, p.75.
22 Kirk's despatches are printed in 'East Coast of Africa: correspondence respecting the slave trade and other matters'. *PP* 1873, LXI [C.867]. Kirk also privately forwarded information on the slave trade to Horace Waller, formerly a UMCA missionary and at that time the incumbent of a London parish. Howell, p.59.

culminated in July in what R.J. Gavin has called 'a minor explosion of feeling on the subject'. Questions in the Lords on the 24th and a supportive *Times* leader on the 25th were followed the same evening by the public meeting at the Mansion House. A deputation to Lord Granville took place the following day, the CMS and LMS secretaries being accompanied by three peers and fifteen MPs.

One of the leaders of this agitation was Sir Bartle Frere, former Governor of Bombay and currently a member of the Indian Council. Frere, a devout evangelical, was fully aware of the Arab slave trade and had come into contact with the CMS settlement for freed slaves at Nasik during his time in Bombay. In 1871-1872 he made a name for himself as a public opponent of the Arab slave trade. Granville's solution was at one stroke both to remove humanitarian opposition and to gain considerable kudos for the government by inviting Frere himself to head a mission to Zanzibar to seek the Sultan's agreement to end the trade. In reporting Frere's appointment, *The Times* indicated 'that a man of so much mark ... should have been appointed to such a post is *prima facie* evidence of the difficulty to be encountered and the importance of the ends to be attained'.[23]

Following Frere's appointment he was fêted at a large public meeting held at the Mansion House with a glittering array of missionary supporters and humanitarians including the bishops of London, Winchester and Rochester, Henry Morton Stanley, Kinnaird, Gilpin, Sir T.F. Buxton, Robert Moffat (LMS) and Horace Waller (UMCA).[24] This meeting had the atmosphere of a victory rally of those who had campaigned for action following the Select Committee's report. Indeed Frere, at ease with the anti-slavery enthusiasts with whom he had been making common cause for the past year, encouraged his hearers to 'keep up the pressure upon us to do our duty' and to 'take care that public attention does not flag on this subject'.[25]

Writing to Kirk on 31 October 1872, Granville summarised the Frere mission's purpose as simply 'the negotiation of fresh and more stringent treaties with the Sultan of Zanzibar and Muscat for the suppression of the slave trade'.[26] As well as his instructions,[27] Frere received a letter from Granville to convey to the Sultan, which explained the purpose of his mission. It was blunt and to the point:

> Should Your Highness, as Her Majesty's Government trust you will, join with them ... in carrying out efficient measures for putting an end to the export of slaves from your dominions in Africa, Your Highness may reckon on the friendship and support

---

23 *The Times*, 24 October 1872, p.10.
24 *The Times*, 5 November 1872, p.4.
25 *Ibid*.
26 Granville to Kirk, 31 October 1872. *PP* 1873, LXI [C.820].
27 Frere had virtually written his own instructions. See Frere to Granville, 9 October 1872. PRO 30/29/103.

of this country and the Government of India; but should on the other hand Your Highness decline the terms which will be submitted to you by Her Majesty's Envoy, Your Highness may be assured that, however much Her Majesty's Government may regret your decision, the subjects which they have in view will none the less be pursued.[28]

Frere arrived in Zanzibar in January 1873 and soon realised that his mission was not going to be as straightforward as he might have imagined.[29] Optimistically looking for stations to place freed slaves, Frere took the opportunity to visit and consult the missions in Zanzibar and on the mainland opposite. All except the CMS expressed a willingness to help; the aged Rebmann was now clearly beyond any new initiatives. Frere commented somewhat sarcastically that Rebmann's 'holy life of ascetic self-denial and indifference to all worldly enjoyments and employments ... have had the usual effect of exciting admiration, without securing the imitation of the people around him'.[30] On 17 January he confessed to Granville that he 'had no idea of the strength of the monopolist opposition (including all the European and Indian traders)'.[31] By 1 February he gloomily reported that 'I very much doubt ... whether I shall get the Sultan to sign any treaty or cooperate in any way in putting down the export of slaves...'. Yet he had not given up hope and hinted that non-diplomatic means might have the desired effect.[32]

Frere's diplomatic mission to Zanzibar was a failure and he left empty-handed in May 1873 having been unable to persuade Sultan Barghash of the wisdom of signing a treaty to abolish the seaborne slave trade. But once at sea on the return journey he turned to non-diplomatic methods as an alternative means of persuasion: on his own authority he gave orders for a blockade of Zanzibar by the Royal Navy to force the Sultan into compliance.[33] From 16 May, HMS *Briton* and HMS *Daphne* blockaded the island and achieved a complete stoppage in the slave trade to and from Zanzibar.

As happened later with disastrous consequences in South Africa in 1879, Frere took the initiative himself and the government was forced to respond to his unauthorised actions. Victorian pro-consuls and 'men on the spot' on the imperial frontier habitually acted on their own initiative. Although it often caused embarrassment and confusion, the home government rarely failed to back them up. After initial hesitation it was decided to underwrite Frere's actions even to the extent of authorising the use of force if Barghash failed to

---

28 Granville to Sultan of Zanzibar, 9 November 1872. *PP* 1873, LXI [C.820].
29 For the Frere Mission see Coupland, *The Exploitation of East Africa* (London: Faber and Faber, 1939), pp.182-205; Gavin, 122-148; Howell, pp.79-99.
30 Quoted in Bennett, 163.
31 Frere to Granville, 17 January 1873. PRO 30/29/103.
32 Frere to Granville, 1 February 1873. PRO 30/29/103.
33 See Granville's Minute for Cabinet, 29 April 1873. PRO 30/29/73.

sign a new treaty.[34] But perhaps this is not so surprising since, having set up Frere's mission somewhat reluctantly the government now required a successful outcome in order to justify it. Gladstone's first ministry had already reached the end of its tether, its Front Bench having become, in Disraeli's words, 'a range of exhausted volcanoes', and with an election imminent, they were in urgent need of the political kudos that a successful outcome to the Frere mission would bring. It should be remembered that in March 1873 Gladstone had tendered to the Queen his government's resignation after the Irish University Bill was defeated in the Commons. Disraeli had refused to take office as a minority government and waited for the dissolution which he knew must come within the year.[35] Thus it was only natural for the Liberal Cabinet to have high hopes that Frere's mission would bolster their flagging popularity in the country and be a potential vote-winner.

Though Sir Bartle Frere, by initiating the naval blockade, may have created the conditions in which the Sultan would be forced to capitulate, it was an official ultimatum from Granville threatening the use of British force, together with the diplomatic pressure applied sensitively but firmly by Kirk that, in due course, paid dividends. Thus on 5 June 1873 Barghash signed the treaty abolishing the seaborne slave trade.[36]

The book by Edward Hutchinson, CMS Lay Secretary, *The Slave Trade of East Africa*, though written for propaganda purposes, contains much useful information on the trade and its doleful effects on East African life, but is not   that it was published in 1874 well *after* the Frere mission and the treaty with the Sultan.[37] The reason was clear – despite the seaborne trade being abolished the trade continued by the overland routes. Hutchinson's information on this continuing trade was derived from Kirk's vice-consul, Captain Frederic Elton, from whose despatches he quoted at length.[38] But rather than missionary publicity in England or warships off the coast of Zanzibar, it was Kirk's patient work in Zanzibar which eventually bore fruit, together with a realisation by the Sultan that he had already passed the point of no-return. Thus, on 18 April 1876 Barghash issued two proclamations, which Kirk had drafted for him, ending the overland slave trade also.[39]

The Sultan's proclamations did not, however, spell an instant end to the slave trade. Its death throes took a number of years and British consuls

---

34 Gavin, 146.
35 Robert Blake, *Disraeli* (London: Eyre and Spottiswoode, 1966), pp.527-528.
36 Treaty between Her Majesty and the Sultan of Zanzibar for the suppression of the slave trade, 5 June 1873. PP 1873, LXI [C.820]. The catalyst for Granville's uncharacteristic display of action was possibly a speech in the Lords on 12 May when Lord Campbell claimed that 'Sir Bartle Frere ... had wholly failed to bend the Sultan to [his] object'. *Hansard*, Third Series, CCXV, cols 1779-1780.
37 Edward Hutchinson, *The Slave Trade of East Africa* (London: Sampson Low, 1874).
38 Reports by Elton, quoted in Hutchinson, pp.57-62.
39 Enc. in Kirk to Derby, 28 April 1876. FO 84/1453.

continued sending reports on the state of the trade to London.[40] Nevertheless, now deprived of official sanction and with the slave market at Zanzibar closed, the trade was in terminal decline.[41]

David Livingstone

No analysis of missionary work in East Africa can ignore the towering personality of David Livingstone. Though he resigned from the LMS in order to be free to explore Central Africa and campaign against the slave trade, Livingstone always regarded himself as primarily a missionary, recognising that 'the end of the geographical feat is but the beginning of the missionary enterprise'.[42] Owen Chadwick precisely captures the missionary philosophy of this highly complex figure who, although he was the most famous, was in many ways the most unusual and atypical of Victorian missionaries:

> He had no interest himself in building up strong congregations, in gathering a nucleus of faithful men, in creating the first beginnings of a church. He believed in the diffused influence of a white and Christian civilization as the Christianizing force of Africa; and he conceived his own travels as the opening of gates for the spread of that influence.[43]

Was his vision wider than the making of individual converts or was he simply unsuited to a humdrum daily routine, a manic depressive who craved constant activity and therefore sought to grace his restlessness with a hint of wider strategy? Certainly, his letter to Dr Tidman parting company with the LMS gave that impression, but with Livingstone one can never be sure since he always seemed to keep one eye on posterity in his copious writings.[44]

Livingstone in many ways came to regard himself as a missionary *above* denominational organisations, though he was never averse to manipulating them in order to achieve his ambitious projects. But unlike Cecil Rhodes in the next generation, Livingstone was not personally ambitious and sought only the good of Africa by cleansing it from 'that open sore ... – the slave trade'. Yet it would seem that, like Shakespeare's Henry V, who did not regard it as a sin to covet

---

40 See, for example, despatches in *PP* 1878, LXVII [C.2139]; 1881, LXXXV [C.3052]; 1882, LXV [C.3160] and 1883, LXVI [C.3547].
41 In a highly symbolic gesture, the UMCA purchased the site of the former slave market on which to build the new Zanzibar Cathedral.
42 Quoted in Stock, II, 138.
43 Owen Chadwick, *Mackenzie's Grave* (London: Hodder and Stoughton, 1959), p.23.
44 He was, he said, with implied criticism of the LMS, leaving to go to 'the untried, remote and difficult fields to which I humbly yet firmly believe God has directed my steps'. Livingstone to Tidman, 12 October 1855, quoted in Seaver, p.249.

honour,[45] Livingstone felt the same about the reputation he was to leave behind for posterity.

Tim Jeal's biography of Livingstone, first published in 1973 on the centenary of his death, could justifiably be described as 'revisionist' had not some previous works been more hagiographical than historical. Jeal portrays Livingstone as a great man, but with feet of clay. So single minded in his objectives and mindful of his reputation, he appeared manipulative, devious, and at times, untruthful. By comparing Livingstone's private correspondence with his published works, Jeal concludes that Livingstone was normally prepared to manipulate his presentation of the facts, routinely resorting to litotes to conceal that which was inconvenient and to hyperbole to highlight that which was advantageous. Jumping on Jeal's bandwagon a reviewer unfairly proclaimed, 'David Livingstone was indeed a chilling and ruthless man who often used pious Christian principles to disguise his worldly ambitions'.[46]

More interestingly, Dr John Kirk who, unlike Jeal, had nothing to gain and no reputation to make by casting aspersions on Livingstone's integrity and who had known him at close quarters over the five years of the Zambesi expedition, paints this unflattering portrait: 'Dr Livingstone ... is about as ungrateful and slippery a mortal as I ever came into contact with, and, although he would be grievously offended to think that anyone doubted his honesty, I am sorry to say that I do'. Kirk continued: 'I think the explanation to be that he is one of those sanguine enthusiasts wrapped up in their own schemes whose reason and better judgment is blinded by headstrong passion'.[47]

Also reacting against the Livingstone legend, but in a more measured assessment, George Shepperson lists Livingstone's faults as neglect of his family, frequent lack of consideration for others (especially Europeans who did not match up to his standards), obstinacy that sometimes became purblindness in the face of situations which did not fit in with his preconceived ideas, and a touch of arrogance. To set against this, however, he credits Livingstone with being 'a very great propagandist' who, 'perhaps more than any other person in human history, drew one particular part of the world to the attention of those who lived outside it'. Shepperson regarded the attack on Livingstone by Jeal and his reviewers as excessive, particularly any suggestion that religion was cynically exploited: 'To me the religious impulse was the basic factor in David Livingstone's life ... a religious impulse which was not a calculated cover for secular ambitions but a central and essential element in him'.[48]

---

45 Henry V, Act IV, Scene iii, 28-29.
46 Graham Lord, 'Ah, the real Dr Livingstone, I presume...', *Scottish Sunday Express*, 29 April 1973, p.6., quoted in George Shepperson, 'David Livingstone, Scotland and Africa', in *David Livingstone and Africa* (University of Edinburgh, Centre for African Studies, seminar 3-5 May 1973), p.20.
47 Quoted in Jeal, p.265.
48 Shepperson, pp.1, 20-21.

A more recent work by Timothy Holmes has sought to explore the 'imperial myth' surrounding Livingstone.[49] Taking as his starting point papers held in the Livingstone Museum in Zambia, Holmes notes the differences between original MSS and published letters which, he alleged, 'had in most cases been doctored to remove anything that might stain Livingstone's image or that of the civilisation of which he had been presented as a model'.[50] To Holmes, the real Livingstone needs to be disentangled from the myth of him presented by others, 'the Men of Empire who used his name'.[51] Yet despite detailed research Livingstone remains an enigma in whom are combined both the highest motives and the pettiest attitudes.

Attention has been drawn to Livingstone's belief in combining Christianity with commerce to fill the gap in African society when the slave trade had been eradicated. For example, writing to Lord Clarendon in 1857, he stated:

> Legitimate commerce breaks up the isolation engendered by heathenism and the slave trade and surely if we take advantage of the very striking peculiarity of the African character (i.e. their fondness for barter and agriculture) we shall eventually bring this people within the sphere of Christian sympathy and the scope of missionary operations ....[52]

He returned to this laudable and very practical theme in his Cambridge speech later in the same year: 'My object in labouring as I have done in Africa, is to open up the country to commerce and Christianity. I propose in my next expedition to visit the Zambesi ... endeavouring to induce them to cultivate cotton and to abolish the slave trade'.[53]

It should, nevertheless, be noted that however original Livingstone's own ideas may have been, he was not first in this particular field. Once again it was the fertile mind of Henry Venn who, without the glare of fame or publicity, had at least partially anticipated him. As early as 1845 Venn, influenced by T.F. Buxton's 'Bible and plough' philosophy, had formed a small committee to advise him on initiating commercial enterprise in West Africa and to provide financial backing. He then brought Africans to London for a three-month course on cultivation at Kew Gardens. Thomas Clegg, a Manchester Cotton merchant, offered his services and by 1859 there were said to be between two and three hundred cotton gins at work in Abeokuta alone.[54]

---

49 Timothy Holmes, *Journey to Livingstone* (Edinburgh: Canongate Books, 1993).
50 *Ibid.*, p.xv.
51 *Ibid.*, p.351.
52 Livingstone to Clarendon, 26 January 1857, quoted in Seaver, p.299.
53 Speech at the Senate House, Cambridge, 5 December 1857, quoted in Groves, II, p.176.
54 Hennell, pp.84-85. See also Stock, II, pp.109-111. It was to Clegg that Venn entrusted Samuel Crowther's son Josiah as an apprentice, hoping that he would acquire

Livingstone and the UMCA

The exercise of Livingstone's influence is clearly seen in the foundation of the Universities' Mission to Central Africa following his Senate House speech in Cambridge in November 1857. But it seems ironic that Livingstone, a Scot and a Nonconformist, should make an appeal that led to the establishment of the most catholic of all the British Protestant missions. Anderson-Morshead suggests that it was Livingstone's good impression of the Church of England, following his break with the LMS that led him to make the Cambridge appeal.[55] After his return to Africa and prior to the arrival of the UMCA missionaries in 1861 Livingstone, perhaps impatient with the time it was taking to start up the new mission, continued to cast his net widely for missionaries to come to the part of Africa he hoped to colonise. Thus in 1859 he wrote to Henry Venn suggesting a CMS mission to the area of the recently discovered Lake Shirwa. After describing the natural beauty of the lake and its surroundings he continued:

> my first thoughts ... was (sic) 'Now this is what the Church Missionary Society has been thinking of for many years – a field in East Africa for planting the gospel beyond the unfriendly coast tribes; I shall write to Mr Venn about it at the first opportunity'.[56]

Livingstone wrote a follow-up letter five months to the day after his first,[57] but Venn's replies to either do not appear to have survived. Of course, Venn would have been only too aware of Livingstone's criticism of the CMS's use of German missionaries to make up the shortfall of British candidates.[58] But it is unlikely that Venn would have allowed such criticism to prejudice him against Livingstone and to use it as an excuse to withhold the co-operation of the CMS from a really viable mission. Indeed Livingstone's criticism was rather more aimed at British Christian manhood for failing to respond to the call of Africa rather than at the CMS for having to make do with Germans to fill their gaps in personnel. But Venn was second to none in his experience of placing missions and was far too prudent to allow a temporary enthusiasm, even from someone as

---

the necessary skills in the Lancashire cotton mills to put into practice in Abeokuta. Yates, p.151.
55 Anderson-Morshead, I, p.3.
56 Livingstone to Venn, 15 May 1859. CMS East Africa Mission papers CA5/01. Unaccountably, Stock (II, p.138) claims that this letter was written to the *Church Missionary Intelligencer*. But Livingstone clearly knew where lay the source of authority and influence in the CMS – Henry Venn. Michael Hennell noted that such was Venn's authority at Salisbury Square that his chair was irreverently referred to by the staff as the 'throne'. Hennell, p.76.
57 Livingstone to Venn, 15 October1859. CMS East Africa Mission papers, CA5/01.
58 Elston, in Pachai (ed.), *Livingstone, Man of Africa: Memorial Essays 1873-1973* (London: Longman, 1973), p.66.

persuasive as Livingstone, to sway more rational considerations. Thus the CMS failed to be persuaded by Livingstone's attempt to manipulate their strategic placement of missions. The UMCA alone was the fruit of his appeal. Here was a new mission founded in a unique way and tapping sources of support from a section of society which, apart from particular individuals, was not normally associated with missionary work. As Philip Elston points out, 'in turning to Cambridge, he was stirring not just the Church of England but also the wealthy and influential sectors of English society'.[59]

The foundation of the UMCA as a direct response to his appeal meant that Livingstone had a personal interest, one might even say a vested interest, in the progress of that mission, whose agenda he had dictated according to his own purposes. Thus Livingstone was not entirely blameless for the death of Bishop Mackenzie who perished in January 1862 in a fruitless attempt to meet up with Livingstone. When Bishop Tozer took the decision to abandon the Shiré highlands and to move initially to Zanzibar to regroup, Livingstone was apoplectic with rage, for it not only meant the end of his dream of a mission-led colony in the Shiré highlands but also called into question his own judgment in promoting it as a location for the mission in the first place. Bitterly, he denounced the UMCA: 'This I believe to be the first instance in modern times in which missionaries have voluntarily turned tail'.[60]

This was no momentary irritation however. Nearly four years later Livingstone was still lambasting Tozer and the UMCA: 'It is almost enough to make Mackenzie turn round in his grave to find his mission degraded to a mere chaplaincy to a consulate, and I fear there is no hope of seeing Central Africa occupied by its own mission in our day'.[61] Clearly he felt a sense of personal betrayal which goes some way to endorsing Jeal's contention that it was really his own judgment and reputation – the thing which he allegedly held most dear – that he felt was threatened by the mission's transfer from the site which he had chosen for them and in which he had invested so much emotional capital.

Just as with the death of Bishop Patteson in the Pacific, so first the death of Bishop Mackenzie in 1862 and then, particularly, the death of Livingstone himself in 1873 turned public attention to central and east Africa in general and to the issue of slavery in particular. Stanley had given Livingstone and his views maximum publicity in the period leading up to his death. If the UMCA owed its existence to Livingstone while he was very much alive, Eugene Stock asserted that directly or indirectly Livingstone's death in the heart of Africa 'led to the great missionary advances that date from the years following 1873'.[62] The more

---

59 *Ibid.*, p.69.
60 Livingstone to Sir Thomas Maclear, 19 December 1862, quoted in Seaver, p.433.
61 Livingstone to Professor Adam Sedgwick, 24 August 1866, quoted in Seaver, p.476.
62 Stock, III, p.73. Roland Oliver observed that, not insignificantly, Livingstone was responsible for 'a new and more numerous class of subscribers on to the [missionary] societies' lists'. Oliver, p.34.

notable of these in the immediate aftermath of the great explorer's death were the CMS Nyanza mission, the Free Church of Scotland Livingstonia mission, the Church of Scotland Blantyre mission and the LMS Central African mission.

The LMS Central African Mission

Whereas the UMCA had been salvaged from its disastrous start at Magomero by Bishop Tozer's strategic withdrawal of the mission to Zanzibar, the LMS Central African Mission was a disaster with few redeeming or redeemable features.[63] After dispensing the obligatory epithets of 'noble ambition', 'great extension of work', 'lofty hope, floated upon the tide of great enthusiasm', Lovett, the Society's official historian became more truthful in his account and characterised the mission as 'one long tragedy' and 'an instructive example of how great missionary enterprises ought not to be attempted'.[64]

The expedition had left Zanzibar in July 1877 and arrived at Ujiji thirteen months later. But only four of the six mission workers who set out finally reached Ujiji and of these two died shortly after. Having drawn no adverse conclusions from this sorry state of affairs, the LMS Directors sent out a relief expedition in 1879 which included no less than the Society's Foreign Secretary, Dr Joseph Mullens.[65] The death of Mullens on the ill-fated expedition did nothing to discourage further expeditions which went, lemming-like, in 1880 and again in 1882.[66]

Lovett (writing in 1899) noted that of thirty-six missionaries sent out between 1877 and 1893, eleven died and fourteen 'retired'. He also noted that the net result of this by the latter date was 'only twenty' converts 'at the most liberal calculation'.[67] Somewhat daringly, since he was writing an official history with their imprimatur, he criticised the LMS Directors, who 'sanctioned the mission without any true conception of the magnitude of the task they were undertaking' and who were 'ignorant of the climate, of the peculiarities of the country, of the nature of the work'.[68] The LMS had failed to heed the lesson of the UMCA who had eventually recognised their inability to maintain supply lines over hundreds of miles of potentially hostile territory without a chain of intermediate mission stations.

---

63 See Lovett, *History of LMS*, I, pp.650-670 and Doug Stuart, *The Making of a Missionary Disaster: the Makololo and the London Missionary Society*, (Cambridge: NAMP, 1997).
64 Lovett, *History of LMS*, I, pp. 649-650.
65 Mullens to Hutchinson, 7 April 1879. CMS Nyanza Mission papers, CA6/04.
66 A.J. Hanna highlighted another flaw in the mission – the lack of adequate leadership. Hanna, *Beginnings of Nyasaland and North-Eastern Rhodesia*, p.47n.
67 The first baptism had not taken place until 1891, thirteen years into the mission.
68 Lovett, *History of LMS*, I, 669-670.

Interestingly, in his chapter on the Central African Mission, Lovett fails to mention that it was a large donation of £5,000 from a wealthy missionary supporter, Robert Arthington of Leeds, that was the spur to the Central African Mission.[69] Eugene Stock, who as an Anglican had no such inhibitions, revealed that the mission was 'projected in consequence of a donation of £5,000'.[70] Though Ujiji was apparently selected as the base for the mission because it was the most easterly point on Lake Tanganyika and thus seemingly the nearest point to the Indian Ocean, it is difficult to believe that sentimental associations – the meeting place of Livingstone and Stanley in November 1871 – did not sway more rational thinking. The large donation from Arthington was in fact conditional on the establishment of the mission in the place he prescribed.[71]

The Troubles at Frere Town

The CMS settlement at Frere Town, near Mombasa, owed its name to Sir Bartle Frere and its existence to the Arab slave trade.[72] Accurately described by Norman Bennett as 'this most troublesome mission',[73] it caused the CMS endless difficulties and embarrassments.

The establishment of Frere Town, near to the existing CMS mission at Rabai, just outside Mombasa, was the response of the CMS to the abolition of the Arab slave trade and the need to care for freed slaves. Though Frere was dismissive of the results of the mission at Rabai when he visited it – 'It has been longer at work, with less apparent result, than any mission on this coast'[74] – he recommended the establishment of settlements for freed slaves in Zanzibar or on the coast opposite. The CMS responded by sending Sparshott and Chancellor at the end of 1873 to Rabai to take over from the aged Rebmann and to persuade him to retire. Their initial lack of progress resulted within a year in a decision from Salisbury Square to second an experienced missionary, William Salter Price, to take charge. Price had been serving at the CMS Nasik mission at Sharanpur, near Bombay, which specialised in the rehabilitation of freed slaves liberated from Arab dhows in the Indian Ocean. Appalled at what he found in

---

69 Lovett does in fact mention the donation, but tucks it away in his second volume in a chapter on Home Administration 1870-1895. Lovett, *History of LMS*, II, p.717. Could this have been on the instructions of the Directors who were prepared to accept his necessary criticisms but did not want the sorry account of this unsuccessful mission juxtaposed with the fact of Arthington's donation lest the (probably correct) conclusion be drawn that their judgment was influenced by this large financial incentive?
70 Stock, III, p.80.
71 Cairns, pp.14-15. Cairns described the four LMS expeditions to Ujiji as 'a continuous attempt to repair the folly evoked by zeal without discretion'.
72 The spellings, Frere Town and Freretown, seem to be used interchangeably.
73 Bennett, p.178.
74 Quoted in Bennett, p.161.

Rabai, he soon procured land adjacent to Mombasa for a settlement. Dr Kirk had visited Salisbury Square during leave from Zanzibar and, with his support, freed slaves began to arrive at Frere Town in 1875.[75]

There were five main problems that undermined the progress of the Frere Town settlement: the lack of control exercised by the missionaries, the brutality of punishments combined with uncertainty of jurisdiction, the harbouring of runaway slaves, chronic disagreements between the missionaries and tensions between white missionaries and the 'Bombay Africans'.

The hurried arrival of a large number of freed slaves who had had no previous contact with Europeans before the mission was really running efficiently, was the beginning of Frere Town's problems. The first shipment consisted of over 250 slaves and was not easy to assimilate since around seventy were adults who could not easily be controlled by the mission staff. Indeed, the population soon rose to 450.[76] Price felt that the work with the children was effective but the adults were 'a lot of idle savages, and until they can be made to understand their position and our feelings towards them we shall have something to do to keep order'.[77]

The real difficulty of keeping order among a large number of often unruly and unwilling ex-slaves led to the greatest crisis and most publicised scandal affecting Frere Town. The post of 'Lay Superintendent' was created in 1876, after the Revd J.T. Last had returned home, as a way of taking the pressure off the missionaries at Rabai by delegating their responsibilities for the inhabitants of Frere Town to an individual specifically charged with its day-to-day running. To counter the unruliness of their charges, both the Lay Superintendents, Captain W. Russell (1876-77) and J.R. Streeter (1877-81) were brutal in their punishment regime,[78] but it was Streeter who reaped the whirlwind of hostility which had built up in the Mombasa area.[79] The problem of discipline amongst the Frere Town residents was compounded by the mission's lack of legal jurisdiction over the Sultan's subjects, and the difficulty of knowing just whose subjects individual recalcitrant ex-slaves actually were.

---

75 Hutchinson to Price, 12 February 1875. CMS East African Mission papers, CA5/L1.
76 Strayer, p.15.
77 Price to Wright, 5 October 1875, quoted in Bennett, p.167.
78 A.J. Temu, *British Protestant Missions* (London: Longman, 1972), p.16. Strayer noted that Price had written that the stocks were the 'most prominent object' in the settlement and that the lash was in frequent use' (p.16). Unfortunately Strayer's method of identifying sources in the CMS archives is, to say the least, idiosyncratic, which makes tracing his references virtually impossible.
79 Even before the Streeter affair became public knowledge, Semler, one of the Bombay Africans had commented obliquely in a letter to CMS headquarters that Streeter 'knows how to rule the Africans'. Semler to CMS, 27 March 1879. CMS East African Mission papers, CA5/01.

A complaint about Streeter's brutality reached the Sultan who referred it to Kirk. Kirk sent his vice-consul, Frederic Holmwood, to investigate.[80] So little did Kirk realise what a can of worms Holmwood was about to open that he wrote a friendly note to Streeter, advising him, because of the complications of jurisdiction, 'to try to have an amicable settlement made of these matters and not allow the case to proceed to trial and I have told Mr Holmwood to do all he can to bring about a compromise'.[81] Streeter had already confessed to Kirk that he *had* used corporal punishment to get at the truth about stolen food [82] when a damning report from Holmwood, confirming the charges of excessive brutality against Streeter, landed on Kirk's desk.[83] Kirk confessed to Granville that he read it 'with the utmost surprise'. Streeter's practice of beating half-naked married women particularly revolted Kirk who was also clearly embarrassed by his own misjudgement, having initially discounted the charges and supported Streeter.[84]

A report on Frere Town from Commander Matthew Byley RN to the senior naval officer on the East coast of Africa was also damning:

> I consider the treatment of natives living in the Church Mission station, Mombasa, a disgrace to the honour of Englishmen, and if the facts were fully known in England, they would very much militate against the prosperity of that great and useful Society, the Church Missionary Society. In the interests of the Church Missionary Society I consider it desirable that as soon as possible all the present white officials be removed and be replaced by those who can carry the Gospel into all parts of the world without bringing disgrace on the name of England.[85]

In explaining the financial implications of such abuses of power, Byley was merely confirming what CMS headquarters already knew. Streeter was recalled and W.S. Price (who had left in 1876) instructed to return to East Africa and take charge once again. As far as the CMS was concerned the points at issue were that, first, 'there [had] been a usurpation of authority on the part of the lay Superintendent over the subjects of the Sultan of Zanzibar' and, secondly, 'undue exercise of authority and an excess of severity in the punishments inflicted on children'. Price was instructed that henceforth 'all grave offences must be brought before the consulate' and the use of both flogging and the stocks was forbidden.[86]

---

80 Kirk to Holmwood, 30 June 1881. FO 84/1600.
81 *Ibid.*, Kirk to Streeter, 1 July 1881.
82 *Ibid.*, Streeter to Kirk, 18 June 1881.
83 *Ibid.*, Holmwood to Kirk, 7 July 1881.
84 *Ibid.*, Kirk to Granville, 21 July 1881.
85 *Ibid.*, Byley to Captain Brownrigg, 12 July 1881.
86 CMS Secretaries to Price, 14 November 1881. CMS East African Mission papers, CA5/L2.

In one sense Streeter's crime was to hit the headlines in Britain shortly after disclosures about the Church of Scotland's Blantyre mission had made missionary brutality a live and contentious issue.[87] Streeter's subsequent attempt to justify his actions made matters worse. A contrite apology would have been more fitting and a better tactical move. Streeter's public dismissal (and, no doubt, the Blantyre revelations which had also received much notoriety) meant that other missions now became more scrupulous in administering punishments, no doubt thankful that their punishment regimes had not been exposed in the media. For example, Bishop Steere of the UMCA wrote to his Archdeacon, Chauncey Maples: 'I have no choice but to forbid altogether all beating of women'.[88] Clearly he would not bother to forbid what was not already taking place, but nevertheless he still allowed men to be beaten.

A further complication to the scandal was the fact that Streeter had openly received runaway slaves at Frere Town, outraging the local Arab population in the same way that his brutal punishments outraged British opinion.[89] When the Wali (Governor) of Mombasa and the Sultan of Zanzibar both complained that Frere Town was becoming a haven for runaway slaves, Kirk was bound to act.[90] Salisbury Square was dragged into a complicated and unedifying dispute, made worse by the inaccurate information they had received from their missionaries.

All in all, the CMS were glad to be rid of an embarrassment when Streeter was recalled in 1881, but the damage to the reputation of Frere Town had been done. In addition to his personal disgrace, Streeter's activities resulted in a loss of confidence in the settlement, and no freed slaves were sent there between the end of 1879 and March 1885. The former date was a clear indication of the harmful effect that Streeter's actions were having on Frere Town's reputation, even before the full range of his activities had been brought out into the open.[91]

The other problems did nothing to make Frere Town an easy mission station in which to work. Indeed, it does seem to have been a particularly quarrelsome one. From the arrival of Price in 1874 and the consequent recall of Sparshott for opposing his new chief,[92] discord seems to have been the order of the day at both Frere Town and Rabai. Missionaries were, of course, notable for their contentiousness. This was hardly surprising in view of the hardships they endured and the proximity to one another far away from civilisation – an

---

87 At Blantyre both floggings and even executions had taken place. See Hanna, Beginnings of Nyasaland and North-Eastern Rhodesia, pp.28-34 and John McCracken, *Politics and Christianity in Malawi 1875-1940* (Cambridge: CUP, 1977), pp.65-68.
88 Steere to Maples, 10 May 1882, quoted in Temu, p.30n.
89 Temu notes that it was hardly surprising that the missionaries aroused Arab hostility by preaching against Islam and slavery, both fundamental elements of Arab culture. Temu p.19.
90 See Kirk to Salisbury, 9 January 1880. *PP* 1881, LXXXV [C.3052].
91 Howell, p.183.
92 Telegram: CMS Secretaries to Price, 22 February 1875. CMS East African Mission papers, CA5/L1.

inevitable part of the missionary's lot. Nevertheless, the CMS archives for this mission seem to have a larger than average number of arguments and complaints aired in their despatches to London.[93] The consequence of their endemic ill feeling is spelled out by R.M. Githige: 'It is clear that personal disagreements between missionaries themselves made the task of maintaining a common mission policy on many issues difficult'.[94]

Further complications were caused by tensions which developed between white missionaries and the so-called 'Bombay Africans' or 'Nasik Christians'. These had been introduced to Frere Town by Price, who brought them with him from India. Not surprisingly, Price and equally (during his superintendency between Price's two tours of duty) James Lamb, worked well with them. On the other hand Sparshott referred to the Bombay Africans on their arrival as 'the very dregs of society, a shame and dishonour to Christianity'.[95] But he was clearly biased and resentful, seeing them as *protégés* of Price, whose very arrival was a vote of no-confidence in himself by the CMS. In contrast, Price and Lamb were of an older generation of missionaries, well-used to working with black Christians on their mission team. More ominous was the attitude of Streeter, the mission schoolmaster John Handford, and the younger mission staff who came on stream in the 1880s.

Their prejudiced attitudes towards the Bombay Africans were symptomatic of the tones of white racial superiority that became more prevalent in missionary circles in the 1880s and 1890s. In many ways, the Bombay Africans were the 'backbone' of the settlement. Used as catechists, teachers, interpreters, preachers and artisans, they formed a recognisable buffer between the white missionaries and the freed slaves, a veritable 'NCO' class. Their presence meant that the missionaries took a more managerial role and often lived in comparative luxury, a point noted by Bishop Hannington on his visit to the Mombasa area.[96] Robert Strayer describes the Bombay Africans as 'an aspiring mission-trained middle class, confident of their abilities, devoted to the mission but anxious to make the most of their new opportunities'.[97] Some of them, educated and enterprising, like Ishmael Michael Semler and George David, were particularly valuable to the mission. James Lamb, who had transferred to Mombasa from Yorubaland, was impressed by David and drew upon his own West African experience when he described him as 'a truly valuable man and if

---

93 See, as examples, Chancellor to CMS Committee, 7 July 1874, CA5/05; Price to Binns, 8 March 1876, CA5/023; Handford to CMS, 24 March 1876, CA5/011; J.T. Last to CMS Committee, 12 April 1876, CA5/01. All CMS East African Mission papers.
94 R.M. Githige, 'The Issue of Slavery: Relations between the CMS and the State on the East African Coast prior to 1895', *Journal of Religion in Africa*, 16 (1986), 214.
95 Sparshott to Wright, 21 May 1874, quoted in Bennett, p.170.
96 It made him 'shudder slightly to see such palatial residences'. Hannington, 9 February 1885, quoted in Strayer, p.15.
97 Strayer, p.16.

his life is spared will be the Bishop Crowther of the East Coast'. He recommended him for ordination to the diaconate.[98]

Thus some were well-educated and able men, and they became increasingly resentful of the constant carping criticism of the younger white mission staff, especially after Lamb's departure in 1878. Their legitimate complaints of the way in which they were stereotyped and their efforts unrecognised by the mission staff initially went unnoticed, eclipsed by the other problems caused by Streeter. By 1881, according to Strayer, 'an incipient rebellion of at least the better educated and more highly placed section of the Bombay Africans was well under way'.[99]

The return of the sympathetic W.S. Price to East Africa in 1881 to resolve the trouble Streeter had caused meant that he was able to reconcile the Bombay Africans to the mission, but he was too late to prevent the resignation of George David and a small exodus to the UMCA mission in Zanzibar. Neither could he solve the long-term problem of how to incorporate educated African Christians into the mission structures in a valued non-subordinate role, an issue that became increasingly difficult in the face of the growth of newly-fashionable white supremacist views.

The Nyanza Mission, Buganda and Bishop Hannington

If David Livingstone stirred the British national conscience with regard to the Arab slave trade and acted as the spur to a resurgence of missionary activity by the UMCA, the LMS, and both the Church and Free Church of Scotland, it was a similar challenge from Henry Morton Stanley that led to the establishment of the CMS Nyanza mission. On 15 November 1875 the London *Daily Telegraph* published a letter, written by Stanley some months earlier, calling for 'pious and practical' missionaries to be sent to Buganda. It appears to be the case that Livingstone's personal magnetism had strangely affected the cynical and hard-bitten journalist and he was more than willing to transmit Kabaka Mutesa's request.[100] Like his mentor, before he became disillusioned by the 'perfidy' of the UMCA, it would seem that Stanley too saw missionaries as potential imperialists.

In 1872, at a time when the Frere mission had been appointed and there was much optimism in missionary circles, the CMS had 'opened a special fund for East Africa'. As Hutchinson had informed Frere at the time, it had 'the two-fold object in view: first to strengthen our Mombas (sic) mission and second to endeavour to reach the interior from Mombas as a base'.[101] The interest aroused

---

98 Lamb to Wright, 4 November 1876. CMS East African Mission papers, CA5/O17.
99 Strayer, p.17.
100 Also spelled M'tesa and Mtesa.
101 Hutchinson to Frere, 19 December 1872. CMS East African Mission papers, CA5/L1.

by Stanley's letter enabled the CMS to consider putting into practice the second part of that objective, having funds in hand to do so. A specially convened CMS Victoria Nyanza Sub-Committee met on 23 November 1875, a week after the publication of Stanley's letter, 'to consider the subject of the invitation conveyed from the capital of Uganda in Mr Stanley's despatch'.[102] The sub-committee minutes go on to reveal, however, that the CMS's commendable haste was motivated not just by Stanley's letter but also by a not insignificant financial consideration. An anonymous letter, written on 17 November was read to the meeting:

> The appeal of the energetic explorer Stanley ... taken in conjunction with Colonel Gordon's occupation of the upper territories of the Nile seems to me to indicate that the time has come for the soldiers of the cross to make an advance into that region. If the Committee of the CMS are prepared at once and with energy to organise a mission to the Victoria Nyanza, I shall account it a high privilege to place £5,000 at their disposal.[103]

The offer was accepted with alacrity, but as the LMS found out in their Central African Mission, the CMS also discovered that it was easy to start a mission with high hopes and a substantial bank balance; to transform that into a viable mission far from the coast would result in an expenditure of lives rather than of pounds sterling.

Hurriedly assembled, the mission party embarked from Southampton in April 1876, arriving in Zanzibar the following month. The long trek inland began in July and six months later the mission party arrived at the southern end of Lake Victoria. In the meantime, Alexander Mackay, who became the most celebrated of the first generation of missionaries in Buganda, fell sick and was obliged to return, for the moment, to the coast.[104] This temporary illness may well have saved his life. The mission party was further reduced in May 1877 when Dr John Smith succumbed to fever.

Welcoming letters from Mutesa indicated that the time was right to make their entry into Buganda, so the small mission party split up. Leaving Thomas O'Neill with most of their supplies, the other two, the Revd Charles Wilson and Lieutenant George Shergold Smith crossed Lake Victoria into Mutesa's domains. An attack with poisoned arrows by tribes on a small island *en route* resulted in Shergold Smith being blinded in one eye. But they pressed forward and on 8 July 1877 were received by Mutesa in his court at Rubaga.

---

102 CMS Victoria Nyanza Sub-Committee Minute Book, 23 November 1875. CMS Nyanza Mission papers, CA6/N.
103 *Ibid.* 'An Unprofitable Servant' to Hutchinson, 17 November 1875. There is no evidence regarding the identity of the donor though Robert Arthington is widely suspected.
104 Shergold Smith to Kirk, 7 November 1876, enc. in Kirk to CMS, 12 December 1876. CMS Nyanza Mission papers, CA6/O13.

Significantly, after expressing interest in the missionaries' religious message, Mutesa enquired about the means to make powder and shot.[105] The following Sunday Wilson led public worship for the Kabaka and his court. With this apparently successful start to the mission, further personnel were sent from England in May 1878. Travelling up the Nile they were warmly welcomed by Colonel Charles Gordon in Khartoum (less than seven years prior to the events that were to inextricably link Gordon's name with that of Khartoum). He wrote personally to notify CMS headquarters of their safe arrival.[106] Gordon, himself an evangelical and supporter of missions, sent the mission party right to the Buganda border by government steamers, at his own expense.[107]

The Zanzibar consulate took a keen interest in the expedition, clearly seeing it as ground breaking insofar as relations with Mutesa were concerned. A few weeks after their arrival in Zanzibar, Vice-Consul Holmwood wrote to CMS headquarters offering his support and his good wishes.[108] Dr Kirk in Zanzibar subsequently kept Salisbury Square informed on news of the expedition.[109] He also intended to use the missionaries for his own purposes to provide information on the incidence of slavery in Buganda.[110]

Thus it was from Kirk that the first news came of the murder of O'Neill and Shergold Smith, by a chief named Lukongeh at Ukerewé, probably on 13 December 1877.[111] It had taken three months for the news to reach Kirk, and over two weeks even to reach Wilson, who had remained at Mutesa's court and who was now the solitary missionary in the interior.[112] By way of encouragement Henry Wright wrote to Wilson that 'We are sending out four picked men by way of the Nile.... At the same time we have directed Mackay ... to push forward to the Lake with another party'.[113] Wilson was alone for twelve months until Alexander Mackay, now fully recovered, reached him and together they restarted the Nyanza mission.

Unaware of this disaster the aged Ludwig Krapf wrote from Kornthal expressing his delight that his vision of a chain of mission stations reaching into the interior of Africa from Rabai was at last, apparently, being realised. But

---

105 Shergold Smith's Journal, entry for 8 July 1877, quoted in Stock, III, pp.101-102.
106 Gordon to Henry Wright, 11 August 1878. CMS Nyanza Mission papers, CA6/O11.
107 Stock, III, p.104.
108 Holmwood to Hutchinson, 19 August 1876. CMS Nyanza Mission papers, CA6/O4.
109 See, for example, Kirk to Hutchinson, 15 July 1877 and Kirk to CMS, 23 August 1877. CMS East African Mission papers, CA5/015.
110 Kirk to Derby, 31 January 1877. *PP* 1878, LXVII [C.2139].
111 Kirk to Hutchinson, 5 March 1878. CMS Nyanza Mission papers, CA6/013.
112 Confirmation of the murders came from the Foreign Office in April: 'I am directed by the Secretary of State for Foreign Affairs to transmit to you ... copies of two despatches with their enclosures from Dr Kirk reporting the assassination of Lieut. Shergold Smith RN and Mr O'Niel (sic) of the CMS expedition at Victoria Lake'. FO to CMS, April 1878. CMS Nyanza Mission papers, CA6/01.
113 Wright to Wilson, 26 April 1878. CMS Nyanza Mission papers, CA6/L1.

Krapf could not have known of the events of the previous month when he concluded, with imagery worthy of the Great War yet to come: 'Though many missionaries may fall in the fight, yet the survivors will pass over the slain in the trenches, and take this great African fortress for the Lord'.[114] When the news of the deaths of Shergold Smith and O'Neill eventually reached Britain one result was that the Sussex clergyman James Hannington felt a call to offer for missionary service.[115]

The motives of the Kabaka in requesting missionaries have been much discussed, but there is no reason to doubt A.J. Temu's conclusion that 'the [inland] Africans had no wish to become Christians but they allowed the missionaries to live among them both for economic reasons and for the prestige and military strength their alliance with the newcomers would bring'.[116] Mutesa also allowed Muslims and Roman Catholic White Fathers at his court and favoured each of the three groups at times according to his whim. Bishop John Taylor quoted from a conversation in Alexander Mackay's journal for 23 December 1879 when Mutesa told Mackay that he wanted the missionaries to teach his people how to make powder and guns. Taylor continued:

> The obvious conclusion is that Mutesa, who regarded all religions as means, not ends, welcomed Christianity as he had once welcomed Islam because he wanted to make use of the secret power of those who professed that faith; but he would turn against Christianity just as readily, as soon as it appeared to require of the Kabaka anything resembling submission to its standards ....[117]

Taylor has also suggested that, as well as desiring their technical skills, Mutesa saw the white missionaries as 'simply the most powerful ally against Egyptian aggression'.[118] It is certainly true that Mutesa was concerned about the Khedive's territorial ambitions. Khedive Ismail sought *lebensraum* to the south of his domains including a port on the Indian Ocean under the pretence of putting an end to the overland slave trade. Indeed the appointment of Gordon as Governor-General of the Sudan and Equatorial Provinces in February 1877 may well have increased his confidence in this respect. But it was Kirk, acting as the channel of communication to interested parties in London, who put an end to Egyptian territorial ambitions concealed under a cloak of anti-slavery sentiment. Information was communicated to London, and at a meeting attended by *inter alia*, the Archbishop of Canterbury and Sir T.F. Buxton, a memorial was drawn

---

114 Krapf to CMS, 22 January 1878, quoted in Stock, III, pp.102-103.
115 E.C. Dawson, *James Hannington, A History of His Life and Work* (London: Seeley & Co., 1887), pp.185-186.
116 Temu, p.8.
117 Taylor, p.30.
118 *Ibid.*, p.29.

up to be sent to Lord Derby in the name of the CMS.[119] This time working independently of the missions, probably for greater effect, the Anti-Slavery and Aborigines Protection Societies submitted a similar memorial. Kirk's effective dissemination of information had assisted both the missions and Kabaka Mutesa. It is therefore probable that Mutesa's favour towards British Protestant missionaries was intended to counterbalance the Muslim Egyptians whom he feared.

James Lamb's prophecy did not come to pass and George David was not destined to become the 'Bishop Crowther of the East Coast'. Perhaps not surprisingly, when a diocesan structure was created in 1884, it was an Englishman with very little East African experience – James Hannington – who became the first bishop of Eastern Equatorial Africa. Hannington's appointment was a curious one. His first visit to East Africa in 1882-83 had been decidedly inglorious. On the trek eastwards to Buganda, overcome by fever and dysentery he had been carried back to the coast, and was twice given up for dead.[120] But despite this inauspicious introduction to the region and despite the previous ruling of the CMS Medical Board that he should never return to the region,[121] Hannington, fully recovered in health, was consecrated by Archbishop Benson in June 1884. An interesting comment on his appointment was made by Charles Stokes, the CMS lay missionary who had been in charge of the caravan to Buganda in 1882 during which Hannington had succumbed to illness:

> It was a great surprise to me, Brother Hannington's appointment. May the Lord strengthen him and make him a blessing. He will certainly be a boon to Frere Town and we too will be glad to receive a visit.... I hope he will take better care of himself.... I cannot refrain from saying if our good brother had listened to advice given he might not have gone through all he did....

Perhaps thinking better of his frankness, Stokes concluded: 'I do not mean to be impertinent in my remarks. I like Bishop Hannington very much and no man would wish him better than myself. I am only a layman...'.[122] Stokes had, however, put his finger on what was to prove Hannington's fatal weakness – an inability to ask for or to take advice.

Hannington's fateful journey to Buganda was along the so-called 'Masai route', only recently discovered and previously unused by missionaries.[123] After the near-fatal discomfort of his previous attempt to reach Buganda by the

---

119 CMS Memorial to Earl of Derby, March 1877, uoted in J.M. Gray, 'Sir John Kirk and Mutesa' *Uganda Journal* (March 1951), 8.
120 Stock, III, 403-404.
121 Hannington to Mrs Hannington, 8 October 1883, quoted in Dawson, *James Hannington,* p.293.
122 Stokes to Lang, 6 October 1884. CMS Nyanza Mission papers, G3/A6/O.
123 A detailed account of Hannington's last days is given in Ch 22 and 23 of E.C. Dawson, *The Last Journals of Bishop Hannington* (London: Seeley & Co., 1890).

northern route, Hannington's rashness may be understood, especially taking into consideration that a newly available alternative route was more direct and enjoyed more favourable climatic conditions than that previously taken by missionaries. Such was Hannington's enthusiasm for this new route that he ignored the advice of Joseph Thomson, its discoverer, who was in London in the later part of 1884. Addressing the CMS at a public meeting Thompson emphatically opposed the hasty adoption of his new route. If Thomson is to be believed, Hannington was in no doubt about his opposition, even to the extent of requesting the CMS secretary not to consult him knowing that his opposition was a foregone conclusion.[124]

Having informed the missionaries in Buganda by letter that he was on his way, by the new route, Hannington left Rabai on 23 July 1885. The reply, warning him not to approach Buganda this way, arrived after he had left. Why was this 'Masai route' so dangerous that even its discoverer strongly advised against its use? Put simply it would seem that Busoga, the territory on this part of Buganda's frontier was the area through which its enemies traditionally passed, a rough equivalent perhaps of the Scottish and Welsh marches to England. Any arrivals from that direction would be treated with suspicion or even hostility. Perhaps this avoidable breach in diplomatic protocol might have been less serious, had it not been for a change of monarch in Buganda following Mutesa's death in October 1884. The new Kabaka, his son Mwanga, had a very different personality, 'fickle, sensuous, nervous and unstable',[125] and persecution of Christians soon began. Whereas Mutesa welcomed white missionaries for the advantages they brought him, Mwanga was suspicious and showed hostility to his subjects, particularly the large number of courtiers, who had converted to the white man's creed. And the timing of Hannington's journey could not have been worse. The incursions of Carl Peters and the Germans had unsettled the Kabaka's courtiers who were seemingly unable to distinguish between different nationalities of white men. Alexander Mackay recorded: 'Alarm was at its height, the Court counselled the killing of all the Missionaries, as we were only forerunners of invasion'.[126]

The reason that the impetuous Hannington was willing to risk the Masai route was a wholly laudable, pastoral one: he had heard of the trials of the missionaries and the converts at the Kabaka's court and wished to be with them as soon as possible.[127] On entering Busoga, Hannington was held by the local

---

124 H.B. Thomas 'The Last Days of Bishop Hannington', *Uganda Journal* (September 1940), 21. He claims that Dawson omitted from his book a vital sentence from Hannington's letter of 7 May 1885 to the CMS Committee (*James Hannington*, pp.376-377) in which he begged the Secretary not to refer his projected route to Joseph Thomson as his opposition was a foregone conclusion.
125 J.A. Rowe, 'The purge of Christians at Mwanga's court', *JAH*, V (1964), p.67.
126 Quoted in Dawson, *Last Journals*, p.427.
127 Early in 1885 the chiefs had begun terrorising the courtiers attached to the mission; three were mutilated and burned to death. Taylor, pp.56-57.

chief who sent to Mwanga for instructions as to the fate of his prisoner, and when the order came, duly despatched him by means of a spear on 29 October. The leader of the Roman Catholic mission, who protested at the outrage, was summarily beheaded and in the great persecution of the following spring at least thirty-two Christians were martyred.[128]

Kabaka Mwanga has had a bad press, not surprisingly in view of his persecuting tendencies in general and in particular his perceived responsibility for the murder of Hannington.[129] To a Victorian public fed on sensational newspaper headlines he was no more than a bloodthirsty sodomite. However, in a 1964 article in the *Journal of African History*, J.A. Rowe undertook a reappraisal of Mwanga and portrayed him less as a cruel and perverted tyrant than as an uncertain and inexperienced ruler thrust into a position of power before he was ready. Rowe claims that Mwanga had Hannington killed because he feared the bishop might be leading the first contingent of a European invading force. The Christian pages in his court undoubtedly passed privileged information to the missionaries and fed Mwanga's paranoia, allowing him to view native Christians, especially those at court, as a treacherous fifth column. Rowe suggests that he was pragmatic rather than anti-Christian, since, when he later sought to destroy the influence of powerful chiefs, Mwanga quickly allied himself with both Christians and Muslims, who enjoyed his favours for a period until the revolution of 1888.[130]

Imperialism in East Africa

Any move from the mere presence of British citizens in East Africa to any kind of formal British control over territory was to be a slow process, initially resisted by the British government and beyond the chronological confines of this study. In the 1870s the Foreign Office was determined to avoid any official entanglements that might lead to formal control. Consequently H.M. Stanley was firmly told to desist from using the Union Jack in his explorations in the region.[131] The LMS Directors were similarly chastised when in 1878 their ill-fated Central African Mission at Ujiji hoisted the British flag. An abject apology was soon forthcoming:

---

128 *Ibid.* p.57. For a detailed reappraisal of the persecution see Rowe, 55-72.
129 Hannington's death received official ecclesiastical sanction as a martyrdom in 1980 when the date of his death – 29 October – was listed in the 'Lesser Festivals and Commemorations' in the Church of England's *Alternative Service Book* (London, Oxford and Cambridge: various publishers, 1980), p.20.
130 A useful short summary of Rowe's argument is printed on p.72, at the end of his article.
131 Kirk to Stanley, 11 December 1876, enc. in Kirk to Derby, 11 December 1876. *PP* 1878, LXVII [C.2139].

> The subject of our missions in Ujiji hoisting the British flag has been considered by the Directors of the Society and they instruct me to request you to assure the Marquis of Salisbury that this action on the part of the missionaries was not in accordance with any instructions on the part of the Directors to that effect, and also to state that they are advising them to avoid for the future giving offence in this matter.[132]

As late as November 1884, when the Berlin Conference was convening and Carl Peters was busy making treaties with chiefs on the East African mainland who were vassals of the Sultan of Zanzibar,[133] the Liberal government seemed to have no real policy on the level of British involvement in East Africa. In a response to a memorandum by Clement Hill of the Foreign Office suggesting that British interests would be best served by propping up the Sultan and, if necessary, paying him a subsidy, minutes indicate that ministers were still only too happy to take the line of least resistance and try to avoid direct involvement.[134] But it was the end of an era and Kirk finally left Zanzibar in July 1886, having tried to the last to protect the Sultan's mainland dominions from annexation by Germany, an effort in which he was largely unsuccessful.[135]

The scramble for East Africa is beyond the remit of this study, yet the shape it took was undoubtedly influenced by the missionary activity which preceded it. While Robinson and Gallagher assert that explorers and missionaries have no importance in the explanation of imperial moves in East Africa,[136] the weight of evidence in this chapter suggests otherwise as far as missionaries were concerned. It was the early CMS missionaries, Ludwig Krapf and his companions who first explored East Africa and Johannes Rebmann who maintained a missionary presence, albeit a tenuous one for many years. It was the CMS which did the spade work in the establishment of the Parliamentary Select Committee out of which came the Frere mission and the treaties with the Sultan. Livingstone single-handedly caught the public imagination in publicising the iniquities of the trade and its effects on Africa. The Livingstone myth lived on after him and his death resulted in the formation of more missions to the area than during his lifetime. It is true that commercial interests, like Mackinnon's Imperial British East Africa Company, were important, particularly towards the end of the century. But even if Mackinnon expected initial dividends to be paid in philanthropy rather than pounds,[137] British

---

132 J.O. Whitehouse to Sir J. Pauncefote, 31 January 1880. *PP* 1881, LXXXV [C.3052].
133 For more details of German involvement see H.P. Merritt, 'Bismarck and the German interest in East Africa 1884-1885', *Historical Journal*, 21 (1978), 97-116.
134 Memorandum by Clement Hill, 29 November 1884 and mins. Granville Papers. PRO 30/29/144.
135 J.M. Gray, 'Sir John Kirk and Mutesa', *Uganda Journal* (March 1951), 14.
136 Robinson and Gallagher, p.25.
137 Galbraith, *Mackinnon and East Africa*, p.14.

investors only followed where they expected a return on their capital in the forseeable future. In other words they did not risk their capital until the slave trade had been eradicated and missionaries had begun the work of civilisation (in some cases actually fostering a market economy to replace the slave trade). Finally, it should be noted that even that most unfortunate of missions, the LMS Central African Mission, had in the view of A.J. Hanna its imperial usefulness, its very presence preventing further German expansion into Nyasaland.[138]

Clearly, the missionary impact on the spread of the British *imperium* in East Africa is a highly contentious matter. As the other case studies in this book have shown, even when it is possible to fathom the *intentions* of the missionaries, the *results* of their actions are still a subject for debate. That missionaries played an influential role in the drama of imperial expansion cannot, however, be disputed.

---

138 A.J. Hanna, 'The role of the London Missionary Society in the opening up of East Central Africa', *TRHS*, 5 (1955), 59.

CONCLUSION

Incidental Imperialists – Missionary Influence on the Growth of Empire

On one of his very rare furloughs in Britain towards the end of his life James Chalmers made a platform speech at the Founders' Week Convention that was the high point of the LMS centenary celebrations in 1895. In the course of a long address he astutely commented that, 'every missionary, even Lawes and Chalmers, if they bring the Gospel to a people, revolutionise that people; you cannot help it'.[1] But Chalmers was not speaking of the spiritual revolution effected in the lives of individuals by the transforming power of the gospel. Rather he was commenting on the revolutionary change brought about in individuals, villages, whole tribes and communities by the presence of western missionaries with their radically different approach to life, an approach which was eagerly imitated by those among whom they settled and whose appetite for things European was quickly kindled. Their lives were also revolutionised by the other Europeans who inevitably followed. For the missionaries did the pioneering work and rendered it relatively safe for white people to live and trade among those who may previously have been savages or even cannibals. And this second wave of Europeans who followed them were generally motivated neither by altruism nor paternalism toward the native population but by their own commercial interests. Indeed they often regarded the natives as stupid or hostile, denigrated them as 'niggers' or 'kaffirs' and meted out violence and death when their often unreasonable demands were not meekly complied with. Missionaries who had no pre-existent imperial agenda sometimes came round to favour imperial solutions by default – the lesser evil after more favoured options had proved untenable – in response to the arrival of white settlers whom they could not effectively control or influence, and whose presence had an adverse effect on the native peoples and the work of the mission. And even if British colonial rule followed, bringing a rule of law to regulate excesses by unruly Europeans, life was never quite the same again.

---

1 Centenary of the LMS: Proceedings of the Founders' Week Convention, Sept 21-27 1895, p.56, quoted in J.M. Hitchen, 'Formation of the Nineteenth Century Missionary Worldview: the case of James Chalmers', unpublished Ph.D thesis (Aberdeen, 1984), p.738.

Those who had put away their old gods and accepted the Christian gospel found that its implications entailed much more than simple religious faith, bringing in its wake much more that was neither simple nor religious.

It would be hard not to agree with Andrew Porter's observation that 'most missionaries were not conscious imperialists'[2]. Although specifically referring to the slightly later period 1880-1914 it is equally applicable to the period of this study with which it overlaps. But the qualifying adjective, 'conscious', is of primary importance. For the actual effect of missionary presence was inevitably imperialist, in that European religion, values, ethics, culture, education and even commerce, were being actively promoted among peoples who were largely unable to resist them.

In their study of *British Imperialism: Innovation and Expansion, 1688-1914* Cain and Hopkins refer, almost in passing, to what they call 'a distinction between an imperialism of intent and an imperialism of result'.[3] Such a helpful distinction may usefully be employed when assessing the impact of the missions and missionaries examined in the foregoing case studies, since the effect that missionaries and their parent societies had on imperial development in this period, while sometimes intentional, was more often incidental. In fact, in most cases where the missions' actions may be said to have aided imperial development, it was very much 'an imperialism of result'. It is therefore appropriate to keep this barely-defined concept in mind for the period 1860 to 1885 as a brief survey of the findings of each of the case studies is considered.

In the south-west Pacific, the missionaries, aided by their contacts in Australia and Britain, effectively opposed the Queensland labour trade. While the New Hebrides and Melanesian missionaries differed in their degree of opposition to indentured labour in general, and abuses in the labour trade in particular, their opposition was sufficient to influence legislation in the imperial Parliament. But though they campaigned against the trade and gave it a high profile, it was the furore attendant on the death of Bishop Patteson which caused the legislation to be enacted at that particular time. Although John Paton later opposed the establishment of French penal colonies in the New Hebrides and lobbied unsuccessfully for annexation by Britain,[4] in the period under discussion the New Hebrides missionaries, and even more so the Melanesian missionaries, simply wanted to be left alone to engage in missionary work with the people to whom they ministered. Their contribution to the development of imperial responsibilities lay in successfully pressing Britain to legislate for the protection of Pacific islanders.

---

2 Andrew Porter, *The Imperial Horizons of British Protestant Missions, 1880-1914* (Grand Rapids and Cambridge: Eerdmans, 2003), p.4.
3 P.J. Cain and A.G. Hopkins, *British Imperialism: Innovation and Expansion, 1688–1914* (London: Longman, 1993), p.43.
4 See Morrell, *Pacific Islands*, pp. 194-204.

In Fiji, on the other hand, from the establishment of Bauan hegemony in 1855, the Wesleyan missionaries used their position of influence with Cakobau, Vunivalu of Bau, to advantage. James Calvert, a true missionary imperialist, repeatedly sought to engineer cessions of Fiji to the British Crown. These were unsuccessful and after the third, in 1861, the Smythe report in effect left the missionaries to rule Fiji. This situation continued for over ten years, but the influx of unruly Europeans whom the missionaries could not control brought dangerous instability and led them, together with John Thurston, to press once again for annexation. This was finally effected in October 1874 following Goodenough and Layard's report and Sir Hercules Robinson's success in obtaining an unconditional offer of cession from Cakobau. A particularly important factor in the government's acceptance of annexation as the best solution was the influence exerted in the House of Commons by William M'Arthur, a leading lay member of the WMMS. However, after a honeymoon period, the missionaries soon became disenchanted with the new colonial government under Sir Arthur Gordon as they resented their inevitable loss of influence. Though annexation by Britain was, to a greater or lesser extent, the favoured option of virtually all the missionaries in Fiji, it was not so much their lobbying as the use of parliamentary pressure by their supporters in Britain that finally brought it about.

The LMS, which was the pioneering mission in Papua New Guinea, had little interest in imperial solutions to the problems it encountered. Paradoxically then, it was the LMS missionaries who played a major part in Britain's involvement in New Guinea. The first person to advocate British involvement, in January 1873, was W. Wyatt Gill of the LMS, though he was at pains to point out that the views he expressed were personal and not those of the Society. Gill's concern was for strategic reasons, fearing that, 'should New Guinea fall into hostile hands, the key of the Torres Straits would be lost ...'.[5] These were precisely the same fears frequently expressed by Robert Herbert in the Colonial Office. Gill's views were not at that time shared by the other missionaries in New Guinea, who feared the aboriginal peoples could be affected adversely if *any* European power took over the territory. But as time passed, prospectors, adventurers and labour traders made their presence felt in New Guinea, and the ambivalence which the Comaroffs have noted in Nonconformist missionary attitudes to colonial governments came to the fore.[6] The missionaries came to realise that some European intervention was inevitable, and it was probably best for the indigenous peoples that this should be British. Their interests were then most likely to be considered in a favourable light. W.G. Lawes' preference was for British 'authority' rather than sovereignty, probably meaning an extension of the powers of the Western Pacific High Commission to protect the native

---

5 Gill to G.A. Lloyd, 28 July 1873. enc. in Lloyd to Robinson, 31 July 1874. Confidential Print Australian No. 47. CO 881/4.
6 Comaroff and Comaroff, I, p.78.

peoples from the depredations of avaricious outsiders. Chalmers favoured the concept of a protectorate, which was eventually established in 1885, seeing it as a kind of trusteeship of the interests of the Papuan people rather than an extension of empire. Though missionary involvement was but one of four factors influencing Britain's proclamation of a protectorate over New Guinea in 1885, the importance of the missionary factor can be seen in the reliance placed upon the missionaries (particularly Chalmers) by both the Special Commissioner for the Protectorate and the first Governor of the Crown colony.

Turning to Africa, the opposition to the Gambia exchange project was ultimately successful, and the scheme was finally abandoned in 1876. But the resident Methodist missionaries have been shown to be largely ineffective contributors to this opposition. Though resolutions were passed and letters written, these lacked real commitment and conviction. Passionate, committed opposition came from those with commercial interests in the territory, who stood to lose financially if the exchange went ahead. It is true that there were missionary supporters and officials on the informal 'Gambia Committee' in London, but it has been ascertained that William M'Arthur's opposition to the exchange was more likely to have been influenced by his membership of the Aborigines Protection Society than his membership of the WMMS. The Gambia agitation is an important example of those occasions when missionaries failed to influence imperial development. In this case they made only a half-hearted effort, failed to take the initiative and allowed other interested parties, more dynamic than themselves, to make the running in a campaign which was ultimately to have a significant effect on the future of the mission and its people.

Things were different in Yorubaland where the CMS had been established since 1846. Keen to destroy the last vestiges of the slave trade and to replace it with legitimate commerce, they encouraged British intervention in the nearby slave port of Lagos in 1851, leading to the establishment of a Crown colony in 1861. But as in the case of Fiji after 1874, the missionaries soon lost confidence in the government for two reasons. First, economically and politically, Lagos came to rival and surpass Abeokuta, thus eclipsing the 'sunrise in the tropics'. Second, for reasons inexplicable to the missionaries, Governor Glover took a dislike to the Egba, the Yoruba tribe with whom the missionaries had been so successful and through whom they hoped to evangelise Yorubaland. In the short term, missionary agitation backfired in that the Egba were actually worse off than before British intervention. Supporting the missionaries and the Egba during the trials of the Yoruba wars, invasion by Dahomey and blockade by the Lagos authorities, was Henry Venn who skilfully used his many contacts to good effect. Venn's 'native pastorate' scheme, which began in the Niger in 1875 (as early as 1861 in Sierra Leone) and only developed at a snail's pace, nevertheless proved, together with missionary education, to be the foundation of later Nigerian nationalism in providing an educated elite to govern the church and, eventually, the state.

In East and Central Africa there was a considerable missionary presence, largely because of the involvement in the region of David Livingstone and the moral legacy he left. The publicising by Livingstone of the deleterious effects of the Arab slave trade on African society was of paramount importance in influencing the involvement of missions in this large area. But since 1844, long before Livingstone with his high-profile approach, the CMS through Ludwig Krapf had been operating a mission station near Mombasa. It was the CMS who did the spade-work behind the lobbying for a Select Committee on the East African slave trade which met in 1871. From this flowed the Frere mission to Zanzibar in 1873 and the Sultan's signature on a treaty abolishing the sea-borne trade in June of that year. CMS interest in the area continued with the establishment of Frere Town as a settlement for freed slaves in 1875. The UMCA, having relocated from the Shiré highlands to Zanzibar was also much involved in work with freed slaves. Livingstone's death revived interest in the area with new missions being founded by the LMS, the Church of Scotland and Free Church of Scotland. The CMS began a second mission, the Nyanza mission, to push further inland than the existing East African mission. Though commercial interests were also highly important in this area it should be noted that entrepreneurs did not risk their capital until the slave trade had been virtually eradicated and the process of civilisation had been begun by the missionaries. Missionary involvement was primary and without it, it is highly unlikely that, following the scramble for Africa, most of East Africa would have been coloured red on the map. The motive for missionary involvement was the extirpation of the Arab slave trade. The result was a large number of mission communities providing extensive British involvement and a vested interest for Britain in acquiring large swathes of territory in this area when Africa was being partitioned in the late 1880s and 1890s.

We have already observed and examined in detail two factors which are crucial to this study of the ways in which missionaries influenced government thinking and action on the development of empire. First, the importance of mission supporters and sympathisers in Parliament, who were prepared to use their influence by speaking in debates and committees, putting down questions to ministers and proposing motions and amendments. Where missionaries were most effective in influencing the decisions of those in government it was usually by means of such influential supporters. Government departments like the Colonial Office were surprisingly open to the consideration of views put to them by informed or interested parties. They were willing to weigh any reasonable arguments and the fact that missionaries were sometimes better informed than the Colonial Office meant that their comments were treated with all due seriousness. Thus missionaries had a real opportunity to influence official thinking and policy. Equally, where it was clear to the Colonial Office that they were merely being used by someone with a personal axe to grind (John Paton, for instance) the authorities could be firm in rejecting proffered opinions.

A second crucial factor was the networking between missions, churches and other evangelical and humanitarian groups, who frequently supported each other and who made use of a common network of wide and influential contacts which included MPs and Peers, merchants and members of imperial societies like the Royal Colonial Institute. The frequent overlap in supporters of these groups and willingness to make common cause to achieve a mutually agreed objective also resulted in the formation of single-issue committees in the cases of Fiji and the Gambia (and also a South Africa committee with a similar membership which followed in 1883). But a number of other significant points also emerge from this study, and these need to be considered as necessary parts of the equation.

To be a missionary far from 'civilization' was to aspire to omnicompetence; multi-tasking and possession of a wide range of specialist skills were not so much optional as a necessity of life. As well as their primary preaching and teaching ministry missionaries frequently demonstrated degrees of expertise in other areas, for example as doctors, botanists and explorers. In this latter capacity, for example, Livingstone, Chalmers, Krapf and Rebmann all added to western knowledge of the parts of the globe they explored and named. Governments and commercial interests clearly benefited since they were able to reap the benefits where the missionaries had previously sown.

The established missionary channels of communication with regular, detailed reports from mission field to mission headquarters were a highly important source of information providing details and evidence of events in far corners of the globe. Missionaries were usually the Europeans closest to the imperial frontier with established channels of communication to Britain. Of course, military and naval personnel also possessed such channels of communication but they were far fewer in number than missionaries, were frequently situated in less propitious locations, were temporary rather than long-term residents and the nature of their work made getting alongside indigenous peoples far more difficult than was the case for missionaries.

It was not surprising then, that missionaries frequently adopted the role of 'advocates for the natives' where indigenous peoples appeared to be suffering adversely from imperial incursions into their lives, whether or not a colonial government was eventually established.[7] Susan Thorne's comment that 'the influx of competing European interests into the mission field forced missionaries to befriend the natives if they were to have a constituency left to proselytize',[8] is no doubt true but in no way negates the fact that many missions were already giving high priority to upholding the rights of indigenous peoples.

---

7 Though Horst Gründer asserts that this only went as far as criticising individual evils but never as far as criticising the colonial system as such. 'Christian Missions and colonial expansion', *Mission Studies*, XII (1995), p.20.

8 Susan Thorne, *Congregational Missions and the making of an Imperial Culture in Nineteenth-Century England* (Stanford: Stanford University Press, 1999), p.156.

Paradoxically, the civilizing presence of missions made it safer for other Europeans to visit, trade and settle in such areas, bringing with them an inexorable threat to indigenous traditions, culture and lifestyle. For even when no formal colonial structure emerged missions were responsible for helping to create conditions that aided the growth of 'informal empire' as much as formal control.[9]

One irony was that for all their good intentions missions and missionaries had no way of foreseeing or controlling the results of their work or influence, which were sometimes far from what might have been intended. Thus they were, in D.C. Gordon's phrase, 'frontiersmen of forces they could not control',[10] and a reverse image of Pandora's box is not an unhelpful one in such cases. Missions opened up many primitive communities to the outside world and, having done so, were unable to prevent the outside world from invading and violating such societies. Another paradox was the authority and influence over secular matters which missionaries often acquired was also lost the moment a colonial government was established

The Christian faith, as presented by European missionaries, came in a package. In addition to the doctrines of Protestant Christianity (presented in various shades dependant on denominational affiliation) they were the purveyors of 'civilised' values, one of their greatest consistent contributions to the growth of European influence in tropical Africa and the Pacific. Amongst them were the promotion of agricultural cultivation and 'legitimate' trade to replace the slave trade, bringing freedom from cruel and superstitious practices and, perhaps most importantly, education.[11] Protestant Christianity was founded on the right of individuals to read the Bible in their own language. Translating the Scriptures and teaching converts to read were thus a top priority for the missionaries. Interestingly, Andrew Porter argues that education was actually *anti*-imperial since, as is well-known, literacy brought political radicalism in its wake and the first generation of nationalist leaders were largely educated at mission schools.[12] And of course Porter is correct in the long perspective of his study from 1700 to 1914. This study, however, is focused on a much shorter time-frame and within it education can be seen to be bringing African and Pacific peoples increasingly into an orbit of religious, ethical and moral values that were nothing if not European.

---

9 J.A. Gallagher, and R.E. Robinson, 'The Imperialism of Free Trade', *Econ HR*, 2nd ser., VI (1953), 1-15.
10 Gordon, p.13.
11 Henry Venn's father, John, had recognised this point back in 1804: 'Man cannot by education be made a real Christian; but by education he may be freed from prejudices and delivered from the dominion of dispositions highly favourable to temptation and sin'. Quoted in Bebbington, *Evangelicalism in Modern Britain*, p.123. See also Ayandele, *Missionary Impact*, p.15.
12 Porter, *Religion versus Empire?*, p.317.

Finally, it may be observed that death, whether through martyrdom, accident or natural causes did not necessarily end a missionary's influence. Some, like Patteson and Hannington and probably even Livingstone, appeared more influential in death than life.

Contemporary theology distinguishes between 'presence' and 'proclamation' in mission, a distinction between two complementary roles, teaching by example of life and by word of mouth. Such was also the imperial influence of Victorian missionaries. Just 'being there' as informal European representatives, 'unconscious agents' as E.A. Ayandele put it, was perhaps their major contribution, imperialist by their presence if not their proclamation. It is clear from their requests for missionaries for the Shiré highlands and Buganda respectively, that both Livingstone and Stanley had no doubts about the imperialistic value of a missionary presence. And Ayandele interestingly brackets missionary converts with the missionaries themselves as 'unconscious agents of British imperialism'.[13]

Alan Cairns considered that 'the missionary tended to see Christianity and imperialism as complementary, with the latter acting as a vehicle for the spread of the former'.[14] Cain and Hopkins go a step further maintaining that, 'missionaries came to see it [the empire] as a crusading vehicle for collective salvation'.[15] There is, however, little evidence from the preceding case studies that many missionaries in this period had a vision of empire, formal or informal, aiding missions on a wide scale. If they had imperialistic thoughts at all they were very much localised: could *my* work, *my* mission, the conditions of the native peoples under *my* care be improved if British traders or naval personnel were regular visitors or if the civil government of this territory was under British control? Essentially, British Protestant missionaries made the furtherance of the gospel their first priority and protecting the interests of the aboriginal people to whom they ministered their second. Recent studies have rightly emphasised the spiritual and theological underpinning of missionary work.[16] And yet it cannot be denied that their presence and sometimes their actions aided that spread of western influence, authority and power that we refer to as 'imperialism'. Nevertheless, where their actions aided the development of the empire it was as a secondary consequence, what may appropriately be described as incidental imperialism.

---

13 Ayandele, *Missionary Impact*, p.15.
14 Cairns, p.243.
15 Cain and Hopkins, p.35. Interestingly, Andrew Porter detects a 'gulf between missionaries and governments' in the early days of the evangelical revival which again emerged in the years before the First World War. Indeed, he states that 'that gulf never disappeared in the intervening years' and declares that 'many of the bridges thrown across it were either fragile or temporary, sometimes both'. A.N. Porter, 'Religion and Empire', 385.
16 Porter, *Religion versus Empire?*, p.13.

On 21 February 1865, the day of Adderley's motion in the House of Commons for a West Africa Select Committee, the Colonial Secretary, Edward Cardwell, paid tribute to missionaries:

> I hold in highest esteem the labours of these men who, denying themselves the comforts and happiness of home, leave their own country and devote themselves to spread the Gospel, in which they sincerely believe, among the most benighted and miserable inhabitants of any portion of the globe.[17]

The missionaries were almost invariably the first resident Europeans in many parts of tropical Africa and many Pacific islands.[18] So where empire, formal or informal, followed, it was in their wake. To return to Cain and Hopkins' categories, it was almost always an 'imperialism of result' rather than an 'imperialism of intent'. Missionaries should be seen first and foremost as messengers of the Christian gospel and its attendant values. Where their presence aided imperial advancement it was always incidental to that primary purpose. Yet, says Bosch, 'Whether they liked it or not the missionaries became pioneers of western imperialistic expansion'.[19] Today, missionaries receive training in the principles of cross-cultural mission but no such training was available or even considered for those missionaries who have appeared in the pages of this book. Some – the more enlightened ones – did seek to respect indigenous cultures where they did not conflict with their understanding of Christianity.[20]

A medical metaphor may be appropriate. Many diseases are passed on by human contacts. But the 'carrier', the person who actually passes on the infection – anything from the common cold to HIV/AIDS – almost certainly has no active intention of doing so and is probably unaware of having infected another person. The analogy is not perfect since some missionaries had difficulty in distinguishing the Christian gospel from Western civilization. Nevertheless, even those who were most concerned to promote indigenous

---

17 *Hansard*, Third Series, CLXXVII, col.553.
18 Though sometimes preceded by traders of various description, missionaries were normally the first Europeans to reside in or near indigenous communities. The Zulu king, Cetshwayo, is said to have observed, 'First a missionary, then a consul, and then come army'. Quoted in Gründer, 20.
19 Bosch, p.304.
20 In the period 1850-75 the instructions issued by the LMS to their missionaries contained the following advice:
> 'Do not Anglicise your converts. Remember that the people are foreigners. Let them continue as such. Let their foreign individuality be maintained. Build upon it, so far as it is sound and good; and Christianise, but do not needlessly change it. Do not seek to make the people Englishmen. Seek to develop and mould a pure, refined and Christian character, native to the soil'.

churches still acted as 'carriers' of those western values and practices that quickly 'infected' tribal societies in both Africa and the Pacific.

To change the metaphor: viewers of the long-running television and film science fiction series, *Star Trek*, will be aware of the 'prime directive'. This fundamental rule of fictional space exploration requires the crew of the Star Ship *Enterprise* to avoid anything that might adversely affect or contaminate the culture of the alien societies with which they come into contact during their mission of exploration beyond edges of the known universe and into uncharted space. And yet, as frequent plot lines make clear, Captain Kirk and his crew found it almost impossible to do this since their mere presence on any inhabited planet with a relatively less advanced culture would, inevitably, have considerable effects on it. The only way to ensure that other cultures remain uncontaminated is to remain at a safe distance, which would negate the purpose of their mission.[21]

Nineteenth-century missionaries were in an almost identical situation. David Bosch's observation, 'there is no such thing as a "pure" gospel, isolated from culture', demonstrates the point precisely.[22] Missionaries were inevitably going to bring their own cultural baggage with them and whether they liked it or not this would influence those to whom they proclaimed the Christian gospel. And if, as we have established, some missionaries had difficulty in differentiating the gospel from Western civilization it is not surprising that unsophisticated indigenous peoples would have difficulty in distinguishing the gospel message from the European packaging in which it was presented. But in most cases this was an incidental imperialism – an 'imperialism of result' rather than an 'imperialism of intent'. Missionaries were primarily messengers of the Christian gospel and its attendant values. Where their presence aided imperial advancement it was always incidental to that primary purpose.

---

21 I am grateful to Anne Noble for this insight.
22 Bosch, p.297

Bibliography

Primary Sources

Manuscripts

GOVERNMENT RECORDS
The National Archives of the UK, Public Record Office, Kew.

Colonial Office
- Fiji Islands — CO 83/1-6
- The Gambia — CO 87/86-98B
- Gold Coast — CO 96/104-5
- New South Wales — CO 201/514, 526, 529, 542, 551, 560, 562-4, 579, 582, 599
- Victoria — CO 309/111
- Natal — CO 179/112-3
- Queensland — CO 234/21-35
- Lagos — CO 147/1, 3-4, 7, 11, 14, 21, 23
- Western Pacific — CO 225/1

Foreign Office
- France — FO 27/2226-7
- Pacific Islands — FO 58/106, 118, 127, 134,139
- Slave Trade — FO 84/1600

PRIVATE PAPERS

Carnarvon Papers,
   The National Archives of the UK, Public Record Office, Kew. PRO 30/6

Church Missionary Society Archives,
   Birmingham University Library.
- Yoruba Mission papers (before 1880) CA2
   (after 1880) G3 A2

- East Africa (Kenya) Mission papers (before 1880) CA5
   (after 1880) G3 A5
   Letter Books /L
   Original papers /0

- Nyanza Mission papers (before 1880) CA6

(after 1880) G3 A6
Letter Books /L
Victoria Nyanza Sub-Committee /N
Original papers /O

Granville Papers,
The National Archives of the UK, Public Record Office, Kew. PRO 30/29.

Council for World Mission (London Missionary Society) Archives,
School of Oriental and African Studies, London.
- Australian Correspondence. Box 7.
- South Sea Correspondence. Boxes 23, 30, 32-3, 35
- South Sea Journals. Box 9.
- Papua Correspondence. Boxes 1-4.
- Papua Personal. Box 1.
- Home Office Papers. Box 12.

Melanesian Mission Archives,
School of Oriental and African Studies, London.
- Minute Books. 1/1.
- Codrington Letters. 2/1-4.
- Bishop Patteson Letters. 2/8.
- Miscellaneous Correspondence. 2/24.

Wesleyan Methodist Missionary Society Archives,
School of Oriental and African Studies, London.
- Australian Correspondence: Fiji Correspondence Files. Box 532-7.
- Biographical, South Seas: Calvert Papers. Box 645-8.
- Gambia Correspondence Files. Box 295.
- Synod Minutes Files for Gambia. Box 297.

Printed Sources

GOVERNMENT CONFIDENTIAL PRINTS
Australian: C.O.881/4.
No.39 The Fiji Islands. July 1874.
No.40 Correspondence respecting the annexation of the Fiji Islands. July 1874.
No.41 Report of Commodore Goodenough and Mr Consul Layard on the Fiji Islands. April 1874.
No.45 Correspondence with Sir H. Robinson KCMG respecting the annexation of the Fiji islands. Dec.1874.
No.47 Correspondence respecting New Guinea. July 1875.

Bibliography

No.49 Correspondence respecting the Colony of Fiji. January 1876.
No.49A Further correspondence respecting the colony of Fiji.
No.50 Further correspondence respecting New Guinea.
No.51 Memorandum on the question of the annexation of New Guinea. October 1875.
No.52 Correspondence respecting New Guinea. November 1875.
No.53 Correspondence respecting New Guinea. July 1876.

Australian: C.O.881/6.
No.84 Labour Trade in the Western Pacific.
No.95 Further correspondence respecting New Guinea, the New Hebrides and other islands.
No.103 Annexation of Protectorate of New Guinea and other islands in the Western Pacific. June 1884.

African: C.O.879/3.
No.23 Correspondence relative to the abandonment of McCarthy's Island, River Gambia. 1866.
No.24 Correspondence respecting French acquisition of territories on the West coast of Africa. Dec. 1869.

PARLIAMENTARY PAPERS

1852	LIV	1455	Papers relative to the reduction of Lagos by H.M. Forces on the West Coast of Africa.
1862	XXXVI	2995	Correspondence relative to the Fiji Islands.
	LXI	2982	Papers relating to the occupation of Lagos.
1863	XXXVIII	512	Letter from the Rev H. Venn respecting the conduct of missionaries at Abeokuta.
		3212	Ditto.
1864	LXVI	3307	Correspondence respecting the removal of the inhabitants of Polynesian Islands to Peru.
1865	V	412	Report from the Select Committee on Africa (Western Coast).
	XXXVII	170	Report of Colonel Ord, Commissioner appointed to inquire into the Condition of the British settlements on the West Coast of Africa.
1867-8	XLVIII	391	Correspondence relating to the importation of South Sea Islanders into Queensland.
1868-9	XLIII	408	Correspondence relating to the importation of South Sea islanders into Queensland.
		438	Correspondence respecting the deportation of South Sea islanders.
1870	L	444	Correspondence respecting the proposed cession of the Gambia to France.

1871	XII	420	Report from the Select Committee on Slave Trade (East Coast of Africa).
	XLVII	435	Correspondence and documents relating to the Fiji Islands.
	XLVIII	468	Further Correspondence relating to the Importation of South Sea Islanders into Queensland.
		245	Further Correspondence respecting the Deportation of South Sea Islanders.
1872	III		Pacific Islanders Protection Bill.
	XXIX	C.542	Report of proceedings of H.M. Ship *Rosario*, during cruise among the South Sea Islands, Nov.1871 – Feb.1872.
	XLIII	C.509	Further Correspondence relating to the Fiji Islands.
		C.496	Further Correspondence respecting the Deportation of South Sea Islanders.
1873	L	C.793	Correspondence relative to the introduction of Polynesian labourers into Queensland.
	LXI	C.867	East Coast of Africa: Correspondence respecting the Slave Trade and other matters, 1872.
		C.820	Correspondence respecting Sir Bartle Frere's Mission to the East Coast of Africa, 1872-3.
1874	XLV	C.983	Fiji Islands: Copy of a Letter Addressed to Commodore Goodenough RN, and E.L. Layard Esq.
		C.1011	Report of Commodore Goodenough and Mr Consul Layard on the offer of the cession of the Fiji Islands to the British Crown.
1875	LII	C.1114	Correspondence respecting the cession of Fiji.
		C.1337	Correspondence respecting the Colony of Fiji.
1876	LII	C.1409	Correspondence respecting the affairs of the Gambia and the proposed exchange with France of possessions on the West coast of Africa.
		C.1498	Copy of petition from the inhabitants of the Gambia praying that that settlement be not ceded to France.
		C.1566	Correspondence respecting New Guinea.
1877	LX	C.1827	Correspondence respecting the limits of British jurisdiction in the River Gambia.
1878	LXVII	C.2139	Correspondence with British representatives and agents abroad and reports from naval officers relating to the slave trade.
1881	LXXXV	C.3052	Correspondence with British representatives and agents abroad and reports from naval officers and the Treasury relative to the slave trade.

1882	LXV	C.3160 Correspondence with British representatives and agents abroad and reports from naval officers relative to the slave trade.
1883	XLVII	C.3617 Further Correspondence respecting New Guinea.
		C.3691 Further Correspondence respecting New Guinea.
	LXVI	C.3547 Correspondence with British representatives and agents abroad and reports from naval officers and the Treasury relative to the slave trade 1882-3.
1884	LV	C.3863 Correspondence respecting New Guinea and other Islands.
		C.3839 Further Correspondence respecting New Guinea and other Islands.
		C.3905 Report of Royal Commission appointed to inquire into the working of the Western Pacific Orders in Council
1884-5	LIV	C.4217 Further Correspondence respecting New Guinea and other islands.
		C.4273 Further correspondence respecting New Guinea and other islands in the Western Pacific Ocean.
		C.4441 Arrangement between Great Britain and Germany relative to their respective spheres of action in portions of New Guinea.
		C.4584 Further correspondence respecting New Guinea and other islands in the Western Pacific Ocean.
1886	LXXIII	C.4656 Declaration between the Governments of Great Britain and the German Empire relating to the demarcation of the British and German spheres of influence in the Western Pacific.
1887	LX	C.4957 Correspondence respecting war between native tribes in the interior and peace negotiations conducted by the Lagos government.
		C.5144 Further correspondence on the same.

OFFICIAL PUBLICATIONS AND OTHER COLLECTIONS OF DOCUMENTS

Hansard's Parliamentary Debates, Third Series. Vols. CLXXV – CCLXXX.

Henderson, G.C., *The Journal of Thomas Williams, Missionary in Fiji, 1840-53* (Sydney: Angus and Robertson, 1931).

Kay, John (ed.), *The Slave Trade in the New Hebrides* (Edinburgh: Edmonston and Douglas, 1872).

Newbury, C.W., *British Policy towards West Africa: Selected Documents*, 2 vols, (Oxford: Clarendon Press, 1965 & 1971).

Ramm, Agatha (ed.), 'The Political Correspondence of Mr Gladstone and

Lord Granville 1868-1876', *Camden Society*, 3rd Series, lxxxii (1952).
Schutz, A.J. (ed.), *The Diaries and Correspondence of David Cargill, 1832-1843* (Canberra: Australian National University Press, 1977).
Warren, Max, *To Apply the Gospel: Selections from the writings of Henry Venn* (Grand Rapids: Eerdmans, 1971).

Contemporary Writings

REPORTS, PERIODICALS, NEWSPAPERS AND JOURNALS
Church Missionary Intelligencer.
London Missionary Society *Annual Reports.*
Wesleyan Methodist Missionary Society *Annual Reports.*
Wesleyan Methodist Missionary Society, *Missionary Notices.*
Proceedings of the Royal Colonial Institute.
Melanesian Mission *Annual Reports.*
The Times.

CONTEMPORARY ARTICLES, BOOKS, MEMOIRS AND PAMPHLETS
Blackmore, E.G., 'South Sea Slavery: Kidnapping and Murder', *Macmillans Magazine*, 27 (March 1873), 370-375.
Boreham, F.W., *George Augustus Selwyn DD* (London: S.W. Partridge, 1911).
Brenchley, Julius L., *Jottings during the Cruise of H.M.S. Curaçoa* (London: Longmans, Green & Co., 1873).
Carey, William, *An Enquiry into the Obligations of Christians to Use Means for the Conversion of the Heathens* [1792] (new edn., ed. E.A. Payne, London: Carey Kingsgate Press, 1961).
Carnarvon, Earl of, 'Imperial Administration', *Fortnightly Review*, XXIV (1878), 751-63.
Chalmers, James, 'New Guinea – Past, Present and Future', *PRCI*, XVIII (1886-7) 88-122.
Chalmers, James, & Gill, W. Wyatt, *Work and Adventure in New Guinea* (London: Religious Tract Society, 1885).
Chesson, F.W., 'The Polynesian Labour Question in Relation to the Islands and Queensland', *PRCI*, III (1871-2), 34-56.
— 'The Past and Present of Fiji', *PRCI*, VI (1874-5), 89-105.
Chirnside, Andrew, *The Blantyre Missionaries: Discreditable Disclosures* (London: William Ridgway, 1880).
Cust, R.N., *An Essay on the prevailing methods of evangelising the non-Christian World* (London: Luzac & Co., 1894).
Dawson, E.C., *The Last Journals of Bishop Hannington* (London: Seeley & Co.,1890).
— *James Hannington, A History of His Life and Work* (London: Seeley & Co., 1887).

Deane, Wallace (ed.), *In Wild New Britain: the Story of Benjamin Danks, Pioneer Missionary* (Sydney: Angus and Robertson, 1933).

Dyson, Martin, *My Story of Samoan Methodism* (Melbourne: Fergusson & Moore, 1875).

Erskine, J.E., *Journal of a Cruise among the Islands of the Western Pacific* (London: Murray, 1853).

Fitzgerald, C., *The Gambia and its Proposed Cession to France* (London: Unwin Brothers, 1875).

Frere, Sir Bartle,'Have we a Colonial Policy?', *The National Review*, II (1883), 1-22.

Gambia Committee, *The Proposed Cession of the Gambia* (London, 1876).

Gill, W. Wyatt, 'Three Visits to New Guinea', *Journal of the Royal Geographical Society*, 44 (1874), 15-30.

Gladstone, W.E., 'England's Mission', *The Nineteenth Century*, IV (1878), 560-84.

Hall, C.M., *Calvert of Cannibal Fiji* (London: WMMS, 1918).

Hinderer, Anna, *Seventeen Years in the Yoruba Country* (London: Religious Tract Society, 1873).

Hutton, J.F., *The Proposed Cession of the British Colony of the Gambia to France* (Manchester, 1876).

Hutchinson, Edward, *The Slave Trade of East Africa* (London: Sampson Low, 1874).

Inglis, John, *In the New Hebrides* (London: Nelson, 1887).

Johnston, H.H., 'British Missions and Missionaries in Africa', *The Nineteenth Century*, XXII (1887), 708-24.

Kimberley, Earl of, 'Journal of Events during the Gladstone Ministry, 1868-74', ed. Ethel Drus, *Camden Miscellany*, XXI (1958).

King, Joseph, *William George Lawes of Savage Island and New Guinea* (London: Religious Tract Society, 1909).

Knatchbull Hugessen, E.H., 'The Fiji Islands', *Edinburgh Review*, 138 (October, 1873), 329-61.

Knight, William, *Memoir of Henry Venn / The Missionary Secretariat of Henry Venn* (London: Longmans, Green & Co., 1880).

Krapf, J.L., *Travels, Researches and Missionary Labours* (London: Trübner and Co., 1860).

Lovett, Richard (ed.), *James Chalmers: his Autobiography and Letters* (London: Religious Tract Society, 1902).

M'Cullagh, Thomas, *Sir William M'Arthur, KCMG, a Biography* (London: Hodder & Stoughton, 1891).

McFarlane, S., *The Story of the Lifu Mission* (London: J. Nisbet, 1873).

— *Among the Cannibals of New Guinea* (London: LMS, 1888).

McFarlane, S., and Chalmers, J., *The Mission to New Guinea* (London, 1879).

Marindin, G.E., *Letters of Frederic, Lord Blachford, Under-Secretary of State for the Colonies, 1860-71* (London: John Murray, 1896).

Markham, A.H., *The Cruise of the 'Rosario' amongst the New Hebrides and Santa Cruz Islands* (London: S. Low, Marston, Low and Searle, 1873).

Martineau, J., *Life and Correspondence of Sir Bartle Frere*, 2 vols (London, 1895).

Maudslay, A.P., *Life in the Pacific Fifty Years Ago* (London: Routledge, 1930).

Moresby, John, *Discoveries and Surveys in New Guinea* (London: J. Murray, 1876).

—*Two Admirals* (London: J. Murray, 1909).

Murray, A.W., *Forty Years' Mission Work in Polynesia and New Guinea* (London, 1876).

Palmer, George, *Kidnapping in the South Seas* (Edinburgh: Edmonston and Douglas, 1871).

Paton, John G., *John G. Paton, Missionary to the New Hebrides: An Autobiography*, 2 vols (London: Hodder & Stoughton, 1889).

Paton, Margaret W., *Letters and Sketches from the New Hebrides* (London: Hodder and Stoughton, 1896).

Patterson, George, *Missionary Life among the Cannibals, being the Life of John Geddie, DD, First Missionary to the New Hebrides* (Toronto, J. Campbell, J. Bain and Hart, 1882).

Powell, Wilfred, *Wanderings in a Far Country* (London: Sampson Low, Marston, Searle and Rivington, 1883).

Pritchard, W.T., *Polynesian Reminiscences* (London: Chapman & Hall, 1866).

Romilly, H.H., *The Western Pacific and New Guinea*, 2nd edn (London: J. Murray, 1887).

Rowe, J.A., 'The Purge of Christians at Mwanga's Court', *JAH*, V (1964) 55-72.

Rowe, S.G., (ed.), *Joel Bulu: the Autobiography of a Native Minister in the South Seas* (London: T. Woolmer, 1871).

Scholes, S.E., *Fiji and the Friendly Islands* (London: C.H. Kelly, n.d.).

Seemann, Berthold, *Viti; an account of a Government Mission to the Vitian or Fijian Islands in the Years 1860-1* (Cambridge: Macmillan, 1862).

Smythe, S.M., *Ten Months in the Fiji Islands* (Oxford: Parker, 1864).

Steel, Robert, *The New Hebrides and Christian Missions* (London: J. Nisbet, 1880).

Wawn, William T., *The South Sea Islanders and the Queensland Labour Trade* (London: Swan Sonnenschein, 1893).

Yonge, Charlotte M., *Life of John Coleridge Patteson, Missionary Bishop of the Melanesian Islands*, 2 vols (London: Macmillan, 1874).

Young, F., 'Report on the Gambia Question' *PRCI*, VII (1875-6), 68-85.

Secondary Sources

Aderibigbe, A.A.B., 'Expansion of the Lagos Protectorate, 1863-1900', unpublished PhD thesis (London, 1959).

Ajayi, J.F.A., 'The British Occupation of Lagos, 1851-1861: a critical review', *Nigeria Magazine,* 69 (August 1961), 96-105.

— *Christian Missions in Nigeria, 1841-1891: the Making of a New Elite* (London: Longmans, 1965).

— *Native Agency in 19th Century West Africa: the case of Bishop Crowther* (Cambridge: NAMP, 1997).

Ajayi, W.O., 'A History of the Yoruba Mission, 1843-1880', unpublished MA thesis (Bristol, 1959).

— 'The beginnings of the West African Bishopric on the Niger', *Bulletin of the Society of African Church History,* 3 (1969), 92-99.

Alpers, Edward A., *The East African Slave Trade* (Nairobi, 1967).

Anderson, W.B., *The Church in East Africa, 1840-1874* (Dodoma: Central Tanganyika Press, 1977).

Anderson-Morshead, A.E.M., *The History of the Universities' Mission to Central Africa,* Vol. 1, 1859-1909, (London: UMCA, 1955).

Armstrong, E.S., *The History of the Melanesian Mission* (London: Isbister, 1900).

Artless, S.W., *The Story of the Melanesian Mission* (Oxford, 1955).

Ayandele, E.A., *The Missionary Impact on Modern Nigeria, 1842-1914* (London: Longmans, 1966).

— 'Christianity in Nigeria', *JAH,* 8 (1967), 362-64.

— *Holy Johnson, Pioneer of African Nationalism* (London: Frank Cass, 1970).

Aydelotte, W.O., *Bismarck and British Colonial Policy* (Philadelphia: University of Pennsylvania Press, 1937).

Baillie Hamilton, W.A., 'Forty-Four Years at the Colonial Office', *The Nineteenth Century and After,* LXV (April 1909), 599-613.

Bebbington, David W., *Evangelicalism in Modern Britain* (London: Unwin Hyman, 1989).

— *William Ewart Gladstone: Faith and Politics in Victorian Britain* (Grand Rapids: Eerdmans, 1993).

Beidelman, T.O., 'Social Theory and the Study of Christian Missions in Africa', *Africa,* XLIV (1974), 235-49.

Bennett, Norman R., 'The Church Missionary Society at Mombasa, 1873-1894', *Boston University Papers on African History* (Boston, 1964).

Bickers, Robert and Seton, Rosemary (eds) *Missionary Encounters: Sources and Issues* (Richmond: Curzon Press, 1996).

Binfield, Clyde, *So Down to Prayers: Studies in English Nonconformity 1780-1920* (London: J. & M. Dent, 1977).

Biobaku, S.O., *The Egba and their Neighbours, 1842-1872* (Oxford: OUP, 1957).

Blake, Robert, *Disraeli* (London: Eyre and Spottiswoode, 1966).

Blakely, B.L., *The Colonial Office, 1868-92* (Durham, N.C.: Duke UP, 1972).
Bodelsen, C.A., *Studies in Mid-Victorian Imperialism* [1924] (London: Heinemann, 1960).
Bosch, David J., *Transforming Mission: Paradigm Shifts in the Theology of Mission* (Maryknoll, N.Y.: Orbis, 1991).
Bradley, Ian, *The Call to Seriousness; the evangelical impact on the Victorians* (London: Jonathan Cape, 1976).
Brantlinger, Patrick, 'Missionaries and Cannibals in Nineteenth Century Fiji ,' *History and Anthropology*, 17:1 (2006), 21-38.
Brendon, Piers, *The Decline and fall of the British Empire 1781-1997* (London: Jonathan Cape, 2007).
Breward, Ian, *A History of the Churches in Australasia* (Oxford: OUP, 2001).
Bridges, Roy C., 'The historical role of British explorers in East Africa', *Terrae Incognitae*, 14 (1982), 1-21.
Brookes, J.I., *International Rivalry in the Pacific Islands, 1800-1875* (Berkeley and Los Angeles: University of California Press, 1941).
Burns, Alan C., *Fiji* (London: HMSO, 1963).
— *History of Nigeria* (London: Allen & Unwin, 7th edn 1969).
Burton, J.W., *Modern Missions in the South Pacific* (London: Livingstone Press, 1949).
Butler, J.R.M., 'Imperial Questions in British Politics, 1868-1880', *CHBE*, vol. 3 (Cambridge, CUP, 1959), 17- 64.
Cain, P.J., and Hopkins, A.G., *British Imperialism: Innovation and Expansion, 1688-1914* (London: Longman, 1993).
Cairns, H.A.C., *Prelude to Imperialism: British Reactions to Central African Society 1840-1890* (London: Routledge & Kegan Paul, 1966).
Causley, Alison, 'Bishop Crowther: aspects of his life and views', unpublished BA dissertation (Wales: Aberystwyth, 1975).
Cell, J.W., *British Colonial Administration in the Mid-Nineteenth Century: the Policy-making Process* (New Haven: Yale University Press, 1970).
Chadwick, Owen, *Mackenzie's Grave* (London: Hodder and Stoughton, 1959).
— *The Victorian Church*, 2 vols (London: A & C Black, 1966, 1970).
Chamberlain, M.E., *The New Imperialism* (London: Historical Association, 1970).
— *The Scramble for Africa* (London: Longman, 1974).
— 'Clement Hill's Memoranda and the British interest in East Africa', *English Historical Review*, LXXXVII (1972), 533-47.
Chapman, J.K., *Arthur Hamilton Gordon, First Lord Stanmore* (Toronto: University of Toronto Press, 1964).
Claridge, W.W., *A History of the Gold Coast and Ashanti* (ed. W.E.F. Ward, London: Frank Cass, 1964).
Comaroff, Jean and Comaroff, John L., *Of Revelation and Revolution*, 2 vols (Chicago: Chicago University Press, 1991, 1997).
Coupland, R., *Kirk on the Zambesi* (Oxford: Clarendon Press, 1928).

— *The British Anti-Slavery Movement,* (London: Thornton Butterworth, 1933).
— *East Africa and its Invaders* (London: OUP, 1938).
— *The Exploitation of East Africa* (London: Faber & Faber, 1939).
— *Livingstone's Last Journey* (London: Collins, 1947).
Cox, Jeffrey, 'Audience and Exclusion at the Margins of Imperial History', *Women's History Review,* 3 (1994), 501-514.
Crowder, Michael, *The Story of Nigeria* (London: Faber & Faber, 1962).
Cumpston, I.M., 'The Discussion of Imperial Problems in the British Parliament, 1880-85', *TRHS,* 13 (1963), 29-47.
Dachs, Anthony J., 'Missionary imperialism – the case of Bechuanaland', *JAH,* 13 (1972) 647-658.
Darch, John H., 'William Cross, David Cargill and the Establishment of the Wesleyan Methodist Mission in Fiji, 1835-1843', unpublished MA dissertation (London: Birkbeck College, 1977).
— 'Missionaries to the Cannibals: the Establishment of the First European Mission in Fiji, 1835-1843', *Trivium,* 17 (1982), 103-117.
— 'The Influence of British Protestant Missionaries on the Development of the British Empire in Africa and the Pacific *circa* 1865 to *circa* 1885', unpublished Ph.D thesis (Wales: Lampeter, 1997).
— 'Love and Death in the Mission Compound: the hardships of life in the Tropics for Victorian Missionaries and their families', *Anvil,* 17 (2000), 22-39.
— 'The Church Missionary Society and the governors of Lagos, 1862-72', *JEH,* 52 (2001), 313-333.
— 'Methodist involvement in the British annexation of Fiji, 1874', *Proceedings of the Wesley Historical Society* 55:5 (2006).
— 'Missionaries as Humanitarians? Opposition to the recruitment of indentured labour for Queensland in the 1860s and 70s',a paper given at the Henry Martyn Centre, Westminster College, Cambridge, 2 March 2006, <http://www.martynmission.cam.ac.uk/CJDarch.html>
Davidson, Allan K., 'The Legacy of Robert Henry Codrington', *IBMR,* 27 (2003), 171-176.
Davidson, J.W., and Scarr, Deryck, *Pacific Island Portraits* (Canberra: Australian National University Press, 1970).
Derrick, R.A., *A History of Fiji* (Suva: Printing & Stationery Dept, 1946).
Dike, K. Onwuka, *Trade and Politics in the Niger Delta, 1830-1885* (Oxford: Clarendon Press, 1956).
— *One Hundred Years of British rule in Nigeria, 1851-1951* (Lagos: Federal Information Service, 1957).
— *Origins of the Niger Mission, 1841-1891* [1957], (Ibadan: Ibadan University Press, 1962).
Ditchfield, G.M., *The Evangelical Revival* (London: UCL Press, 1998).
Docker, E.W., *The Blackbirders: the recruiting of South Sea labour for*

Queensland, 1863-1907 (Sydney : Angus and Robertson, 1970).

Don, Alexander, *Peter Milne of Nguna* (Dunedin: Foreign Missions Committee of the Presbyterian Church of New Zealand, 1927).

Donovan, Vincent J., *Christianity Rediscovered: an Epistle from the Masai* (London: SCM, 1978).

Drus, Ethel, 'The Colonial Office and the Annexation of Fiji', *TRHS,* XXXII (1950), 87-110.

Durrans, Peter J., 'The House of Commons and the British Empire, 1868-1880', *Canadian Journal of History,* IX, (1974), 19-44.

— 'A Two-Edged Sword: the Liberal attack on Disraelian Imperialism', *JICH*, 10 (1982), 262-284.

— 'Beaconsfieldism', *Trivium,* 24 (1989), 58-75.

Elbourne, Elizabeth, 'The Foundation of the Church Missionary Society: the Anglican Missionary Impulse,' in Walsh, J., Haydon, C., & Taylor, S., (eds), *The Church of England, c.1689 – c.1833: From Toleration to Tractarianism* (Cambridge: CUP, 1993), 247-264.

Eldridge, C.C., 'The Imperialism of the "Little England Era": The Question of the Annexation of the Fiji Islands, 1858-61', *NZJH*, I (1967), 171-84.

— 'Newcastle and the Ashanti war of 1863-64: a failure of the policy of "Anti-Imperialism"', *Renaissance and Modern Studies,* XII (1968), 68-90.

__ 'The Myth of Mid-Victorian "Separatism": the Cession of the Bay Islands and the Ionian Islands in the early 1860s', *Victorian Studies,* XXI (1969), 331-346.

— *England's Mission: the Imperial Idea in the Age of Gladstone and Disraeli, 1868-1880* (London: Macmillan, 1973).

— *Victorian Imperialism* (London: Hodder and Stoughton, 1978).

— 'Mid-Victorian Imperialism Reconsidered', *Trivium, 15* (1980), 63-72.

— (ed.), *British Imperialism in the Nineteenth Century* (London: Macmillan, 1984).

— *Disraeli and the Rise of a New Imperialism* (Cardiff: University of Wales Press, 1996).

Etherington, Norman A., 'Frederic Elton and the South African Factor in the making of Britain's East African Empire', *JICH,* IX (1980), 255-274.

— 'Missionaries and the intellectual history of Africa: a historical survey', *Itinerario,* 2 (1983), 116-143.

— 'Missions and Empire', in Winks, Robin W., (ed.) *OHBE, V, Historiography* (Oxford: OUP, 1999), 303-314.

— (ed.) *Missions and Empire* (Oxford: OUP, 2005).

Fage, J.D., *An Introduction to the History of West Africa* (Cambridge: CUP, 1955).

Falconer, James W., *John Geddie* (Toronto: Board of Foreign Missions, Presbyterian Church in Canada, 1915).

Farnsworth, Susan H., *The Evolution of British Imperial Policy during the mid-Nineteenth Century* (New York: Garland, 1992).

Ferguson, Niall, *Empire: How Britain Made the Modern World* (London: Allen Lane, 2003).
Fiedler, Klaus, *The Story of Faith Missions* (Oxford: Lynx Regnum, 1994).
Fieldhouse, D.K., *Colonialism 1870-1945: An Introduction* (London: Weidenfeld and Nicolson, 1981).
Findlay, G.G. and Holdsworth, W.W., *The History of the Wesleyan Methodist Missionary Society*, 5 vols (London: Epworth, 1921-4).
Fitzmaurice, Lord Edmond, *The Life of Granville George Leveson Gower, Second Earl Granville KG*, 2 vols (London: Longmans, Green, 1905).
Flint, J.E., *Sir George Goldie and the making of Nigeria* (London: OUP, 1960).
Folsom, Avaline, *The Royal Empire Society* (London: George Allen and Unwin, 1933).
Fox, C.E., *Lord of the Southern Isles, being the Story of the Anglican Mission in Melanesia, 1849-1949* (London: Mowbray, 1958).
France, Peter, *The Charter of the Land* (Melbourne: OUP, 1969).
Frederiks, Martha T., *We have Toiled all Night: Christianity in the Gambia, 1456-2000* (Zoetermeer: Uitgeverij Boekencentrum, 2003).
Frost, Alan and Samson, Jane (eds), *Pacific Empires* (Melbourne: Melbourne University Press, 1999).
Gailey, H.A., *History of the Gambia* (London, Routledge & Kegan Paul, 1964).
Galbraith, John S., 'The "Turbulent Frontier" as a factor in British expansion', *Comparative Studies in Society and History*, II (1960), 150-168.
— 'Gordon, Mackinnon, and Léopold: the Scramble for Africa, 1876-1884', *Victorian Studies*, 14 (1971), 369-88.
— *Mackinnon and East Africa, 1878-1895* (Cambridge: CUP, 1972).
Gallagher, J.A., *The Decline, Revival and Fall of the British Empire* (Cambridge: CUP, 1982).
Gallagher, J.A. and Robinson, R.E., 'The Imperialism of Free Trade', *Econ HR*, 2nd ser., VI (1953), 1-15.
Gann, L.H. & Duignan, P., (eds), *Colonialism in Africa, 1870-1960*, 2 vols (Cambridge: CUP, 1969-70).
Garrett, John, *To Live among the Stars: Christian Origins in Oceania* (Geneva and Suva: World Council of Churches, 1982).
— *A Way in the Sea: aspects of Pacific Christian history with reference to Australia* (Melbourne: Spectrum Publications, 1982).
Gavin, R.J., 'The Bartle Frere Mission to Zanzibar', *Historical Journal*, 5 (1962), 122-48.
Gilley, Sheridan & Stanley, Brian (eds.), *World Christianities c.1815 – c.1914* (Cambridge: CUP, 2006).
Githige, R.M., 'The Issue of Slavery: relations between the C.M.S. and the State on the East African Coast prior to 1895', *Journal of Religion in*

Africa, 16 (1986), 209-25.

Glover, E. and Temple, R., *The Life of Sir John Hawley Glover* (London: Smith and Elder, 1897).

Gordon, D.C., *The Australian Frontier in New Guinea 1870-1885* (New York: Columbia University Press, 1951).

Gray, John M., *A History of the Gambia* [1940] (London: Frank Cass, 1966).

— 'Correspondence Relating to the Death of Bishop Hannington', *Uganda Journal*, (March 1949), 1-22.

— 'Sir John Kirk and Mutesa', *Uganda Journal*, (March 1951), 1-16.

Gray, Richard, *Black Christians and White Missionaries* (New Haven and London: Yale University Press, 1990).

Greenlee, James G. &. Johnston, Charles M., *Good Citizens: British Missionaries and Imperial States, 1870-1914* (Montreal: McGill-Queen's University Press, 1999).

Groves, C.P., *The Planting of Christianity in Africa*, 4 vols (London: Lutterworth Press, 1948-1958).

Gründer, Horst, 'Christian Missions and colonial expansion', *Mission Studies*, XII (1995), 18-29.

Gunson, W.N., 'Missionary Interest in British Expansion in the South Pacific in the Nineteenth Century', *JRH*, III (1965), 296-313.

— 'On the incidence of alcoholism and intemperance in early Pacific Missions', *Journal of Pacific History*, I (1966), 43-62.

— 'The Theology of Imperialism and the Missionary History of the Pacific', *JRH*, V (1969), 255-65.

— 'Victorian Christianity in the South Seas: a Survey', *JRH*, VIII (1974), 183-197.

— *Messengers of Grace* (Melbourne: OUP, 1978).

Hall, Henry L., *The Colonial Office: A History* (London, 1937).

Hamilton, C.I., 'Naval hagiography and the Victorian hero', *Historical Journal*, 23 (1980) 381-398.

Hamilton, W.B., *Barbados and the Confederation Question, 1871-1885* (London: Crown Agents, 1956).

Hanna, A.J., 'The role of the London Missionary Society in the opening up of East Central Africa', *TRHS*, (5th series) 5 (1955), 41-59.

—*The Beginnings of Nyasaland and North Eastern Rhodesia, 1859-1895* (Oxford: Clarendon Press, 1956).

Hansen, Holger Bernt & Twaddle, Michael (eds.) *Christian Missionaries and the State in the Third World* (Oxford and Athens, Ohio: James Currey and Ohio University Press, 2002).

Harcourt, Freda, 'Gladstone, Monarchism and the "New" Imperialism, 1868-74', *JICH*, 14 (1985), 20-51.

Hardinge, A., *Life of Henry Howard Molyneaux Herbert, Fourth Earl of Carnarvon, 1831-90*, 3 vols (London: OUP, 1925).

Hargreaves, J.D., *Prelude to the Partition of West Africa* (London: Macmillan,

1963).
— *West Africa Partitioned*, 2 vols (London: Macmillan, 1974, 1985).
Hastings, Adrian, *A History of English Christianity, 1920-1985* (London: Collins, 1986).
— *The Church in Africa, 1450-1950* (Oxford: Clarendon Press, 1994).
Hempton, David, *Methodism: Empire of the Spirit* (New Haven & London: Yale University Press, 2005).
Henderson, G.C., *History of Government in Fiji* (1941, 2 vols, typescript, on microfilm in School of Oriental and African Studies, London).
— *Fiji and the Fijians, 1835-1856* (Sydney: Angus and Robertson, 1931).
Hennell, Michael, *Sons of the Prophets* (London: SPCK, 1979).
Hicks Beach, Lady Victoria, *Life of Sir Michael Hicks Beach*, 2 vols (London, 1932).
Hilliard, David, *God's Gentlemen: a history of the Melanesian Mission, 1849-1942* (St Lucia, Queensland: Queensland University Press, 1978).
— 'The making of an Anglican martyr: Bishop John Coleridge Patteson of Melanesia', in Wood, D. (ed.), *Martyrs and Martyrologies: Studies in Church History* 30 (Oxford, 1993), 333-35.
Hinchliff, Peter, 'Voluntary Absolutism: British Missionary Societies in the Nineteenth Century,' in Shiels, W.J., & Wood, Diana, *Voluntary Religion: Studies in Church History 23* (Oxford: Blackwell, 1986), 363-379.
Hitchen, J.M., 'Formation of the Nineteenth Century Missionary Worldview: the case of James Chalmers', unpublished Ph.D thesis (Aberdeen, 1984).
Holmes, Timothy *Journey to Livingstone* (Edinburgh: Canongate Books, 1993).
Hopkins, A G., *An Economic History of West Africa* (London: Longman, 1973).
Howell, Raymond, *The Royal Navy and the Slave Trade* (London: Croom Helm, 1987).
Howse, E.M., *Saints in Politics: the 'Clapham Sect' and the Growth of Freedom* (Toronto: University of Toronto Press, 1952).
Hyam, Ronald, *Britain's Imperial Century* (London: B.T. Batsford, 1976).
Hylson-Smith, Kenneth *The Churches in England from Elizabeth I to Elizabeth II*, 3 vols, II. 1688-1833 (London: SCM Press, 1997).
Hynes, William G., *The Economics of Empire: Britain, African and the New Imperialism, 1870-95* (London: Longman, 1979).
Isichei, Elizabeth, *Varieties of Christian Experience in Nigeria* (London: Palgrave Macmillan, 1982).
— *A History of Christianity in Africa* (London: SPCK, 1995).
Jacobs, M.G., 'Bismarck and the Annexation of New Guinea', *HSANZ*, V (1951), 14-26.
— 'The Colonial Office and New Guinea, 1874-84', *HSANZ*, V (1952), 106-118.
Jeal, Tim, *Livingstone* (London: Heinemann, 1973).

Kaniku, J.W., 'James Chalmers at Su'ua Island' *Oral History,* 3:9 (1975) 71-76.
Kent, Graeme, *Company of Heaven,* (Wellington: A.R. & A.W. Reed, 1972).
Kent, John, *Wesley and the Wesleyans* (Cambridge: CUP, 2002).
King, Joseph, *William George Lawes of Savage Island and New Guinea* (London: Religious Tract Society, 1909).
Knaplund, Paul, *Gladstone's Foreign Policy* (New York: Harper & Bros, 1935).
— *Gladstone and Britain's Imperial Policy* [1927] (New York: George Allen & Unwin, 1947).
— 'Sir Arthur Gordon and the New Guinea Question, 1883', *HSANZ,* VII (1956), 328-333.
— 'Sir Arthur Gordon and Fiji: some Gordon – Gladstone letters', *HSANZ,* VIII (1958), 281-296.
Knox, Bruce A., 'Reconsidering Mid-Victorian Imperialism', *JICH, I* (1973), 155-172.
— 'The Earl of Carnarvon, Empire, and Imperialism, 1855–90,' *JICH,* 26 (1998), 48-66.
Koebner, R., and Schmidt, H.D., *Imperialism: The Story and Significance of a Political Word, 1840-1960* (Cambridge: CUP, 1964).
Koskinen, A.A., *Missionary influence as a political factor in the Pacific Islands* (Helsinki: Academia Scientiarum Fennica, 1953).
Koss, Stephen, 'Wesleyanism and Empire', *Historical Journal,* XVIII (1975), 105-118.
Langmore, Diane, *Tamate – a king: James Chalmers in New Guinea 1877-1901* (Melbourne: Melbourne University Press, 1974).
— *Missionary Lives: Papua 1874-1914* (Honolulu: University of Hawaii Press, 1989).
Legge, J.D., *Britain in Fiji, 1858-1880* (London: Macmillan, 1958).
Lennox, Cuthbert, *James Chalmers of New Guinea* (London: Melrose, 1902).
Lloyd, Christopher, *The Navy and the Slave Trade* (London: Longmans, Green, 1949).
Lovett, Richard, *The History of the London Missionary Society, 1795-1895*, 2 vols (London: Henry Frowde, 1899).
Low, D.A., *Buganda in Modern History* (London: Weidenfeld & Nicolson, 1971).
McCracken, John, *Politics and Christianity in Malawi 1875-1940* (Cambridge: CUP, 1977).
McIntyre, W.D., 'Disraeli's Colonial Policy: the creation of the Western Pacific High Commission, 1874-77', *HSANZ,* IX (1960), 279-294.
— 'New Light on Commodore Goodenough's Mission to Fiji, 1873-74', *HSANZ,* X (1962), 270-288.
— 'Commander Glover and the Colony of Lagos, 1861-1873', *JAH,* IV (1963) 57- 79.

— *The Imperial Frontier in the Tropics, 1865-75: a study of British Colonial Policy in West Africa, Malaya and the South Pacific in the Age of Gladstone and Disraeli* (London: Macmillan, 1967).
Magnus, Philip, *Gladstone, a Biography* (London: John Murray, 1954).
Martin, K.L.P., *Missionaries and Annexation in the Pacific* (Oxford: OUP, 1924).
Matthews, Basil J., *Dr Ralph Wardlaw Thompson* (London: Religious Tract Society, 1917).
Maude, H.E., *Slavers in Paradise: The Peruvian Slave Trade in Polynesia, 1862-1864* (Canberra: Australian National University Press, 1981).
Merritt, H.P., 'Bismarck and the German interest in East Africa, 1884-1885', *Historical Journal,* 21 (1978), 97-116.
Miers, Suzanne, *Britain and the Ending of the Slave Trade* (London: Longman, 1975).
Miller, Char (ed.), *Missions and Missionaries in the Pacific* (New York and Toronto, 1985).
Millington, John, 'Life of Sir John Thurston, 1836-1897', unpublished MA thesis (London, 1951).
Monypenny, W.F. and Buckle, G.E., *The Life of Benjamin Disraeli, Earl of Beaconsfield,* 6 vols (London: John Murray, 1910-20).
Moorhouse, Geoffrey, *The Missionaries* (London: Eyre Methuen, 1973).
Morley, John, *The Life of William Ewart Gladstone,* 3 vols (London: Macmillan, 1903).
Morrell, W.P., *Britain in the Pacific Islands* (Oxford: Clarendon Press, 1960).
— *British Colonial Policy in the Mid-Victorian Age* (Oxford: Clarendon Press, 1969).
Munro, J. Forbes, 'Shipping Subsidies and Railway Guarantees: William Mackinnon, Eastern Africa and the Indian Ocean, 1860-1893', *Journal of African History,* 28 (1987), 209-230.
— 'Scottish Overseas Enterprise and the Lure of London: the Mackinnon Group, 1847- 1893', *Scottish Economic and Social History,* 8 (1988), 73-87.
Neill, Stephen C., *A History of Christian Missions* (Harmondsworth: Penguin, 1964).
— *Colonialism and Christian Missions* (London: Lutterworth Press, 1966).
Newbury, C.W., 'The development of French policy on the Lower and Upper Niger', *Journal of Modern History,* 31 (1959), 16-26.
— *The Western Slave Coast and its Rulers* (London, 1961).
Noll, Mark A., *The Rise of Evangelicalism* (Leicester: Apollos, 2004).
O'Connor, Daniel *et al., Three Centuries of Mission: the USPG, 1701-2000* (London: Contiuum, 2000).
Oddie, G.A., 'India and Missionary motives, c.1850-1900,' *JEH,* 25 (1974), 61-74.
Oliver, Roland, *The Missionary Factor in East Africa* (London: Longmans,

Green, 1952).

Pachai, B. (ed.), *Livingstone, Man of Africa: Memorial Essays 1873-1973* (London: Longman, 1973).

Page, Jesse, *The Black Bishop: Samuel Adjai Crowther* (London: S.W. Partridge, 1908).

Parnaby, O.W., 'The Regulation of Indentured Labour to Fiji, 1864-1888', *The Journal of the Polynesian Society*, 65 (1956), 58-60.

— 'Aspects of British Policy in the Pacific: the 1872 Pacific Islanders Protection Act', *HSANZ*, VIII (1957), 54-65.

— *Britain and the Labor Trade in the Southwest Pacific* (Durham, N.C.: York University Press, 1964).

Paton, F.H.L., *The Kingdom in the Pacific* (London: Young People's Missionary Movement, 1913).

Pettifer, Julian & Bradley, Richard, *Missionaries* (London: BBC Books, 1990).

Piggin, Stuart, 'Halevy Revisited: The Origins of the Wesleyan Methodist Missionary Society: An Examination of Semmel's Thesis', *JICH*, 9 (1980), 17-37.

— *Making Evangelical Missionaries, 1789-1858* (Sutton Courtenay: Marcham Manor, 1984).

Pinnington, John, 'Church Principles in the early years of the Church Missionary Society: the problem of the "German" missionaries', *Journal of Theological Studies*, NS 20 (2) (1969), 523-532.

Pope Hennessy, James, *Verandah: some episodes in the Crown Colonies 1867-1889* (London: George Allen and Unwin, 1964).

Porter, Andrew, 'Cambridge, Keswick, and late-nineteenth-century attitudes to Africa', *JICH*, 5 (1976), 5-34.

— 'Evangelical enthusiasm, missionary motivation and West Africa in the late Nineteenth century: the career of G.W. Brooke,' *JICH*, 6 (1977).

— '"Commerce and Christianity": the Rise and Fall of a Nineteenth-Century Missionary Slogan', *Historical Journal*, 28 (1985), 597-621.

— 'The balance sheet of empire, 1850-1914', *Historical Journal*, XXXI (1988), 685-699.

— 'Religion and Empire: British Expansion in the Long Nineteenth Century, 1780-1914,' *JICH*, 20 (1992), 370-390.

— '"Cultural Imperialism" and Protestant Missionary Enterprise, 1780-1914', *JICH*, 25 (1997), 367-391.

— 'Trusteeship, Anti-Slavery, and Humanitarianism' in Porter, Andrew (ed) *OHBE, III, The Nineteenth Century* (Oxford, 1999), 198-221.

— *The Council for World Mission and its Archival Legacy* (London, 1999).

— 'Religion, Missionary Enthusiasm, and Empire' in Porter, Andrew (ed.) *OHBE, III, The Nineteenth Century* (Oxford: OUP, 1999), 222-246.

— 'Church History, History of Christianity, Religious History: Some Reflections on the British Missionary Enterprise since the Late Eighteenth Century', *Church History*, 71:3 (2002), 555-584.

— 'The Universities' Mission to Central Africa: Anglo-Catholicism and the Twentieth-Century Colonial Encounter', in Stanley, Brian (ed.), *Missions, Nationalism and the End of Empire* (Grand Rapids and Cambridge: Eerdmans, 2003).

— (ed.), *The Imperial Horizons of British Protestant Missions, 1880-1914* (Grand Rapids and Cambridge: Eerdmans, 2003).

— *Religion versus Empire?: British Protestant Missionaries and Overseas Expansion, 1700-1914* (Manchester: Manchester University Press, 2004).

Porter, Bernard, *The Lion's Share, a short history of British Imperialism 1850-1970* (London: Longman, 1975).

— *The Absent-Minded Imperialists: Empire, Society and Culture in Britain* (Oxford: OUP, 2004).

Prochaska, Frank K., 'Little Vessels: Children in the Nineteenth Century English Missionary Movement,' *JICH*, VI (1978), 112-118.

Rack, Henry D., *John Wesley and the Rise of Methodism*, [1989] 3rd edn (London: Epworth, 2002).

Ransford, Oliver, *The Slave Trade* (London: J. Murray, 1971).

— *Livingstone: the dark interior* (London: J. Murray, 1978).

Reese, Trevor R., *The History of the Royal Commonwealth Society, 1868-1968* (London: OUP, 1968).

Robert, Dana L., *Converting Colonialism: Visions and Realities in Mission History, 1706-1914* (Grand Rapids and Cambridge: Eerdmans, 2008).

Robinson, R.E., and Gallagher, J., with Denny, A., *African and the Victorians* (London: Macmillan, 1961).

Robson, William, *James Chalmers of New Guinea* (London: Pickering & Inglis, n.d.).

Rosman, Doreen, *Evangelicals and Culture* (London: Croom Helm, 1984).

Ross, Andrew C., *David Livingstone: Mission and Empire* (London: Hambledon, 2002).

— Christian Missions and Mid-Nineteenth-century Change in Attitudes to Race: the African Experience', in Porter, Andrew, (ed.), *The Imperial Horizons of British Protestant Missions, 1880-1914* (Grand Rapids and Cambridge: Eerdmans, 2003), 85-105.

Rouse, Ruth, 'Missionary Vocation', *International Review of Missions,* (April 1917), 244-257.

Routledge, David, 'The Negotiations leading to the Cession of Fiji, 1874', *JICH*, I (1974), 278-293.

Rowbotham, Judith D., 'Edward Knatchbull-Hugessen and the British empire', unpublished PhD thesis, (Wales: Lampeter, 1982).

Rowe, J.A., 'The Purge of Christians at Mwanga's Court', *JAH*, V (1964), 55-72.

Rowell, Geoffrey, *The Vision Glorious: themes and personalities of the Catholic revival in Anglicanism* (Oxford: OUP, 1983).

Safitoa, J., 'Chalmers at Iokea', *Oral History,* 1:7 (1973), 46-49.

Said, Edward W., *Culture and Imperialism* (London: Chatto & Windus, 1993).
Samson, Jane, *Imperial Benevolence: making British authority in the Pacific Islands* (Honolulu: University of Hawai'i Press, 1998).
— *Race and Empire* (London, 2004).
Scarr, Deryck, 'John Bates Thurston, Commodore J.G. Goodenough, and rampant Anglo-Saxons in Fiji', *HSANZ,* XI (1964), 361-382.
— 'Recruits and Recruiters, a Portrait of the Pacific Islands Labour Trade', *JPH,* 2 (1967), 5-24.
—*Fragments of Empire: A History of the Western Pacific High Commission, 1877-1914* (Canberra: Australian National University Press, 1968).
—*The Majesty of Colour: a life of Sir John Bates Thurston,* 2 vols (Canberra: Australian National University Press, 1973 & 1980).
Scholefield, G.H., *The Pacific, its Past and Present* (London: John Murray, 1919).
Searing, James F., *'God Alone is King': Islam and Emancipation in Senegal* (Oxford: James Currey, 2002).
Seaver, George, *David Livingstone: his life and letters* (London: Lutterworth, 1957).
Semmel, Bernard, *The Methodist Revolution* (London: Heinemann, 1974).
Shaw, A.G.L., 'British Attitudes to the Colonies, ca.1820-1850', *Journal of British Studies,* IX (1969), 71-95.
Shenk, Wilbert R., 'Rufus Anderson and Henry Venn: a special relationship?', *IBMR,* 5 (1981), 171.
— *Henry Venn, Missionary Statesman* (Maryknoll, NY: Orbis, 1983).
— 'The Contribution of Henry Venn to Mission Thought', *Anvil,* 2 (1985), 25-42.
Shepperson, George, 'David Livingstone, Scotland and Africa', in *David Livingstone and Africa* (University of Edinburgh, Centre for African Studies, 1973).
Sibree, James, *London Missionary Society: a register of missionaries, deputations, etc, from 1796 to 1923* 4th edn, (London: LMS, 1923).
Sillery, Anthony, *John Mackenzie of Bechuanaland,1835-1899: a study in humanitarian imperialism* (Cape Town: A.A.Balkema, 1971).
Smith, Paul, 'Disraeli's Politics', *TRHS,* 37 (1987), 65-85.
Snelling, R.C. and Barron, T.J., 'The Colonial Office and its Permanent Officials 1801-1914' in Sutherland, G., (ed.) *Studies in the Growth of Nineteenth- Century Government* (London: Routledge and Kegan Paul, 1972), 139-66.
Stanley, Brian, '"Commerce and Christianity": Providence Theory, the Missionary Movement, and the Imperialism of Free Trade, 1842-1860' *Historical Journal,* 26 (1983), 71-94.
— 'Nineteenth-century liberation theology; Nonconformist missionaries and imperialism', *Baptist Quarterly,* 32 (1987) 5-18.
— *The Bible and the Flag* (Leicester: Apollos, 1990).

— *The History of the Baptist Missionary Society* (Edinburgh: T&T Clark, 1992).
— 'The future in the past: eschatological Vision in British and American Protestant missionary history', *Tyndale Bulletin*, 51:1 (2000), 101-120.
— (ed.), *Christian Missions and the Enlightenment* (Grand Rapids & Richmond: Eerdmans & Curzon Press, 2001).
— (ed.), *Missions, Nationalism and the End of Empire* (Grand Rapids & Cambridge: Eerdmans, 2003).
Stembridge, S.R., 'Disraeli and the Millstones', *Journal of British Studies*, V (1965), 122-139.
— *Parliament, the Press, and the Colonies, 1846-1880* (New York: Garland, 1982).
Stock, Eugene, *A History of the Church Missionary Society*, 4 vols (London: CMS, 1899-1916).
Stokes, Evelyn, 'The Fiji Cotton Boom', *NZJH*, 2 (1967), 165-77.
Strayer, Robert W., *The Making of Mission Communities in East Africa* (London: Heinemann, 1978).
Stuart, Doug, *The Making of a Missionary Disaster, the London Missionary Society and the Makololo*, (Cambridge: NAMP, 1997).
Stuart, Ian, *Port Moresby, Yesterday and Today* (Sydney: Pacific Publications, 1970).
Swartz, Marvin, *The Politics of British Foreign Policy in the era of Disraeli and Gladstone* (Basingstoke: Macmillan, 1985).
Tasie, G.O.M., 'The story of S.A. Crowther and the CMS Niger Mission Crisis of the 1880s: a reassessment,' *Ghana Bulletin of Theology* IV: 7 (1974), 47-60.
Taylor, John V., *The Growth of the Church in Buganda* (London: SCM, 1958).
Temperley, H., *British Antislavery 1833-1870* (London: Longman, 1972).
— *White Dreams, Black Africa; the Antislavery Expedition to the Niger, 1841-1842* (New Haven and London: Yale University Press, 1991).
Temu, A.J., *British Protestant Missions* (London: Longman, 1972).
Thomas, H.B., 'The Last Days of Bishop Hannington', *The Uganda Journal*, (September 1940), 18-27.
Thompson, H.P., *Into all Lands: the history of the Society for the Propagation of the Gospel in Foreign Parts, 1701-1900* (London: SPCK, 1951).
Thorne, Susan, *Congregational Missions and the making of an Imperial Culture in Nineteenth-Century England* (Stanford: Stanford University Press, 1999).
Thornley, A.W., '"Heretics and Papists": Wesleyan-Roman Catholic Rivalry in Fiji, 1844-1903', *JRH*, 10 (1979), 294-312.
Thornton, A.P., *The Imperial Idea and its Enemies* (London: Macmillan, 1959).
Tiller, John, *A Strategy for the Church's Ministry* (London: CIO Publishing,

1983).

Tinker, H., *A New System of Slavery: export of Indian labour 1830-1920* (London: OUP for The Institute of Race Relations, 1974).

Tippett, A.R., *The Christian (Fiji, 1835-1867)* (Auckland: The Institute Printing and Publishing Dept, 1954).

Townsend, M.E., *Origins of Modern German Colonialism, 1871-1885* (New York: Columbia University, 1921).

Trainor, Luke, 'Policy-making at the Colonial Office: Robert Meade, the Berlin Conference, and New Guinea 1884-5,' *JICH,* VI (1978), 119-143.

Vickers, John, *The Genesis of Methodist Missions*, (Cambridge: NAMP, 1996).

Vidler, A.R., *The Church in an Age of Revolution* (Harmondsworth: Penguin, 1961).

Walls, Andrew F., 'The Legacy of Samuel Ajayi Crowther', *IBMR,* 16:1 (1992) 15-21.

— 'The Evangelical Revival, the Missionary Movement and Africa', in Noll, M.M., Bebbington, D.W., and Rawlyk, G.A., *Evangelicalism: comparative studies of popular Protestantism in North America, the British Isles and beyond, 1700-1990* (Oxford & New York: OUP, 1994).

— *The Missionary Movement in Christian History* (Maryknoll, & Edinburgh, 1996).

Ward, John M., *British Policy in the South Pacific, 1786-189?* (Sydney: Australian Publishing Co., 1948).

Ward, Kevin and Stanley, Brian (eds), *The Church Mission Society and World Christianity 1799-1999* (Grand Rapids & Richmond: Eerdmans & Curzon Press, 1999).

Ward, W.E.F., *The Royal Navy and the Slavers* (London, 1969).

Ward, W.R., *The Protestant Evangelical Awakening* (Cambridge, 1992).

Warren, Max, *The Missionary Movement from Britain in Modern History* (London: SCM Press, 1965).

— *Social History and Christian Mission* (London: SCM Press, 1967).

Webster, J.B., *The African Church Movement among the Yoruba* (Oxford: Clarendon Press, 1964).

Whiteman, Darrell, *Melanesians and Missionaries* (Pasadena: William Carey Library, 1983).

Williams, C.P., '"Not Quite Gentlemen": An Examination of "Middling Class" Protestant Missionaries from Britain c.1850-1900', *JEH,* 31 (1980), 301-315.

— *The Ideal of the Self-Governing Church: a Case Study in Victorian Missionary Strategy* (Leiden: E.J.Brill, 1990).

— '"Grand and capacious Gothic Churches": Pluralism and Victorian Missionaries', *Tyndale Bulletin,* 43:1 (1992), 139-153.

— 'British Religion and the Wider World: Mission and Empire 1800-1940', in Gilley, S. and Sheils, W.J., (eds), *A History of Religion in Britain*

(Oxford: Blackwell, 1994).
Willmington, Susan M.K., 'The activities of the Aborigines Protection Society as a pressure group on the formulation of colonial policy, 1868-80', unpublished PhD thesis (Wales: Lampeter, 1973).
Wilson, G.H., *The History of the Universities' Mission to Central Africa* (London: UMCA, 1936).
Wolffe, John (ed.), *Evangelical faith and public zeal: Evangelicals and society in Britain 1780-1980* (London: SPCK, 1995).
— (ed.), *Religion in Victorian Britain, Vol. 5, Culture & Empire* (Manchester: Manchester University Press, 1997).
Worsfold, W.B., *Sir Bartle Frere* (London: Butterworth, 1923).
Yates, T.E., *Venn and Victorian Bishops abroad* (Uppsala & London: SPCK, 1978).

Index

Abeokuta, 45, 176, 179-82, 184-5, 190, 194, 204-7, 219, 240
Aberdeen, Earl of, 107
Aborigines Protection Society, 29, 68-74, 94, 95, 98-100, 104, 107, 130, 133, 156, 158, 164, 232, 240
Adcock, George, 162
Adderley, Charles B., 120, 149-50, 157, 172, 196, 201, 245
Aderibigbe, A.A.B., 187, 190
Admiralty, 65, 121, 161
Ajayi. J.F.A., 36, 173, 178, 206
Ajayi, W.O., 7
Akitoye, 178-9, 183
Alake, 175
Albert, Prince, 173
Allgemeine Zeitung, 130
Aniwa, 58, 60
Aneiteum, 50, 54
Angra Pequeña, 136
Anti-Slavery Society, 29, 68-73, 95, 96, 120, 164, 232
Archibald, Isaac, 39
Armit, R.H., 120
Arthington, Robert, 223
Arthur, William, 100
Asbury, Francis, 10
Ashanti, 149, 202
Ashley, Evelyn, 131-2
Atai, 21
Auckland, 15
Australian Intercolonial Convention, 137
Ayandele, E.A., 179, 202, 205, 208, 244
Azikiwe, Nnamdi, 207

Badagry, 179, 186-7
Badcock, John, 162
Baikie, W.B., 189
Baillie-Cochrane, Alexander, 106
Baker, John, 145
Baker, Shirley, 12
Baker, Thomas, 44
Banner, Capt., 114
Baptist Missionary Society, 3, 40
Barff, Charles, 38
Barghash, Sultan, 215-16
Baring, Sir Francis, 150
Barrow, Sir George, 182
Basilisk, H.M.S., 112, 116
Basle Seminary, 7
Bathurst, 145, 148-9, 162
Bau, 80-1, 83
Bau Constitution (1867), 91
Bau Constitution, Amended (1869). 91
Bechuanaland, xix
Beecroft, John, 176-7
Bell, J.W., 45
Belmore, Lord, 94
Benin, Bight of, 172, 176
Bennett, Norman, 210-11, 223
Benson, Archbishop E.W., 232
Berlin Conference, 235
Berlin Seminary, 7
Beswick, Thomas, 43
Biafra, Bight of, 176
Binner, John, 84
Biobaku, S.O., 187
Bishopsgate Street, London, 12
Bismarck, Otto von, 28, 136-7
Blackall, Samuel, 191-2
Blackwood, Capt., 112

Index

Blantyre, Nyasaland (Church of Scotland mission), 34, 222, 226
Blomfield Street, London, 4
'Bombay Africans', 223-8
Border Maid, 27
Bosch, David, 19, 245-6
Bowen, Sir George, 119
Bowen, Bp John, 43, 45
Boyce, W.B., 12, 92, 95, 100, 104, 163
Bramble, H.M.S., 112
Bravo, Major Alexander, 153
Breadfruit Church, Lagos, 203
Brendon, Piers, 196
Breward, Ian, 82
Brisbane, 57, 67, 74, 116, 136
British and Foreign Bible Society, 95
Brooke, Charles, 40
Brown, George, 32, 142
Brown, Thomas, 154, 156-7, 162-3, 168, 170
Bruce, Commodore, 177-8, 183
Buckingham and Chandos, Duke of, 120, 191
Bulu, Joel, 21,
Buganda, 25, 44, 209, 228-30, 232-3, 244
Burns, Alan, 91
Burton, J.W., 20
Buxton, Thomas Fowell, 173, 175, 194, 214, 219, 231
Buzzacott, Aaron, 120
Byley, Commander Matthew, 225

Cabinet, The, 60, 93, 98, 105, 127, 129, 132-3, 136-8, 161, 166-8, 216
Cain, P.J., 238, 244
Cairns, H. Alan C., 27, 31, 244
Cakobau (Seru), 81-5, 87, 89, 94, 96, 100, 104, 106, 110, 124, 137, 239
Calvert, James, 38, 41-2, 81-2, 84-5, 87, 92-3, 95-6, 98, 101, 110, 158, 239
Cambridge, 7, 18, 21, 31, 180, 219-21
Campbell, A.J., 74-5
Campbell, Benjamin, 179
Canterbury Cathedral, 18
Cape Colony, xix, 136
Cardwell, Edward, 149, 151, 184, 186, 191, 245
Carew, W.S., 108
Carey, William, 3, 4, 10, 50
Cargill, David, 39, 79
Carl massacre, 93-4, 98
Carnarvon, Earl of, 100, 104-7, 109, 117-20, 122, 126-7, 132, 147, 152, 159, 161, 165-70, 201-2
Central African Mission (LMS), 24, 222-3, 229, 236
Chadwick, Owen, 217
Chalmers, James, 5, 15, 22, 27, 33, 37, 39, 43, 44, 116, 123, 125-6, 130-1, 134-5, 139-40, 237, 240, 242
Chancellor, William, 41, 223
Cheetham, Bishop, 204
Chesson, F.W., 69, 100, 119, 163, 164, 170
Chester, Henry, 116, 131, 134
Chirnside, Andrew, 34
Chown, T.C., 156-7
Church of England, 2, 6-7, 19, 22, 30, 105, 181, 220-1
Church of Scotland, 34, 222, 226, 241
Church Missionary Society (CMS), 4, 6-10, 26-8, 31-2, 41, 104, 150, 173-4, 176, 178-9, 181, 185-6, 195, 203-4, 206-7, 209-16, 220-3, 225-30, 232-3, 235, 240-1
Clapham, 8, 175
Clapham Sect, 6, 47
Clarendon, Earl of, 156, 169, 219

Clarke, Captain Andrew, 149
Clegg, Thomas, 219
Clement, Yorke, 39
Codrington, R.W., 63, 66, 77
Coke, Thomas, 10
Colonial Office, xxii, 8, 29, 48, 53, 55-7, 59, 69, 70-2, 74, 76-7, 78, 84, 86, 91, 93, 95, 96, 100, 103-4, 113-14, 117, 120-1, 126, 128-9, 130-3, 139, 140-2, 149, 151-2, 154-9, 161, 166-7, 176, 182, 185, 187-8, 190, 195, 199, 201, 239, 241
Comaroff, Jean 108, 239
Comaroff, John L., 108, 239
Commons, House of, 5, 12, 65, 72, 96, 131-2, 151, 160, 176, 212, 216, 239
Confederation (Fiji, 1865), 91
Congregational Churches, 4-5, 13, 134
Constitutional Monarchy (Fiji, 1871), 91
Cook, James, 49
Cottesloe, Lord, 168
Coupland, Reginald, 211
Cross, William, 79-81
Crowder, Michael, 178, 207
Crowther, Bishop Samuel Adjai, 22, 29, 38, 173-4, 177, 180-2, 189, 204, 207
Curaçoa, H.M.S., 33
Cust, R.N., 24, 35

Dahomey, 172, 175, 179, 182, 184-5, 240
Danks, Benjamin, 28, 33-4, 52, 142
Daphne, 65, 92
David, George, 227-8, 232
D'Arcy, George, 151
Dealtry, William, 55, 72
Denham, Captain, 84
Derby, Earl of, 121, 129-30, 132-2, 136-8, 142, 147, 159, 166, 232
Derrick, R.A., 89
Disraeli, Benjamin, 105, 129, 159-61, 167, 170, 196, 216
Docker, E.W., 68
Durrans, P.J., 212-13
Dosumu, 182

Eddy, C.W., 100
Edgerley, Rose, 40
Efik, 179
Egba, 170, 175, 179, 182, 184, 186, 189-93, 197, 206-8, 240
Egba United Board of Management, 195, 204
Eldridge, C.C., 160
Ellengowan, 116
Elliot, T.F., 151, 155, 187
Emma Bell, 62
Enfield, Viscount, 97, 212
Erromanga, 44, 50, 55
Erskine, Admiral J.E., 79, 81, 92, 96, 98, 100, 138-9, 163-4
Eton College, 16, 21, 60, 72
Evangelical Alliance, 95
Evans & Brewer, 89
Exeter, 144
Exeter Hall, London, 5

Faidherbe, Louis, 147, 151
Farnsworth, Susan, 87
Fieldhouse, James, 162
Fiji, xxii, 21, 25-6, 30, 38, 78-111, 117, 120, 124, 132, 146, 158-9, 160-4, 170, 240
Fiji Committee, 29, 104, 163, 242
Finden, Harry, 157
Fison, Lorimer, 52, 83, 91
Fison, William, 91
Fitzgerald, Captain Charles, 163
Flanders, x
Flint, J.E., 202
Fly, H.M.S., 112
Foreign Missions, Day of Intercession for, xx

Index 273

Fordham, John, 84
Foreign Office, xxi, xxii, 56, 71, 88, 97-8, 121, 156, 164, 167, 176, 182, 184, 190, 212, 234-5
Forrest, A.E.C., 63
Forster & Smith, 155-6
Fortescue, Chichester, 150
Fowler, R. N., 156, 212
Franco-Prussian War, 157
Frederiks, Martha, 146
Free Church of Scotland, 222, 228, 241
Freeman, Henry S., 184-7, 189-90
Freeman, J., 6
Freeman, T.B., 174
Fremantle, Capt., 84
Frere, Sir Bartle, 212, 214-5, 228, 235, 241
Frere Town, 34, 36, 41, 209, 223-8, 232, 241

Gailey, H.A., 146
Galbraith, J.S., xxi, 30
Gallagher, J., 150, 208
Gambia, xxii, 144-71, 172, 191, 201-2, 207, 240, 242
Gambia Committee, 29, 163-5, 167, 169, 240, 242
Garrett, John, 52, 134
Gavin, R.J., 211
Geddie, John, 12-14, 24, 27, 33, 35, 39-40, 50, 54, 69
Gelele, King of Dahomey, 184-5
George Tubou, King of Tonga, 82
Gill, W. Wyatt, 118-9, 123, 133, 239
Gilpin, Charles, 212, 214
Githige, R.M., 227
Gladstone, W.E., 60, 96-8, 106-8, 129, 132, 136, 173, 200, 205, 216
Glasgow Theological Academy, 5
Glover, John Hawley, 186, 189-98
Gold Coast, 149, 159, 161, 166, 174, 202

Goldie, Andrew, 127
Gollmer, Charles, 7, 32, 38, 174, 176-80,
Goodenough, Commodore J.G., 99-100, 103-4, 110, 239
Gordon, Sir Arthur, 32, 101, 107-8, 123, 128, 132, 134
Gordon, Colonel Charles, 230-1
Gordon, D.C., 123, 141, 243
Gordon, George, 44
Gordon, James, 44
Gorrie, Sir J., 37
Gosport (LMS Missionary Training College) 5
Granville, Earl, 65, 130, 133, 137, 151, 156, 166, 206, 213-6, 225
Gray, Richard, xx, 3
Grenfell, George, 40
Grey, 3rd Earl, 176
Griffith, Edward, 74
Grimshaw, William, 2
Groundnut farming and trade, 147-8
Groves, C.P., 183
Gunson, W. Niel, 39, 135
Gurney, Russell, 212

Hamilton, Archdeacon, 206
Hammerton Treaty (1847), 211
Handford, John, 227
Hanea, 21
Hanna, A.J., 236
Hannington, Bishop James, 35-6, 41, 212, 214-5, 228, 235, 244
Harcourt, Sir William, 136
Hargreaves, J.D., 148, 154, 157, 160, 162, 169, 189, 196
Hastings, Adrian, 25
Havannah, H.M.S., 81
Hay, Sir John, 131-2, 150, 152, 157, 212
Hemming, A.W.L., 166
Hempton, David, 11
Henderson, G.C., 39, 82, 109
Herald, H.M.S., 84

Herbert, Robert, 48, 72, 91, 99, 106, 117, 122, 127, 130, 136, 139-40, 143, 157, 239
Hicks Beach, Sir Michael, 128-9,
Hill, Clement, 235
Hill, Bishop Joseph, 45
Hilliard, David, 62-3, 146
Hinderer, Anna, 42, 182, 193
Hinderer, David, 7, 42, 180, 182, 193
Holland, Henry, 159
Holmes, Timothy, 219
Holmwood, Frederic, 225, 230
Hopkins, A.J., 238, 244
Horsley, John F., 38, 89
Hoxton (LMS Missionary College), 5
Huddersfield, 8
Hutchinson, Edward, 10, 29, 212-13, 216, 228
Hutt Select Committee, 176

Ibadan, 180-3, 186, 193
Ifole, 195-6
Ijaye, 179, 182, 193, 195
Ijebu, 32
Ikorudu, 190
Ilesha, 179
India Office, 212
Inglis, John, 13, 27, 53, 73, 76
Irish University Bill, 216
Irvine, Dr Edward, 183
Islington, (CMS Missionary College), 7

Jaggar, Thomas, 39
Jeal, Tim, 23, 218, 221
Jobson, Dr., 104
Johnson, Bishop James 'Holy', 203-5
Johnson, Samuel, 206
Jones, John, 114
Jones, H.M., 92

Kaba, Battle of (1855), 83, 89

Kadavu, 100
Kalo massacre, 34, 116
Kay, John, 13, 29, 55, 96
Keble, John, 17
Kennedy, Sir Arthur, 148, 152-3, 196
Kilham, Hannah, 145
Kimberley, Earl of, 69, 70, 72, 93-4, 96-7, 99, 100, 103, 129, 156, 158, 169, 192, 196, 198-9, 201-2, 205
King, Joseph, 114
Kinnaird, Arthur, 5, 55, 65, 69, 70, 96, 98, 100, 104, 119, 212, 214
Kirk, Dr John, 213, 214, 216, 218, 224, 230-2, 235
Knatchbull-Hugessen, Edward, 72-3, 76-6, 98, 103, 132, 157, 169, 192, 198-201
Knight, Charles, 162
Koskinen, A.A., 23
Kosoko, 177
Krapf, Ludwig, 7, 43, 209-10, 230-1, 241-2

Labilliere, Francis P. de, 117-9, 129, 133, 142
Lagos, 22, 29, 171, 173, 175-9, 182-4, 186-9, 193, 202, 204-5, 206, 208-9, 240
Lakeba, 79
Lamb, James, 41, 227-8, 232
Lander, Richard, 173
Langham, Frederick, 95, 100-4, 107
Langmore, Diane, 139-40
Last, J.T., 224
Lau Group, 79-80, 85
Lawes, W.G., 24, 36-7, 41, 49, 114, 122-8, 131, 134, 138, 239
Layard, Edgar L., 22, 99, 100, 102-4, 106, 110, 239
Legge, J.D., 31, 84-5, 87
Leke, 187

Index 275

Levuka, 30, 75, 90-1
Lifu, 22, 114, 122
Livingstone, David, xx, xxi, 7, 15, 18-9, 23-4, 36-7, 40, 42, 124, 210-2, 217-23, 228, 235, 241, 242, 244
Livingstonia, Nyasaland (Free Church of Scotland mission), 222
Lloyd, Christopher, 211
Lloyd, G.A., 118
London Missionary Society (LMS), xix, 4-6, 13-14, 26-7, 29, 31-2, 37, 53, 104, 113-16, 118-19, 120, 122-6, 128, 131, 133-6, 140-3, 209, 237, 239, 241
Lords, House of, 32, 73, 104-5, 109, 129, 133, 151, 157, 165, 167, 214
Lovett, Richard, 114, 222
Lowther, James, 103
Loyalty Islands, 24, 26, 54, 114, 142
Lüderitz, 136
Lugard, Frederick, 208
Lukongeh, 34, 230
Lyttona incident, 55-7, 69, 70

Ma'afu, 83, 85
Màbba, 148
Macdonald, Duff, 35
Macgregor, Sir William, 123, 139-40
Mackay, Alexander, 34, 229-31, 233
Mackenzie, Bishop Charles F., 18-9, 24, 45, 221
Mackenzie, John, xix
Macaulay, Herbert, 207
Maclay, Count de Miklouho, 130
Madras, 8
Majuba Hill, Battle of (1881), 129
Malcolm W.R., 121-2
Manchester, Duke of, 157, 166

Mann, Adolphus, 7, 180, 182
Mansion House, London, 213-14
Maples, Chauncy, 226
March, Henry, 90, 94, 99
Markham, Albert, 63-4, 66
M'Arthur, Alexander, 12, 93, 100, 104, 163-4,
M'Arthur, William, 12, 29, 92, 95-9, 100-4, 106-7, 110, 119, 158, 163-4, 170, 207, 239-40
Martin, K.L.P., 84
Mathieson, J.W., 64
Maude, H.E., xxi
Maughan, Stephen, 14, 170
McCarthy, Charles, 145
McCarthy's Island (Lemaine), 145-6, 148-50
McCoskrey, William, 175, 189
McFarlane, Samuel, 24, 37-8, 41, 54, 114-5, 122, 124-7
McIlwraith, Sir Thomas, 131, 137, 141
McIntyre, W. David, xix, 93, 101-2, 150, 160, 169, 183, 189, 199, 200
McNair, James, 35, 55-7, 70
Melanesian Mission, 7, 14-18, 21-2, 26, 30-2, 40, 66, 94, 238
Methodist Churches, 2-4, 10-12, 25-8, 45
Methodist Conference, 10-11
Michie, Archibald, 119
Mills, Arthur, 167
Milne, Peter, 42
Moffat, John S., 43
Moffat, Robert, 124, 163, 214
Moloney, Alfred, 206
Monsell, William, 69, 156-7
Moore, William, 89
Mombasa, 209-10, 223-7, 241
Moresby, Captain John, 22, 112, 116, 119, 140
Moresby Treaty (1822), 211
Morgan, John, 145
McBrair, Robert, 146

Morrell, W.P., xxi, 82, 85, 87, 114, 140
Mota, 15
Mudgee Liberal, The, 47
Mullens, Joseph, 5, 29, 73, 96, 114, 119-20, 126, 128, 222
Munster, Count, 137
Murdoch, Sir Clinton, 56
Murray, A.W., 115-6, 120, 122, 124
Mutesa, 44
Mwanga, 44-5

Napoleon III, Emperor, 26
Native Pastorate, 9, 22, 174, 181, 203, 240
Neale, R.S., 21
Neill, Stephen, 22, 85
Nelson, H.M.S., 139
New Britain, 22, 36
Newbury, C.W., 176, 198
New Caledonia, 49
Newcastle, Duke of, 65, 86, 110, 185-6, 190
New Guinea, *see* Papua New Guinea
New Guinea Colonizing Association, 120-1
New Guinea Company, 120
New Guinea Prospecting Association, 120
New Hebrides (Vanuatu) 12, 24, 33, 35, 48, 238
New Hebrides Mission, 12-14, 26, 29, 33, 35, 37, 50-60, 76, 238
New South Wales, 12, 65, 93, 95, 97, 101, 104, 118, 120, 144
New Zealand, 13-15, 19, 54, 61, 73, 78-80, 90, 95
Nicholson, Lancelot, 197-8
Niger Expedition, 174, 189
Niger Mission, 180, 189
Niger, River, 144, 166, 172-3, 176, 179
Niue (Savage Island), 36, 49, 122

Nggela, 40
Nguna, 59
Norfolk Island, 14, 22, 125
Nova Scotia, 12-13, 54
Nukapu, 32, 62-3
Nyanza Mission (CMS) xix, 25, 34, 209, 222, 228-32, 241

Oliver, Roland, xx, 10, 211-12
Ondo, 28, 204
Oneata, 79
O'Neill, Thomas, 34, 44, 229-31
Onslow, Earl of, 139
Ord, Sir Harry, 29, 149-50, 195
Osborn, Dr, 104
Ovalau, 81, 84
Owl, The, 200
Oyo, 179
Onitsha, 180
Oxford, 21, 31, 60
Oxford Movement, 4, 17, 18

Pacific Islanders' Protection Act (1872), 69, 72-3, 93-4, 96, 116, 119, 213
Pacific (Queensland) Labour Trade, 13, 17, 23, 29, 47-77, 238
Paddon, James, 50
Paley, Richard, 45, 180
Palmer, Commander George, 37, 64-5
Palmer, George, (M.P.), 130
Palmerston, Viscount, 149, 176, 182-3, 188
Papua New Guinea, xxii, 22, 24, 27, 36, 112-43, 239
Park, Mungo, 173
Parnaby, Owen W., 71
Patey, Admiral, 191
Paton, John, 20, 23, 37, 42, 57-60, 64, 67, 69, 76, 238
Patteson, Bishop John Coleridge, xx, 15-17, 26, 32, 44, 60-6, 68, 70-2, 75, 77, 92, 115, 124-5,

Index 277

213, 238, 244
Pelly, Colonel, 210
Peters, Carl, 233, 235
Phillips, Bishop Charles, 28, 41, 206
'Pity Poor Feejee' Appeal, 78-80, 110
Plimsoll, Samuel, 150, 160
Polynesian Company, 89
Polynesian Labourers Act (Queensland), 52, 57, 65, 71, 107
Pope-Hennessy, John, 42, 196-9
Porter, Andrew N., xix, 1, 14, 238, 243
Port Moresby, 22, 113, 127, 129
Porto Novo, 191-2, 197
Powell, Thomas, 13, 54
Powell, Wilfred, 23
Price, W.S., 223-5, 227-8
Pritchard, W.T., 84, 87, 92, 98, 101, 107, 110
Public Worship Regulation Bill, 105
Punshon, Morley, 163

Queensland, 43, 47-77, 238
Quilter, Henry, 153
Quin, T.F., 156-7

Rabai, 209-10, 223-4, 226, 230, 233
Rankin, Dr, 134
Rarotonga, 22, 115, 118, 120, 123, 133
Rattlesnake, H.M.S., 112
Rebmann, Johannes, 7, 209-11, 215, 223, 235, 242
Reformed Presbyterian Church in Scotland, 13, 29, 33
Rewa, 39
Rhodes, Cecil, 217
Rigg, James, 164
Robinson, Sir Hercules, 97, 104, 106, 107, 110, 118, 122, 142, 239
Robinson, Ronald E., 129, 150, 208
Rogers, Sir Frederic (Lord Blachford), 56, 71, 99, 155, 166, 190
Rogers, Joseph, 45
Romilly, Hugh, 123, 138
Rosario, H.M.S., 32, 37, 64, 66
Rothery, H.C., 72,212
Rouse, Ruth, 20
Rowbotham, Judith, 200-1
Rowe, J.A., 234
Royal Colonial Institute, 69, 100, 130, 133, 139, 157, 165, 168, 241
Rupert, Prince, 144
Russell, Earl, 49, 184, 190
Russell, Capt. W., 224
Ryan, Bishop 212

Salisbury, Marquess of, 105
Salisbury Square, London (CMS headquarters), 7-8, 175, 194, 224
Samson, Jane, 76-7
Scarr, Deryck, 62, 102
Schön , J.F., 173
Schütz, Albert J., 39
Scratchley, Sir Peter, 139
Selbourne, Earl of, 136
Semler, Ishmael Michael, 227
Selwyn, Bishop George A., 12, 14, 15, 26-7, 32, 39, 50, 63, 73
Semmel, Bernard, 11
Seven Years' War, 144
Sharanpur, 224
Shenk, Wilbert, 207
Shepperson, George, 218
Shiré highlands, 221, 241, 244
Shirwa, Lake, 220
Sidmouth, Lord, 11
Sierra Leone, 9, 22, 174, 240
Simpson, Alexander, 38
Slave Trade:

1807 Act, 144
1871 Select Committee, 209, 212-14, 235, 241
Atlantic, 172, 183, 207, 211
East African, 10, 29, 207, 211-17, 219, 221-4, 226, 228, 231
Smith, George Shergold, 34, 44, 229-31, 241
Smythe, Lt Col. W.J., 51, 65, 86-7, 89, 95, 98, 102, 110, 239
Society for Promoting Christian Knowledge (SPCK), 1-3
Society for the Propagation of the Gospel (SPG) 1-3, 7
Solomon Islands, 15, 38, 40, 60, 73, 79
South American Missionary Society (SAMS) 7
Sparshott, T.H, 223, 226-7
Spion Kop, xx
Stanley, Brian, 170
Stanley, H.M., xx, 36, 214, 221, 223, 228-9, 244
Stanley, Capt. Owen, 112
Steel, Robert, 13, 29, 55
Steere, Bishop Edward, 19, 212, 226
Stephen, Sir James, 175
St George's Cathedral, Cape Town, 18
Stirling, Commodore, 99
St Mary's Island (Banjul) 145
Stock, Eugene, 28, 221, 223
Stokes, Charles, 43, 232
Strayer, Robert, 227-8
Streeter, James, 34, 224-8
Suez Canal, 212
Sunderland, J.P., 29, 55, 57, 76, 114
Surprise, 115
Surrey Chapel, London, 213
Swedi, John, 23
Sydney, 13, 29, 55, 57, 64-5, 76, 118, 120, 127, 131, 137-8
Sydney Morning Herald, 116

Tahiti, 27, 38
Talbot, E.S., Bishop of Rochester, 25
Tanganyika, 28
Tanganyika, Lake, 28
Tanna, 37, 50, 58, 60
Tanoa, 80-1
Taveuni, 94
Taylor, James Hudson, 14, 124
Taylor, J.C., 30
Taylor, J.V., 231
Taylor, P.A., 56, 71
Taylor, Thomas, 184
Temu, A.J., 231
Thompson, Ralph Wardlaw, 5, 37
Thorne, Susan, 242
Thurston, John B., 26, 85, 91-2, 94-5, 97, 101-3, 106-7, 239
Tidman, Arthur, 3, 217
Tiller, John, 30
Times, The, 166
Tinnevelly, 9
Tomkins, Oliver, 44
Tonga, 12, 21, 27, 39
Torres Straits, 114-16, 118, 121, 124, 129, 131, 239
Towns, Robert, 49, 51
Townsend, Henry, 22, 38, 45, 174-6, 180-2, 184, 188, 193-5, 198, 204
Tozer, Bishop W.G., 19, 24, 221-2
Tranquebar, 3
Tregaskis, Benjamin, 13, 154, 162
Transvaal, 129
Tui Viti, 83-5, 91

Uganda, xix, 229
Ujiji, 222-3, 234-5
Ukerewé, 44
Universities. Mission to Central Africa (UMCA), 7, 18-19, 21, 23-4, 31-2, 40, 45, 209, 212, 214, 220-2, 226, 228, 241

Venn, Henry, Snr 2, 8

Venn, Henry, 8-10, 15, 22, 29-31, 36, 38, 175, 179, 180-1, 183-8, 194-5, 203, 207-10, 219-20, 240
Venn, John, 8, 19
Victoria, Queen, 177
Vidal, Bishop Owen E., 45
Vunivalu, 81

Waller, Horace, 212, 214
Walls, Andrew, 2
Ward, J.M. 71, 87
Warren, Max, xx
Waterhouse, John, 87, 101
Watsford, John, 81
Wawn, William, 67-8
Wesley, Charles, 2
Wesley, John, 2, 8, 10
Wesleyan Methodist Missionary Society (WMMS), 10-12, 27, 31, 40, 79-90, 95, 99-100, 104, 107, 141, 145-6, 153-4, 157-8, 162-4, 170, 174, 239-40
West African Settlements, Select Committee on (1865), 29, 149-51, 157, 172, 181, 188, 191, 199, 201, 245
Western Pacific High Commission, 32, 134, 137, 239
'White Fathers', 25
White, James, 30
Whitefield, George, 2, 8
Wilberforce, William, 24, 47, 173, 175

Williams, C. Peter, 20
Williams, John, 21, 44, 50, 53
Williams, J.B., 83
Willmington, Susan, 69, 71, 93, 158
Wilmot, Commodore, 185
Wilson, Charles, 229-30
Windsor Castle, 177
Windward Islands, 167
Wingfield, Sir Charles, 98, 100, 168
Wiseman, Commodore, 33
Wolverine, H.M.S., 34
Woods, G.A., 93, 101
Wright, Henry, 9, 203

Yelling, 8
Yonge, Charlotte, M., 16, 61
Yorubaland, 9, 22, 28, 32, 172, 174, 176-7, 180, 182-3, 189, 227, 240
Yoruba Mission, 38, 174, 179, 183, 193, 197, 203-4, 207
Yoruba Wars, 28, 182, 206
Young Australian, 92
Yule, Lieutenant, 112

Zambesi, 45, 211
Zambesi Expedition,
Zanzibar, 34, 64, 210-17, 221-6, 228-30, 235, 241

www.ingramcontent.com/pod-product-compliance
Lightning Source LLC
Chambersburg PA
CBHW061433300426
44114CB00014B/1665